J. A. I. I. B./D.B.F.

Workbook on

- **Principles and Practices of Banking**
- **Accounting and Finance for Bankers**
- **Legal and Regulatory Aspects of Banking**

INDIAN INSTITUTE OF BANKING & FINANCE

Taxmann

November 2009

Price : Rs. 485

Published by :
Taxmann Publications (P.) Ltd.

Sales & Marketing :
59/32, New Rohtak Road, New Delhi-110 005 India
Phone : +91-11-45562222 Fax : +91-11-45562223

Regd. Office :
21/35, West Punjabi Bagh, New Delhi-110 026 India

Taxmann on Internet http://www.taxmann.com
Email sales@taxmann.com

Printed at :
Tan Prints (India) Pvt. Ltd.
44 Km. Mile Stone, National Highway, Rohtak Road
Village Rohad, Distt. Jhajjar (Haryana)

ISBN : 978-81-7194-647-1

FOREWORD

The Institute is not able to provide the previous question papers to the candidates. Therefore, the Institute has decided to bring out workbooks under the revised syllabus for the benefit of the candidates appearing for the JAIIB/DBF/CAIIB examinations in order to provide educational support to the students appearing for these examinations.

Candidates are aware that comprehensive study kits have been brought out for JAIIB/DBF/CAIIB examinations and published through M/s Macmillan Co. Ltd. The Institute also arranges classes through accredited institutions in many centres. The Institute also offers live interactive web based tutorial classes as another mode of study support. The workbook is one more effort in that direction. The purpose of the workbook is to serve as additional self-study material with exercises designed to assist the students in achieving the learning objectives and help them in their examinations.

As the question pattern for JAIIB/DBF/CAIIB subjects is fully objective type, the workbook has been prepared having due regard to course content, question pattern, target group etc. This workbook would enable the student to study the subject at his/her own pace and convenience and apply the various techniques and concepts of the subject in the examination and workplace. Students are advised to study the courseware/books thoroughly. These workbooks are not intended to be stand-alone materials or a substitute for studying of textbooks. They complement well with the textbook.

The Institute acknowledges with gratitude the valuable services rendered by all the resource persons who have developed revised the workbooks. *M/s Taxmann Publishers* have published this workbook in record time.

We welcome suggestions for improvement of the book.

MUMBAI

(R. BHASKARAN)
CHIEF EXECUTIVE OFFICER

AUTHORS

JAIIB/DBF
Originally prepared **By Shri O.P. Agarwal** (Paper 1) **Shri S.P. Oberoi (Paper 2) and Shri K.G. Mallya & Shri Ajay Balan** (Paper 3) and updated/revised by the IIBF's faculty.

CONTENTS

PAPER 1

PRINCIPLES AND PRACTICES OF BANKING

CONTENTS

PAPER - 1

CHAPTER

1

MULTIPLE CHOICE - QUESTIONS AND ANSWERS

Banker-Customer relationship

Q.1. ABC Bank Ltd. has made aggressive publicity for locker facilities to new bank customers due to occurence of many thefts in the locality. Number of new customers availed of the facility. Bank was closed half day on Saturday, Sunday and also on Monday (due to Ganpati Day) and there was percolation of rainwater, inside the basement area, where lockers were kept, due to overflow of rainwater nallah, which was flowing near the bank premises. Resultantly, all paper material inside the lockers got spoiled. All the customers complained for the loss suffered by them due to bank's negligence. Bank expressed regret for the loss suffered by them but stated (choose the correct one) :

(*a*) Bank is not responsible since it was an act of God.

(*b*) Bank is not responsible as a bailee since bank had taken enough care of the articles bailed in the lockers as a man of ordinary prudence, under similar circumstances, would take of his own goods. Overflow of nallah water was not a regular feature and bank had taken enough care in protecting the premises from any mishaps or insecurity as covered under section 151 of Contract Act, 1872.

(*c*) Bank was not responsible since the bank had given on hire the place in the locker, which is not destroyed or spoiled at all, due to overflow of water inside the locker-cabinets. Bank does not know the contents of the locker and hence is not responsible for any loss suffered by customers under section 177 of Contract Act, 1872 as pawnor.

(*d*) It is not the duty of the bank to return the goods bailed/or stored in the safe deposit lockers, and the customer would be responsible for the loss, destruction or deterioration.

Q.2. Mohammed Aslam Shah who does not like to earn any interest on his money, entered the ABC Bank Ltd., and desired to open an account without payment of interest for deposits for withdrawal sometimes but not as a trader, but for saving and liquidity. The Branch Manager offered to open Savings Bank A/c but expressed inability to exempt payment of interest thereon. What can the branch manger do in this case?

(*a*) To open current account in the name of Mohammed Aslam Shah and go on depositing the money for liquidity and savings.

(*b*) To open Savings Account in the name of the depositor and take an undertaking from Mohammed Aslam Shah that no interest be paid in the account and interest credit be blocked in the computers.

(*c*) To refuse to open such account, without interest. However an arrangement could be made by him for awarding scholarships to needy students out of the interest earned on deposits; if agreed to by Mohammed Aslam Shah.

(*d*) R.B.I. be approached for making regulations for such depositors, who are unwilling to earn any interest thereon.

Credit/Debit Cards

Q.3. Banks and other institutions have issued debit and credit cards; the purpose of both are:

(*a*) the same, to make paperless payments

(*b*) different, since in credit card, the account is credited with the amount while in debit card the account is debited.

(*c*) the same, there is risk weightage of 125% in both the cards

(*d*) different, since in debit cards interest for delayed period is charged while in credit cards no such interest is charged by banks.

Banker's Special Relationship

Q.4. A Joint savings (Non-Resident) account in the names of R and S, with instructions of "former or survivor" is in a bank where garnishee order is received in the name of R only. What can the bank do?

(*a*) Return the order with the remark "No such account in the name of R".

(*b*) Attach the account, with the garnishee amount, since R is the exclusive owner of the account, during his lifetime.

(*c*) Inform the authorities the account is in two names and bank can attach the account only on assent by S only.

(*d*) Cannot be attached since it is a non-resident account, return with this remark to authorities.

Q.5. When does an automatic right of set-off arise?

(*a*) on death, insanity or insolvency of the customer

(*b*) on receipt of garnishee order

(*c*) on receipt of assignment of credit balance

(*d*) on the happening of an event as in a, b, or c

Negotiable Instruments Act, 1881

Q.6. What are the circumstances when though there is sufficient and adequate funds in the bank account, the cheques are returned unpaid by banks?

(*a*) when payment is stopped

(*b*) when funds are attached by garnishee or are set-off by bank

(*c*) when balance is not clear balance for payments

(*d*) combination of (a) to (c)

Q.7. Out of various kinds of endorsements, in which endorsement does the endorser waive the right of receiving the notice of dishonour

(*a*) Facultative

(*b*) Conditional

(*c*) Sans recourse

(*d*) Restrictive

Q.8. In the case of bouncing of cheques, which of the following as per the provisions of section 138 of NI Act could be considered reasons for offence?

(*a*) Insufficient funds, not arranged for, exceeds arrangement, refer to drawer, closure of account by drawer etc.

(*b*) Non-presentation of cheques, without prior permission.

(*c*) Present again since funds are uncleared, death of the drawer, attachment by garnishee order

(*d*) Combination of (a) and (b)

Q.9. Can the cheque-returning memo be treated as evidence in offences under Negotiable Instruments Act?

(*a*) It is Secondary evidence, banker could be called in court

(*b*) It is Prima facie evidence, banker need not be called in court

(*c*) It is Affidavit evidence, banker to tender affidavit

(*d*) None

Q.10. The Negotiable Instruments Act defines the holder in due course as

(*a*) Holder of a negotiable instrument.

(*b*) A person who is entitled to hold before it becomes due for payment.

(*c*) A person who is possessor of the Negotiable instrument for consideration

(*d*) Combination of (a) to (c)

Q.11. When could the operation in the account be stopped by the bank?

(*a*) Insanity of the account holder

(*b*) Insolvency of the account holder

(*c*) Death of the account holder

(*d*) Combination of (a) to (c)

Q.12. As per the provisions of section 138 of Negotiable Instruments Act, 1881, payee of a cheque may initiate criminal action, if the cheque is returned for the reason......

(*a*) Refer to drawer

(*b*) Payment stopped by the drawer

(*c*) Post-dated

(*d*) Insufficient funds

Partnership Firm Accounts

Q.13. Partners are mutual agents. It applies to sleeping or secret partners also. The rights of other partners—

(*a*) can be restricted and entrusted to one partner

(*b*) cannot be restricted and not be entrusted to one partner

(*c*) can be enjoyed jointly

(*d*) can be enjoyed severally

Securitisation Act

Q.14. Under which Act can a financial corporation retain the right of taking over the management or possession or both of the industrial concern and realise the property pledged, mortgaged or hypothecated under the law

(*a*) Debt Recovery Act.

(*b*) S.A.R.F.A.E.S.I. Act, 2002

(*c*) R.D.D.B.S.F.I. Act, 1993

(*d*) Non-Performing Assets Act

Other new products/services by banks

Q.15. Bancassurance means

(*a*) bank assures the customer of best services

(*b*) bank has to be assured or guaranteed repayment of advances

(*c*) a package of financial services that can fulfil both banking and insurance needs of the customer at the same time.

(*d*) a kind of insurance policy.

e-Banking services

Q.16. Name any e-banking service, which is based on voice processing facility -

(*a*) Anytime banking

(*b*) Tele-banking

(*c*) Anywhere banking

(*d*) On line banking

Non-performing assets

Q.17. Non-Performing Assets are those assets which are overdue for a period of more than—

(*a*) 90 days in interest and/or instalments in term loan

(*b*) 90 days out of order in case of overdraft/cash credit (hypothecation), Bills Purchased and Bills Discounted

(*c*) 2 harvest seasons for advances for cultivation of short duration crops

(*d*) combination of (a) to (c)

Co-operative banking

Q.18. When Co-operative banks are functioning in more than one State, then they are governed by

(*a*) Multi State Co-operative Societies Act, 1984

(*b*) Multi Units Co-operative Societies Act

(*c*) Multi State Co-operative Societies Act, 2002

(*d*) Banking Laws (Application to Co-operative Societies) Act, 1965

Banking Regulation Act, 1949

Q.19. Banking Regulation Act, 1949 deals with

(*a*) The regulation of banking companies

(*b*) The control over the management of banking companies

(*c*) Suspension and winding up of banking companies

(*d*) Combination of (a) to (c)

Obligations of Bankers

Q.20. The banker is justified in refusing to honour a cheque on account of

(*a*) Insufficient funds, cheque improperly drawn, not properly signed, death of drawer.

(*b*) Cheque is post-dated/cheque presented for payment other than at the branch at which payable/stop payment of cheque by drawer.

(*c*) Crossed cheque presented for counter payment/drawer's signature different as per record/amount in words and figures differ.

(*d*) Combination of (a) to (c)

Q.21. In which of the following, bankers' general lien is not applicable -

(*a*) Safe custody articles/documents/money deposited with specific purposes.

(*b*) Securities/documents/valuables left by oversight at the bank premises.

(*c*) Stolen goods given as specific security to bank/where right of set off is available.

(*d*) Combination of (a) to (c)

Right of Set-off

Q.22. There is no need to give notice to the customer, of bank's intention to exercise

(*a*) Right of set-off

(*b*) Right to sell the pledged goods

(*c*) Bankers' lien

(*d*) Contingent contracts

Q.23. In which case or cases, Rule of Clayton does not apply ?

(*a*) For transactions relating to two accounts of the same person.

(*b*) Fixed deposits, savings bank, recurring deposit accounts

(*c*) Current deposit accounts with overdraft facility.

(*d*) Combination of (a) and (b)

Partnership Firm Accounts

Q.24. Under what circumstances can the bank close a partnership account?

(*a*) Death of Partner

(*b*) Retirement of a partner

(*c*) Insolvency of a partner

(*d*) Combination of (a) to (c)

Power of Attorney

Q.25. Power of attorney is a stamped document and generally executed in the presence of

(*a*) A Notary Public

(*b*) A Magistrate of a Court

(*c*) An Authorised Government official

(*d*) Combination of (a) to (c)

Garnishee order

Q.26. What is attachable under Garnishee Orders?

(*a*) The specified amount in the garnishee order

(*b*) If the amount is unspecified, then the account is frozen and no payment is allowed

(*c*) Any amount payable on demand or time deposits.

(*d*) Combination of (a) to (c)

NRI Accounts

Q.27. A non-resident person under the Non-Resident Rules in India means

(*a*) A person is away from India for more than 182 days or more for taking up employment/vocation

(*b*) For any other purposes, it would indicate his stay outside India for uncertain period.

(*c*) A body incorporated/registered outside India or controlled by a person resident outside India.

(*d*) Combination of (a) to (c)

Bank Lending

Q.28. Can banks lend below their PLR? If so, to which sectors ?

(*a*) No - because the PLR is the minimum lending rate for banks

(*b*) No - because due to competition, and the high cost of funds, the banks cannot afford to lend below PLR (*c*) Yes - banks can lend below PLR to special category of borrowers *i.e.* exporters, public enterprises, agriculture, education loans and women entrepreneurs.

(*d*) Yes - banks can lend below PLR for advance below Rs. 2 lakhs.

Bank Inspection

Q.29. Onsite inspections of banks and financial institutions is based on ......

(*a*) CAMELS - Capital adequacy/asset quality/management/earnings appraisal/liquidity and system controls.

(*b*) ACB - Audit Committee of the Board.

(*c*) K.Y.C. - Know your customer

(*d*) OSMOS - On site monitoring system.

Winding up of Banking Companies

Q.30. Winding up of a banking company is done under the provisions of the Banking Regulation Act, 1949. The reasons for such winding up can be

(*a*) Inability to pay its debts.

(*b*) Moratorium placed on the bank/failure to comply with minimum capital adequacy.

(*c*) Failure to comply with requirements of Banking Regulation Act/disentitled to carry on banking business/compromise or arrangement by the court cannot be worked/continuance is prejudicial to the interests of the depositors.

(*d*) Combination of (a) and (c)

Bank computerisation

Q.31. Define the main objectives of computerisation at the branch level -

(*a*) Improvement in customer service and quality of house keeping.

(*b*) Generation of data for better management control.

(*c*) Improvement in productivity and profitability.

(*d*) Combination of (a) to (c)

Q.32. The advantages of Local Area Network to banks are: -

(*a*) Sharing of expensive resources by several users.

(*b*) Availability of stored information to all users.

(*c*) All the terminals are intelligent terminals; the processing load is shared by computers in LAN.

(*d*) Combination of (a) to (c)

Q.33. Large scale computer network spread over the sizable geographic area is called:

(*a*) Local Area Network

(*b*) Wide Area Network

(*c*) Topology

(*d*) RDBMS

Q.34. Core Banking is computerisation in which branches are connected to a central host server and its advantages are: —

(*a*) Reliable centralised data repository

(*b*) Provision of Online ATM, tele-banking, internet banking

(*c*) Quick adoption of software changes and relief from data backup, 24 × 7 service to customer.

(*d*) Combination of (a) and (c)

Payment system and e-banking

Q.35. Name the card which is having features of accumulation of transactions over a period of time and the total amount charged to the account, once a month?

(*a*) Debit card

(*b*) Charge card

(*c*) Credit card

(*d*) Smart card

Q.36. Which is that card that looks like any other plastic card or an ATM card with integrated circuit (IC-Chip)?

(*a*) Member card

(*b*) Charge card

(*c*) Credit card

(*d*) Smart card

Mobile Banking

Q.37. .... are the features of Mobile Banking

(*a*) Encryption with 128 bit

(*b*) Open internet technology

(*c*) Dependent on any specific service provider

(*d*) Combination of (a) and (b)

Electronic Funds Transfer Systems

Q.38. The methods of data transmission for communication can be:—

(*a*) Simplex, capable of transmitting data in one direction,

(*b*) Half-duplex, data movement in both the directions,

(*c*) Full duplex, simultaneous two way transmission,

(*d*) Combination of (a), (b) and (c)

Q.39. .... is the largest wide area network, provides access to the satellite and operates from 650 VSAT terminals, access is through leased lines as well as dial up connectivity :—

(*a*) INET

(*b*) NICNET

(*c*) INDONET

(*d*) INFINET

Q.40. .... is a country-wide network which has host computers at Hyderabad and 4 metro centres and access points at Pune, Vizag, Bangalore and Ahmedabad. It provides a gateway to INET for wider geographical spread in India and connectivity to other international networks.

(*a*) NICNET

(*b*) Telenet

(*c*) Indonet

(*d*) Tymnet

Q.41. The following applications are possible on VSAT Network for banks

(*a*) Anywhere/Anytime banking/Electronic Fund Transfer

(*b*) Plastic cards implementation/Treasury Management

(*c*) Inter branch Reconciliation or transfer like DD/TT/MT advice, accounting and transfer, e-mail, circulars-corporate website for employees, MIS for credit risk management.

(*d*) Combination of (a) to (c)

Q.42. Name a system/organisation which operates with an objective of creating a unified international transaction processing and transmission to meet the ever-growing telecommunications requirements of the banking industry.

(*a*) SWIFT

(*b*) Internet

(*c*) CHIPS

(*d*) CHATS

Q.43. As per Information Technology Act, 2000, the importance of electronic transmission of message has gone up heavily in e-commerce. The digital images are required for authenticity, integrity and non-repudiation. The concept is known as ?

(*a*) RTGS

(*b*) Electronic Fund Transfer

(*c*) Packet assembler/dissembler

(*d*) Digital signature

Role of technology upgradation

Q.44. The data stored have got characteristics of customer oriented/integrated and absence of inconsistencies/non-volatile and time variant for longer storage of say 5 to 10 years in banks. This data base system is called.

(*a*) Data Mining

(*b*) Data Warehousing

(*c*) Gateway for Electronic Data Interchange services

(*d*) Data Message

Q.45. Name the concept/system of paperless office extensively used for inter office and intra office correspondence ?

(*a*) e-Banking

(*b*) e-B to B

(*c*) e-Mail

(*d*) e-Commerce

Q.46. Banks are using through .... new avenues to market their products and services, dissemination of information, financial advice, non-banking activities, node for commerce, etc.; name this platform —

(*a*) Web-sites

(*b*) MIS

(*c*) DSS

(*d*) EDI

Q.47. .... is useful in situations which cannot be predicted. The system allows creation of simulations under various conditions and helps the management in analysing situations under different conditions. *e.g.* in CRR/SLR requirements, pricing of services and products, etc.—

(*a*) Computer based decision systems

(*b*) Data Mining

(*c*) Decision Support system

(*d*) Management Information System

Q.48. Data Mining is a technique to reveal the strategic information hidden in Data Warehouses. It helps in exposing the patterns that are critical to business and provides an advantage through insight and knowledge of: —

(*a*) Predictions of customer behaviour, highly targeted market focus, maximised operational effectiveness.

(*b*) Unsound predictions of customer behaviour, optimal return on investment and minimum operational effectiveness.

(*c*) Allows banks to capitalise on the investments made in constructing and managing data warehouses and maximising return on investments.

(*d*) None

Security consideration

Q.49. .... is involved in establishing and running computerised systems, and which is exposed to the risk of stagnation in knowledge and skill levels, high turnover due to inappropriate match of tasks with capabilities or on account of allurements:

(*a*) Hardware

(*b*) Software

(*c*) People ware

(*d*) Data ware

Q.50. Which types of threats are there in a computerised system ?

(*a*) Errors and omissions in data and software

(*b*) Unauthorised disclosure of confidential information/frauds/computer abuse and mis-utilisation of banks' assets.

(*c*) No humidity, flood proof area, free from radio transmissions over data, no intercepting during transmissions.

(*d*) Combination of (*a*) and (*b*)

Q.51. The fraud prone area in a computerised environment is

(*a*) Unauthorised changes to records, manipulations to programs or data, bypass of password, amendments as to payment instructions, etc.

(*b*) Unauthorised changes to programs during routine maintenance, ignoring control checks on specified or selected transactions and transport of data to another computer and returned with manipulations.

(*c*) Authorised amendments to the payment instructions after their entry into the computer

(*d*) Both (a) and (b) above

Q.52. Review of operations of the established policies, standards and procedures, quality of efficiency of operations, integrity review focused at fraud detection/ prevention and monitoring of employees activities is called —

(*a*) Audit approaches in computer

(*b*) Audit Trails

(*c*) Computer Audit

(*d*) Computer operations accounting Trails

Marketing of Banking services

Q.53. Marketing is

(*a*) The process of sale of goods or services to the customers.

(*b*) The process of serving as a link between a society's needs and its pattern of industrial response.

(*c*) The process of planning and executing, the conception, pricing, promotion and distribution of goods, service and ideas that satisfy customer.

(*d*) The process of Converting customer needs into profitable dis-opportunities.

Q.54. Distinction between marketing and selling is

(*a*) Marketing relates to producing or creating goods or services needed by the customers while in selling the objective is to sell whatever is available.

(*b*) Marketing is operational activity whereas the selling is a total management concept.

(*c*) Marketing is product focussed while selling is customer focussed.

(*d*) Marketing is oriented to the needs of the seller whereas selling is oriented to the needs of the buyer.

Q.55. Functions of marketing management are

(*a*) Scientific analysis of data to understand the needs of customers, planning for long-term marketing, implementation of plans for staffing, budgeting and financing, control and evaluation of goals and targets.

(*b*) Planning and distributing goods to customers or service oriented towards the needs of the seller.

(*c*) Conversion of customer needs into profitable opportunities and encashment of the same.

(*d*) Combination of (a) and (b)

Q.56. Which one is true in respect of bank marketing ?

(*a*) Bank marketing deals with providing services to satisfy customers' financial needs and wants.

(*b*) Bank marketing has to discover/ascertain/anticipate the financial needs of the corporates.

(*c*) Bank marketing may be required to satisfy the corporates, and institutions, other related needs and wants.

(*d*) Bank marketing means competitive element, efficiency and effectiveness in the process.

Q.57. A Bank Product comprises a brand name and packaging which means—

(*a*) Brand is a name, term, sign, a symbol or design/combination of these.

(*b*) Brand name has become important part of the product and represents consumer's perception and feelings.

(*c*) Brand can be positioned in the minds of the consumers or products, benefits and values.

(*d*) Combination of (a) and (b)

Q.58. The labelling functions can be -

(*a*) Integrated part of packaging for identifying the product or brand, promoting the product through graphics.

(*b*) Describing information about the product, manufacturer, user instructions and other prescribed particulars.

(*c*) Labelling is reviewed and redesigned periodically as they become stale over a period of time.

(*d*) Combination of (a) and (b)

Pricing

Q.59. The objectives of pricing are

(*a*) Profit optimisation, adjustment of prices due to competition, increasing the market share, improved cash flows to avoid cash crunch, stabilisation of demand and sales, improvement in product quality, communicates an image of the value.

(*b*) Understanding with price cartels, bargaining power of suppliers, government controls and regulations, buyers' behaviour, customer demand and competition.

(*c*) Price elasticity of the demand of the product, cost of manufacturing the product, characteristics of the product.

(*d*) Combination of (b) and (c)

Q.60. For new products which pricing strategy may not be effective ?

(*a*) Discriminatory pricing where different prices are charged to different buyers, depending upon their intensity of demand, lower price for buyers of a large volume, and different classes of buyers.

(*b*) The product is initially priced higher and over a period of time, it is reduced to attract more buyers, with a view to "Skimming" the revenues layer by layer, from the market.

(*c*) The price is initially low in order to penetrate the market quickly and deeply attracting a large market share. High volumes give benefit of lower costs, allowing further reduction in price.

(*d*) Product mix pricing - in case of products which are a part of product mix, the pricing becomes more complex. This involves developing a set of prices for optimising the profit for the entire mix.

Distribution Channel

Q.61. Distribution Channel refers to

(*a*) Short-term commitments on the producer to various firms.

(*b*) Sets of independent organisations involved in the process of making a product or service available for use or consumption.

(*c*) More than one independent entity to take care of various tasks besides the job of selling of the product to the ultimate consumer.

(*d*) The function of distribution becomes a little complex for the procedures, in as much as, they are required to build relationships, not only with the consumers but also with key suppliers.

Q.62. The functions of the distribution (marketing) channel are -

(*a*) To gather market information/to promote and spread persuasive communications/physical proximity to consumer/matching the buyers' needs/ negotiate and settle the final price.

(*b*) To provide the consumers with the required technical information about the products/physical distribution to consumers/acquire and use funds for financing the channel/intermediaries provide the deposit or buy the goods on cash basis./Assume the risk of carrying out the channel tasks.

(*c*) To bring the product ownership to the final buyer.

(*d*) Combination of (a) and (b)

Q.63. Features of channels for banking services are

(*a*) Intangibility/inseparability from the seller/variability in customer experiences.

(*b*) Perishability and non-storability/personal contacts with clients.

(*c*) Banking services have no physical and personal channels of distribution.

(*d*) Combination of (a) and (b)

Q.64. Requirements of distribution outlets for banking services are -

(*a*) Bank branches, fixed in location and the consumers are normally required to visit the branch for transacting their business. Place should be convenient to the customers. The layout of the branch and its internal décor should also make an impact on the customer.

(*b*) Telephone banking and call centres - some of the services are made available round the clock, thus giving the customer the benefit of 24 × 7 services. ATM services are other outlet. Off site ATMs provide a value addition and enables branches to tap business. Home banking and personal computers, plastic cards and automated video banking are for certain transactions to be done by clients.

(*c*) Intermediaries for increasing the availability of convenience of a service, help maintaining existing users and attract new users *viz.*, direct sales agents/automobile dealers/merchant establishments/physical distribution.

(*d*) Combination of (a) to (c)

Promotion in Marketing

Q.65. The role of promotion in marketing is based on —

(*a*) Persuasion seeks to bring about a change in attitude.

(*b*) Reminding seeks to remind the customers about the offerings for retaining their business.

(*c*) Reinforcing aims at reinforcing the customer satisfaction for increasing the number of habitual customers.

(*d*) Combination of (a) to (c)

Q.66. The components of Promotion Mix are —

(*a*) Advertising; a paid form of non-personal promotion/personal selling; personal presentation to prospective clients.

(*b*) Sales campaign; to encourage sales/public relations; for building good relations with clients/direct marketing; is making direct connect with individual customers.

(*c*) Sampling and coupons

(*d*) Combination of (a) and (b)

Q.67. Promotion mix strategies can be

(*a*) Push strategy - is directed at the channel members to induce them to purchase the products and sell them to the final consumer.

(*b*) Pull strategy - efforts are directed to the final consumer to induce them to buy the product.

(*c*) Hang strategy - efforts are directed to hang the services and attract the customers towards them

(*d*) Combination of (a) and (b)

Marketing Information System

Q.68. The meaning of marketing information system is —

(*a*) A system for providing accurate information for use by marketing decision makers, to improve their marketing planning, execution and control.

(*b*) A system to off-set uncertainty, improve economy of operations, to focus on objectives and to promote device for connecting the managed operating systems by exchange of information.

(*c*) Plan, organise and control the major activities of the business in order to have classified and interpreted data that are being used for decision making.

(*d*) Generation of information required for timely use and relevant for the business.

Q.69. The main features of Marketing Information System (MIS) are —

(*a*) Creation of master plan for information flow, coordination between functional departments and specialist executives, future orientation for anticipating and preventing marketing problems and solving them.

(*b*) Facilitation for developing decisions in planning, organising, controlling and initiating.

(*c*) Decision making, organising and controlling the major activities of the business and initiating action.

(*d*) None.

Q.70. The functions of collecting and assembling data, its processing, analysing, storage and dissemination of information is called —

(*a*) Mechanised information system.

(*b*) Marketing information system.

(*c*) Master processing strategy.

(*d*) Computerisation of clerical work.

Q.71. Need for Marketing Information System is due to —

(*a*) Better understanding of the market ups and downs.

(*b*) Better knowledge of customer behaviour and expectations.

(*c*) Information explosion, and avoidance of communication gap and to take prompt decisions and to face non-price competition.

(*d*) Competition in modern market, like branding, packaging and advertising only.

Q.72. The advantages of Marketing Information System are —

(*a*) Provision of procedure and methods for regular purpose oriented and systematic collection of data, its analysis, checks for reliability, tailor made information for specific needs.

(*b*) Facilitation of repetitive use of same information for different purposes, sorting out conflicting information, cross sharing of data for better customer service.

(*c*) Better customer relationships. It also serves as total knowledge management mechanism, making the knowledge flow, where it is required.

(*d*) Combination of (a) to (c)

Home Loans

Q.73. Direct finance to the housing sector up to ...... is treated as part of priority sector lending:

(*a*) Rs. 5 lakh

(*b*) Rs. 10 lakh

(*c*) Rs. 15 lakh

(*d*) Rs. 20 lakh

Q.74. The limit on housing loans for repairing damaged houses has been raised to .... in rural and semi-urban areas and to .... in urban areas:

(*a*) Rs.25,000 and Rs. 50,000

(*b*) Rs. 50,000 and Rs. 1 lakh

(*c*) Rs. 1 lakh and Rs. 2 lakh

(*d*) Rs. 2 lakh and Rs. 5 lakh

General Banking

Q.75. The ability of a commercial bank to increase its loans and investment depends on its:

(*a*) holding of Government securities

(*b*) profitability

(*c*) excess cash/liquidity position

(*d*) outstanding loans and investments

Q.76. Who manages the Rural Infrastructure Development Fund (RIDF):

(*a*) Reserve Bank of India

(*b*) NABARD

(*c*) Rural Development Ministry

(*d*) SIDBI

Risk Management

Q.77. Basel II norms are associated with .... sector/s among the following sectors:

(*a*) Banking sector

(*b*) Insurance sector

(*c*) Share markets

(*d*) All of the above

Banking technology

Q.78. What is John Shephard Baron's contribution to banking, the idea of which struck him as he stretched out in his bath after a long wait at the bank counter:

(*a*) ATM

(*b*) Credit Card

(*c*) Debit Card

(*d*) Plastic Money

Q.79. 'National Financial Switch' has been set up to facilitate connectivity between the Bank's switches and their ATMs, and inter bank payment gateway for authentication and routing the payment details of various e-commerce transactions. Which organisation has set up this switch:

(*a*) IBRD

(*b*) IDRBT

(*c*) SBI

(*d*) SIDBI

Credit Cards

Q.80. Disadvantages to Credit Card holders include:

(*a*) Over Spending ending in Debt Trap

(*b*) Frauds due to loss or theft of cards

(*c*) Forged signatures

(*d*) All of above

Q.81. The bank which pays the merchant for the transactions is called as.......

(*a*) Issuer bank
(*b*) Clearance bank
(*c*) Acquirer bank
(*d*) None of the above

Securities and their mode of charging

Q.82. The nature of charge created on the intangible securities like 'accounts receivable' is ....

(*a*) Assignment
(*b*) Mortgage
(*c*) Lien
(*d*) None of the above

Q.83. Under the provisions of ...., banks can sell the mortgaged property, without the intervention of the court after observing formalities mentioned therein.

(*a*) SARFAESI Act, 2002
(*b*) Transfer of Property Act
(*c*) Banking Regulation Act, 1949
(*d*) Negotiable Instruments Act, 1881

Q.84. Banks advance loans against the security of assets and the nature of charge created while doing so is .... (Take odd man out)

(*a*) Pledge
(*b*) Hypothecation
(*c*) Mortgage
(*d*) Assignment

Q.85. The provisions of SARFAESI Act, 2002 can be applied while taking possession of goods ....to the bank and selling them without intervention of the court and after observing the required formalities:

(*a*) Pledged
(*b*) Hypothecated
(*c*) Assigned
(*d*) Mortgaged

Q.86. In the case of pledge and hypothecation, the title in the goods is .... to the bank making the advance:

(*a*) Transferred

(*b*) Not transferred

(*c*) It can be either (*a*) or (*b*) above.

(*d*) None of the above

Q.87. As per section 2(4) of the Sale of Goods Act, goods represented by the documents create a right by virtue of either law or trade or usage, to possess the goods represented by the documents. The said goods represented by the documents are transferable by .... and/or delivery of the documents:

(*a*) Assignment

(*b*) Hypothecation

(*c*) Pledge

(*d*) Endorsement

Q.88. The banks can grant advances to employees for purchase of shares of their own companies under the ESOP to the extent of 90 per cent of the purchase price of shares subject to a limit of ....

(*a*) Rs. 10 lakh

(*b*) Rs. 20 lakh

(*c*) Rs. 50 lakh

(*d*) None of the above

Q.89. A................, though appears to be a negotiable instrument, is not a negotiable one, but only quasi-negotiable, since the *bona fide* transferee for value can be affected by defects in the title of the transferor:

(*a*) Document of Title to Goods

(*b*) Cheque

(*c*) Bill of Exchange

(*d*) Promissory Note

Q.90. The assignment shall not be operative as against the insurance company until the notice in writing is given to the insurance company. This notice may be given by......

(*a*) The assignee

(*b*) The assignor

(*c*) The nominee

(*d*) Either (*a*) or (*b*) of the above.

Q.91. Banks finance Book Debts by .... (Take odd man out) :

(*a*) Factoring
(*b*) Forfaiting
(*c*) Overdraft and Cash Credit against Hypothecation of book debts
(*d*) Cash Credit against pledge of book debts

Q.92. In a ...., there is transfer of interest in the property to the creditor but in ...., there is only obligation to repay money and no transfer of interest:

(*a*) Mortgage, hypothecation
(*b*) Pledge, Mortgage
(*c*) Both (*a*) and (*b*) above
(*d*) None of the above.

Q.93. The possession of the mortgaged property is normally given to the mortgagee in the case of ....

(*a*) Simple mortgage
(*b*) English Mortgage
(*c*) Usufructuary Mortgage
(*d*) None of the above

Q.94. The limitation period for filing a suit for sale of mortgaged property from the date the mortgage debt becomes due is ....

(*a*) 12 years
(*b*) 30 years
(*c*) 3 years
(*d*) None of the above.

Banking Regulation

Q.95. RBI performs diverse functions of .... of the monetary and banking system. (Pl. state what is not true)

(*a*) Supervision
(*b*) Control
(*c*) Development
(*d*) Transacting banking business with the general public

Q.96. RBI has been playing its role of supervision, control and development of the monetary and banking system in the country through its following functions: (Pl. state what is not true)

(*a*) Public Debt Management

(*b*) Banker to Government

(*c*) Bankers' Bank

(*d*) Banker to the general public

Q.97. Under the R.B.I. Act, 1934, it has the sole authority to issue coins/currency notes of denominations of ....

(*a*) Currency Notes of Rs. 2 and above

(*b*) One Rupee Note

(*c*) One Rupee Coin

(*d*) Fifty Paisa Coin

Q.98. The instruments used by RBI under general credit control are:

(State what is not correct)

(*a*) Bank Rate

(*b*) CRR

(*c*) SLR

(*d*) Exchange Control

Q.99. ....is a tool for general credit control used by RBI which not only influences the flow of liquidity for the purpose of expansion or contraction of credit but also helps RBI to stabilize money supply and prices of Government securities:

(*a*) Bank Rate

(*b*) CRR/SLR

(*c*) OMO

(*d*) Direct Auction

Q.100. Exchange control may be affected by various methods like .... (Pl. state what is not true)

(*a*) Exchange rate interventions

(*b*) Exchange restrictions

(*c*) Changes in CRR/SLR

(*d*) Changes in interest rates

Q.101. Exchange control methods adopted by RBI include:

(Pl. state what is not true)

(*a*) Bilateral settlement of mutual claims

(*b*) Import restrictions and tariffs

(*c*) Export subsidies and changes in interest rates

(*d*) Changes in Bank Rate

Q.102. The FEMA Act, 1999 was enacted to prohibit, restrict and regulate the following: (Pl. state what is not true)

(*a*) Any borrowing or lending in foreign exchange

(*b*) Any borrowing or lending in rupees between a resident in India and a person outside India

(*c*) Any borrowing or lending between residents in India

(*d*) Export, import or holding of currency notes or currency.

Q.103. The FEMA Act, 1999 was enacted to prohibit, restrict and regulate the following: (Pl. state what is not true)

(*a*) Transfer or issue of any foreign security by an Indian resident or by a person residing outside India

(*b*) Any borrowing or lending in rupees between a resident in India and a person outside India

(*c*) Any borrowing or lending between residents in India

(*d*) Deposits between residents in India and those residing outside India.

Q.104. RBI was instrumental in promoting the following financial institutions and providing them with continuous flow of credit: (State what is incorrect)

(*a*) NABARD

(*b*) IDBI

(*c*) SIDBI

(*d*) HDFC

Q.105. State which one amongst the following is not a tool of Monetary Control used by RBI?

(*a*) CRR

(*b*) SLR

(*c*) Branch Licensing Policy

(*d*) Open Market Operations

Q.106. The percentage of SLR currently in force is .....

(*a*) 25

(*b*) 24

(*c*) 23

(*d*) 22

Q.107. A decrease in CRR and SLR will ....the liquidity in the banking system:

(*a*) Decrease

(*b*) Improve

(*c*) Not impact

(*d*) Decrease and improve respectively

Capital Market

Q.108. A bond issued at a discount and redeemable at face value may be which of the following?

(*a*) Preference bond

(*b*) Zero Coupon Bond

(*c*) Convertible Bond

(*d*) Perpetual bond

Q.109. The demutualised exchanges in India do not include:

(*a*) Bombay Stock Exchange

(*b*) National Stock Exchange

(*c*) OTCEI

(*d*) Ahmedabad Stock Exchange

Mutual Funds

Q.110. The Mutual Funds in India are regulated by:

(*a*) RBI

(*b*) SEBI

(*c*) AMFI

(*d*) IRDA

Risk Management

Q.111. The Basel II Accord provides a spectrum of approaches from simple to advanced methodologies for the measurement of both .... and .... in determining capital levels.

(*a*) Credit Risk and Operational Risk

(*b*) Currency Risk and Forex Risk

(*c*) Regulatory and Reputational Risk

(*d*) None of the above

Q.112. The Basel II Accord is based on the concept of a capital ratio where the numerator represents the required amount of capital by a bank and the denominator:

(*a*) The risk-weighted assets

(*b*) Non-performing assets
(*c*) Both (*a*) and (*b*) above
(*d*) None of the above

Q.113. Under Basel II Accord, the minimum required capital ratio as stipulated by RBI continues to be :

(*a*) 8%
(*b*) 9%
(*c*) 10%
(*d*) 12%

Q.114. The Basel II Accord differs from the earlier accord by the introduction of an explicit treatment for .... in the definition of risk-weighted assets:

(*a*) Credit Risk
(*b*) Operational Risk
(*c*) Market Risk
(*d*) None of the above

Mergers and consolidation

Q.115. The mergers involving two or more companies which are producing similar products or rendering the same type of services competing directly with each other are called .....

(*a*) Horizontal Mergers
(*b*) Vertical Mergers
(*c*) Concentric Mergers
(*d*) Cogeneric Mergers

CIBIL

Q.116. .... has been set up for exchange of credit information among its members:

(*a*) DICGCI
(*b*) CIBIL
(*c*) ECGC
(*d*) EXIM Bank

Banking Codes and Standards

Q.117. The Banking Codes and Standards Board of India (BCSBI) is functioning as ....

(*a*) a Department of the RBI

(*b*) a Company incorporated under the Indian Companies Act, 1956.

(*c*) a Society under the Societies Registration Act, 1860

(*d*) none of the above

Banker-Customer Relationship

Q.118. A bank received the payment of an outstation bill on behalf of its customer, but before the money could be credited to the customer's account the bank failed. What is the relationship between the bank and the customer?

(*a*) Creditor & Debtor

(*b*) Principal & Agent

(*c*) Bailer & Bailee

(*d*) Trustee & Beneficiary

Know Your Customer

Q.119. Which one of the following is a valid document available to the bank for customer identification?

(*a*) Voter's ID Card

(*b*) Ration Card

(*c*) Bank's Pass Book

(*d*) All the above

AML

Q.120. All cash transactions of the value of more than .... or its equivalent in foreign currency are to be reported by banks to the Financial Intelligence Unit - India :

(*a*) Rs. 5 lakh

(*b*) Rs. 10 lakh

(*c*) Rs. 25 lakh

(*d*) None of the above

Priority Sector Lending

Q.121. The export finance made by .... is reckoned as priority sector advance:

(*a*) Domestic scheduled commercial banks

(*b*) Co-operative banks

(*c*) Foreign Banks

(*d*) Regional Rural banks

Q.122. The Export Credit target for foreign banks in India is ..... of ANBC:

(*a*) 40 per cent

(*b*) 32 per cent

(*c*) 12 per cent

(*d*) 10 per cent

Micro Finance

Q.123. Provision of credit not exceeding .... per borrower, either directly or through SHG/JLG mechanism will constitute micro credit:

(*a*) Rs.10,000

(*b*) Rs. 25,000

(*c*) Rs. 50,000

(*d*) Rs. 1 lac

Q.124. A micro enterprise in the service sector is one where the investment in equipment does not exceed ......

(*a*) Rs. 10 lakh

(*b*) Rs. 20 lakh

(*c*) Rs. 25 lakh

(*d*) Rs. 50 lakh

SARFAESI Act, 2002

Q.125. The Securitization & Reconstruction of Financial Assets and Enforcement of Security Interest Act, 2002 allowed the banks to take possession of assets of defaulting borrowers and charged to the bank.......

(*a*) With the legal process

(*b*) Without the legal process

(*c*) With the permission of Lok Adalat

(*d*) None of these

Non-Performing Assets

Q.126. An NPA is an advance, where Interest and/or instalment of principal remains overdue for a period of more than ..... days in respect of a term loan and the account remains "out of order" for a period of ......days in respect of an Overdraft/Cash Credit:

(*a*) 90 days

(*b*) 120 days

(*c*) 180 days

(*d*) None of the above

Q.127. An account should be treated as "out of order" if the outstanding balance remains continuously in excess of the sanctioned limit/drawing power. In cases where the outstanding balance is less than the sanctioned limit/drawing power, but there are no credits continuously for .....days or the credits are not enough to cover the interest during the same period, then the account should be treated as "out of order".

(*a*) 90 days

(*b*) 120 days

(*c*) 180 days

(*d*) None of the above

Q.128. A stock statement displays the current assets owned by a borrower against which working capital is provided by the bank. The outstanding in the account, based on the drawing power calculated from stock statements older than .... would be deemed as irregular and such accounts should be treated as "out of order":

(*a*) 1 month

(*b*) 2 months

(*c*) 3 months

(*d*) None of the above

Q.129. The bill remains overdue for a period of 90 days, in the case of bills purchased and discounted. If one bill purchased/discounted by a bank is overdue for more than 90 days, the total outstanding .... is treated as NPA:

(*a*) Of the overdue bill.

(*b*) In the account towards all the bills purchased/discounted.

(*c*) In the borrower's various advances accounts with the Bank.

(*d*) None of the above.

Q.130. A loan granted for short term crops will be treated as NPA, if the instalment of principal or interest thereon or both remain overdue for .... crop season/s:

(*a*) one
(*b*) two
(*c*) three
(*d*) four

Q.131. ABC Bank has advanced Rs. 50,000 to a farmer for cultivation of sugarcane crop in June, 2007. The borrower has repaid Rs. 25,000 plus interest accrued on the entire loan promptly after the harvest of sugarcane in June, 2008 and informed the bank that he could not pay the balance amount of loan as the crop was affected by the disease resulting in a poor yield just sufficient to pay a half of the loan availed by him from the bank. How would the bank recognise the balance loan outstanding in his account for the purpose of asset classification as on 30-6-2008?

(*a*) As a Standard Asset
(*b*) As a Sub-Standard Asset
(*c*) As a Doubtful Asset
(*d*) As a Loss Asset

Q.132. Which of the following assets may be included for the purpose of NPA classification?

(*a*) Loan against the bank's fixed deposits
(*b*) Loan against life policies
(*c*) Crop Loan granted to farmers
(*d*) Staff loan

Q.133. The sub-standard accounts subjected to restructuring would be eligible to be upgraded to the standard category only after a specified period of .... after the date on which the first payment of interest or principal, whichever is earlier, falls due:

(*a*) 90 days
(*b*) 180 days
(*c*) One year
(*d*) None of the above

Q.134. A borrowal account is classified as sub-standard if it is overdue for more than 90 days. It means that the account has to be overdue at the maximum for........., in order to be classified in the doubtful category:

(*a*) 12 months

(*b*) 15 months

(*c*) 18 months

(*d*) None of the above

Q.135. In cases where the loan is sanctioned by the bank against the borrower submitting the fake/forged documents and thus playing fraud on the bank, such a loan is to be treated in the bank's books as a .... asset, even when there is recovery in the account as per the repayment schedule approved by the bank at the time of sanctioning the loan.

(*a*) Standard

(*b*) Sub-standard

(*c*) Doubtful

(*d*) Loss

Q.136. In case of a personal loan where there is default in repayment, say for 90 days, the account may be classified as .... asset:

(*a*) Sub-standard

(*b*) Doubtful

(*c*) Loss

(*d*) None of the above.

Q.137. Banks shall make 100% provision against the unsecured portion of a doubtful asset. In regard to the secured portion and if the asset remained in doubtful category for less than a year, a provision of .... may be made on the amount of advance so secured:

(*a*) 20%

(*b*) 30%

(*c*) 50%

(*d*) 100%

Financial Inclusion

Q.138. When was the 'Self Help Group' bank linkage programme started ?

(*a*) 1992

(*b*) 1995

(*c*) 1998

(*d*) 2001

Q.139. By Financial Inclusion, we mean provision of .... by the formal financial system to those who are hitherto excluded:

(*a*) Affordable financial services

(*b*) Savings and insurance services alone

(*c*) Payments and remittance facilities alone

(*d*) Small-value credit facilities

Q.140. The RBI has continued to lay stress on the need for financial inclusion and advised banks to make available a basic banking ....with nil or very minimum balance:

(*a*) Savings account

(*b*) No-frills savings account

(*c*) Current account

(*d*) Deposit account

Q.141. The RBI, in its efforts towards faster financial inclusion both in the rural and urban areas, has also advised banks to simplify the KYC procedure for opening accounts for those persons with balances not exceeding .... and credits in the accounts not exceeding .... in a year:

(*a*) Rs. 1000 and Rs. 10000

(*b*) Rs. 5000 and Rs. 25000

(*c*) Rs. 25000 and Rs. 50000

(*d*) Rs. 50000 and Rs. 1 lakh

Q.142. Under the Business Facilitator Model, banks may use intermediaries such as:

(*a*) NGOs/Farmers' Clubs

(*b*) Post Offices

(*c*) KVIC/KVIB Units

(*d*) All the above

Q.143. In addition to organizations such as NGOs/MFIs set up under the Societies/Trust Acts etc., certain individuals like .... may also act as Business Correspondents :

(*a*) Retired bankers

(*b*) Retired Government Employees

(*c*) Ex-servicemen

(*d*) All the above

Q.144. The scope of the activities undertaken by the business correspondents will include:

(*a*) Disbursal of small-value credit

(*b*) Recovery of loans and interest

(*c*) Collection of small-value deposit

(*d*) All the above

Q.145. Banks cannot use the services of the following persons as Business Facilitator/Business Correspondent:

(*a*) Village Sarpanchs

(*b*) Insurance Agents

(*c*) Ex-servicemen

(*d*) Retired Government Officials

Documentation

Q.146. When banks make advances to limited companies against their assets, the required forms are to be presented to the Registrar of Companies within .....from the date of execution:

(*a*) 21 days

(*b*) 30 days

(*c*) 1 month

(*d*) None of the above

Q.147. In the case of creation of registered mortgages, the mortgage deed should be presented for registration with Registrar of Assurances within .... month/s from the date of execution of the deed:

(*a*) 1 month

(*b*) 2 months

(*c*) 3 months

(*d*) 4 months

Q.148. Take the odd man out:

(*a*) D.P.N.

(*b*) Hypothecation Agreement

(*c*) Term Loan Agreement

(*d*) Application Form

Indian Financial System

Q.149. Primary Dealers (PDs) deal in .... in both primary and secondary markets:

(*a*) Equities

(*b*) Debentures

(*c*) Corporate Bonds

(*d*) Government Securities

Q.150. Urban Co-operative banks are controlled by .... and ....

(*a*) State Governments and RBI.

(*b*) State Governments and NABARD

(*c*) Both State and Central Government

(*d*) RBI and NABARD

Q.151. ....regulates all aspects of insurance business:

(*a*) RBI

(*b*) IRDA

(*c*) AMFI

(*d*) None of the above

Q.152. Among the following, which one is not a regulator?

(*a*) RBI

(*b*) SEBI

(*c*) AMFI

(*d*) IRDA

Q.153. RBI is popularly known as a lender ....

(*a*) To Central Government

(*b*) To State Government

(*c*) Of Foreign Currency

(*d*) Of the last resort

ANSWERS					
1. (b)	2. (a)	3. (a)	4. (b)	5. (d)	6. (d)
7. (a)	8. (a)	9. (b)	10. (d)	11. (d)	12. (d)
13. (a)	14. (b)	15. (c)	16. (b)	17. (d)	18. (c)
19. (d)	20. (d)	21. (d)	22. (a)	23. (d)	24. (d)
25. (d)	26. (d)	27. (d)	28. (c)	29. (a)	30. (d)
31. (d)	32. (d)	33. (b)	34. (d)	35. (b)	36. (d)
37. (d)	38. (d)	39. (b)	40. (c)	41. (d)	42. (a)
43. (d)	44. (b)	45. (c)	46. (a)	47. (c)	48. (a)
49. (c)	50. (d)	51. (d)	52. (c)	53. (c)	54. (a)
55. (a)	56. (a)	57. (d)	58. (d)	59. (a)	60. (a)
61. (b)	62. (d)	63. (d)	64. (d)	65. (d)	66. (d)
67. (d)	68. (a)	69. (a)	70. (b)	71. (c)	72. (d)
73. (d)	74. (d)	75. (c)	76. (b)	77. (a)	78. (a)
79. (b)	80. (d)	81. (c)	82. (a)	83. (a)	84. (d)
85. (b)	86. (b)	87. (d)	88. (b)	89. (a)	90. (d)
91. (d)	92. (a)	93. (c)	94. (a)	95. (d)	96. (d)
97. (a)	98. (d)	99. (c)	100. (c)	101. (d)	102. (c)
103. (c)	104. (d)	105. (c)	106. (b)	107. (b)	108. (b)
109. (d)	110. (b)	111. (a)	112. (a)	113. (a)	114. (b)
115. (a)	116. (b)	117. (c)	118. (b)	119. (a)	120. (b)
121. (c)	122. (c)	123. (c)	124. (a)	125. (b)	126. (a)
127. (a)	128. (c)	129. (c)	130. (b)	131. (a)	132. (c)
133. (c)	134. (b)	135. (d)	136. (c)	137. (a)	138. (a)
139. (a)	140. (b)	141. (d)	142. (d)	143. (d)	144. (d)
145. (a)	146. (b)	147. (d)	148. (d)	149. (d)	150. (a)
151. (b)	152. (c)	153. (d)			

CHAPTER

2

MULTIPLE CHOICE - PROBLEMS AND SOLUTIONS

Q.1. Can a commercial bank acquire, construct and maintain buildings for indefinite period ?

(*a*) No, it is not permitted as per section 6(1) of B.R. Act. It is allowed for its own use. The bank can acquire, hold and deal with any property (but cannot construct), which may form the security of any loan, not for a period exceeding 7 years (sec. 8)

(*b*) No, this is not possible as it is prohibited under section 8 of B.R. Act. However the bank can realise the securities given to it or held by it for a loan, if need arises [as per section 6(1)].

(*c*) Yes, this is permitted under section 6(1) of B.R. Act.

(*d*) Yes, this is permitted under section 8 of B.R. Act.

Q.2. .... are the various types of risks in Internet banking.

(*a*) Operational or transactional, reputational, legal, credit, liquidity, interest rate risks.

(*b*) Money laundering, cross border terrorism, strategic system not working up to expectations, security breach, criminal activities.

(*c*) Non-Compliance of different countries laws, absence of consumer protection laws and privacy laws.

(*d*) Risk arising from access to critical information, by hackers.

Q.3. Which of the following statement/s is/are true?

(*a*) Securitisation can provide much needed liquidity to an originators' balance sheet, make room for fresh asset creation, and obtain better pricing than through a debt-financing route. It also allows investors to improve their yields.

(*b*) Small business loans can be securitised only if there is government guarantee and thus help the originator in proactively managing its asset portfolio.

(*c*) Under securitisation, although the bank does not choose to service the loans, customers are concerned with control of credit by bank.

(*d*) Securitisation does not transfer the credit and other risks.

Q.4. Which of the following statement/s is/are true regarding Banker's duty of maintaining confidentiality?

(*a*) A banker has a duty to keep confidential certain affairs and this duty is non-contractual.

(*b*) The duty is absolute and under several circumstances a banker can disclose otherwise privileged information.

(*c*) It does not apply where disclosure is compelled under law, or duty to disclose, or in the banks interest and with the consent of the parties.

(*d*) The duty does not extend beyond the information obtained from customer account.

Q.5. You are an official of ABC Bank served with a garnishee order by the Court regarding the accounts of Neha Agarwal. Which of the following is most appropriate action?

(*a*) As soon as the garnishee order "NISI" is served, the bank should freeze the entire balance standing to the credit of customers account unless the order directs otherwise.

(*b*) The bank would handover the order to banks' advocate for his opinion.

(*c*) Inform the customer about the court order and ask her to bring vacation of order.

(*d*) The bank may send a notice to the court as to why it should not pay the amount to the creditor.

Q.6. Which of the following factors spurred the growth of the housing finance industry in India?

(*a*) Improved demand and rising affordability, low interest rates on advances, rising income levels of persons, fiscal incentives, increasing urbanisation and higher deduction for company's quarters by employers, etc.

(*b*) Every rupee spent on housing leads to a 78 paise increase in Gross Domestic Product (GDP), increase in real estate price compared to bank deposit rates and free housing to middle and lower class families.

(*c*) Availability of open lands of closed textile mills and other SSI units at lower prices to builders.

(*d*) Sharp rise in income levels and inflation index.

Q.7. Which instrument comes as a protection for the importer/exporter ?

(*a*) Factoring

(*b*) Guarantees issued by banks to clients

(*c*) Letter of credit, a document issued by a bank guaranteeing a client's ability to pay for goods or services.

(*d*) Deferred payment guarantee. No cash is tied up in the process. This is particularly helpful when the importer is unfamiliar with the overseas laws and suppliers.

Q.8. As a Credit Officer considering a loan application from a customer, what are the questions that must be satisfactorily answered before you recommend for the approval of the loan?

(*a*) Credit officer will check the purpose of loan, amount of loan, duration, repayment period, availability of technical know-how, market stability, financial soundness, bank's exposure to the industry, securities and their valuations, and bank's ability to monitor the advance.

(*b*) Credit officer will usually look at capacity to repay, cash flow projections, amount of capital invested, collateral security and its valuation, local economic conditions and industry trends.

(*c*) Assessment of the risks and rewards of sanctioning a loan, ratio analysis and due diligence.

(*d*) All the above.

Q.9. Mr. Wani has been forging his wife's signature on cheques that were paid by bank which was discovered by her. On Mrs. Wani's reprimand on an occasion, Mr. Wani expressed regret and promised not to repeat.

A year later, Mrs. Wani found out that Mr. Wani had again forged her signature and bought shares wherein he suffered losses in the stock market. Mrs. Wani then complained to the bank for passing of forged cheque, and demanded refund of a total sum of Rs. 25,27,29,000 *plus* interest thereon @ 3.5% p.a. from the day the account was opened by her. Will Mrs. Wani be able to recover the money from the bank?

(*a*) A customer would be failing in his/her duty, if he/she remained silent about the forgery and thus, allowed the forger to escape. In such a situation, the customer cannot claim from the bank the money paid by the bank on the forged cheques.

Mrs. Wani owed a duty to the bank to notify it promptly of any forgeries. Failure to do gives rise to estoppels.

(*b*) She cannot recover the amount lost by forgeries, since the culprit was her husband.

(*c*) She can recover the amount from the bank if she hands over her husband to the police.

(*d*) None of the above.

Q.10. Under which of the following circumstances, a bank can dishonour the cheque?

(*a*) Death/incapacity/bankruptcy or insolvency of the customer, serving of Garnishee order/countermand/insufficient funds/account is closed/defect in the presenter's title.

(*b*) A Garnishee NISI order is served for lesser amount compared to credit balance/cheque's payee is a minor, etc.

(*c*) When payee is imprisoned.

(*d*) Combination of (*b*) and (*c*)

Q.11. Mr. Chhaganlal Gupta and Mr. P.C. Jain, are partners in M/s. C.P.C. Television. The firm enjoys a cash credit hypothecation limit of Rs. 10 lakhs from ABC Bank. Account is operative by any of the partners singly. On 7th January 2005, Mr. P.C. Jain and the wife of Mr. M.C. Gupta informed the bank that Mr. Gupta had died two days ago. Mr. P.C. Jain has requested the bank to continue operations in the account since the account was in debit. On September 9, 2005 Mr. P.C. Jain became bankrupt. On the date of bankruptcy of Mr. P.C. Jain, the C/C Hyp. A/c. (since old account was continued by bank) was having a debit balance of Rs.10,50,000.

Advise the bank whether it can sue the wife of Mr. Gupta as heirs of the estate of Mr. Gupta for recovery of amount.

(*a*) ABC Bank can recover the amount since the death of a customer terminates the mandate or authority given to the banker. The rights and interest of the customer are passed on to the legal representative of the deceased customer.

(*b*) Bank cannot sue the estate of the Mr. Gupta, the deceased, because of the operation of Clayton's Rule (Devaynes v/s Noble). As the account was in debit balance, the bank should have frozen the account on information of death of Mr. Gupta. There were substantial credits after the notice of death; the estate of the deceased was no longer liable for the firm's debt. The wife of Mr. Gupta is not liable for the firm's debt.

(*c*) Mrs. Gupta is having the means to repay. Thus, the bank may succeed.

(*d*) None of the above.

Q.12. The basic foundation of a bank's appraisal for working capital is based on the needs of creditors and the level of current assets. Which of the following statements is true in respect of working capital finance?

(*a*) The working capital limit is fixed on an annual basis. However since such limit is provided to meet specific requirements, utilising the limits is subjected to the Drawing power, which is decided on a daily/weekly/monthly/quarterly basis. The effective bank financing is, therefore, to the extent of the lower of working limit - determined on the assessment of the current year's projection and the actual for the previous year.

(*b*) Drawing power - linked to the quantum of current assets (and the current liabilities) owned by the business with appropriate margins. Amount allowed to be drawn is equal to MPBF or drawing power, whichever is less.

(*c*) Working capital includes the amounts and expenses incurred for purchase of raw materials, manufacturing, selling and administration until such goods are sold and the monies realised.

(*d*) Combination of (*a*) and (*b*).

Q.13. ATM cardholder wants to operate the card, but he forgets the number for feeding in the ATM machine. What is that number called?

(*a*) PAN (Permanent Account Number)

(*b*) FIN (Financial Information Number)

(*c*) PIN (Personal Identification Number)

(*d*) PIN (Personal Introduction Number)

Q.14. A large scale computer network spread over a span of sizeable geographic area utilising the telecommunication network is called -

(*a*) LAN

(*b*) WAN

(*c*) Offline

(*d*) Online

Q.15. Shrikant drew a cheque payable to Smt. Shubha on ABC Bank Ltd., for Rs. 7000. When Shubha presented the cheque to the bank, the bank refused to pay the cheque, because the teller entered the wrong account number, which had a balance of less than Rs.7000. In fact there were sufficient funds in Shrikant's account. The bank would be liable for —

(*a*) Stop payment orders

(*b*) Insufficient funds

(*c*) Wilful dishonour

(*d*) Wrongful dishonour

Q.16. A customer deposits shares of MTNL and jewellery in the safe deposit vaults/lockers of a bank for safety against payment of rent. What is the role of the bank?

(*a*) Debtor

(*b*) Drawee

(*c*) Depository

(*d*) Lessor

Q.17. Which of the following is NOT a part of the fundamental principles, which guide lending?

(*a*) Safety

(*b*) Security

(*c*) Liquidity

(*d*) Legality

Q.18. If there were a probability/likelihood for the borrower to use money towards unproductive or unsuccessful activities, the bank would not sanction the credit to such borrower. This is based on .... principle.

(*a*) Safety

(*b*) Security

(*c*) Liquidity

(*d*) Profitability

Q.19. If an exporter is doubtful about an issuing bank's ability to pay under LC, he will expect a domestic bank to join the transaction. This type of LC is called - - - LC.

(*a*) Revolving

(*b*) Revocable

(*c*) Irrevocable

(*d*) Confirmed

Q.20. The distance between two branches of Zero Bank Plc. is 300 metres. What computer network will link computers and peripherals of both the branches?

(*a*) LAN

(*b*) WAN

(*c*) DDP

(*d*) UPS

Q.21. Your branch is having LAN system of network. Uninterruptible power supply can be attached with the file server. Which of the following is correct?

(*a*) 230-volt input current converted into 48 V-DC and then converted to a 230 V-AC. It comes back automatically, to the normal status when the main supply recovers.

(*b*) When the power is on, the battery charger is only charging the battery and the inverter is on standby. It supplies raw power and does not regulate the input frequency.

(*c*) Both A&B are applicable

(*d*) Neither A nor B is applicable

Q.22. There has been crowding at bank counters in ABC Bank. The Bank desires to improve the service at reduced cost. Which of the following is the best alternative?

(*a*) Increase counters at the branch.

(*b*) Take new premises for additional counters.

(*c*) To install automatic teller machines.

(*d*) To provide Home Banking (personal).

Q.23. Which credit card is useful exclusively by members of a club or chain of hotels?

(*a*) Member card

(*b*) Smart card

(*c*) Charge card

(*d*) Chip card

Q.24. Data movement in both the directions is possible through ....

(*a*) Siplex method of transmission

(*b*) Modems

(*c*) Full duplex

(*d*) COMET

Q.25. What of the following techniques is applied in analysing predictions of customer behaviour, highly targeted market focus, maximised operational effectiveness, and optimal return on investment?

(*a*) Data Warehousing

(*b*) SWIFT

(*c*) VSAT

(*d*) Data Mining

Q.26. Which is the place or site for Corporates to market their services/products for dissemination of information, financial advice, node for commerce, gateway to the Internet?

(*a*) Website
(*b*) Indonet
(*c*) VSAT
(*d*) Mobilenet

Q.27. For increasing organisational productivity, efficiency, better control, reducing the hierarchical tier systems, change in managerial attitudes, addition to the changes in organisational structure and orientation, which of the following technology is the best ?

(*a*) Management technology
(*b*) Software technology
(*c*) Credit Risk management
(*d*) Information technology

Q.28. The main characteristics of intangibility, inseparability, heterogeneity, perishability pertain to?

(*a*) Services
(*b*) Product
(*c*) Management
(*d*) MIS

Q.29. Anything that can be offered to satisfy a want or need is called a product. Out of the following, which cannot be considered a product?

(*a*) Pilgrimage tour to Bangladesh
(*b*) "Green New Delhi" call
(*c*) Spring Leaf Co-operative Housing Society
(*d*) Discourse for public by Shri Sudhanshu Maharaj at Azad Maidan.

Q.30. There are four stages in a product life cycle *viz.*, introduction, growth, maturity and decline. From the following which products is in its introductory stage in modern banking?

(*a*) Home banking through personal computers and debit cards.
(*b*) Home loans and tractor loans.
(*c*) Savings bank account.
(*d*) Demand drafts.

Q.31. The landline telephone connections are in large volume in our country but because of cellular phones, the volume of land line connections is affected. Under which category of product life cycle does the landline phone service stand?

(*a*) Introduction

(*b*) Decline

(*c*) Growth

(*d*) Maturity

Q.32. The product life cycle concept has introduction, growth, maturity and decline stages. What shall be the profit position of a product in the maturity stage?

(*a*) Low margin

(*b*) Marginal

(*c*) Rapid rise

(*d*) Falling margins

Q.33. The position of competition in the declining stage of the product life cycle would be?

(*a*) Limited competitors

(*b*) Extensive

(*c*) Few competitors

(*d*) Inefficient competitors

Q.34. In the maturity stage of its life cycle, the sales of a product declines. At this stage, efforts are made to stimulate sales of the products; by modifying the product's characteristics. This is achieved to improve the functional performance *viz.*, durability, reliability and/or speed of the product. What would such modification be called?

(*a*) Feature improvement

(*b*) Style improvement

(*c*) Quality improvement

(*d*) Loyalty improvement

Q.35. Pizza-hut is the name of the retail chain in the country and overseas, although all pizza shops are located not in any hut but in a posh and decorated building, but are still called Pizza-hut. It is—

(*a*) Personality

(*b*) Product mix

(*c*) Brand name

(*d*) Brand location

Q.36. The value of a brand is its power to capture consumer preference and loyalty. The positive differential effect that knowing a brand name has on consumer response to a product or service, is called as brand equity. Brands represent consumers' perceptions and feelings about a product and its performance. Which of the following would be the most appropriate for branding in the case of a bank ?

(*a*) Banks' name

(*b*) Banks' staff as brand ambassador

(*c*) Banks' number of years of services

(*d*) Banks' chairman

Q.37. ABC Bank Ltd., has a special product for senior citizens which provides cheque book on savings account with customers' name on cheque book, free of cost debit card with overdraft facility of Rs.25,000, a special pouch for holding passbook, cheque book and debit card facility for withdrawal and deposits at any branch of the bank, free of cost remittance to any branch of the bank and free of cost remittance to any branch of another bank covered under RTGS facility. Which of the following is the core product in this offering?

(*a*) Overdraft

(*b*) Debit card

(*c*) Remittances

(*d*) Savings account

Q.38. ABC Bank Ltd. finds that its savings account which requires a Rs. 400 minimum balance, costs the banks Rs.3.13 per month in servicing costs, Rs. 1.18 per month in overhead expenses and a profit margin of Re. 0.50 is added per month. What monthly fee should the bank charge for each customer?

Further analysis of customer accounts reveals that for each additional Rs. 100 maintained in average balance in its savings account, the bank saves about 5% in operating expenses associated with each account. For a customer who consistently maintains an average balance of Rs. 1000 per month, how much should the bank charge so as to protect its profit margin?

(*a*) Monthly fee = Rs. 3.13 + Rs. 1.18 + Re. 0.50 = Rs. 4.81
Fee for customer = Rs. 3.13 - 30% + 1.18 + 0.50
= Rs. 2.19 + 1.18 + 0.50
= Rs. 3.87 per month

(*b*) Monthly fee = Rs. 3.13 + Rs. 1.18 + Re. 0.50 = Rs. 4.81
Fee for customer = 30% (Rs. 3.13 + 1.18) + 0.50
= Rs. 3.02 + 0.50
= Rs. 3.52 per month

(*c*) Monthly fee = 30% of Rs. 4.81
Fee for customer = Rs. 3.37 per month

(*d*) None of the above.

Q.39. Which is the rate, the banks quote to their most trusted and creditworthy customers?

(*a*) Floating rate

(*b*) Prime Lending rate

(*c*) Inter bank rate

(*d*) Bank rate

Q.40. Mr. & Mrs. X maintain a joint saving account with ABC Bank Ltd., with mandate 'either or survivor'. On 21-9-2005, Mr. X had a heart attack and died in the premises of ABC Bank Ltd. One week after Mr. X's death, Mrs. X wants to withdraw the entire sum standing in the credit of the joint account. Which of the following is the most appropriate action

(*a*) The bank cannot make the payment unless there is nomination in favour of Mrs. X.

(*b*) Relationship with the customer terminates on account of death of the depositor. When operation is either or survivor, the balance can be paid to Mrs. X on production of death certificate.

(*c*) The credit balance cannot be paid to the deceased wife, unless Certificate of Probate is produced.

(*d*) B or C only

Q.41. Shrikant is a current account holder of ABC Bank Ltd. Shrikant is dissatisfied with the bank service as he claimed that the bank had wrongfully returned his cheque for Rs. 300, citing the reason as "account closed" when there was sufficient credit balance Rs.350 in his account. Bank claimed that the account of Shrikant was closed, based on his telephonic conversation with the branch manager of the bank for closing the account. Bankers' cheque for Rs.350 was posted to Shrikant recently by the bank. Shrikant denied having had any such conversation and threatened to sue the bank. Which of the following is the most appropriate action :

(*a*) Based on telephonic conversation with the customer the bank may close the account as a normal service provided to customers. Hence bank has done nothing wrong.

(*b*) If the bank manager has closed the account on the basis of telephonic conversation, then definitely the bank has committed a mistake, because the customer can dispute as to whether there was any written instruction, as has happened in this case. Only written instructions to close the account should be given to the bank along with details of unused cheque leaves. The bank here is liable for damages.

(*c*) Bank on receipt of verbal instructions, should have given adequate notice to its customer before closing the account, hence it is liable for unauthorised closure of account and is liable for damages by the use of the words "no account" or "account closed".

(*d*) None of the above

Q.42. Miss Neha Agarwal issues an order cheque to Natwarlal. One Rajaram signs on the back of the cheque (Rs.5000) and then approaches the bank for payment. The bank's teller asked the holder "your endorsement is required on the back of the cheque before I encash it".

Rajaram signs at the back of the cheque and the bank encashes it. Later on it was found that the signature of the payee was forged. Which of the following is correct in this case ?

(*a*) A banker who pays an order cheque containing a forged endorsement, in good faith and in the ordinary course of business, is deemed to have made payment in due course and as such not liable in this case.

(*b*) If the order cheque is presented for encashment and it does not contain an endorsement, the cheque should be returned with the remark, "payee's endorsement required". If the presenter then in the presence of the teller endorses the cheque by signing the payee's name on the reverse of the cheque, the teller should insist on positive identification. Since the same is not done by the teller, the bank will not be protected.

(*c*) A teller when confronted with an order cheque containing an endorsement in blank, should not ask the presenter whether he/she is the payee but should merely proceed and assume that the endorsement is valid and that the presenter is the payee. If it turns out that the endorsement was forged and the payee is not a customer of the bank, the bank will be protected.

(*d*) None of the above

ANSWERS

1. (a)	2. (a)	3. (a)	4. (c)	5. (a)	6. (a)
7. (c)	8. (d)	9. (a)	10. (a)	11. (b)	12. (d)
13. (c)	14. (b)	15. (d)	16. (d)	17. (d)	18. (a)
19. (d)	20. (b)	21. (a)	22. (c)	23. (a)	24. (b)
25. (d)	26. (a)	27. (d)	28. (a)	29. (b)	30. (a)
31. (b)	32. (c)	33. (a)	34. (c)	35. (c)	36. (a)
37. (a)	38. (a)	39. (b)	40. (b)	41. (b)	42. (b)

CHAPTER

3

APPLIED THEORY (QUESTIONS AND ANSWERS IN MULTIPLE CHOICE)

Q.1. Management of working capital is of crucial importance considering the dynamic nature of operations of an enterprise. Which of the following factors affect the composition of working capital ?

(*a*) Nature of business, nature of raw materials used, process technology and its stages, nature of finished goods and degree of competition in the market.

(*b*) Period of inventory, industry, whether seasonal or regular, liquidity of cash in the business, finished goods shelf life, (short or long), bills receivable for long period or short period and the security offered in the loan sanction.

(*c*) Demand of the borrower, MPBF as carried out by banks, bridge loans for the time gap, use of current ratio of 1:1 or 1.33:1

(*d*) All of the above

Q.2. Which of the following statement best illustrates a bank guarantee ?

(*a*) A commercial instrument in the nature of a contract, intended to secure compliance with the contract. A guarantee can be given by the buyer to a seller for the present payments.

(*b*) A contract of guarantee is a contract to perform the promise made or discharge liability incurred by a third party in case of his default.

(*c*) A guarantee may be given by the contractor as a guarantee for any amount advanced.

(*d*) The promisee in a contract of guarantee indemnifies to perform the promise made of discharge or liability incurred by a third person. A guarantee is given to safeguard against the interest and as for due payments

Q.3. Which of the following statement is true in respect of Small Manufacturing Enterprises ?

(*a*) Small Manufacturing Enterprise means a manufacturing unit in which investment in plant and machinery does not exceed Rs. Five Crore.

(*b*) For all small and medium enterprises, bank limits should not exceed Rs. One crore.

(*c*) Small Manufacturing Enterprises can have investment of less than Rs. 25 lacs in plant and machinery.

(*d*) In case of Small Manufacturing Enterprises, the total employment does not exceed 50 (fifty) and most of the process is manual only.

Q.4. Which of the following statement is true in respect of SSI units ?

(*a*) Rangarajan Committee devised norms for SSI units for assessing the working capital requirements and pegged it at 20% of the projected turn-over.

(*b*) Small scale industries have a distinct set of characteristics such as low bargaining power leading to problem of receivable and lower credit on purchases, poor financial strength, high level of variability due to dependence on local factors. The Nayak Committee has assessed the working capital requirement of SSI and pegged it at 20% of the projected annual turnover.

(*c*) SSI have distinct set of characteristics and Laxminarayan Committee has opined that the turnover method for working capital is based on 20% of the projected annual turnover.

(*d*) None of the above

Q.5. Off balance sheet activities undertaken by banks generate good return for a bank and they are more risky too. Which of the following are off-balance sheet items

(*a*) Deposits

(*b*) Loans and Advances

(*c*) Loan commitments, Standby Letter of Credit, derivatives contract (futures + forwards + swaps and options)

(*d*) All the above

Q.6. Which of the following 6 C's of credit are correct ?

(*a*) Character, capacity, capital, conditions, cardinal, compliance with laws.

(*b*) Character of applicant, capacity to progress, capital adequacy, conditions to repay, collateral assets for security, compliance with laws and regulations.

(*c*) Creditworthiness, cash balance, character, capacity, collateral assets and compliance with laws.

(*d*) All the above

Q.7. Which of the following statements is applicable to a form of topology ?

(*a*) This topology is quite easy to set up. If one station on the LAN fails, it will not affect the rest of the network. It offers limited flexibility for change.

(*b*) It circulates when all stations are idle. A station wanting to transmit must wait until it detects a token passing by.

(*c*) It provides signal from several communication line and pass on to one communication line and *vice versa*.

(*d*) All the above

Q.8. Core banking is a centralised branch computerisation model in which branches are connected to a central host. In it, there is a central database for the bank and transactions done centrally, on line. It offers integrated products and services to customers round the clock. Which of the following is an advantage under core banking?

(*a*) Easy implementation of integrated customer centric services like online ATM, telebanking, internet banking efficient and effective MIS, ALM, risk management, etc.

(*b*) Do not attract higher investment initially and no core infrastructure.

(*c*) Lacking of data ware-housing and data mining technologies and their drawbacks. Off-line implementation to any branch banking, kiosk banking cash management services.

(*d*) None of the above.

Q.9. The major routine processing in day-to-day banking operations originates at the cash counter. Essentially the idea behind the electronic payment system is that one or few activities related to the payment should be done with the help of a computer. Name the system, which is available all 24 × 7 hours to users without going to the bank.

(*a*) Core banking

(*b*) Automatic Teller Machine

(*c*) Tele banking

(*d*) All the above

Q.10. Name the scheme in Mutual Funds which is akin to recurring deposits?

(*a*) A fixed sum is regularly paid by investors and invested in mutual fund schemes of investors' choice. It is called Systematic Investment Plan.

(*b*) A fixed sum is regularly paid by investors on monthly basis and the scheme is called ULIP.

(*c*) A fixed sum is regularly paid by investors on monthly basis and it is called open ended scheme.

(*d*) All the above

Q.11. Various investment and security schemes are available in mutual funds and insurance business. These provide insurance of life and also high return on investments. ELSS, ULIP and Life Gold Policy are three such schemes. Which of the following offers the highest return on investments?

(*a*) ELSS (Equity Linked Saving Scheme) provides return on full amount of investment hence, total return is higher.

(*b*) ULIP (Unit Linked Insurance Plan) provides return on a portion of investment since other part goes to fees and other loadings but provides insurance to ULIP holder in case death occurs within 5 to 10 years, hence return is higher.

(*c*) LIC Gold Policy is a money back policy and 20% of sum assured is payable with every 5 years, hence return is higher.

(*d*) All the above

Q.12. The way in which the devices are interconnected is known as topology or layout. There are three centralised networks are star, ring and bus topology. In which networks all devices are connected to a single continuous cable?

(*a*) Star

(*b*) Bus

(*c*) Ring

(*d*) All the above

Q.13. Credit cards are small plastic cards. The card issuer should normally get the cardholder to sign on the back of credit card before parting with the card. What is mode of acceptance of credit card in EDC machines?

(*a*) Manual mode to verify the genuineness of the card.

(*b*) Electronic mode to verify the card and its credit limit.

(*c*) Imprint machine mode to get the imprint of the credit card.

(*d*) a or c only

Q.14. Remote banking has become very popular among metro customers. More and more banks are providing customer terminals right in the customer's office, which will facilitate the customers to operate the account without physically coming to the bank. Customers, who are having modems and a personal computer at home can have direct connectivity with bank's computer. This system is called ?

(*a*) Internet banking.

(*b*) Personal banking

(*c*) Tele-banking

(*d*) Mobile banking

Q.15. The signature of customer is verified through a device called

(*a*) Spanner.

(*b*) Smart device

(*c*) Signature device

(*d*) Scanner

Q.16. There are some public data networks developed for information processing. What is the name of the communication device for exclusive use by banks ?

(*a*) Very Small Aperture Terminal network.

(*b*) Magnetic Ink character recognition

(*c*) Bankwire.

(*d*) FED wire

Q.17. Name the fund transfer system which is directly connected with the retailer's terminal?

(*a*) Fed wire

(*b*) Bank wire

(*c*) EFTPOS

(*d*) EDI

Q.18. Name the payment system where payment instructions are processed on a continuous basis?

(*a*) Protocol Conversion Device

(*b*) RTGS

(*c*) EFT Point of sales

(*d*) ATM

Q.19. Data Mining is defined as?

(*a*) A technique wherein data from heterogeneous sources is stored to generate critical information for decision.

(*b*) A technique to reveal the strategic information hidden in large databases. It helps in exposing the patterns that are critical to business and provide an advantage.

(*c*) The transmission of data and messages is one of the fundamental activities of any business system.

(*d*) All the above.

Q.20. Electronic Data Interchange (EDI) is the inter—organisational exchange of business documentation which can be processed by computers. It takes form of interchange of standard formatted data between the computer application systems of the trading partners with minimal manual intervention. Which is the gateway in India for EDI?

(*a*) Satyam Online

(*b*) M.T.N.L.

(*c*) V.S.N.L.

(*d*) Reliance Infocomm.

Q.21. An audit trail is a chronological record of all events occurring in a system. This record is maintained for tracing irregularities and to detect the consequences of error. Which type of audit trial is good for an institution?

(*a*) Accounting audit trail - it maintains a record of processes that update the data and information.

(*b*) System audit trail - it processes the consumption of resources.

(*c*) Checksum audit trail - to ensure the integrity of data stored in a computer.

(*d*) All the above

Q.22. The approach followed in computer audit is

(*a*) Collection of records and evidence.

(*b*) Logic and controls within the system.

(*c*) Computer aided audit approach.

(*d*) All the above

Q.23. Destroying, deleting or altering any information residing in a computer resources or diminishing its value or utility by any means, with the intent to cause wrongful loss or damage to the public or person is called what?

(*a*) Frauds

(*b*) Violation of privacy

(*c*) Hacking

(*d*) Mis-application

Q.24. What is the final stage of a product in product development ?

(*a*) Screening

(*b*) Testing

(*c*) Commercial launch

(*d*) Sampling

Q.25. In a product development, there are various stages. But there is a stage which is an important part of the product as it imparts a perceived value to the product and generates income for the firm/company. It is known as :—

(*a*) Branding

(*b*) Packing

(*c*) Labelling

(*d*) Testing

Q.26. In pricing, there are several objectives. They would normally be determined by or emanate from the corporate and marketing objectives of the firm. Which of the following is a major objective in pricing?

(*a*) Maintaining or increasing the market share.

(*b*) Survival in the market.

(*c*) Optimisation of profit over a long term.

(*d*) All the above.

ANSWERS					
1. (a)	2. (b)	3. (a)	4. (b)	5. (c)	6. (b)
7. (a)	8. (a)	9. (b)	10. (a)	11. (a)	12. (b)
13. (b)	14. (b)	15. (d)	16. (a)	17. (c)	18. (b)
19. (b)	20. (c)	21. (a)	22. (b)	23. (c)	24. (c)
25. (a)	26. (c)				

CHAPTER

4

CASE STUDIES AND CASE-LETS (PROBLEMS AND SOLUTIONS IN MULTIPLE CHOICE)

Q.1. The wave of global consolidation process blurred the distinction between the commercial banks, investment banks and insurance companies. The banking system is in the midst of a technological revolution with banks offering anywhere banking and any time banking and also attempting to become a one stop financial shop offering all financial solutions. New technology, globalisation, non-bank competition, deregulation and the opening up of protected markets are combining to force banks to re-examine their business. Read the case let and answer.

- Which of the following forces are going to transform commercial banking?
  - (*a*) Traditionally banks have long been exposed to strong external pressures. The most fundamental force responsible for change in the financial sector has been the evolution of technology. The technology and deregulation of the financial services have enabled banks to develop an entire new range of financial products including insurance policies selling.
  - (*b*) Deregulation combined with increased competition has dramatically increased the real average cost of selling/marketing the deposits. Deregulation of financial sector has expanded the range of opportunities for bankers, mergers and amalgamation in more number.
  - (*c*) Heavy investments of money for technologies upliftment has created pressure on banks to increase their charges for providing better service to their customers. The spread between income and expenses

is reducing and banks have to shift to other sources of income like insurance marketing, merchant banking.

(*d*) None of the above.

Q.2. Banks in many countries, including India are permitted to engage in securities business as well as insurance. The story of bancassurance, or banks taking over insurance, is documented. India's new policy on insurance has been one of the most hotly debated. It is, therefore, of utmost importance that the new experiment, initiated as a result of the latest round of reforms, succeeds in giving both better service and larger spread of insurance benefits without leaving any loopholes for abuse of financial powers inherent in owning and managing an insurance company. Read the case let and answer—

- Which is the specific advantage that can be reaped by a bank under bancassurance

(*a*) Bancassurance is a form of distribution of insurance products through a bank's channel. It is a means of product diversification and a source of additional fee incomes.

Specific advantage of bancassurance to a bank is increased return on assets through fee income which can cover more of their operating expenses.

(*b*) Bancassurance (also known as All finanz) is a package of financial services that can fulfil both banking and insurance needs at the same time. Insurance companies see bancassurance as a tool for decreasing their market penetration and premium turnover.

Specific advantage to banks lower cost per sale of insurance policy but sharing of corporate commissions with employees working or entire staff of the branch.

(*c*) Bancassurance is a means of product diversification and source of additional fee income.
Sales productivity of banks increases because with the same staff the additional work of insurance can be serviced, hence more or better future of the bank branch.

(*d*) None of the above.

Q.3. Banks have over a long period of time, been using electronic and telecommunication networks for delivering a wide range of value added products and services. The delivery channels are used for anytime banking, anywhere banking, home banking, internet banking, mobile banking, e-commerce, ATMs, easy access to World Wide Web (WWW). The increasing attractiveness of internet banking can be attributed to several factors. E-banking delivers new services through additional capabilities, but these services themselves carry new risks. These risks can be characterized by the velocity of innovation in the technological change and attendant customer service. Read the case let and answer:

- Which type of risk a bank is prone to, through Internet Banking?
    - (*a*) The major driving force behind the rapid spread of e-banking is its acceptance as an extremely cost effective delivery channel. The channel has also brought about a new orientation to risks *viz.*, operational risk (transactional risk) security risk/reputational risk (negative public opinion)/legal risk/money laundering risk/cross border risk/strategic risk and other risks like credit-liquidity-interest rate-market risks.
    - (*b*) E-banking removes the traditional geographical barriers through internet. However internet is not an unmixed blessing to the banking sector. The various limited number of risks are inaccurate processing of transactions/crackers-hackers/infringing customer's privacy/risk of customer's account accessibility.
    - (*c*) E-banking has enabled banks and other financial institutions to increase the use of internet banking for receipt and delivery of their products and services. The only and main risk are exposure to money laundering resulting in legal punishments for non-compliance with Know Your Customer (KYC) rules of RBI.
    - (*d*) None of the above.

Q.4. You are an employee of ABC Bank. Your bank has been served with a garnishee order by the Court regarding the savings accounts in the name of Shri Ajay Banerjee. Read the case let and answer:

- Which of the following is correct
    - (*a*) There are two stages (*i*) order NISI and (*ii*) order absolute. In order NISI, the court first issues a garnishee order NISI to show cause by the bank as to payment of the amount, to the creditor mentioned in the order. Order absolute, is a final order. Any payment made prior to absolute order would be without authority and may result in wrongful debit.
    - (*b*) There are three stages (*i*) order for submission of details by bank *ab initio* (*ii*) order for financial standing of the customer and (*iii*) order finale - for payments to creditor.
    - (*c*) There is only one stage that is final order and the bank is bound to proceed to pay the sum stated in the order to either the judgment creditor or the court.
    - (*d*) None of the above.

Q.5. As per section 10 of Negotiable Instruments Act, 1881, the payment in due course means payment in accordance in good faith and without negligence to any person in possession thereof. One of the primary duties of a banker is to honour the cheques issued by the customer but in certain circumstances the bank can dishonour the cheques presented.

- Which of the following is correct ?
  - (*a*) Bank cannot refuse payment when payment of cheque is stopped or where there is defect in the presenter's title.
  - (*b*) Bank can return the cheques unpaid by informing the reasons of
    - (*i*) Insolvency of the payee or
    - (*ii*) Bankruptcy of the payee.
  - (*c*) Bank can dishonour the customer's cheque for
    - (*i*) Assignment of the account balance to the credit of third party by the drawer of the cheque.
    - (*ii*) If garnishee order is received by the bank from the court, the bank can refuse payment.
  - (*d*) None of the above.

Q.6. Canara Sales Corporation Ltd., had a current account with ABC Bank which was operated by the company's M.D. The company's accountant, in whose custody the cheque book was, forged the signature of the M.D. in 42 cheques totalling Rs.3,26,047.92 over a period of time. This was detected by another accountant. The company, immediately on detection of the fraud, demanded the amount from the bank. The ABC Bank refused payment and as such company filed a suit against the bank. The bank lost the suit and Supreme Court decided the case in 1987.

- Which one is most appropriate?
  - (*a*) When the signature on the cheque is forged, there is no mandate to the bank to pay and as such it is not entitled to debit the customer's account on such forged cheques.
  - (*b*) Since the relationship of the customer and the bank is that of a creditor and debtor, the bank had no authority to make payment of a cheque containing a forged signature. However, there was a mandate to pay since there was estoppel.
  - (*c*) There is no liability to refund the amount to the Canara Sales Corporation since there was a mandate to pay as the forgeries is committed by employee of the company.
  - (*d*) None of the above.

Q.7. In *Bihta Co-operative Development and Cane Marketing Union Ltd.* v. *Bank of Bihar Ltd.* AIR 1967 SC 389, the Co-operative Marketing Union had an account with the bank, which was authorised to be operated by the Joint Secretary and treasurer of the Co-operative Marketing Union. On 16-4-1948 the bank made payment of Rs.11,000 on a loose leaf cheque and not on a cheque from the cheque book issued to the society. Though two signatures appeared on the cheque, one of them, the signature of the Joint Secretary was forged. The bank made payment. The Co-op. Marketing Union sued the bank for recovery of the money.

- Which one is most appropriate?
  - (*a*) One of the signatures was forged so that there never was any mandate by the customer to the banker and the question of negligence of the customer never arose.
  - (*b*) In a joint account operation if one of the signatures is forged then there is no mandate and no liability on the banker for the payment made.
  - (*c*) There is negligence on the part of the bank of issue of loose cheque for payment to the company and it is liable as a contributory.
  - (*d*) None of the above.

Q.8. Bank of Bihar had agreed to grant to the firm cash credit facility against pledge of cloth bales on the firm fulfilling certain conditions, one of which was that the money for purchasing the cloth would not be directly given to the firm, but instead the supplier would be paid, by the bank and the cloth bales would be kept by the bank as pledge for the loan. The firm, thereafter, was required to draw a cheque on itself, which was handed over to the bank. The bank instead of handing over cash to the firm's partner, entrusted it with one of their employees, who accompanied the partner to the wholesalers. However, before the money could be paid to the wholesalers, the employee absconded. The bank sought repayment of the money, which was refused by the firm. (*Bank of Bihar Ltd.* v. *Mahabirlal* AIR 1964 SC 377)

- Which one of the following is correct?
  - (*a*) The bank can seek protection under section 118 of the N.I. Act., since payment to the firm has been made to the holder, his servant or agent.
  - (*b*) The bank can seek protection under section 85 of N.I. Act, only when payment has been made to the holder, his servant or agent. The bank in the case, handed over the cash not to the partner of the firm, but to the employee of the bank, hence payment was not made in due course.
  - (*c*) Payment to a person who had nothing to do with the firm or a payment to an agent of the bank would not be a payment to the firm under section 89 of N.I. Act.
  - (*d*) None of the above.

Q.9. A partnership firm opened a current account with the Wagle Industrial Estate, Thane (Maharashtra) branch of the Bank of Maharashtra (*Bank of Maharashtra* v. *Automotive Engineering Co.* 1993 (2) SCC 97), an area where forgery of cheques were rampant and although all other branches of the bank were provided with ultraviolet ray lamps, the said branch was not provided with such a lamp.

- The question, which arose for consideration, was whether the paying banker was bound to keep an ultraviolet ray lamp, to scrutinise the cheques, even if no infirmity on the face of the said cheque on visual scrutiny was found. Which one of the following is correct ?
  - (*a*) Since ultraviolet ray lamp was not kept in the branch and the said cheque was not subjected to such lamp, the bank was guilty of negligence in payment in due course u/s 10 of N.I. Act.
  - (*b*) It is not a correct legal proposition that the bank in order to get absolved from the liability of negligence was under an obligation to verify the cheque under advanced technology apart from visual scrutiny in order to avail protection u/s 10 of N.I. Act.
  - (*c*) By not providing the facility of ultraviolet ray lamp, the bank had failed to discharge proper care and was there lack of diligence hence liable for such negligence.
  - (*d*) None of the above.

Q.10. Refer to the Calcutta High Court in *Krishna Kishore Kar* v. *United Commercial Bank* AIR 1982 Cal. 62. The facts of the case are that the bank had issued a guarantee on behalf of a borrower and the borrower had (*i*) deposited margin money for the guarantee with the bank and (*ii*) executed a counter guarantee undertaking to reimburse the bank on demand and in default the bank was authorised to recover the amount paid under the guarantee from the balances or securities held or to be held by the bank.

- From the above case law, you have to explain whether the bank could exercise its right of general lien on the margin money held in fixed deposit and reimburse itself out of those monies after it had paid under the guarantee when properly invoked by the beneficiary? State which one of the following is correct ?
  - (*a*) An express contract between the parties creating a lien or security would exclude the operation of the statutory general lien under section 171. Therefore, where the borrower and the bank had an express contract by way of counter guarantee providing the method of reimbursement. However, if default was committed in making reimbursement on demand as stipulated in the counter guarantee, section 171 would become applicable and the bank could exercise its general lien.
  - (*b*) A general lien being a right of defence and not a right of action (that is, it can be exercised without the intervention of a court of law) and extends over time barred debts also. The bank could not exercise its

right of general lien on the surplus margin money in deposit and recover the outstanding balance in the cash credit or overdraft account.

(*c*) The banker has the right to set-off one account against the other. The use of the word "lien" in this context is misleading.

(*d*) None of the above.

Q.11. Porbandar Commercial Co-operative Bank Ltd., had advanced two separate loans to a proprietorship firm on the basis of security furnished by two partnership firms and guarantees signed by one partner of each firm. The partnership firms were not carrying on any business of underwriting loan transactions of the third parties by standing as surety. (*Porbandar Commercial Co-operative Bank Ltd.* v. *Bhanji Lavji* AIR 1985 Guj. 106)

◆ Which one of the following is correct?

(*a*) Merely because the concerned two partners signed on behalf of their respective firms, they cannot bind any other partners of the firms.

(*b*) Even though the other partners of the firms were not liable and no decree can be passed against the concerned two firms, the respective two partners would remain personally liable to answer the suit claim as such decree can be passed against.

(*c*) A guarantee is valid if there is lawful consideration. Anything done or any promise made for the benefit of the surety may be sufficient consideration. Hence both the partners of the two firms are liable on behalf of their partnership firms for the guarantee given.

(*d*) None of the above.

Q.12. Any instrument evidencing a lawful contract or agreement whereby two parties make reciprocal promises needs to be executed under Indian Stamp Act, 1989 by both the consenting parties. If only one of them signs the instruments, the instrument would fall under the description of a bond, indemnity or undertaking rather than a simple agreement. (*State Bank of India* v. *Laishram Mohansingh* (1987) Gauhati)

◆ Which of the following is correct?

(*a*) The High Court decided that as the agreement was duly stamped as a bond it was to be treated as a hypothecation bond which means a written obligation to repay loan under a specific term. Hence the document is a bond of credit and as such the absence of signature of the bank manager would not invalidate the document.

(*b*) Documents, executed as per State Stamp Acts are called agreements while executed as per Indian Stamp Act, 1989, are not agreements.

(*c*) In case of a bank advance, letter of sanction of terms and conditions once accepted by the customer along with other documents is treated as an agreement since there are signatures and offer and acceptance by both parties. The cash credit agreement need not have to be executed by the bank also; though the bank's signature is affixed, it would nullify the document.

(*d*) None of the above.

Q.13. Syndicate Bank opened an account in the name of M/s. Axle Conductor Industries Ltd., with proprietor R.K.Vyas. The introduction was given by one Nanjunde Gowda, who was having a small shop at just opposite the bank's branch. No information was sought or inquiry held, as to the incorporation certificate of the Ltd. Company nor any memo/articles copies were obtained. One demand draft for Rs.2,51,125 was deposited into the account of the company on 5-10-1979 and was collected by Syndicate Bank for the account holder company. The High Court of Karnataka (*Syndicate Bank* v. *Jaishree Industries* AIR 1994 Kar. 315) decided the case.

◆ Which of the following is correct?

(*a*) In order to get protection under section 131 of N.I. Act, an essential requirement is that the bank should receive payment for a customer and the account opening procedure should be done properly and be verified (which was missing in the case). Hence bank was negligent in collecting draft.

(*b*) In order to get protection under sec.10 of N.I. Act, wherein two conditions must be satisfied (*i*) in good faith and without negligence and (*ii*) entitled to receive payment. Both the conditions are satisfied and Syndicate bank will be protected.

(*c*) In order to get protection for drafts collected by Syndicate Bank, protection is available under section 85A of N.I. Act, to the bank. Court decided the case in favour of bank.

(*d*) None of the above.

Q.14. In the case law of *M.R. Utensils* v. *Union of India* (2003) 113 Comp. Cas. 667 enforcing of security interest created in financial institution's favour is valid or not under Article 14 of the Indian Constitution, Gujarat High Court decided the case. The fact of the case was whether section 17 of the SARFAESI Act, 2002 without intervention of any court or tribunal is valid.

◆ Which of the following is correct?

(*a*) It is valid and not in dissonance with the provisions of article 14 of the constitution. Though there is a condition u/s 17(2) that no appeal shall be entertained by DRT unless the borrower deposits with DRT 75% (now reduced to 50% in 2005) the embargo of deposit with the DRT is not absolute and the tribunal is empowered to waive or reduce the said amount.

(*b*) The Gujarat High Court came to the conclusion that the impugned ordinance (subsequently turned to Act) did suffer from vice of arbitrariness and that it is in dissonance with the Article 14 of the constitution.

(*c*) The Gujarat High Court decided that the compulsion of deposit of 75% of the amount with DRT is a hardship with the petitioner and should be reduced to protect the interest of Justice.

(*d*) None of the above.

Q.15. In the case of *Muthukumara Ramalingam* v. *State of Andhra Pradesh* (2002) 114 Comp. Cas. 372, the High Court of Andhra Pradesh decided the case. The petitioner was in charge of and was responsible for the conduct of the business of the company and issued cheques to M/s. Velan Textile Ltd., which was dishonoured by the bank. While of the following is the correct decision?

(*a*) The complaint does not disclose the specific duties of the petitioner and his role in issuing of cheques that were dishonoured. As such the petitioner cannot be made liable for an offence u/s 138 of N.I. Act.

(*b*) Section 141 of the N.I. Act provides that every person, who at the time when the offence was committed, was in charge of and was responsible for the conduct of the business of the company and the company also are liable to be proceeded against for the offence u/s 138 of the Act. The court held that the Board of Directors of the company were under a legal obligation to make provision for payment of the amount due to the complainant. Therefore, the petitioner also by virtue of sec. 141 could be proceeded.

(*c*) The Board of Directors of the company are under a legal obligation to make provision for payment of the amount due on a cheque, issued by the company. But the burden of proof would not be on the director to establish that he was not responsible for the offence.

(*d*) None of the above.

Q.16. Customer's relationship with their bankers may be terminated by closure of the accounts by the bankers or the customers themselves. Sometimes the relationship is terminated by *Operation of Law.* Which one of the following is correct regarding termination of relationship by operation of law ?

(*a*) Assignment of balance to third party,
Stop payment, and
when Account is closed.

(*b*) Where there is defect in the present title,
Compulsion of law, and
Bank's own interest.

(*c*) Bankruptcy or liquidation,
Death of the account holder,
Mental incapacity of the account holder.

(*d*) None of the above.

(The term operation of law covers where both the customer and the banker neither intend nor desire to terminate the relationship).

Q. 17. ABC Bank has sanctioned certain credit limits to XYZ Company Ltd. The operations in the Company's various accounts with the bank are satisfactory as on 31-3-2008. However, on 30-4-2008, a Letter of Guarantee (LG) issued by the bank for Rs. 25 lacs (with 20% cash margin) on behalf of the Company to Maharashtra State Electricity Board (MSEB) was invoked for payment within 15 days, consequent to which the bank has made payment of Rs. 25 lacs to MSEB on 15-5-2008 by debit to a separate account maintained by the bank for such purposes. Though called upon by the bank to pay the amount of invoked guarantee, the Company has not made payment, as a result, the amount remained unrecovered by the bank as on 30-6-2008. The operations in the Company's other borrowal accounts are however satisfactory with the Company servicing monthly interest debited in their Cash Credit and Term Loan accounts promptly.

The limits and the balances outstanding in the Company's various accounts with the bank as on 30-6-2008 are as under :

(Amount in Rs.)

	Limit	*Bal. Outstanding*
a. Cash Credit (Hypothecation)	75,00,000	71,25,700
b. Term Loan (Machinery)	40,00,000	30,50,750
c. Outstanding under Invoked Guarantee (Overdue)		26,45,000
Total Outstanding		**1,28,21,450**

Please state how would you recognise the balances outstanding in the Company's various accounts for asset classification and income recognition purposes as on 30-6-2008 and as on 30-9-2008, if the Company maintains status quo regarding the guarantee liability devolved on them, till that date?

a. Entire outstanding in the Company's various accounts, (including the amount guaranteed by the bank and paid on devolvement) will be treated as Standard asset as on 30-6-2008. The devolved guarantee outstanding *minus* cash margin will however be treated as sub-standard asset as on 30-9-2008 and a provision of 10% will be made thereagainst.

b. Entire outstanding in the Company's various accounts, (including the amount guaranteed by the bank and paid on devolvement) will be treated as Standard asset as on 30-6-2008, which will have to be downgraded as Sub-standard asset as on 30-9-2008, in view of the guarantee outstanding remaining unrecovered for a period of more than 90 days. A provision at 10% will be made on the Company's total outstandings after adjusting the cash margin paid against Bank Guarantee as on 30.9.2008.

c. Entire outstanding in the Company's various accounts, (including the amount guaranteed by the bank and paid on devolvement) will be treated as Standard asset as on 30.6.2008 as well as on 30.9.2008 and no provision will therefore be necessary.

d. Entire outstanding in the Company's various accounts, (including the amount guaranteed by the bank and paid on devolvement) will be treated as Sub-standard asset as on 30.6.2008 as well as on 30.9.2008 and 10% provision will therefore be made during both quarters.

ANSWERS

1. (a)	2. (a)	3. (a)	4. (a)	5. (c)	6. (a)
7. (a)	8. (b)	9. (b)	10. (a)	11. (a)	12. (a)
13. (a)	14. (a)	15. (b)	16. (c)	17. (b)	

CHAPTER 5

MODEL QUESTION PAPER IN OBJECTIVE MODE

The model question paper consists of four parts A, B, C and D. Part A is intended to test the conceptual understanding of the candidates while Part B contains problems. Part C consists of essay type questions with emphasis on practical applications, the fourth Part D includes case laws and case lets for broader understanding about laws and of the subject. The multiple choice questions carry a score of one point from A to C parts and three points in Part D, totalling to 100 points.

Part A - Basic Concepts (Points 16)

Q.1A Financial institutions are typically classified into

(*a*) Depository and non-depository institutions

(*b*) NBFC and commercial banks

(*c*) Insurance companies and deposit banks

(*d*) Commercial banks and investment banks.

Q.2A Which of the following is not the right of a bank against its customer?

(*a*) Right of Lien.

(*b*) Right of set off in case of garnishee order.

(*c*) Right to charge interest and service charges.

(*d*) Right to set-off in the account containing trust funds.

Q.3A While evaluating credit card requests, the officer addresses all the following issues except

(*a*) Character

(*b*) Use of loan proceeds.

(*c*) The primary and secondary sources of repayment.

(*d*) The limit of amount borrowed at a time.

Q.4A Which of the following statement/s is/are true with respect to aggressive pricing?

(*a*) The aggressive pricing of private banks for high balance and low activity deposits.

(*b*) To improve the demand for existing products.

(*c*) It is done according to the number of services used by the customer.

(*d*) None of the above.

Q.5A Working capital margin is

(*a*) Difference between current assets and current liabilities.

(*b*) Increase in working capital requirement as a result of increased production.

(*c*) The portion of working capital requirement that is financed through bank loans.

(*d*) The portion of working capital which is financed through the long term sources.

Q.6A Which of the following problems a firm or company faces in case of inadequate working capital?

(*a*) It may not be able to take advantage of cash discounts.

(*b*) It may not be able to take advantage of profitable business opportunities.

(*c*) There may arise an imbalance between liquidity and profitability.

(*d*) May not be able to take advantage of cash discounts + take advantage of profitable business opportunities.

Q.7A Which of the following relations exists between a banker and customer after opening a saving account?

(*a*) Debtor and creditor

(*b*) Principal and agent

(*c*) Executor and trustee

(*d*) Bailor and bailee

Q.8A Bank rate is the rate at which

(*a*) RBI lends to banks.

(*b*) Commercial banks lend to borrowers.

(*c*) Scheduled banks accept deposits.

(*d*) Term lending institutions lend to borrowers.

Q.9A The best method for assessing working capital limit used by the bank for seasonal industries is

(*a*) Operating cycle method.

(*b*) Projected networking method.

(*c*) Projected turnover method.

(*d*) Cash budget method.

Q.10A Which of the following is/are correspondent banking services?

(*a*) Data processing services.

(*b*) Portfolio analysis and investment advice.

(*c*) Federal funds trading.

(*d*) Cheque collection/funds transfer/loan participation assistance/securities safe keeping and trading.

Q.11A Electronic Fund Transfer (EFT) enables

(*a*) Transfer of funds within and across cities.

(*b*) Collection of consolidated account wise and centre wise position.

(*c*) Transmission of intra-bank and inter bank messages.

(*d*) Transfer of funds through ECS.

Q.12A Which of the following is not an approach to improve service productivity?

(*a*) If employees work more skilfully.

(*b*) If there is surrender of some quantity.

(*c*) Harness the power of technology.

(*d*) Design a more effective service.

Q.13A Which of the following committees is not related to working capital finance?

(*a*) Chore Committee (1979)

(*b*) Laxminarayan Committee (1973)

(*c*) Nayak Committee (1993)

(*d*) Kannan Committee (1997)

Q.14A Banker customer relationship stands terminated in which of the following cases?

(*a*) Garnishee order.

(*b*) Insanity or death of the customer.

(*c*) Attachment order for income tax office.

(*d*) All of the above.

Q.15A Which of the following is/are the characteristics of a good collateral security?

(*a*) Durability

(*b*) Marketability/standardization

(*c*) Identification/stability of value

(*d*) All of the above.

Q.16A Which of the following problems does a firm face in case of excess of working capital?

(*a*) May not be able to take advantage of cash discount.

(*b*) Since funds are idle, there is no profit; hence lesser rate of return on investment.

(*c*) Imbalance between liquidity and profitability.

(*d*) Reduced profit/over supply of products and crash of prices.

Part B - Problems (Points 17)

Q.1B Lupin Pharmaceuticals Ltd. Mumbai is having information of production as under (Amt. in crore)

Raw materials	(Opening stock)	Rs. 40	(Closing stock)	Rs. 45
Finished goods	(Opening stock)	Rs. 80	(Closing stock)	Rs. 90
Debtors	(Opening stock)	Rs. 90	(Closing stock)	Rs. 100
Purchases 20% of sales		Rs. 140		
Sales		Rs. 700		

Find out raw material storage period

(*a*) Average stock

$$\frac{80 + 90}{2} = 85$$

Consumption of stock per year

$80 + 140 - 90 = 130$

$$\text{Daily consumption} = \frac{130}{360} = 0.361$$

$$\text{Raw material storage period} = \frac{85}{0.361}$$

$$= 235 \text{ days}$$

(*b*) Average Stock

$$\frac{40 + 45}{2} = 42.5$$

Consumption of materials per year

$40 + 140 - 45 = 135$

$$\text{Daily consumption} = \frac{135}{360} = 0.375$$

$$\text{Raw material storage period} = \frac{42.5}{0.375} = 113.3 \text{ days}$$

(*c*) Average Stock

$$\frac{90 + 100}{2} = 95 \text{ and}$$

$$+ = 90$$

$$\frac{80 + 90}{2} = 85$$

Consumption of stocks

$90 + 140 - 100 = 130$

and $+ = 260$

$80 + 140 - 90 = 130$

$$\text{Daily consumption} = \frac{260}{360} = 0.722$$

$$\text{Raw material storage period} = \frac{90}{0.722} = 124 \text{ days}$$

Q.2B Mr. A and Mrs. B have been married for 10 years. Mr. A has been forging his wife's signature on cheques that were paid by the bank. Mrs. B discovered the forgeries and threatened to reveal them to the bank, but Mrs. B agreed not to do so after Mr. A told her that the money was used for helping a sick friend. One year later Mrs. B found out that Mr. A had used the money to buy shares and had suffered losses in that.

Will Mrs. B be able to recover the money from the bank? Give reasons.

(*a*) Mrs. B cannot claim from the bank the money paid on the forged cheques since she remained silent after knowledge of forgery.

(*b*) Mrs. B owes a duty to the bank to notify about forgeries within 3 months (which is period of limitation) from knowledge and she failed to do so hence, bank is not liable.

(*c*) Mrs. B's husband has done forgeries (who is residing with her) knowledge of husband is considered implied to wife and as such bank is not liable.

Q.3B Mr. and Mrs. Acharya maintain a joint savings account with ABC Bank Ltd. The instructions for operation of the account were "payable to either or survivor". On 7th Jan. 2006. Shri Acharya had a heart attack and died in the premises of the bank. One week after Mr. Acharya death *i.e* on 14th Jan. 2006 Mrs. Acharya desired to withdraw the entire sum from the savings account Rs.1,07,300. How will you pay?

(*a*) When the bank has notice of the customer's death, it would freeze the account and inform Mrs. Acharya to submit death certificate and a request letter for removal of the name of the deceased Mr. Acharya from the account and thereafter she can operate the account and till then operation was not possible.

(*b*) Since the credit balance in the account is substantial, the payment will not be made except on production of succession certificate.

(*c*) Stamped Indemnity Bond duly signed by all the heirs of the deceased stating therein to make payment to Mrs. Acharya be submitted with two sureties for enabling bank to affect payment. Legal heirs include even all the married and unmarried daughters of the deceased, if any.

Q.4B Mr. Kehar Singh who does not maintain any account with ABC Bank, purchased foreign currencies from the bank. Can Kehar Singh be called a customer of the bank?

(*a*) Entering into the contract for exchange of currencies is banker customer relationship. However, Kehar Singh is the bank's customer for the duration of that transaction only.

(*b*) Kehar Singh is not a customer of the bank as the bank is merely rendering a casual service to Kehar Singh *i.e.* exchange of currencies. Hence Kehar Singh is not a customer of ABC Bank. Customers must have some sort of account with the bank.

(*c*) There are no regular transactions by Kehar Singh with the bank; hence he is not a customer.

Q.5B K. M. Adam is having overdraft account with ABC Bank up to Rs. 50,000. The present debit balance in the account was 30,570. The bank received attachment order from Income Tax Department for Rs.17,570. What can the bank do in this situation?

(*a*) Debit the demand of the I.T.D. since there is enough overdraft limit available with bank.

(*b*) Inform the I.T.D. that the monies lying in the overdraft account cannot be attached since it was not customer's money.

(*c*) The bank which has offered overdraft facility to its customer does not hold the amount specified as the amount up to which the customer may draw, as either "a debtor" of the customer nor holds that money on behalf or on account of the customer. Unless the bank is a debtor, there can be no attachment and an unutilised overdraft account does not render the bank a debtor in any sense.

Q.6B ABC Bank noted a lien on the amount of the credit of the joint account of A and B for the debt due from one of the account holders i.e. A. Discuss how far it is valid?

(*a*) Valid - since A and B both are owners of the credit balance of the account and lien can be marked over it since A's share would not be less than ½ of it.

(*b*) Invalid - since lien on the exclusive account of the holder can only be marked and not on the joint account. Lien marking on joint account is improper and invalid.

(*c*) Invalid - money lying in the deposit account with the bank ceases to be the property of the depositor and constitutes a debt of the banker to the depositor. Banker is to take care as bailee for the depositor.

Q.7B The guarantees are issued by banks and if invoked by the beneficiary, the bank is bound to pay on demand without contestation, demur or protest and without reference to the customer. This has been decided by the Supreme Court in *Texmaco Ltd.* v. *State Bank of India* AIR 1979 Cal. 44 Are there any exceptions to it?

(*a*) No- there are no exceptions and the bank is under bounden duty to honour its commitment once the guarantee is invoked.

(*b*) Yes - in clear case of fraud of which banks have notice, the courts will leave the merchants to settle their disputes under the contracts by arbitration or as stipulated in the contracts.

(*c*) Egregious nature as to vitiate the entire underlying transaction. If the fraud of beneficiary is there and not the fraud of somebody else. This should enable the bank to obtain injunction order from court.

Q.8B ABC Bank Ltd. issues a guarantee in favour of Greater Mumbai Municipal Corporation on 7-1-2000 for Rs. 50 crore for 2 years *i.e.* upto 6-1-2002. Joshi Realities Ltd. is the party who have paid margin amount of Rs. 10 crores. On 6-1-2002 M/s Joshi Realities requested the bank to release the margin money, since there was no claim/invocation by Greater Mumbai Municipal Corporation. On asking about the original guarantee, they stated that since the guarantee period was over, there was no necessity and Corporation takes more time in returning the guarantees, even 5 to 10 years. Should the bank refund the margin money after 3 months of guarantee period?

(*a*) Yes- ABC bank can refund since there is a clause in the guarantee bond itself that the bank's liability extinguishes after the expiry of guarantee period and can refund the money after waiting normal period of 3 months.

(*b*) No-ABC Bank Ltd. cannot do so since as per the law of Limitation Act, 1963 the period for Government Department or Municipal Body is 30 years. Hence the liability continues for next 30 years for a default committed by the debtor *i.e.* Joshi Realities Ltd. during the validity period, in case the bank did not make payment, the beneficiary can sue the bank.

(*c*) No-ABC Bank Ltd. cannot refund the margin money since as per Contract Act section 28, standard limitation clauses in the bank guarantee incorporates extinction of bank liability for 3 years.

Q.9B A promissory note is an instrument in writing containing an unconditional undertaking, signed by the maker to pay a certain sum of money only to, or to the order of, a certain person, or to the bearer of the instrument. In which of the following cases, the instrument is promissory note.

(*a*) I promise to pay to B Rs.50,000 and all other sums which shall be due to him.

(*b*) I promise to pay Rs.70,000 seven days after my marriage with Chintamani.

(*c*) I promise to pay Veena or order Rs.67,000.

Q.10B If a promissory note is invalid because it is unduly stamped or otherwise defective and not admissible in evidence, then can the bank recover the money?

(*a*) No - bank cannot recover the amount since the only legal course is invalid.

(*b*) Yes - bank can always sue on the original cause of action *i.e.* money had been received by the borrowers, when the negotiable instrument becomes inadmissible in evidence under section 35 of the Stamp Act.

(*c*) No-where the promissory note incorporates all the terms of the contract of loan and it was executed as a collateral security. When such instrument is improperly stamped, no suit on debt will lie.

Q.11B Why is it essential for the hypothecatee to give or display a public notice of his charge, affix and keep displayed at all times? Could there be any problem to bank if no such display is made?

(*a*) The official assignee/receiver or official liquidator may on the doctrine of reputed ownership take the property into his custody on the insolvency or winding up of the hypothecator.

(*b*) Hypothecatee may fraudulently pledge or charge the property to another creditor who may acquire priority of charge if he parts with valuable considerations in good faith.

(*c*) Hypothecated property, even if not displayed under public notice, cannot be acquired by or sold to another creditor since it belongs to banking industry.

Q.12B If the bank's claim is barred by limitation, the implication is that the bank cannot seek to enforce the claim in a court by filing a suit against the debtor. What should the bank do?

(*a*) Debit the amount to Profit & Loss A/c of the bank and forget.

(*b*) To recover the amount from the employee/officer of the bank, during whose regime and fault this happened.

(*c*) Right of the bank to recover does not extinguish. Recourse may be had to sec. 25 (3) of the Contract Act. If the debtor or his agent has made, in writing, a promise to pay after the expiry of the limitation period of the debt, the debt is revived.

Q.13B The authorised officer is appointed under Securitisation and Reconstruction of Financial Assets and Enforcement of Security Interest Act, 2002 by the Board of Directors of the Public sector banks who should not be less than

(*a*) Deputy General Manager

(*b*) Assistant General Manager

(*c*) Chief Manager

Q.14B Which one of the following is the possession - notice under Securitisation and Reconstruction of Financial Assets and Enforcement of Security Interest Act, 2002?

(*a*) In the presence of the above mentioned Panchs, Shri ...., the authorised officer of ....(institution) in exercise of the powers conferred under section 13(4) of the said Act, entered the premises ....

(*b*) The undersigned being the authorised officer of the .... (institution) under the SARFAESI Act, 2002 and in exercise of powers conferred under section 13(12) issued a demand notice dated .... calling upon the borrower .... to repay the amount mentioned in the notice.

(*c*) The undersigned being the authorised officer of the .... (institution) under SARFAESI Act, 2002 and in exercise of the powers conferred under sub-section (12) of section 13, in consideration of the payment of Rs........... on behalf of the ....(secured creditor)

Q.15B Which financial assets can be sold to Securitisation Company or Reconstruction Company (created under SARFAESI Act, 2002)?

(*a*) A non-performing asset including a non-performing bond/debenture.

(*b*) A standard asset where it is under consortium/multiple banking arrangements and 75% by value of asset under NPA.

(*c*) Combination of (*a*) and (*b*).

Q.16B SARFAESI Act, 2002 bars which of the following laws of their applicability?

(*a*) Companies Act, 1956 and Securities Contracts (Regulation) Act, 1956.

(*b*) SEBI Act, 1992 and D.D.B & F.I Act, 1993.

(*c*) None.

Q.17B Passing of SARFAESI Act, 2002 has been .... to the exercise of powers by administrative officers to ensure rule of law and prevent failure of justice.

(*a*) Supplementary

(*b*) Complementary

(*c*) Derogatory

Part C - Applied Theory (Points 16)

Q.1C Management of working capital is of crucial importance considering the dynamic nature of operations of an enterprise. What are the factors that affect the composition of working capital?

(*a*) Nature of business/raw material used/process technology and degree of market competition.

(*b*) Share in market/monopoly status brand name/nature of finished goods

(*c*) Market competitions, period of conversion to finished goods/transportation time required for supplies/bank's ceilings on advances.

Q.2C With the bank guarantee, a borrower can mobilise funds on terms and conditions significantly better than it could do on its own. Which of the following is the instance when a bank guarantee can be given.

(*a*) Guarantee for future payment of an amount advanced (for its security).

(*b*) Can be given by an importer to safeguard against political changes and for due payment.

(*c*) Combination of (a) and (b).

Q.3C Banks are called financial intermediaries since they collect deposits and deliver the same to borrowers. Can you distinguish between Core-deposits and purchased funds?

(*a*) Core deposits are deposits from regular customers (*viz.* business firms, government undertaking and householders) while purchased deposits are obtained at higher competitive interest rates.

(*b*) Core deposits provide a stable/long term funds whereas purchased deposits serve to overcome liquidity crunch.

(*c*) Both (*a*) and (*b*) above.

Q.4C Financial Institution wish to have the money lent by them repaid in time. Secured advances sanctioned by banks possess what kind of security?

(*a*) Secured advances have impersonal security *i.e.* tangible asset.

(*b*) Secured advances have personal security like third party guarantee.

(*c*) Charge on the immovable properties is secured advances.

Q.5C Branch level computerisation is the need of the hour where every person/ corporate wants accurate, clear, fast and quickest services. In view of above, which network is used largely in bank branches?

(*a*) Wide Area Network

(*b*) Local Area Network

(*c*) Data Base Management Network

Q.6C Most of the large banks in European countries and the U.S.A have their independent communication networks. The banks use distributed data processing techniques with central system acting as the main data base server. This has enabled them to provide certain specialized functions like transfer of funds, which of the following EFT network is present in India?

(*a*) CHIPS

(*b*) CHATS

(*c*) RTGS

Q.7C Core banking is a centralised branch computerisation model in which branches are connected to a central host. In it, there is central database for the bank and transactions are done centrally, online. It offers integrated products and services to customer round the clock. Can you explain any one advantage of Core banking?

(*a*) No core infrastructure.

(*b*) No drawbacks of data mining and data warehousing.

(*c*) Easy implementation of integrated customer centric services like online ATM/tele-banking/internet banking.

Q.8C As a feature of credit cards, customer can avail cash for routine requirements for smaller payments. Now most of major credit card issuers have started offering 5% cash back points to the credit holder on payments made through credit cards. Since cash withdrawal is also one of the ways of payments, whether 5% cash back scheme applies to cash withdrawals also?

(*a*) Yes - the regulations are equally applicable and 5% cash back could be given by issuing bank.

(*b*) No- there is no 5% cash back scheme. On the contrary, there would be minimum charge payable @ 2½% for every transaction with minimum Rs.300 per transaction.

(*c*) Yes - there is cash back scheme for cash withdrawals above Rs.20,000 at a time.

Q.9C Various investment and security schemes are available in mutual funds. When it comes to investing in mutual funds, investors have literally hundreds of choices. There are various kinds of mutual funds open to investors. If an investor is interested in modest risk and reasonable rate of return, in assets with mixture of industrial stocks and bonds, which kind of mutual fund is best suited?

(*a*) Open ended schemes

(*b*) Growth funds

(*c*) Balanced funds

Q.10C Now Electronic Funds Transfer System has been adopted by most of the major banks in India. Legal regulations till now have been governed under N.A. Act, 1881. But after adoption of electronic banking, what could be the position for EFT, in case the funds transfer is not effected, due to any reason, by banks?

(*a*) Customer should be refunded money back.

(*b*) Beneficiary be paid even though delayed and no money back to sender.

(*c*) Customer should be refunded the amount with interest on the debited amount.

Q.11C In EFT there are 7 parties involved in transactions (i) sender (ii) sender bank (iii) receiving bank or beneficiary and others. In case of non-receipt of funds by the beneficiary, the litigation can start and there could be multi-party litigations. What measures have been accepted by RBI in this regard?

(*a*) Sending bank only should be made responsible to its customers.

(*b*) Receiving bank only should be made responsible to its customers.

(*c*) RBI - EFT only should be made responsible to sending bank's customers.

Q.12C When a bank extends to a customer an EFT facility, the relationship would be that of principal and agent. In an EFT system, payment is put through another bank, which may be beneficiary's bank. Here the relationship of the beneficiaries and his bank would be that of principal and agent or till the beneficiaries bank holds the amount, the relationship of the sender and the beneficiary bank would be that of principal and agent. Then in case of insolvency or bankruptcy of the bank, who would be responsible?

(*a*) Sending bank only.

(*b*) Beneficiary's bank only.

(*c*) Receiving EFT centre.

Q.13C Name the system wherein the computers are based on centralised processing concept. All the information is kept and processed at main central machines and various terminals are attached to the main computer?

(*a*) Microcomputers.

(*b*) Multi-user computer networking.

(*c*) Super computers.

Q.14C Topology or layout is the way in which the devices are inter-connected. The popular centralised control networks are star, tree, loop, ring and bus topologies. Each topology has its advantages as well as disadvantages. If one station on the LAN fails, it will not affect the rest of the network. What we call this network?

(*a*) Star Topology.

(*b*) Ring Topology.

(*c*) Bus Topology.

Q.15C The advantages of using LAN in banks are various viz., sharing of expensive resources by several users, reduction in overall cost of computerisation, availability of information to all users and no overloading on any single machine. Is there any disadvantage of LAN to banks?

(*a*) High security risks due to independent access to users and high maintenance cost.

(*b*) Complicated software for data management but low maintenance cost.

(*c*) Security risks are higher but regular maintenance cost is low

Q.16C There is a card, which has space for the storage of an amount. These can be used for different types of account of the user. In addition, there is space for user data such as address, branch where the user has his/her account and even last 30 to 50 transactions. Can you name it?

(*a*) Electronic cheque

(*b*) Bank card

(*c*) Electronic purse.

Part D - Case-let/Case Studies (Points 48)

Q.1D Money laundering is a great threat to the country in general and the banking industry in particular. It is a process of hiding ill-gotten money earned from crime and corruption in black holes, with an intention to dodge investigators chasing the criminal. The money is later dug up in such a way that its source is lost. Money launderers use normal banking channels very often to convert illegally received money and make it appear as though it originated from legitimate source. Bankers can do a great deal to help the Government in its anti-money laundering efforts. How the banks can help the Government and public in this regard?

(*a*) Establish an effective Know Your Customer (KYC) screening; beware of large value funds transfer or cash withdrawals.

(*b*) Obtaining of duly completed account-opening forms should not be treated as formality but be viewed as measures to safeguard banks' interest and monitoring of heavy clearing transactions.

(*c*) Non-opening of accounts by undesirable person such as terrorists/extortionists/arms and drugs trafficking, etc. in banks.

Q.2D Economic development of a country to a large extent depends upon agricultural and industrial sectors. Development of agriculture depends upon irrigation facilities while industrial development on availability of power, good transport and fast communication facilities. All these are called infrastructure. Read the case-let and explain which industries constitute infrastructure?

(*a*) Energy + transport + communication.

(*b*) Irrigation, construction of bridges and dams over rivers and stable Government at the centre.

(*c*) Availability of funds for Prime Minister Rozgar Yojna and Swarn Jayanti Rural Housing Finance Scheme.

Q.3D We are hearing in India about the globalisation of economy. World Trade Organisation (WTO) was established in 1995, with its objective to increase overall world trade. The measures identified by WTO are to produce for exports, to balance foreign exchange out-go on importing inputs and not to export more than specified proportions. Read the case-let and explain/define which are the services brought within the ambit of WTO, recently?

(*a*) Trade in services like banking services, travel, maritime, transportation, mobility of labour etc.

(*b*) Trade in services like factoring, lease financing, book writing, and call centres services.

(*c*) Trade in services retail marketing, air passenger services, house building services etc.

Q.4D There is worldwide debate about the fast growing integration of financial services. Nowadays banks in many countries are permitted to engage in securities business as well as insurance. Bancassurance in its simplest form is the distribution of insurance products through a bank's distribution channels. In April, 2000 the RBI permitted banks in India, to enter the insurance market. Read the case-let and point out the specific advantages that are reaped by banks from bancassurance?

(*a*) Banks are selling Personal Accident and Lost Baggage Insurance directly to their credit card members as a value addition to their products.

(*b*) Fee income base has increased under bancassurance giving a higher income without investment or expenses. But at a cost of dissatisfaction among employees; not doing selling of insurance policies.

(*c*) Success of a bancassurance venture requires change in approach, thinking and work culture. However, this change has resulted in deterioration of marketing of its own bank services.

Q.5D ABC Bank Ltd. is having a current account in the name of Ajay Banerjee. On 7th November, 2005 the credit balance in the account is Rs.57,775. The same day bank received a garnishee order from the court at 3 p.m. for payment of Rs.50,000 from the account of Shri Ajay Banerjee. Read the case let and explain which is the correct option available to the bank?

(*a*) Since the name and account number of Ajay Banerjee are tallying with the details in the garnishee order and there is enough balance is available in the account, the bank should debit the account and send pay order to the court.

(*b*) Since bank's business hours end at 2.30 p.m. and garnishee order is received at 3 p.m. (received after business hour) any payment by transfer from Banerjee account could be made to oblige the account holder and escape from garnishee order.

(*c*) The bank, after matching the account number and name should check if the garnishee order is order NISI or order absolute. If it is an order NISI, the court be informed about attaching the amount since the judgment debtor is entitled to enforce that order, when a final order will be issued by the court, known as order absolute. Under order absolute, the bank is authorised to pay the monies to the judgment creditor or the court only.

Q.6D In the legal decision of *Sadanandan Bhadran* v. *Madhavan Sunil Kumar* AIR 1998 SC 3043 the plaintiff issued cheque, which was dishonoured for want of funds. The defendant contacted the drawer who requested the payee to re-lodge the cheque for payment, but this time also the cheque returned unpaid. Now the question arose as to whether the payee can approach the court when cheque is lodged more than one time under section 138 of N.I. Act. Examine the correct position out of the followings.

(*a*) Rights under bouncing of cheque under sec. 138 is applicable/available once only *i.e.* for the first time only because the cause of action starts from the date of return of the instrument.

(*b*) Right against the drawer of the cheque, which is returned unpaid is available anytime from the last date of return of instrument under section 141 N.I. Act.

(*c*) Right against the drawer is not on continuous basis and is available only once in an instrument. If the cheque is dishonoured and is substituted by fresh cheque by the drawer, payee does not possess right under N.I. Act for lodging a complaint under section 138, under first dishonour and if the fresh cheque is also dishonoured.

Q.7D R issued 8 cheques to A, bearing various dates from 9th April, 1995 to 30th April, 1995 for a sum totalling Rs. 4 lakhs. The cheques were presented for payment on 15th May, 1995 but were dishonoured. R requested for more time to pay. Accordingly, A granted time. In January 1996, R changed the dates of the cheques from 1995 to 1996 and made necessary endorsement on the cheques at that time and also requested A to present the cheques after a period of 3 months. Accordingly, A presented the cheques on 18-7-1996 for payment, but the said cheques were again dishonoured. Therefore A filed a complaint. Case law on the subject is *Vira Exports* v. *T. Kalavathy* AIR 2002 S.C. 38. Read the caselet and explain as to whether there can be revalidation of cheques under N.I. Act and if not, could there be any fresh life to cheques?

(*a*) Yes, there is no provision in the N.I. Act. But it is always open to the drawer to voluntarily revalidate a negotiable instrument.

(*b*) As per section 87 of N.I. Act, the party who consents to the alteration as well as the party who make alterations, are disentitled to complain against such alterations. If the drawer himself has altered the cheque for validating, he cannot take advantage of it later by saying that the cheque became void as there is material alteration.

(*c*) Combination of (a) and (b)

Q.8D Annapoorna Finance had tendered a cheque for collection on 10-4-1985 for Rs.10,000 to Indian Bank, drawn by one S in favour of the finance company. The bank credited the cheque in the account on the same day. Company sent cheque for withdrawal of Rs.10,000 on 12-4-1985. On 16-4-1985 the appellant bank informed the respondent that the cheque issued by S had been returned unpaid and consequently debited Rs. 10,000 in the respondent's account. The respondent filed a suit for recovery of sum of Rs.10,000 from the bank. (*Indian Bank* v. *Annapoorna Finance Co.* 2000 Comp. Cas) Read the above and decide on the correct decision in the matter out of the following options.

(*a*) Right of set-off in relation of debtor and creditor relationship exists, hence bank can debit and recover the amount from the customer.

(*b*) There exists a right of lien in respect of money; securities and properties in the banks' custody hence it is covered under it.

(*c*) The conduct of the bank was a glaring example of negligence and hence its acts of withholding the plaintiff's money and making a debit of Rs. 10,000 in his account was unlawful and illegal. The bank was liable to return the said sum of Rs. 10,000 to the plaintiff with interest 12% p.a. from 11-4-1985 till realisation.

Q.9D In the case of *Dr. T.K. Srinivasalu* v. *Union of India* AIR 2002 AP 335. In this case question was whether banks are entitled to charge penal rate of interest on credit card, Plaintiff stated that rate of interest charged were to the extent of 60% to 84% p.a. while the statement of Standard Chartered Bank was that credit card facility was unsecured overdraft facility. Transaction cost was 2.5% of value with minimum of Rs.75. As regards interest, the charges are levied @ 2.95% per month on the plaintiff card account, as per acceptance of terms by the plaintiff. Read the case-let and decide which is correct out of the following options.

(*a*) Since the payments made by the plaintiff were irregular, the bank was entitled to charge penal rate of interest as per terms and conditions.

(*b*) Since the charging of exorbitant interest @ 60% to 84% was illegal, unauthorised and void. Further the Standard Chartered Bank should refund the excess of interest and other charges charged on the plaintiff's account since beginning.

(*c*) Held that the bank was entitled to charge maximum interest @ 18% on the loan availed by the plaintiff in June 2000 for Rs. 28,000 till date of decision of this court and refund the excess amount charged to the account.

Q.10D Marketing management is the process of planning and executing the conception, pricing, promotion and distribution of goods, services and ideas to create exchanges with target groups that satisfy customers and organisational objectives. These are four key functional aspects in marketing management. Read the case let and decide which is the main functional aspect for understanding the need of the customer, out of the following options?

(*a*) Analysis of data for trends and changes.

(*b*) Planning the goals and target segments and actions required.

(*c*) Use of budgetary control, marketing mix and marketing audit for controlling.

Q.11D A brand is a name, term, sign and symbol or design or the combination of these. Brand has become an important part of the product. One does not ask for toothpaste but asks for Colgate Total or Pepsodent Active Salt. Often brands take the position of generic names. Read the case let and explain what involves in building brand out of the following options?

(*a*) Brand positioning, brand name selection and brand development.

(*b*) Line extension, identity of product and segmentation of markets.

(*c*) Awareness and loyalty to consumers.

Q.12D Retail banking is going through an active metamorphosis, thanks to the number of consumers who have migrated from paper to plastic and of course also due to changes in banks themselves. For a bank to succeed and profit, it has to learn from and actively respond to customer's needs. There is an enormous proliferation of ATMs deployed by banks. Private banks are increasing their branches and ATMs aggressively for the simple reason that they are cost effective and consumer effective. In the prevailing scenario, a number of banks have adopted a new deployment strategy of infrastructure out sourcing, to lower the cost of service channels. Read the case-let and decide the future of retail banking in 2020 Indian banking :

(*a*) In the next decade, there would be large-scale shift to online banking because it is the simplest way to integrate low cost financial services. However, the branch network may not disappear. Customer will always find solace in the sense of assurance that a blue chip brand is embodied by a physical presence.

(*b*) In the next 15 years, there would be large-scale shift to online banking when 60% of urban customers and large number of customers will forget to regularly drop into the branch for face-to-face interaction. To save cost in branch expansion, ATMs will be to the extent of 5 times of existing number of branches *i.e.* about 3,25,000 in number (65000 × 5) to cater the needs of cash requirements of often than online customers.

(*c*) New development would be in the areas of ATMs, mobile banking and online Internet banking. There would be large consumer market and more competition. Human touch will be replaced with computers, which will decide the requirements of depositors and borrowers without any human intervention. Number of bank employees will reduce to 4 lakh as against 8 lakh today.

Q.13D In recent years, off balance sheet activities have been growing in importance for banks. These are activities that affect bank's profit and yet do not appear on bank balance sheets. A significant chunk of a bank's non-fund based incomes come from these activities. Such business often creates contingent liability - a liability that comes into existence only when triggered by a specific event. After reading the above case-let, choose any option as to how a bank can manage credit risk incurred through off balance sheet activities?

(*a*) Banks should classify their off-balance sheet exposures into 3 categories (*i*) credit substitutes. (*ii*) stand by letter of credit, money guarantees (medium risk) (*iii*) reverse repos, currency swaps options and futures etc. (low risk).

The current and potential credit exposures may be measured on a daily basis to evaluate the impact of potential changes in market conditions on the value of counterparty positions.

(*b*) Contingent liabilities such as Letters of Credit and financial guarantees represent potentially significant cash drains. A bank should be able to ascertain normal level of cash outflows on an ongoing basis, and then estimate the scope for an increase in these flows during period of stress.

(c) Swaps, interest rate and foreign exchange rate contracts are the potential source of cash outflows. A bank would need to review its written options together with any hedges against these positions.

Q.14D Read the case-let and give your option for correct answer. Which of the following restrictive loan covenants are negative covenants?

i. Restrictions on payment of dividends.

ii. Requirement to insure selected assets.

iii. Restrictions against taking on new debt.

iv. Requirement of submitting financial statements on quarterly/half yearly and yearly basis.

v. Requirement of securing bank approval before adding to a borrower's stock of fixed assets.

vi. Maintaining of current ratio not lower than 1.33

(a) Loan sanctions between customer and bank generally contain conditions, which require the borrowers 'to do', and also 'not to do'. Negative conditions prohibit acts of borrower that would jeopardise its continued credit worthiness. Negative covenants are

(i) restrictions on payments of dividends.

(ii) restrictions on taking on new debt.

(iii) securing bank approval for increase in fixed assets.

(b) Breach of many negative conditions may also create rights in third parties for which there is no remedy in the lenders' hands. These covenants require borrower to maintain corporate existence and property. The restrictions are

(i) restrictions on payments of dividends.

(ii) requiring to maintain current ratio.

(iii) requirement of periodic financial statements.

(c) Covenants requirement can be extensive depending upon the amount and term of the loan and credit standing of the borrower. Negative covenants typically address issues affecting fundamental nature of borrower's business. Breaching of negative covenants usually constitutes immediate default under most loan sanctions. The negative covenants are

(i) restrictions on payments of dividends.

(ii) requirement of insure assets.

(*iii*) requiring a borrower customer to maintain a current ratio - a liquidity measure.

Q.15D Apart from financing for investing in fixed assets, every business also requires funds on an essential basis for carrying on its operations. These include the amounts and expenses incurred for purchase of raw material, manufacturing, selling and administration until such goods are sold and the monies realised. Business transactions are generally carried on credit with a number of days elapsing subsequent to the sale being affected for realization of proceeds. Read the case-let and decide which is the correct option as to main factors considered in the estimation of working capital requirement?

(*a*) The main factors considered in the estimation of working capital requirement are

(*i*) Annual sales and cost of production.

(*ii*) Quantum of current assets.

(*iii*) Turnover of manufacturing unit.

(*b*) Seasonality of raw materials or demand

(*i*) inventories and receivables levels

(*ii*) level of production and debtors, nature of business and sector wise norms.

(*c*) Industry norms of credit allowed to buyers determine the level of debtors of the company in the normal course of business.

Q.16D Loan pricing takes a variety of information to calculate the lending rate needed to meet the institution's goals. What is a prime lending rate (PLR) ? Do banks prefer to charge fixed rate or floating rates?

(*a*) PLR refers to the interest rate that is charged to the bank's most credit worthy customers. This can also be called a base rate around which pricing varies according to risk factor. Banks prefer floating rates for term loans while borrowers prefer fixed rates.

(*b*) PLR is a base rate around which pricing varies primarily as a function of risk, as risk increases premiums are added to the base rate. Sophisticated borrowers have many ways to hedge hence prefer fixed rates in order to avoid uncertainties, while banks also prefer fixed rate of interest.

(*c*) PLR is the rate at which banks generally lend fund to borrowers. In some instances, the banks may even lend at rates below base rate (in case of priority sector advances)

Banks feel that giving or fixing of PLR is not economical and operationally feasible for medium size and smaller banks. Such banks cannot compete with larger banks at floating rates of interest.

Q.17D Diversification refers to entering attractive opportunities, which are outside the existing business of the firm. When a firm identifies a highly attractive industry the requisite business strengths for which are already present with the company, it has an attractive business opportunity for diversification. Read the case-let and decide the proper conglomerate diversification.

(*a*) The new products have technological or marketing synergies with existing product lines, though the target groups of customers are entirely different.

(*b*) The new products appeal to the existing customers, though the products are technologically unrelated to existing product line.

(*c*) The new products or business have no relationship to the existing technology, products or market of the firm. An audio cassette manufacturer enters into fax machines or food products business.

ANSWER TO MODEL QUESTIONS

Q.1A		(*a*)
Q.2A		(*d*)
Q.3A		(*b*)
Q.4A		(*a*)
Q.5A		(*d*)
Q.6A		(*d*)
Q.7A		(*a*)
Q.8A		(*a*)
Q.9A		(*d*)
Q.10A		(*d*)
Q.11A		(*a*)
Q.12A		(*b*)
Q.13A		(*b*)
Q.14A		(*b*)
Q.15A		(*d*)
Q.16A		(*b*)
Q.1B		(*b*)
Q.2B		(*a*)
Q.3B		(*a*)
Q.4B		(*a*)
Q.5B		(*c*)
Q.6B		(*b*)
Q.7B		(*b*)
Q.8B		(*b*)
Q.9B		(*c*)
Q.10B		(*b*)
Q.11B		(*a*)
Q.12B		(*c*)
Q.13B		(*c*)
Q.14B		(*b*)
Q.15B		(*c*)
Q.16B		(*c*)
Q.17B		(*b*)

Q.1C		(*a*)
Q.2C		(*c*)
Q.3C		(*c*)
Q.4C		(*a*)
Q.5C		(*b*)
Q.6C		(*c*)
Q.7C		(*c*)
Q.8C		(*b*)
Q.9C		(*c*)
Q.10C		(*a*)
Q.11C		(*a*)
Q.12C		(*a*)
Q.13C		(*b*)
Q.14C		(*c*)
Q.15C		(*a*)
Q.16C		(*c*)
Q.1D		(*a*)
Q.2D		(*a*)
Q.3D		(*a*)
Q.4D		(*a*)
Q.5D		(*c*)
Q.6D		(*a*)
Q.7D		(*c*)
Q.8D		(*c*)
Q.9D		(*a*)
Q.10D		(*a*)
Q.11D		(*a*)
Q.12D		(*a*)
Q.13D		(*a*)
Q.14D		(*a*)
Q.15D		(*b*)
Q.16D		(*a*)
Q.17D		(*c*)

PAPER 2

ACCOUNTING & FINANCE FOR BANKERS

CONTENTS

PAPER - 2

MODULE D

FINAL ACCOUNTS

MODULE

A

BUSINESS MATHEMATICS

CHAPTER

1

CALCULATION OF INTEREST

Introduction

Q1. Which of the following are true about Interest?

(*a*) When a lender lends some money to a borrower, the borrower pays a fee to the lender, which is called interest.

(*b*) When a depositor deposits some money in the bank, he receives a fee as consideration, which is known as interest.

(*c*) It is the change in the value of money deposited or lent because of inflation.

(*d*) (a) & (b)

Q2. In the formula, Interest = Principal × Rate × Time, Interest is —— and Principal is——:

(*a*) Total interest, initial amount borrowed or lent

(*b*) Rate of interest, Total amount Payable

(*c*) Interest per annum, Amount which is principally agreed to be paid

(*d*) Minimum interest, Total amount payable

Q3. In the formula, Interest = Principal × Rate × Time, Rate is —— and Time is——:

(*a*) Bank rate of interest, One year period of time

(*b*) Rate of interest percent per annum, period expressed in years for which some amount is borrowed or lent

(*c*) Average rate per annum, Periodicity of applying interest

(*d*) Market rate of interest, Initial period fixed for repayment

Q4. While calculating simple interest the interest rate % is expressed as:

(*a*) Rate ×100

(*b*) Rate/100

(*c*) Rate - 1/100

(*d*) (1+ Rate/100)

Q5. A purchased a scooter by obtaining a loan of Rs. 30,000 at the rate of 15% simple interest p.a. How much interest in total will he pay if the loan is taken for 3 years?

(*a*) Rs. 4500

(*b*) Rs. 10,500

(*c*) Rs. 12,500

(*d*) Rs. 13,500

Q6. Total repayment is:

(*a*) Total interest payable

(*b*) Total principal payable

(*c*) Total of principal and interest

(*d*) Total amount payable per year

Q7. Equated instalment is:

(*a*) Equated Fixed amount, that is to be repaid regularly in a specified period.

(*b*) Fixed amount, that is repaid at will of the borrower during any period.

(*c*) Fixed amount of interest repaid by the borrower during any specified period.

(*d*) Fixed amount of repayment of the principal amount only

Q8. Monthly instalment may be calculated as:

(*a*) Total amount divided by time

(*b*) Total amount divided by total period converted into months.

(*c*) Principal divided by total period converted into months.

(*d*) Principal divided by number of years

Q9. Ramesh has borrowed some money for one year at a specified interest. If he wants to repay the amount weekly, the instalment will be:

(*a*) Borrowed Amount/12

(*b*) Borrowed Amount/24

(*c*) Borrowed Amount/2

(*d*) Borrowed Amount/52

Q10. Amount is———whereas principal is——-

(*a*) Present value, Future value

(*b*) Past value, present value

(*c*) Future value, Present value

(*d*) Present value, Past value

Q11. Which of the following is true?

(*a*) Amount = (Principal + Interest) or (A = P+I)

(*b*) Amount = (Principal + Principal×Rate×Time) or(A=P+Prt)

(*c*) Amount = {Principal(1+ Rate×Time)} or {A= P(1+rt)}

(*d*) All of the above

Q12. Which of the followings are true?

(*a*) P=I/RT Principal=Interest/Rate×Time

(*b*) R=I/PT Rate= Interest/Principal×Time

(*c*) T=I/PR Time=Interest/Principal×Rate

(*d*) All of the above

Q13. If a sum of Rs. 10,000 accumulates to Rs. 16,000 after 3 years at simple interest, what is the rate of Interest?

(*a*) 10%

(*b*) 5%

(*c*) 15%

(*d*) 20%

Q14. In how many years Rs. 10,000 will mature to 11,100 if the simple rate of interest is 5.5% per annum?

(*a*) 1 year

(*b*) 2 years

(*c*) 3 years

(*d*) 4 years

Q15. A deposit matures to Rs. 24,200 after 3 years at simple interest of 7% per annum. What is the principal amount of the deposit?

(*a*) 12,000

(*b*) 15,000

(*c*) 20,000

(*d*) 18,000

Q16. What is the formula for calculating compound interest with annual compounding?

(*a*) $A=P(1+r)^n$

(*b*) A=Prt

(*c*) A=Prt + P(1+r)

(*d*) None of the above

Where A=the total amount *i.e.*, principal + interest thereupon, P is the original principal amount, r is the rate of interest(annual), n is the number of years for which the interest is charged.

Q17. Ramesh has deposited Rs. 10,000 for 3 years. The interest is compounded annually at 10%. What will be the amount receivable by Ramesh at the end of the 3 years period?

(*a*) 13,000

(*b*) 12,000

(*c*) 13,110

(*d*) 13,310

Q18. In the above question, $(1+r)^3$ becomes $(1+10/100)^3 = (1+0.10)^3 = (1.10)^3$. How is this figure calculated?

(*a*) By manual calculation, as $(1.10)^3 = 1.10 \times 1.10 \times 1.10$

(*b*) Using Calculator

(*c*) Using MS-Excel and applying ^ function (exponential function) *i.e.*, $(1.10)^3$=(1.10)^3

(*d*) All of the above

Q19. Ramesh has deposited Rs. 10,000 for 3 years. The interest is compounded annually at 10%. At the end of the 3 years Ramesh received Rs. 13,310 in total.

The amount originally invested (Rs. 10,000) is also known as——— and the amount received by Ramesh at the end of 3 years (Rs. 13,310) is also known as—

————.

(*a*) Past value, Present value

(*b*) Present value, Future value

(*c*) Present value, Long-term value

(*d*) Future value, past value

Q20. In the terms Present value or Future value, the term 'value' is also known as:

(*a*) Principal

(*b*) Investment

(*c*) Cash flow

(*d*) None of these

Q21. The relationship between Present value and Future value (for single cash flow) is:

(*a*) $FV_n = PV(1+r)^n$

(*b*) $PV = \frac{FV_n}{(1+r)^n}$

(*c*) $PV = FV_n(1+r)^{-n}$

(*d*) All of these

Where, PV= Present value, FV_n = Future value, r = rate of interest, n= time period

Q22. The formula $PV = FV_n(1+r)^{-n}$ can also be written as:

(*a*) Present value = Future value × $(1 + r^n)$

(*b*) $PV = FV \times (1^n + r^n)$

(*c*) $PV = \frac{FV_n}{(1+r)^n}$

(*d*) None of the above

Where, FV_n = Future value, n = period, r = rate of interest

Q23. If you want to receive Rs. 40,000 at the end of 10 years, how much have you to invest to-day, considering the interest rate is 10% p.a (yearly compounding).

(*a*) 20,000

(*b*) 15440

(*c*) 14878

(*d*) 19253

Q24. How compound interest is calculated for other compounding periods, like, Half-yearly, quarterly, monthly or weekly?

(*a*) By using the formula, $A=P(1+r/n)^{nt}$

(*b*) By using the formula, $A=P(1+r)^{nt}$

(*c*) By using the formula, $P=A(1+r/n)^{nt}$

(*d*) By using the formula, P=A(1+r)nt

Where A = Future value, P= Present value, r = interest rate, n= number of times interest is compounded in a year, t = period expressed in years.

Q25. In the formula, $A=P(1+r/n)^{nt}$:

(*a*) n is the number of compounding in a year (Half-yearly =2, Quarterly=4 etc.)

(*b*) nt is the number of compounding in a year multiplied by the number of years the money is invested or lent.

(*c*) A is the total amount accumulated along with interest at the end of a period

(*d*) All of the above

Q26. Ram borrowed an amount of Rs. 20,000 for 4 Years with half-yearly compounding interest of 12% per annum. How much amount has he to pay back, if he pays the entire amount with interest at the end of the 4 years period?

(*a*) 31,000

(*b*) 29,600

(*c*) 31,877

(*d*) 32,353

Q27. The rule of 72 allows you to,

(*a*) Calculate interest if interest rate is multiple of 72.

(*b*) Determine the number of years approximately by which your money doubles whether in investment or in debt.

(*c*) Calculate compound interest more easily and quickly.

(*d*) Determine the interest charged or earned in your debt or investment in 72 years.

Q28. How to apply rule of 72?

(*a*) Divide your amount of investment or debt with 72 multiplied by the rate percentage on your debt or investment and you will get the approximate period in years by which your debt or investment gets doubled.

(*b*) Multiply your investment with 72 and apply on it, the interest you are paying on your debt or earning on your investment and you will get the approximate period in years by which your debt or investment gets doubled.

(*c*) Divide the number 72 by the percentage rate you are paying on your debt or earning on your investment and you will get the approximate period in years by which your debt or investment gets doubled.

(*d*) None of these

Procedure to calculate the monthly instalments

Q29. Shyam borrowed Rs. 9,600 from you at monthly compounded interest of 12% per annum for one year. He wants to pay you back in equal monthly instalments along with interest.

(*a*) Divide 9,600 by 12 and you get Rs. 800. So Shyam will pay every month Rs. 800.

(*b*) First month he has to pay interest of 1% on Rs. 9600 i.e., Rs. 96. So the total instalment will be Rs. 896.

(*c*) In the second month the interest will be 1% on Rs. 8800 (9600-800) i.e., Rs. 88 and the instalment will be Rs. 888. The next months, principal amount will be Rs. 8000 and so on.

(*d*) Will apply the Formula EMI $= 9600 \times .01 \times \frac{(1.01)^{12}}{(1.01)^{12} - 1}$

Q30. A deposit is carrying 12% compound interest, compounded quarterly. What will be the effective annual rate?

(*a*) 11%

(*b*) 12%

(*c*) 12.55%

(*d*) 13%

Annuities

Q31. Annuities are:

(*a*) Series of payments (Many number of cash flows) made at a specified frequency over the course of a fixed period of time.

(*b*) Lump sum payments made anytime during the course of a fixed period of time.

(*c*) The annual interest payable or receivable in a debt or an investment.

(*d*) The total amount payable annually in respect of a debt or investment.

Q32. An annuity is ordinary annuity:

(*a*) If payments are required to be made at the beginning of each period.

(*b*) If payments are required to be made at the middle of each period.

(*c*) If payments are required to be made at the end of each period.

(*d*) If payments are required to be made at ordinary instalments.

Q33. An annuity is annuity due:

(*a*) If payments are required to be made at the beginning of each period.

(*b*) If payments are required to be made at the middle of each period.

(*c*) If payments are required to be made at the end of each period.

(*d*) If payments are required to be made at ordinary instalments.

Q34. Which of the followings are calculations involved in calculation of annuity:

(*a*) Calculating the future value of an ordinary annuity

(*b*) Calculating the present value of an ordinary annuity

(*c*) Calculating the future value of an annuity due

(*d*) All of the above

Q35. By calculating the future value of an ordinary annuity:

(*a*) One may come to know, how much he will get in future by investing certain some of money at specified intervals for a certain time period at a given interest rate.

(*b*) One may come to know, how much a loan would cost to him by paying certain amount of instalment at specified intervals for a given interest rate.

(*c*) One may come to know the future value of an ordinary annuity.

(*d*) All of the above

Q36. The formula for calculating future value (FV) of an ordinary annuity is:

(*a*) $FV(\text{ordinary annuity}) = \dfrac{C \times [(1+I)^n - 1]}{I}$

(*b*) $FV(\text{ordinary annuity}) = \dfrac{C / [(1+I)^n - 1]}{I}$

(*c*) $FV(\text{ordinary annuity}) = \dfrac{C \times [(1+I)^n]}{I}$

(*d*) $FV(\text{ordinary annuity}) = \dfrac{C - [(1+I)^n]}{I}$

Where C= cash flow per period, I= Interest rate, n=Number of Payments

Q37. Vinod is investing Rs. 1500 at the end of every year for the next three years @10% per annum. How much amount will he be getting at the end of three years?

(*a*) 3150

(*b*) 4580

(*c*) 4965

(*d*) 5461

Q38. By calculating the present value of an ordinary annuity:

(*a*) One may come to know, to-day's value of a series of future payments.

(*b*) One may come to know, the present value of the coupon payments that he will be receiving in future.

(*c*) None of the above.

(*d*) (*a*) and (*b*)

Q39. The formula for calculating the Present value (PV) of an ordinary annuity is:

(*a*) $\frac{C\times[(1+I)^{n}-1]}{I}$

(*b*) $\frac{C\times[1-(1+I)^{-n}]}{I}$

(*c*) $\frac{C\times[(1+I)^{n}+1]}{I}$

(*d*) $\frac{C\times[(1-I)^{n}-1]}{I}$

Where C= cash flow per period, I= Interest rate, n=Number of Payments

Q40. Vinod is planning to invest Rs. 1500 at the end of every year for the next three years @10% per annum. What is the present value of the amount he is going to get at the end of three years.

(*a*) 3150
(*b*) 4580
(*c*) 3730
(*d*) 5125

Q41. The formula for calculating the Future Value (FV) of an annuity due is:

(*a*) FV(annuity due) = $\frac{C\times[(1+I)^{n}-1]\times(1+I)}{I}$

(*b*) FV(annuity due) = $\frac{C/[(1+I)^{n}-1]\times(1+I)}{I}$

(*c*) FV(annuity due) = $\frac{C\times[(1+I)^{n}]\times(1+I)}{I}$

(*d*) FV(annuity due) = $\frac{C-[(1+I)^{n}]\times(1+I)}{I}$

Where C= cash flow per period, I= Interest rate, n=Number of Payments

Q42. Vinod is planning to invest Rs. 1500 every year at the beginning of the year for the next three years @10% per annum. How much amount he will be getting at the end of three years?

(*a*) 4965.5
(*b*) 5461.5
(*c*) 4567.2
(*d*) 5460

Q43. The formula for calculating the Present Value (PV) of an annuity due is:

(*a*) $\frac{C \times [(1+I)^{n}-1]}{I} \times (1+I)$

(*b*) $\frac{C \times [1-(1+I)^{-n}]}{I} \times (1+I)$

(*c*) $\frac{C \times [(1+I)^{n}+1]}{I} \times (1+I)$

(*d*) $\frac{C \times [(1-I)^{n}-1]}{I} \times (1+I)$

Where C= cash flow per period, I= Interest rate, n=Number of Payments

Q44. Vinod is investing Rs. 1500 every year at the beginning of the year for the next three years @10% per annum. What is the present value of the amount he is going to get at the end of three years.

(*a*) 4103

(*b*) 5175

(*c*) 3975

(*d*) 4323

Q45. The present value of an ordinary annuity is:

(*a*) Less than the present value of an annuity due

(*b*) More than the present value of an annuity due

(*c*) Same as the present value of an annuity due

(*d*) Nothing can be said conclusively

Q46. For calculation of annuity which variables are required to be accounted for?

(*a*) Payment frequencies

(*b*) Number of payments

(*c*) Timing of payment (beginning or end of period)

(*d*) All of the above

Q47. The formula for Present value of an ordinary annuity, i.e.,

$$PV = C \times \frac{[1-(1+I)^{-n}]}{I}$$

Can also be expressed as:

(*a*) PV(ordinary annuity) = $C \times \left[\frac{1}{I} - \frac{1}{I(1+I)^{n}},\right]$

(*b*) Present Value (ordinary annuity) = Cash Flow× present value of an annuity factor of Rs. 1

(*c*) $PV = C \times PVFA_{n,I}$

(*d*) All of the above

Where PVFA is present value annuity factor.

Amortisation of a debt

Q48. Which of the following are true about amortisation of debt:

(*a*) It is an application of annuities in business transactions.

(*b*) It is used to liquidate an interest-bearing debt by making a series of periodic payments, usually equal.

(*c*) When a debt is amortised by equal payments at equal intervals, the debt becomes the discounted value of an annuity.

(*d*) All of the above

Q49. Rajan wants to take a loan of Rs. 30,000 for purchasing fridge. The rate of interest on loan per annum is 8%. If Rajan wants to pay back the money along with interest in four equal yearly instalments, what should be the yearly instalment?

(*a*) Rs. 7500

(*b*) Rs. 9058

(*c*) Rs. 8036

(*d*) Rs. 9435

Q50. Ranjan wants to receive Rs. 15,000 every year for 15 years by investing in an annuity. When the interest rate is 8%, the amount he needs to invest in annuity is:

(*a*) Rs. 1,25,000

(*b*) Rs. 1,25,392

(*c*) Rs. 1,28,000

(*d*) Rs. 1,28,392

Q51. Ramesh wants to get quarterly payment of Rs. 500 for 5 years. How much amount he has to invest now, assuming 10% quarterly compounding rate of interest?

(*a*) Rs. 7,800

(*b*) Rs. 8,125

(*c*) Rs. 7,794

(*d*) Rs. 7,500

Q52. Ajay has borrowed a sum of Rs. 40,000 repayable in 10 years. What monthly repayment Ajay has to make at 15% interest compounded monthly?

(*a*) Rs. 545

(*b*) Rs. 500

(*c*) Rs. 783

(*d*) Rs. 645

Q53. The amortisation formula is:

(*a*) $R = \frac{Ar,}{[1-(1+r)^{-n}]}$

(*b*) $R= Ar[1-(1+r)^{-n}]$

(*c*) $R= \frac{[1-(1+r)^{-n}]}{Ar}$

(*d*) $R= \frac{Ar,}{[1-(1+r)^{n}]}$

Where R is the periodic payment of an annuity whose present value is A for n periods at the rate r per period.

Q54. The formula for Future value of an annuity i.e., $FV = C\times \frac{[(1+I)^n-1]}{I}$

Can also be expressed as:

(*a*) $FV = C\times \left[\frac{(1+I)^n}{I} - \frac{1}{I}\right]$

(*b*) Future value = Annuity cash Flow×Compound value factor for annuity of Re. 1

(*c*) $FV_n = C \times CVFA_{n,i}$

(*d*) All of the above

Where FV is future value of annuity, C is annuity amount, CVFA is compound value factor of an annuity, n is the period of years, i is the interest rate.

Sinking Fund

Q55. Sinking fund is characterized by:

(*a*) When some specified amount is needed in future, accumulation of the fund by means of equal periodic deposits is known as sinking fund

(*b*) Sinking funds may be used to redeem bond issues

(*c*) Sinking funds may be used to replace worn out equipments or to buy new equipments

(*d*) All of the above

Q56. The sinking fund may be calculated by the formula:

(*a*) Sinking Fund (annuity)

$$= \frac{\text{Future value}}{\text{Compound value factor of an annuity of Rs. 1}}$$

(*b*) $A = F_n \left[\frac{i,}{(1+i)^n - 1} \right]$

(*c*) $F = A \left[\frac{(1+i)^n - 1}{i} \right]$

(*d*) All of the above

Where F is the value of an annuity A, with rate of interest i for n number of years.

Q57. A firm is planning to purchase a machinery worth Rs. 50,000 after 4 years. They have planned to make savings right from this year. Calculate the yearly savings, they are required to make to purchase the machinery if the return on investment is 12%.

(*a*) 10321

(*b*) 10462

(*c*) 12000

(*d*) 12163

Q58. In relation to paying of long term loans the sum of the interest payments and the sinking fund payment is called:

(*a*) Book value

(*b*) Periodic expense

(*c*) Cost of the debt

(*d*) b & c

Q59. Sinking fund amount can be calculated by:

(*a*) Formula for present value of annuity

(*b*) Formula for present value of annuity due

(*c*) Formula for future value of annuity

(*d*) Formula for present value of annuity due

Q60. State whether True or False:

1. Simple interest is costlier than compound interest.

2. The more the frequently of compounding per year, more is the interest charged.
3. PVIF is the value of one rupee to be received after a specified period, when discounted at a specified rate of discount.
4. In compound interest, the effective annual rate is always less than normal annual rate.
5. Present value of an amount is the discounted value of its future value.

Ans. 1. False (compound interest is costlier because of charging interest on interest)

2. True (More interest is charged repeatedly on the same amount)

3. True

4. False (Because of compounding, interest charged is more)

5. True

Q61. A home loan with a floating rate of interest is repayable in 120 EMIs of Rs. 5000 each. If the rate of interest increases, which of the following will be done by the bank, in the normal course:

(*a*) The amount of EMI will become more than Rs. 5000

(*b*) The amount of EMI will remain Rs. 5000 but the number of EMIs will be more than 120

(*c*) Both amount and number of EMIs will increase

(*d*) Both amount and number of EMIs will remain same and bank will charge a one time additional amount

Q62. If P is the loan amount, *r* is the monthly interest, and *n* is the No. of instalments, EMI is equal to which the following:

(*a*) $P \times r \times \dfrac{(1+r)^n}{(1+r)^n - 1}$

(*b*) $\dfrac{P \times r}{1-(1+r)^n}$

(*c*) $\dfrac{P \times r}{1+\dfrac{1}{(1+r)^n}}$

(*d*) None of the above

ANSWERS					
1. (d)	2. (a)	3. (b)	4. (b)	5. (d)	6. (c)
7. (a)	8. (b)	9. (d)	10. (c)	11. (d)	12. (d)
13. (d)	14. (b)	15. (c)	16. (a)	17. (d)	18. (d)
19. (b)	20. (c)	21. (d)	22. (c)	23. (b)	24. (a)
25. (d)	26. (c)	27. (b)	28. (c)	29. (d)	30. (c)
31. (a)	32. (c)	33. (a)	34. (d)	35. (d)	36. (a)
37. (c)	38. (d)	39. (b)	40. (c)	41. (a)	42. (b)
43. (b)	44. (a)	45. (a)	46. (d)	47. (d)	48. (d)
49. (b)	50. (d)	51. (c)	52. (d)	53. (a)	54. (d)
55. (d)	56. (d)	57. (b)	58. (d)	59. (c)	60. —
61. (b)	62. (a)				

CHAPTER 2

CALCULATION OF YTM - DURATION - BOND PRICING - PREMIUM AND DISCOUNT - BASEL II

Q.1. Which of the following are true about Debentures:

(*a*) Debenture holders are entitled to receive a guaranteed amount during the period of the debenture.

(*b*) Debenture holders are entitled to be paid the guaranteed amount irrespective of the fact that the debenture issuing company runs into loss or not.

(*c*) Debenture holders do not normally get any voting right in the company.

(*d*) All of the above.

Q.2. Which of the following are true:

(*a*) For a company, debt capital is a source of Funds

(*b*) Interest payments on debt capital are tax-deductible for the companies

(*c*) Bonds are negotiable promissory notes

(*d*) All of the above

Q.3. Bonds may be secured by:

(*a*) Floating charge on assets

(*b*) Fixed charge on assets

(*c*) Unsecured bonds are also issued

(*d*) All of the above

Q.4. What do you mean by 'debt capital provides a tax shield'?

(*a*) Interest payments cannot be deducted from total income to arrive at the taxable income of the company.

(*b*) Interest payments can be deducted from total income to arrive at the taxable income of the company.

(*c*) By issuing debt capital, companies are eligible for lower tax slabs.

(*d*) By issuing debt instruments companies are totally exempted from Income-tax.

Q.5. Mix of debt and equity is known as:

(*a*) Organizational structure of the firm

(*b*) Financial structure of the firm

(*c*) Capital structure of the firm

(*d*) Bond equity structure of the firm

Q.6. Coupon rate is:

(*a*) Market rate of return of a debenture

(*b*) The rate at which a bond is purchased

(*c*) The total amount which one gets on maturity of debenture

(*d*) Specific rate of interest at which a bond is issued

Q.7. The value which a bondholder gets on its maturity is called:

(*a*) Redemption value

(*b*) Coupon value

(*c*) Terminal value

(*d*) Bond value

Q.8. The intrinsic value of bond is:

(*a*) Face value

(*b*) Present value of cash flows in future

(*c*) Market price

(*d*) Issue price

Q.9. A Bond may be issued at par when:

(*a*) Coupon rate of the bond and expected return on the bond is same

(*b*) Coupon rate of the bond is more than expected return on the bond.

(*c*) Coupon rate of the bond is less than expected return on the bond.

(*d*) Coupon rate of the bond is more than market value of the bond.

Q.10. When the expected rate of interest is lower than the coupon rate a Bond may be issued:

(*a*) At par

(*b*) At discount

(*c*) At premium

(*d*) At any rate

Q.11. The price at which a bond is bought or sold in the market is known as its:

(*a*) Face value

(*b*) Redemption value

(*c*) Market value

(*d*) Bond value

Q.12. The value which is stated on the face of a bond is known as its:

(*a*) Market value

(*b*) Real bond value

(*c*) Face value

(*d*) Price value

Q.13. A bond may be redeemed:

(*a*) At market value

(*b*) At par

(*c*) At premium

(*d*) b & c above

Q.14. Zero coupon Bonds:

(*a*) Do not carry any interest. It is issued at a lower price than its redemption value

(*b*) Carry a fixed rate of interest payable at the time of redemption of the bond

(*c*) Bears zero risk

(*d*) All of the above

Q.15. In perpetual Bonds:

(*a*) Interest is paid even beyond maturity period

(*b*) Only interest is paid and has no maturity value

(*c*) Interest and maturity value is paid in advance

(*d*) All of the above

Cost of debt capital

Q.16. Which of the following are true about the cost of debt capital:

(*a*) A security/bond may be regarded as an asset that pays a series of interest payments receivable over a period of time (*b*) Value of any security can be defined as the present value of the future cash streams.

(*c*) The bond holder receives a fixed annual interest payment and redemption value at the time of maturity.

(*d*) All of the above

Q.17. The formula for calculating intrinsic value or present value of a bond is:

(*a*) $V_0 = \sum_{t=1}^{n} \frac{I}{(1+kd)^t} + \frac{F}{(1+kd)^n}$

(*b*) $V_0 = \Sigma I (1+ kd)^t + F(1+kd)^n$

(*c*) $V_0 = \Sigma I (1- kd)^t + F(1-kd)^n$

(*d*) $V = \sum_{t=1}^{n} \frac{I}{(1-kd)^t} + \frac{F}{(1-kd)^n}$

Where V is the intrinsic or present value of the bond, I is annual interest payable on the bond, F redeemable value of the bond, n is maturity period of the bond and kd is cost of capital.

Q.18. The above formula can also be expressed as:

(*a*) Present value of interest = Bond value + present value of maturity value

(*b*) Bond value = Present value of interest + present value of maturity value

(*c*) Present value of maturity value = Present value of interest + Bond value

(*d*) All of the above

Q.19. A bond whose par value is Rs. 5000 bears a coupon rate of 15% and has a maturity period of 5 years. The required rate of return on the bond is 10%. What is the value of the bond?

(*a*) Rs. 5948

(*b*) Rs. 5235

(*c*) Rs. 6534

(*d*) Rs. 5987

Q.20. The steps involved in calculating the bond value in Q.19 above, are :

(*a*) The formula for calculating bond value is $V_0 = \sum_{t=1}^{n} \frac{I}{(1+kd)^t} + \frac{F}{(1+kd)^n}$,

(*b*) The above formula can also be written as,

Bond value = Present value of interest + present value of maturity value

(*c*) Annual interest payable is Rs. 750 (15% of Rs. 5000).

(*d*) To find out the Present value of interest, we have to refer the Present value interest factor of an annuity (PVIFA) table. In this case we have to see the value of Re.1 for 10% (expected return) in 5 years, which is 3.791(approx.).

(*e*) To find out the Present value of maturity value, we have to refer to the Present value interest factor of a lump sum (PVIF) table. In this case we have to see the value of Re.1 for 10% in 5 years, which is 0.621(approx.).

(*f*) Now the formula becomes,

The value of the bond = 750 (PVIFA 10%, 5 yrs.) + Rs. 5000 (PVIF 10%,5 yrs.)

Or, The value of the bond = 750 × 3.791 + 5000 × 0.621 = 5948 (approx.)

Bond value with semi-annual interest

Q.21. The characteristics of Bond value with semi-annual interest are:

(*a*) Interest is paid half-yearly which is further invested.

(*b*) The value of such bonds will be more than the value of bonds with annual interest payment.

(*c*) The period for such bonds will be number of years multiplied by 2.

(*d*) All of the above

Q.22. A Bond with par value Rs. 5000 has a coupon rate of 10% payable semi-annually with maturity of 4 years. The required rate of return is 8%. What is the value of this Bond?

(*a*) Rs. 5500

(*b*) Rs. 5984

(*c*) Rs. 5337

(*d*) Rs. 5126

Current yield on Bond

Q.23. If a Bond is purchased at its current market price and if the coupon interest is received, the rate of return on it is measured by:

(*a*) Yield-to-maturity of Bond

(*b*) Current yield of Bond

(*c*) Current present value of Bond

(*d*) Future yield of Bond

Q.24. The formula for calculating current yield is:

(*a*) Current yield = Current Market Price/Coupon Interest

(*b*) Current yield = Present Value/Coupon Interest

(*c*) Current yield = Coupon Interest/Market Price

(*d*) Current yield = Coupon Interest/Present value

Q.25. A Bond of face value Rs. 5000 carries a coupon interest rate of 12%. It is quoted in the market at Rs. 4500. What is the current yield of the bond?

(*a*) 12%

(*b*) 10%

(*c*) 13.3%

(*d*) 14.2%

Yield-to-maturity of Bond

Q.26. Which of the following are true about yield-to-maturity of Bonds:

(*a*) By Yield-to-maturity (YTM), a Bond's rate of return that takes into account interest income as well as capital gain or loss can be measured.

(*b*) YTM is Bond's internal rate of return.

(*c*) It calculates Bond's yield or rate of return, when its current price and cash flows are known.

(*d*) All of the above

Q.27. There is a Rs. 5000 par value bond. Its current price is Rs. 4000 and coupon rate is 10%. It has maturity of 6 years. What would be the rate of return that an investor will earn if he purchases the bond and holds till maturity.

(*a*) 12.1%

(*b*) 14.3%

(*c*) 15.34%

(*d*) 11.32%

Theorems for Bond value

Q.28. Which of the following are true:

(*a*) When the required rate of return is equal to the coupon rate, the value of the bond is equal to its par value.

(*b*) When the required rate of return is greater than the coupon rate, the value of the bond is less than its par value.

(*c*) When the required rate of return is less than the coupon rate, the value of the bond is greater than its par value.

(*d*) All of the above

Q.29. Which of the following are true:

(*a*) A Bond price is inversely proportional to its yield to maturity.

(*b*) For a given difference between YTM and coupon rate of Bonds, the longer the term of maturity, the greater will be the change in price with change in YTM.

(*c*) Given the maturity the change in Bond price will be greater with a decrease in the Bond's YTM than the change in Bond price with an equal increase in the Bond's YTM.

(*d*) All of the above

Duration of Bond

Q.30. The holding period for which interest rate risk disappears is known as:

(*a*) Safety of Bond

(*b*) Duration of the Bond

(*c*) Maturity of the Bond

(*d*) Due holding period

Q.31. Steps to calculate the desired holding period of a Bond:

(*a*) Determine the cash flows from holding the Bond

(*b*) Determine the present value of all cash flows by discounting the flows with discount rate (YTM).

(*c*) Multiply each of the present values by respective number of years left before the present value is received.

(*d*) Sum these products up and divide by the present value to get the duration of the Bond.

Q.32. Duration of a Bond can be calculated by the formula:

(*a*) $\frac{\Sigma(PV \times T)}{\Sigma PV}$

(*b*) $\frac{\Sigma PV}{\Sigma(PV \times T)}$

(*c*) $\frac{\Sigma PV}{T}$

(*d*) $\frac{\Sigma PV \times \Sigma T}{\Sigma PV}$

Q.33. Consider a Bond which matures after 3 years with face value of Rs. 100, carrying a coupon of 8% payable annually. What is the duration of the Bond?

(*a*) 3 years

(*b*) 3.2 years

(*c*) 2.5 years

(*d*) 2.8 years

Q.34. The concept of duration is also known as:

(*a*) Mcgregor Duration

(*b*) Macaulay Duration

(*c*) Mozart Duration

(*d*) Moler Duration

Q.35. Properties of duration.

(*a*) Duration is less than the term to maturity.

(*b*) Bond's duration will be equal to its term to maturity if and only if it is a zero coupon bond.

(*c*) The duration of a perpetual Bond is equal to $1 + r/r$, where r = current yield of the Bond.

(*d*) Longer the term to maturity of a coupon paying Bond, the greater the difference between its term to maturity and duration.

(*e*) Duration and YTM are inversely related.

(*f*) Larger the coupon rate, smaller the duration of a Bond.

(*g*) An increase in the frequency of coupon payments decreases the duration, while decrease in frequency of coupons increases it.

(*h*) Duration of a Bond declines as the Bond approaches maturity.

Bond Price Volatility

Q.36. The sensitivity of Bond price to changes in interest rates is called:

(*a*) Bond sensitivity

(*b*) Price Volatility

(*c*) Bond Volatility

(*d*) Bond-Price bondage

Q.37. Bond price and YTM are:

(*a*) Directly proportional to each other

(*b*) Absolutely the same

(*c*) Inversely related

(*d*) Not related to each other

Q.38. Which of the following is true:

(*a*) The extent of change in Bond prices for a change in YTM measures the interest rate risk of a Bond.

(*b*) Interest rate risk is a function of the interest rate elasticity.

(*c*) Interest rate elasticity is always a negative number.

(*d*) All of the above.

Q.39. Interest rate elasticity is defined as:

(*a*) $\text{IE} = \dfrac{\text{Percentage change in yield to maturity for a Bond I}}{\text{Percentage change in price for Bond in period t}}$

(*b*) $\text{IE} = \dfrac{\text{Percentage change in price for Bond in period t}}{\text{Percentage change in yield to maturity for a Bond I}}$

(*c*) $\text{IE} = \dfrac{\text{Present value of Bond}}{\text{Percentage change in yield to maturity for a Bond}}$

(*d*) $\text{IE} = \dfrac{\text{Percentage change in yield to maturity for a Bond}}{\text{Present value of Bond}}$

Q.40. Bond price elasticity can be calculated as:

(*a*) $\text{IE} = \dfrac{\text{D} \times \text{YTM}}{1 + \text{YTM}}$

(*b*) $\text{IE} = \dfrac{1 + \text{YTM}}{\text{D} \times \text{YTM}}$

(*c*) $\text{IE} = \dfrac{\text{YTM}}{\text{D} + \text{YTM}}$

(*d*) $\text{IE} = \dfrac{\text{D}}{1 + \text{YTM}},$

Q.41. Duration and interest rate elasticity of a Bond are:

(*a*) Inversely related

(*b*) Directly related

(*c*) Not related to each other

(*d*) Absolutely the same

Q.42. A Bond has a face value of Rs. 5000. Its coupon rate is 8% and period of maturity is 10 years. If the current market rate 8% is changed to 10%, the price of the Bond will change to:

(*a*) 25% increase in YTM would bring -12.29% change in the price

(*b*) 2% increase in YTM would bring -12.29% change in the price

(*c*) 25% increase in TYTM would bring 12.29% change in the price

(*d*) 2% increase in YTM would bring 12.29% change in the price

Q.43. State whether true or false:

1. An irredeemable bond is one, which will be paid back by the company at the end of the specified period
2. The zero coupon bonds are issued at a price lower than the face value
3. Yield to maturity and the internal rate of return of a bond is the same thing
4. Irredeemable debentures are perpetual bonds
5. The maturity and duration of a zero coupon bond are different

Ans. 1. False (There is no repayment of principal)

2. True (issued at lower price but no interest is payable)

3. True

4. True (perpetual debt is that which is not repayable during the lifetime of the company)

5. False (In case of zero coupon bond only one payment is made on the maturity date)

Q.44. Basel Committee on Banking Supervision (BCBC) was set up by—

(*a*) United Nations

(*b*) RBI and Central Banks of some other countries

(*c*) G-10 countries

(*d*) None of the above

Q.45. Which of the following correctly states the 3 main pillars of Basel II accord;

(*a*) Credit Risk, Operational Risk, Market Risk

(*b*) Minimum capital Requirement, Supervisory Review Process, Market Discipline

(*c*) Standard Approach, Internal rating Based approach, Securitisation Framework

(*d*) Income Recognition, Asset Classification, Provisioning

Q.46. Capital Adequacy is defined as—

(*a*) Capital as a percentage of all risk weighted assets including non-fund based and non-performing assets

(*b*) Capital as a percentage of all risk weighted assets excluding non-performing assets

(*c*) Capital as percentage of risk weighted assets excluding non-fund based and non-performing assets

(*d*) Capital as a percentage of risk weighted assets excluding non-fund based assets

ANSWERS					
1. (d)	2. (d)	3. (d)	4. (b)	5. (c)	6. (d)
7. (a)	8. (b)	9. (a)	10. (c)	11. (c)	12. (c)
13. (d)	14. (a)	15. (b)	16. (d)	17. (a)	18. (b)
19. (a)	20. —	21. (d)	22. (c)	23. (b)	24. (c)
25. (c)	26. (d)	27. (c)	28. (d)	29. (d)	30. (b)
31. —	32. (a)	33. (d)	34. (b)	35. —	36. (c)
37. (c)	38. (d)	39. (b)	40. (a)	41. (b)	42. (a)
43. —	44. (c)	45. (b)	46. (a)		

CHAPTER

3

CAPITAL BUDGETING

Introduction

Q.1. Ravi wants to invest Rs. 20,000 in a scheme for 3 years. At the end of three years, he is expected to receive Rs. 32,000. The current rate of interest available in the market for 3 years is 10% per annum compounded annually. Decide whether Ravi should go in for the investment or not. If he goes for the investment, what will be his loss/profit?

(*a*) No, Rs. 6000 loss

(*b*) Yes, Rs. 5380 profit

(*c*) No, Rs. 5000 loss

(*d*) Yes, Rs. 7000 profit

Q.2. The concept of time value of money means:

(*a*) A sum of money received to-day has more value than the same amount of money to be received in future, because the money received to-day can be invested to-day to get some more earning.

(*b*) Since there is risk involved in future, an individual would always like to receive money to-day than to wait for future and be under risk.

(*c*) The money received to-day can be used for any consumption which one may not be able to do because of future inflation and price rise.

(*d*) All of these

Q.3. If one investor wants to take decision about going in for an investment out of many he has to calculate:

(*a*) What the value of money to be received now will be at any point in future.

(*b*) What will be the present value of the sum of money to be received in future.

(*c*) The time value of money and to discount the future sums to be received to their present values before making a decision whether a particular investment opportunity is worth.

(*d*) All of these

Q.4. Capital Budgeting involves:

(*a*) Searching new investment ideas.

(*b*) Estimating the cost-benefit relationships of an investment.

(*c*) Selecting the most profitable investment for implementation.

(*d*) All of these.

Q.5. Time value of money is relevant in:

(*a*) Accounting rate of return method

(*b*) Pay back period method

(*c*) Internal rate of return method

(*d*) All of these

Present value and discounting

Q.6. The formula for calculating the present value of a sum of money to be received in future is:

(*a*) $P = F/(1+r)^n$

(*b*) $P = F^n x (1+r)$

(*c*) $P = F^n/(1+r)$

(*d*) $P = Fx(1+r)^n$

Q.7. Which one is true of the following:

(*a*) If two projects are to be compared, with different expected lives, it is easier to convert cash flows at different points of time to their future values than to the present values.

(*b*) If two projects are to be compared, with different expected lives, it is easier to convert cash flows at different points of time to their present values than to their future values.

(*c*) If two projects are to be compared, with different expected lives, neither the present values of cash flows nor the future values of cash flows are of any help to take the right decisions about investments to be made.

(*d*) All of these.

Q.8. Calculating present value of a future sum of money is known as:

(*a*) Compounding

(*b*) Yielding

(*c*) Discounting

(*d*) Hedging

Q.9. Calculating future value of cash flows is known as:

(*a*) Compounding

(*b*) Yielding

(*c*) Discounting

(*d*) Hedging

Present value tables

Q.10. The present values of the stream of cash flows can be calculated by:

(*a*) Using formulas and calculating manually.

(*b*) Using formulas and calculating with the help of computer applications

(*c*) Using formulas and calculating with the help of calculator.

(*d*) Using ready made discount tables

Q.11. Present value of Re1(lump sum) and present value of annuity of Re1 are the types of:

(*a*) Compounding tables

(*b*) Annuity tables

(*c*) Discount tables

(*d*) Future value tables

Discounted techniques for investment appraisal

Q.12. Which of the following are the two main discounting techniques of investment appraisal?

(*a*) Compounding method

(*b*) Net present value method (NPV)

(*c*) Internal rate of return method (IRR)

(*d*) b & c

Q.13. The assumptions made in the discounting techniques of NPV and IRR are:

(*a*) The money that is accrued in future from an investment is known with certainty.

(*b*) The present value of a cash flow decreases as the time of accrual of that cash flow increases.

(*c*) Cash flows resulting from an investment are sufficient to make investment worthwhile.

(*d*) a & b

Q.14. For a project, the difference between the sum of the present value of cash flows of the project and the cash outlays for financing the project is its:

(*a*) Future value

(*b*) Internal rate of return

(*c*) Net present value

(*d*) Cash outflow

Q.15. If the total of the present value is less than the cash outlay of a project, then the project is:

(*a*) Viable

(*b*) Not viable

(*c*) At no risk

(*d*) Nothing can be concluded

Q.16. The steps involved in using the NPV method are:

(*a*) Estimating all future net cash flows (revenue minus cost) associated with the investment opportunity.

(*b*) Converting the net cash flow figures to their present value equivalents by discounting at the appropriate discount rate.

(*c*) Adding all the present value figures for future cash flows.

(*d*) Subtracting from this value the initial cost of investment

Q.17. The formula for calculating NPV is:

(*a*) $NPV = \sum \frac{C}{(1+r)^n} - I$

(*b*) $NPV = \frac{(1+r)^n}{\sum C} - I$

(*c*) $NPV = \frac{(1+r)^n}{\sum C} \times I$

(*d*) $NPV = \frac{(1+r)^n}{\sum C \times I}$

C= net cash flow per year, n is number of years generating cash flows, I is the initial investment, r is the discount rate.

Q.18/19. The yardstick for evaluation of a project by NPV method is:

(*a*) NPV= I

(*b*) NPV< 0

(*c*) NPV> 0

(*d*) NPV< I

Example: The cash flows of project A and project B are as under:

	Project A	Project B
Investment:	Rs. 7,000	Rs. 7,000
Cash flow:		
1 year	6,000	3,000
2 year	6,000	3,000
3 year	0	3,000
4 year	0	3,000

Calculate net present value at discount rates of 15% and 20%.

Solution:

Net present value at the discount rate of 15%

		Project A		*Project B*	
Year	*Discount Factor*	*Cash Flow*	*Present value*	*Cash Flow*	*Present value*
		Rs.	*Rs.*	*Rs.*	*Rs.*
0	1.000	- 7,000	-7,000	-7,000	-7,000
1	0.870	6,000	5,220	3,000	2,610
2	0.756	6,000	4,536	3,000	2,268
3	0.658			3,000	1,974
4	0.572			3,000	1,716
		NPV	2,756		1,568

Net Present value at the discount rate of 20%

		Project A		*Project B*	
Year	*Discount Factor*	*Cash Flow*	*Present value*	*Cash Flow*	*Present value*
		Rs.	*Rs.*	*Rs.*	*Rs.*
0	1.000	- 7,000	- 7,000	-7,000	-7,000
1	0.833	6,000	4,998	3,000	2,499
2	0.694	6,000	4,164	3,000	2,082
3	0.579			3,000	1,737
4	0.482			3,000	1,446
		NPV	2,162		764

At both the discount rates Project A is preferable because of higher NPV

Internal Rate of Return (IRR) method of Investment Appraisal

Q.20. Fill in the blank:

Internal rate of return is the rate of ——— in NPV equation at which the present value of cash flows of a project equals its initial outlay.

(*a*) Cash flow

(*b*) Investment

(*c*) Discount

(*d*) Years

Q.21. IRR is the value of the discount rate at which the NPV of a project is:

(*a*) More than zero

(*b*) Less than zero

(*c*) Equal to zero

(*d*) Double of zero

Q.22. How is the internal return calculated?

(*a*) It is calculated on the basis of present value tables.

(*b*) First step is to calculate NPV of the project at a rate of discount chosen randomly.

(*c*) If the NPV calculated is positive, then it should be understood that surplus will be generated at a higher rate.

(*d*) A new higher rate of discount is chosen to calculate NPV.

(*e*) If the NPV becomes negative, it should be understood that the IRR is in between these two rates where NPV is zero.

(*f*) By trial and error the rate of return should be chosen where NPV is zero or closest to zero.

(*g*) The trial and error method is tedious and so, alternatively, the IRR may be calculated by interpolating the two randomly chosen rates, one where the NPV is positive and the one where NPV is negative.

Q.23. What is the formula for interpolation in calculating IRR?

(*a*) $$IRR = R_1 + \frac{NPV_1}{(NPV_1 - NPV_2)} \times (R_2 - R_1)$$

(*b*) $$IRR = R_1 + \frac{(NPV_1 - NPV_2)}{NPV_1} \times (R_2 - R_1)$$

(*c*) $IRR = R_2 + \frac{(NPV_1 - NPV_2)}{NPV_1} \times (R_1 - R_2)$

(*d*) All of these

Where, R_1 = Discount rate which is low
R_2 = Discount rate which is lower
NPV_1 = NPV at discount rate which is low
NPV_2 = NPV at discount rate which is higher

Q.24. The cash flows of project A and project B are as under:

	Project A	*Project B*
Investment:	Rs. 7,000	Rs. 7,000
Cash flow:		
1 year	6,000	3,000
2 year	6,000	3,000
3 year	0	3,000
4 year	0	3,000

What is the internal rate of return of Project B.

(*a*) 23.21%

(*b*) 24.35%

(*c*) 23.75%

(*d*) 24.50%

Q.25. Which one of the following is true?

(*a*) Variation on the NPV equation provides the basis for calculating the IRR.

(*b*) NPV and the IRR associated with an investment are actually the same.

(*c*) NPV and IRR are two independent measurements of investment appraisal and have no connection with each other.

(*d*) All of the above.

Q.26. Which of the following is true?

(*a*) IRR calculation deals with a predetermined rate of discount whereas NPV attempts to find out a rate that equals the rate of return on the investment.

(*b*) NPV calculation deals with a predetermined rate of discount whereas IRR attempts to find out a rate that equals the rate of return on the investment.

(*c*) IRR as well as NPV deals with a predetermined rate of discount.

(*d*) IRR as well as NPV do not deal with rate of discount.

Q.27. A project should be undertaken if its IRR is:

(*a*) Less than the cost of capital

(*b*) More than the cost of capital

(*c*) Half of the cost of capital

(*d*) No relevance

Q.28. Which of the following is true for mutually exclusive investment opportunities:

(*a*) Undertake the investment, which has highest IRR, provided the IRR is less than the cost of capital.

(*b*) Undertake the investment, which has lowest IRR, provided the IRR is less than the cost of capital.

(*c*) Undertake the investment, which has lowest IRR, provided the IRR is greater than the cost of capital.

(*d*) Undertake the investment, which has highest IRR, provided the IRR is greater than the cost of capital.

Q.29. Which of the following are the advantages of NPV and IRR method:

(*a*) They give exact results

(*b*) They take into account time value of money

(*c*) They focus on cash flows rather than on accounting profits

(*d*) b & c

Q.30. Where there are cash outflows in between cash inflows in a project:

(*a*) IRR method will give appropriate decision guidance

(*b*) IRR method may not give appropriate decision guidance

(*c*) IRR method will not be applicable

(*d*) IRR is the only applicable method

Q.31. In comparing two projects where their cash flows are not same in terms of volumes and sign:

(*a*) IRR method is helpful

(*b*) Not very helpful

(*c*) Not applicable at all

(*d*) Not relevant

Q.32. Even when two projects are mutually exclusive, capital rationing:

(*a*) Results in accurate ranking by NPV method only

(*b*) Results in accurate ranking by IRR method only

(*c*) Results accurate ranking by NPV as well as IRR method.

(*d*) Results in accurate ranking by NPV as well as IRR method.

Investment decision-making under condition of uncertainty

Q.33. The techniques that can be suggested to the decision-maker, who is faced with the problem of appraising investments where the future cash flows are not certain:

(*a*) Expected NPV rule

(*b*) Risk adjusted discount rate approach

(*c*) Sensitivity analysis

(*d*) All of these

Q.34. As per expected NPV (ENPV) rule, in a situation where cash flows are not known with certainty:

(*a*) Investment appraisal decisions should be made on a single set of cash flow estimates on the basis of single set of assumptions related to the results of investment.

(*b*) Investment appraisal decisions should not be made on a single set of cash flow estimates on the basis of single set of assumptions related to the results of investment.

(*c*) Decision-maker should make number of sales estimates based on various scenarios.

(*d*) b & c

Q.35. The risk adjusted discount rate approach for NPV determination makes a balance between:

(*a*) Degree of risk and rate of return

(*b*) Degree of profitability and investment

(*c*) Degree of risk and degree of uncertainty

(*d*) Average risk and average return

Q.36. The steps involved in the risk adjusted discount rate approach method for NPV determination are:

(*a*) Determine the rate of return required, to make investment with zero risk.

(*b*) To the above rate of return, add a risk premium taking into account the risk factors of the investment under consideration.

(*c*) The resulting rate of return is then to be used as the discount rate in the usual NPV calculation.

Q.37. Sensitivity analysis for NPV determination:

(*a*) Identifies areas of concern in an investment opportunity.

(*b*) Identifies those factors, which are sensitive to the profitability of the investment opportunity.

(*c*) Identifies areas where more efforts are required to be made to explore more information.

(*d*) All of these.

Q.38. The decision tree analysis for NPV estimation recognizes that:

(*a*) Environment is always certain

(*b*) Environment is uncertain

(*c*) Environment is dynamic

(*d*) b & c

Q.39. The characteristics of payback method are:

(*a*) It is a simple and straight forward method of evaluating projects where the time period by which total investment is received back in a project in the form of cash inflows is calculated

(*b*) It measures the net cash flows resulting from the project being undertaken

(*c*) It can be used to rank projects where the investment opportunities are mutually exclusive by choosing the projects that have shortest payback period

(*d*) All of these

Q.40. The shortcomings of payback method are:

(*a*) It does not take into account the time value of money.

(*b*) The choice of payback period is arbitrary

(*c*) Only those cash flows are considered which fall in the payback period.

(*d*) All of these.

Q.41. State whether true or false:

(*a*) Capital budgeting relates to plan for future capital outlay and its financing

(*b*) NPV is the difference between the sum of the present value of cash inflows and cash outlay

(*c*) Internal rate of return method of project appraisal is not based on the time value of money

(*d*) Trial and error method used in internal rate of return method is accurate

(*e*) Pay back method of project appraisal is based on the time value of money

Ans.

1. True
2. True
3. False (It is based on time value of money)
4. True (It is tedious but accurate)
5. False

ANSWERS					
1. (b)	2. (d)	3. (d)	4. (d)	5. (c)	6. (a)
7. (b)	8. (c)	9. (a)	10. —	11. (c)	12. (d)
13. (d)	14. (c)	15. (b)	16. —	17. (a)	18/19. (c)
20. (c)	21. (c)	22. —	23. (a)	24. (b)	25. (a)
26. (b)	27. (b)	28. (d)	29. (d)	30. (b)	31. (b)
32. (d)	33. (d)	34. (d)	35. (a)	36. —	37. (d)
38. (d)	39. (d)	40. (d)			

CHAPTER

4

DEPRECIATION - DIFFERENT TYPES - METHODS OF CALCULATION/FOREIGN EXCHANGE ARITHMETICS

Introduction

Q.1. The depreciation expense is:

(*a*) Cash expense

(*b*) Non-cash expense

(*c*) Long term cash expense

(*d*) Short term cash expense

Methods of calculating depreciation

Q.2. Which of the following are the characteristics of straight line method of calculating depreciation?

(*a*) It assumes that the asset will lose an equal amount of value each year.

(*b*) It is calculated by subtracting salvage value of asset from purchase price and dividing by the estimated number of years of life of the asset.

(*c*) It spreads the depreciation cost evenly over the useful life of the asset.

(*d*) All of the above

Q.3. Equal amount of value of depreciation is charged every year in:

(*a*) Declining balance method of calculating depreciation

(*b*) Sum-of-year's digit method of calculating depreciation

(*c*) Straight line method of calculating depreciation

(*d*) Accelerated depreciation method

Q.4. Accumulated depreciation is the:

(*a*) Total amount of depreciation, which is decided to be charged on an asset.

(*b*) The remaining book value of the asset after charging the depreciation

(*c*) The amount of depreciation, which has accumulated over time.

(*d*) The accumulated interest on the depreciation value of the asset

Q.5. The value of an asset is Rs. 30,000 and rate of depreciation is decided as 10%, then the depreciation charged (as per declining balance method), at the end of second year will be:

(*a*) 3,000

(*b*) 2,700

(*c*) 5,400

(*d*) 2,500

Q.6. Steps involved in double declining method for calculating depreciation are:

(*a*) Use the straight line method of calculating depreciation and find out the amount of depreciation.

(*b*) Calculate the percentage of the above amount of depreciation in relation to the total value of the asset to be depreciated and double it.

(*c*) Charge the above percentage (double) every year on the remaining book value of the asset.

(*d*) When the remaining book value of the asset goes below the amount of depreciation that could have been charged by straight line method, use straight line method.

Q.7. On January, 2000, a machinery costing Rs. 50,000 was purchased. Its working life is estimated to be 5 years and salvage value at Rs. 5,000. The depreciation to be charged (by double declining balance method) at the end of the second year and at the end of the fifth year will be:

(*a*) 20,000 and 20,000

(*b*) 10,000 and 20,000

(*c*) 12,000 and 1480

(*d*) 20,000 and 10,480

Q.8. Which of the following are true for the Sum of year's digit(SYD) method of calculating depreciation:

(*a*) The amount of depreciation is evenly distributed over the useful life of the asset.

(*b*) With the diminishing years of useful life the rate of depreciation increases.

(*c*) The depreciation amount of the earlier years of the useful life of the asset is greater than those in the later years.

(*d*) All of these

Q.9. The steps used in calculating depreciation by using sum of year's digit method is:

(*a*) Estimate an asset's useful life in years.

(*b*) Assign consecutive numbers to each year, count back, total these numbers (for five years useful life it will be, 5+4+3+2+1=15), and get SYD(15).

(*c*) Divide the original depreciation value by SYD and multiply by remaining useful life.

Q.10. The formula for calculating depreciation by sum of year's digit method is:

(*a*) $\text{(Original cost - Salvage value)} \times \dfrac{\text{SYD}}{\text{remaining useful life}}$,

(*b*) $\text{(Original cost - Salvage value)} \times \dfrac{\text{remaining useful life}}{\text{SYD}}$

(*c*) $\dfrac{\text{SYD}}{\text{(Original cost - Salvage value)} \times \text{remaining useful life}}$,

(*d*) $\dfrac{\text{(Original cost - Salvage value)}}{\text{SYD} \times \text{remaining useful life}}$

Q.11. An asset valuing Rs. 20,000 has a salvage value of Rs. 5,000 and useful life of 5 years. The depreciation at the end of the second year by using sum of year's digit method will be:

(*a*) 1,000

(*b*) 5,000

(*c*) 4,000

(*d*) 6,000

Q.12. What are the issues in selecting a method of depreciation?

(*a*) Management should make comparison among various methods of depreciation.

(*b*) Different method affects bottom-line of the company differently.

(*c*) Level of attention on the method of depreciation will depend on the asset intensity of the business.

(*d*) If one company have two asset-intensive businesses, the methods used should be adjusted to be comparable to get accurate picture.

Q.13. How the Excel Worksheet can be used for calculating depreciation:

(*a*) Keep your data ready for calculation of depreciation like,

- Cost of asset
- Salvage value
- Useful life

(*b*) Open Excel worksheet

(*c*) In the first column, type in year1, year 2, etc. up to end of useful life. (Leave one or two rows from the top to give headings).

(*d*) In the second column, Give heading of the method you are going to use (straight line method. Double decline method etc.) just above the row of year1.

(*e*) Select the cell just below this heading in the Year1 row.

(*f*) Click on f_x (Paste Function) on the tool bar. A window will appear. In the left hand box (Function category) click on 'Financial'. In the right hand box (Function name) you will find various abbreviations representing various types of function that you can use under 'Financial' category. Click on the appropriate function that you want to use. For example, see that SLN is for Straight line depreciation method and DDB for Double Declining method for depreciation. When you select any abbreviation the purpose of the function is described. So you may always try and see the purpose of any abbreviation.

(*g*) On clicking any particular function type and clicking on 'OK', another window will come up which is meant for feeding the Data. Fill up the data relevant to that function. For example, the following Data requires to be filled up for Straight Line method of Depreciation:

- Cost
- Salvage
- Life

When you put your cursor in any of these Data fields, description of the type of data is given and you can fill up the data accordingly.

(*h*) When you finish entering Data, click on 'OK'. The results of the calculations will appear in the cell selected earlier by you.

(*i*) You may find problem with currency. The result may come in 'dollars'.

(*j*) To avoid this, keep the cell in which data is displayed in dollars, click on 'format' in tool bar, click on currency and select the appropriate currency (For Rs. click on none).

Q.14. State whether true or false:

1. Under straight line method of depreciation the value of the asset can be reduced to zero or its scrap value
2. Scrap value under double declining method cannot be taken as zero
3. Depreciation is a charge against profit
4. In the straight line method of depreciation the rate of depreciation remains same throughout
5. MACRS is an example of accelerated depreciation method

Ans.

1. True
2. False
3. True
4. False
5. True

Q.15. Which of the following is a Direct Quote:

(*a*) In India : 1 US$ = Rs. 43.2350

(*b*) In USA : 1 Euro = US $ 1.9200

(*c*) In Germany : 1 DM =US $ 1.2450

(*d*) All the above

Q.16. Market quotes are : US $ 1 = Rs. 42.8450/545, Euro 1 = US $ 1.9720/40, By selling Euro 1,00,000, you will get :

(*a*) Rs. 84,59,478

(*b*) Rs. 84,50,907

(*c*) Rs. 84,49,034

(*d*) None of the above

Q.17. Market quote is; 1 Euro = US $ 1.5780/90, 3 month forward; 110-105. If you have to buy Euro, the rate of 1 Euro will be—

(*a*) US $ 1.5890

(*b*) US $ 1.5895

(*c*) US $ 1.5680

(*d*) None of the above

Q.18. If the Spot rate is Euro 1 = US $ 1.500 and the interest rate in Europe is higher by 3% p.a. then in USA, what will, theoretically, be Euro's 90 days forward rate, assuming 360 days in a year?

(*a*) 1.51125

(*b*) 1.48875

(*c*) 1.50750

(*d*) 1.49250

ANSWERS					
1. (b)	2. (d)	3. (c)	4. (c)	5. (b)	6. (—)
7. (c)	8. (c)	9. (—)	10. (b)	11. (c)	12. (—)
13. (—)	14. (—)	15. (a)	16. (c)	17. (d)	18. (b)

MODULE

B

PRINCIPLES OF BOOK KEEPING

CHAPTER

5

NATURE AND PURPOSE OF ACCOUNTING

Meaning of Accountancy

Q.1. Accounting is an art of :

a. Recording, classifying, summarizing and interpreting the monetary transactions

b. Recording the business transactions in the books of original entry and in the ledgers

c. Providing information about the financial position of an enterprise

d. Providing results of business performance to various users

Q.1A. Non-monetary transactions of the business are

a. Recorded in the subsidiary books

b. Converted into monetary transactions and recorded in the books of account

c. Recorded alongwith monetary transactions

d. Not recorded in books of account

Historical Aspects

Q.2. "Financial Accounting is an extension of Stewardship Accounting". Comment.

A.: In the earlier days, wealthy people used to employ stewards to manage their property, who in turn submit their account to the owners at periodic intervals regarding the property they owned, debts they owed and the debts others owed to them. In the present financial system also the same type of reporting is required with a systematic recording as per the basic rules of accountancy.

Q.3. Accounting information is derived from :

(*a*) Record of transactions in books of account

(*b*) Record of cash flows in the business

(*c*) Final accounts of the concern

(*d*) Auditors report

Q.4. Book-keeping differs from accounting in the following manner :

(*a*) Book-keeping and accounting are based on different data.

(*b*) Book-keeping deals with recording of transactions and accounting with their interpretation.

(*c*) Book-keeping is done by non-profit making organizations and accounting by business organizations.

(*d*) Book-keeping is the function of Librarian and accounting is the function of accountant.

Q.5. State Whether the following statements are True or False :

1. Accounting and book keeping are as old as money itself :
2. In earlier days Stewards managed the property of wealthy people and used to prepare statements of their property at periodical intervals.
3. In 1494 at Venice, Luca De Bargo Pacioli, an Italian Monk, propounded the concepts of modern accounting in his book called Summa.
4. The Italian method was adopted by other European countries during 19th and 20th Centuries.
5. In India Accountancy was introduced by Kautilya in his book named Arthasastra in 4th Century B.C.
6. Accountancy refers to the art of recording the business transactions in analytical form.
7. Accountancy and book keeping are same.
8. Accountancy records all types of transactions including quarrels between the management and workers, etc.
9. In Mercantile system of accounting, incomes and expenses are recognized as and when they are due irrespective of their actual receipts or payments.
10. In Cash Method of Accounting, Profit represents excess of receipts over expenditures.
11. Single Entry System of book keeping is a scientific method of accounting.
12. Inflation accounting is concerned with the adjustment in the value of all types of assets and of profits in the light of changes in the price level.
13. In financial accounting the assets are not recorded at their historic cost but are recorded at their market value

14. Human Resource Accounting seeks to report and emphasise the importance of knowledge, training and loyality of employees working in a company

A: 1.True: 1, 2, 3, 4, 5, 6, 9,10,12, 14,

False 7 (*Book keeping refers to the systematic classification of business transactions and recording these events and transactions in the Journal, Cash book, Subsidiary books, etc. and their ledger posting. Accounting starts where book keeping ends. It refers to summarizing of the recorded events, i.e. Preparation of Trial Balance, Balance Sheet and Profit & Loss Account and interpreting the financial transactions.*)

False 8 (*Accounting records transactions in terms of money, to make them meaningful. Events which cannot be expressed in terms of money are not recorded in the books of account*)

False 11 *(Double Entry System of book keeping is a scientific method of accounting.)*

False 13 *(Assets are recorded at their historic cost or market price, whichever is less.)*

ANSWERS					
1. (a)	1A. (d)	2. (—)	3. (a)	4. (b)	5. (—)

CHAPTER

6

ORIGINS OF ACCOUNTING PRINCIPLES, CONCEPTS AND CONVENTIONS

Need, Role and List of Accounting Concepts

Q.1. What was the need for Accounting concepts?

A.: Accounting is a language of business, using which the business world communicates with the outside world. To make this communication understood by all, it is based on certain uniform scientifically laid down standards, which have arisen from

(*i*) Common experience

(*ii*) Historical precedents,

(*iii*) Statements of individuals and professionals, and

(*iv*) Regulations by Government agencies.

Q.2. What is the role of accounting concepts in the preparation of Financial Statements?

A.: Accounting concepts are the fundamental ideas or basic assumptions underlying the theory and practice of financial accounting and are the broad working rules for all accounting activities developed and accepted by the accounting profession. These rules and conventions are known as Generally Accepted Accounting Principles (GAAP) or Basic Accounting Concepts.

Q.3. The acronym 'GAAP' stands for:

(*a*) Generally Accepted Accounting Practices

(*b*) General Agreement on Accounting Principles

(*c*) General American Accounting Practices

(*d*) Generally Accepted Accounting Principles

Q.4. 'GAAP' implies that:

(*a*) The principles are to be followed by all in the profession.

(*b*) The accounts prepared by all the organizations shall be in the same format.

(*c*) The principles have been accepted by majority in the profession.

(*d*) they have backing of law.

Q.5. Give a list of the various accounting concepts.

A.: On the basis of the usage of the various concepts, they can be classified under two broad heads:

A. Concepts observed at recording Stage, and

B. Concepts observed at reporting stage.

Following table shows the various concepts:

A. Concepts observed at recording stage	B. Concepts observed at reporting stage
1. Business Entity Concept	1. Going concern Concept & assumption
2. Money Measurement Concept	2. Accounting Period Concept
3. Objective Evidence Concept	3. Matching Concept
4. Historical Record Concept	4. Conservatism Concept & Convention
5. Cost Concept	5. Consistency Concept & Convention
6. Dual aspect Concept	6. Full Disclosure Concept & Convention
7. Revenue recognition, & Accrual Concept	7. Materiality Concept & Convention

Q6. The proprietor of a firm withdrew Rs. 50,000 for his personal use. This was shown as an expense of the firm. Profits were reduced to pay a lower tax. Is this right from accounting point of view?

A.: The amount withdrawn by the proprietor should be debited to his drawings account and cannot be shown as an expense. He is a separate entity different from the business and as such any amount withdrawn for his personal use cannot be booked as an expense of the concern. Therefore, the action taken here is wrong.

Q.7. The Proprietor is treated as a creditor to the extent of his capital according to :

(*a*) Cost concept

(*b*) Business Entity Concept

(*c*) Going concern Concept

(*d*) Accounting Period Concept

Q.8. Suppose the Managing Director of a company is killed in a plane crash. To the extent 'an organization is the lengthened shadow of a man', the real value of the company will be reflected in the market price of the company's shares. Will this have any effect as far as the accounts of the company are concerned?

A.: As per Money Measurement Concept, every transaction, which is recorded in books of account, must be measured in terms of money. This is a very important information affecting the goodwill of the company, but this cannot be measured in terms of money, and as such, this will have no effect as far as the accounts of the company are concerned.

Q.9. According to Money Measurement Concept which one of the following will be recorded in the books of Account:

(*a*) Health of the Chairman of the Company

(*b*) Quality control in the business

(*c*) Value of the building

(*d*) Good staff relations

Cost concept

Q.10. What is Cost concept and what is its necessity?

A.: Every business transaction is recorded in the books of account at cost price. The concept states that an asset is worth the price paid for or cost incurred to acquire it. Therefore, all the assets are recorded at their original cost and this becomes the basis of all subsequent accounting for the assets.

When an asset is recorded at cost price, the changes in the real worth, with the passage of time, is not ordinarily recorded in the account books. For example, if a land is purchased for Rs. 1 lac and if its market price is 10 lacs at the time of preparation of final accounts, it will not be considered.

However, the cost concept does not mean that assets are always shown year after year at the cost price. They are systematically reduced by the process of depreciation. These assets ultimately disappear when their economic life is over and they have been fully depreciated and sold as scrap.

Q.11. The system of recording transactions based on dual concept is called:

(*a*) Double Account System

(*b*) Double Entry System

(*c*) Single Entry System

(*d*) Single Account System

Q.12. Which of the following is not an accounting convention

(*a*) Conservatism

(*b*) Materiality
(*c*) Dual aspect
(*d*) None of the above

Q.13. As per the realization concept, Closing Stock should be valued at
(*a*) The realizable value
(*b*) Cost price or realizable value, whichever is less
(*c*) Sales less gross profit
(*d*) Cost price plus proportionate expenses till the goods reach to his godown or Saleable value, whichever is less.

Q.14. The practice of providing for unpaid expenses and prepaid expenses is based on:
(*a*) Matching concept
(*b*) Realisation concept
(*c*) Convenience of accounting
(*d*) Accrual basis of accounting

Q15. Under the accrual concept of accounting
(*a*) Only the amounts unpaid are recorded
(*b*) Expenses due are recorded, but incomes due are not included
(*c*) Incomes due are included, but expenses due are not provided for
(*d*) Expenses due are invariably recorded, incomes due but not received are included only when they are certain to be received.

Q.16. The matching concept means:
(*a*) The expenses should be equal to income.
(*b*) Assets should equal liabilities
(*c*) The expenses should be included in the accounting period when the relevant revenues were included.
(*d*) The size of the business should match with its resources.

Q.17. The convention of conservatism is applicable
(*a*) In providing a discount on creditors
(*b*) Adopting straight line method for providing depreciation
(*c*) Showing Joint Life Policy at Surrender Value as against the Premium amount paid.
(*d*) In valuing inventory at higher of cost or market rate

Q.18. Making the provision for doubtful debts in anticipation of actual bad debts is on the basis of

(*a*) Convention of disclosure

(*b*) Convention of consistency

(*c*) Convention of conservatism

(*d*) Money Measurement Concept

Q.19. The practice of appending note regarding contingent liabilities in the accounting statements is pursuant to

(*a*) Convention of Consistency

(*b*) Money Measurement Concept.

(*c*) Convention of Disclosure

(*d*) Convention of conservatism

Q.20. Market value of Investments is shown as a footnote according to

(*a*) Convention of disclosure

(*b*) Convention of consistency

(*c*) Convention of conservatism

(*d*) Money Measurement Concept

Q.21. State whether the following statements are True or False:

1. Accounting Principles are the general laws or rules followed in the preparation of Financial statements.
2. Usefulness, objectivity and feasibility are the three basic norms generally found in Accounting Principles.
3. In keeping with the principle of materiality, unimportant items are either left out or merged with other items.
4. In Accountancy, all business transactions are recorded as having dual aspect.
5. According to money measurement concept, working conditions in which the workers of the business have to work must be clearly recorded in the books of account.
6. The convention of disclosure implies that all material information should be disclosed in the accounts.
7. The convention of conservatism takes into account all prospective profits but leaves all prospective losses.
8. According to the convention of conservatism, the stock in trade is valued at market price, or cost price, whichever is less.

9. The entity concept does not consider the business and the proprietor as distinct from each other.
10. The Proprietor has a separate existence from the business.
11. It is on the basis of the entity concept that money brought by the proprietor into the business is credited to Proprietor's Capital Account.
12. According to periodic matching of cost and revenue concept, a businessman is not only to measure revenues in a particular accounting period but also has to calculate expenses which can be assigned in earning such revenue.
13. It is on the basis of going concern concept that the assets are always valued at market price.
14. Since the life of the business is assumed to be indefinite, the financial statements of the business should be prepared only when it goes into liquidation.
15. As per the going concern concept, until and unless the business has entered into a state of liquidation, it is viewed as having indefinite life.
16. Rupee is the common unit of measurement.
17. A businessman needs to know the statement of affairs of his business at frequent intervals, normally 12 months. This period is called Financial year.
18. The "verifiable objective evidence" concept means that all accounting transactions should be evidenced by business documents.
19. The materiality concept refers to the process of ignoring small items and values from accounts.
20. The generally accepted accounting principles prescribe a uniform accounting practice.
21. The conservatism concept leads to the exclusion of all unrealized profits.
22. The system of recording transactions based on dual aspect concept is called Double Entry.

Ans.: True: 1, 2, 3, 4, 6, 8, 10, 11, 12, 15, 17, 18, 19, 20, 21, 22

False 5 *(Working conditions cannot be measured in terms of money, and as such they are not accounted for)*

False 7 (*The essence of convention of conservatism is to anticipate no profit, but to provide for all possible losses).*

False 9 (*An accounting entity is held to be separate and distint from its owners).*

False 13 (*Assets are valued at cost price or market price, whichever is less, under the principle of conservatism).*

False 14 *(As per the going concern concept, the results of operations can be known only after the liquidation of the business. But accounting period assumption suggests that the entire life of the business be divided into time intervals to check the progress. Therefore a distinction is made between expenditure that will render the benefit for a long period-called assets, and those whose benefits will be exhausted quickly- called expenses).*

False 16 (*Money is the common unit of measurement. This money is converted into the name of the currency for different countries like Rupees in India, or Pounds in UK or Dollars in USA or Yen in Japan, etc.)*

ANSWERS					
1. (—)	2. (—)	3. (d)	4. (c)	5. (—)	6. (—)
7. (b)	8. (—)	9. (c)	10. (—)	11. (b)	12. (d)
13. (b)	14. (d)	15. (d)	16. (c)	17. (c)	18. (c)
19. (c)	20. (a)	21. (—)			

CHAPTER

7

ACCOUNTING STANDARDS, ITS DEFINITION AND SCOPE

Q.1: Accounting Standards are statements prescribed by:

(*a*) Law

(*b*) Government Regulatory bodies

(*c*) Bodies of Shareholders

(*d*) Professional Accounting Bodies

Q.2: In India the Accounting Standards are issued by:

(*a*) The Government of India, Ministry of Finance

(*b*) Reserve Bank of India

(*c*) The Institute of Chartered Accountants of India

(*d*) The Indian Standards Institute

Q3: Which Accounting Standard discusses about the valuation of Inventories?

A.: AS 2 (Revised), which is mandatory since 1-4-1993, deals with the determination of the value at which, the inventories are valued. It states that :

(*a*) Inventories are to be valued lower of cost or net realizable value.

(*b*) Weighted Average Cost or First in First out methods are permitted in general.

Q.4: The cost formulae recommended by Accounting Standard 2 for valuation of inventory are :

(*a*) FIFO or Weighted Average

(*b*) Standard Cost

(*c*) LIFO or latest Purchase price

(*d*) Average market value

Q.5: Is there any Accounting Standard regarding Contingencies and events occurring after the Balance Sheet date?

A: Yes AS 4 (revised), effective from 1-4-1998 deals with such cases.

A. Contingencies means the events whose outcome will be known only on their occurence, *e.g.* pending cases in the court of law.

B. Events occurring after the Balance Sheet date are those which occur between the B/S date and the date on which the accounts are approved at a later date by the Board of Directors.

Q.6: Accounting Standard 28 deals with :

(*a*) Impaired Assets

(*b*) Intangible Assets

(*c*) Contingent Assets

(*d*) Non-Performing Assets

Q.7: Which of the following Indian companies are required to prepare their accounts under USGAAP.

(*a*) All Public Limited Companies

(*b*) Companies borrowing from US banks

(*c*) Companies listed in US Stock Markets

(*d*) None of the above

Q.8: Transfer Pricing relates to :

(*a*) Pricing of goods and services within the divisions of a company or from parent company to a subsidiary

(*b*) Transfer of funds from one bank to another

(*c*) Transfer of funds from one branch to another branch of the same bank

(*d*) Both (a) and (c) above

Q.9: State whether the following statements are True or False :

1. Accounting Standard 1 deals with Depreciation.
2. Accounting Standard 2 is mandatory.
3. The ICAI is a member of the International Accounting Standards Committee.
4. Financial statements are prepared using accounting standards.
5. Accounting standards issued are reviewed regularly and are subject to revision.
6. Accounting standards are like rules of accounting issued by an apex accounting body.

7. In India Accounting concepts are issued by the Accounting Standard Board.
8. There are 29 Accounting Standards in India.
9. Compliance with the Accounting Standards is the duty of the Auditors.

True: 2, 3, 4, 5, 6, 8

False 1 *(AS 1 deals with disclosure of Accounting Policies. It is AS (6) revised which deals with Depreciation Accounting).*

False 7 *(Accounting Standards are like rules of accounting issued by an apex accounting body).*

ANSWERS					
1. (d)	2. (c)	3. (—)	4. (a)	5. (—)	6. (a)
7. (c)	8. (a)	9. (—)			

CHAPTER

8

DOUBLE ENTRY SYSTEM OF BOOK KEEPING

Accounting Equation

Q.1: What is accounting equation? Explain it with illustrations.

A.: At any point of time, the total assets are always equal to the total claims (Liabilities + Capital) = Assets.

This relationship is called accounting or balance sheet equation. If there is any change in the amount of assets or the liabilities, the capital is bound to change correspondingly.

Q. 2: Complete the following accounting equations:

1. Capital Rs. 40,000, Liabilities Rs. 15,000, Assets Rs. ______
2. Capital Rs. 65,000, Liabilities Rs. ________, Assets Rs. 80,000
3. Assets Rs. 90,000, Liabilities Rs. _________, Capital Rs. 50,000
4. Capital Rs. _____, Liabilities Rs. 20,000, Assets Rs. 90,000.

A.: 1. 55000 Assets (40,000 Capital + 15,000 Liabilities),

2. 15,000 Liabilities (80,000 Assets - 65,000 Capital),

3. 40,000 Liabilities (90,000 Assets - 50,000 Capital),

4. 70,000 Capital (90,000 Assets - 20,000 Liabilities).

Q.3: Give your answers to the following situations:

(*a*) If the capital of a business is Rs. 2,00,000 and Liabilities Rs. 50,000, Loss Rs. 70,000. What is the amount of Total Assets of the business.

(*b*) If total Assets of a business are 1,30,000 and net worth is Rs. 80,000. Profit Rs. 10,000. Calculate its creditors.

(*c*) X started his business with Rs. 3,00,000. At the end of the year his Assets worth Rs. 5,00,000 and Liabilities Rs. 1,00,000. Find his closing capital and profits earned during the year.

(*d*) Calculate total Liabilities and total capital:

(*i*) Capital at the beginning Rs. 6,00,000

(*ii*) Creditors Rs. 5,00,000

(*iii*) Revenue Rs. 7,00,000

(*iv*) Expenses Rs. 6,50,000

A.: a. Assets Rs. 1,80,000; b. Creditors Rs. 40,000; c. Capital Rs. 4,00,000 Profit 1,00,000; d. Total Liabilities Rs. 11,50,000 and Capital Rs. 6,50,000.

Q.4: Find out the two accounts involved in the following transactions:

1. Purchased goods on credit from Ramesh.
2. Paid rent to Landlord.
3. Received interest on Government Securities.
4. Purchased a typewriter from Godrej.
5. Proprietor paid tuition fees of his son from the cash box of the shop.
6. Goods given as free samples.
7. Proprietor took certain goods from the shop for his personal consumption.
8. Goods lost in transit.
9. Insurance claim accepted by the insurance company against goods lost in transit.
10. Insurance claim received from the Insurance Company.

A.:
1. Purchases and Ramesh.
2. Rent and Cash
3. Cash, Interest
4. Office Equipment and Godrej
5. Drawings and Cash
6. Advertisement and Purchases
7. Drawings and Purchases
8. Abnormal Loss and Trading
9. Insurance Company and Abnormal Loss
10. Bank and Insurance Company.

Q.5: Following is the list of various accounts. Find out which are Personal, Real or Nominal accounts.

a. Capital, b. Land & Machinery, c. Cash in hand, d. Bank, e. Rent, f. Sales, g. Customer, h. Interest i. Stock in hand j. Wages due but not paid k. Insurance premium paid in advance., l Insurance premium, m. Drawings, n. Charity

A.:(*a*) Capital is a personal account as it relates to the proprietor

(*b*) Land & Building is an Asset and is Real account

(*c*) Cash is an Asset and it is real Account

(*d*) Bank is an Institution and as such it is a Personal account

(*e*) Rent is a nominal account. Rent paid is an expense and rent received is an income.

(*f*) Sales is a revenue and a Nominal account

(*g*) Customer is our Debtor as well as Asset. It is a Personal Account

(*h*) Interest received is an income and interest paid an expense. It is a nominal account.

(*i*) Stock in hand is a real account.

(*j*) Wages due but not paid shows the amount payable to the labourers, therefore it is a Personal account as our Liability, as contrary to only Wages account, which represent an expense of the factory and that is a nominal account.

(*k*) Insurance premium is paid in advance to the Insurance Company, an Institution from whom we have yet to receive the service. It is our Asset in the shape of a Personal Account.

(*l*) Insurance Premium is an expense and is covered under nominal accounts.

(*m*) Drawings are the amount withdrawn by the proprietor from the business for his personal use. It is a personal account to be deducted from the capital.

(*n*) Charity is an expense and is a nominal account.

Q.6: Explain the nature of account and show which account will be debited and which will be credited.

(i) Rent paid, (ii) Interest received, (iii) Machinery purchased, (iv), Discount allowed, (v) Building sold, (vi) Capital introduced, (vii) Goods purchased, (viii) Taken loan from Bank, (ix) Goods purchased from Ram, (x) Salary paid to Ramesh.

A.:

Sl. No.	*Transaction*	*Accounts involved*	*Type of A/c*	*Rule applicable*	*A/c Debited*	*A/c Credited*
(i)	Rent paid	Rent Cash	N R	Dr. expenses Cr. Goes out	Rent	Cash
(ii)	Interest received	Interest Cash	N R	Cr. All incomes Dr. comes in	Cash	Interest

Sl. No.	*Transaction*	*Accounts involved*	*Type of A/c*	*Rule applicable*	*A/c Debited*	*A/c Credited*
(iii)	Machinery purchased	Machinery Cash	R R	Dr. Comes in Cr. Goes out	Machinery	Cash
(iv)	Discount allowed	Discount Cash	N R	Dr. expenses Cr. Goes out	Discount	Cash
(v)	Building sold	Building Cash	R R	Cr. Goes out Dr. comes in	Cash	Building
(vi)	Capital introduced	Capital Cash	P R	Cr. The giver Dr. Comes in	Cash	Capital
(vii)	Goods purchased	Purchases Cash	N R	Dr. Expenses Cr. Goes out	Purchases	Cash
(viii)	Taken loan from Bank	Cash Bank Loan	R P	Dr. Comes in Cr. The giver	Cash	Bank
(ix)	Goods purchased from Ram	Purchases Ram	N P	Dr. All expenses Cr. The giver	Purchases	Ram
(x)	Salary paid to Ramesh	Salary Cash	N R	Dr. All expenses Cr. What goes out	Salary	Cash

Q.7:. What is a Nominal account:

(*a*) An account of each person or firm with whom the trader deals

(*b*) An account of each head of expense or source of income

(*c*) An account of each property or possession dealt in by the trader in his business

(*d*) None of these

Q.8: What is the fundamental rule of debit and credit with regards to Assets or Real accounts:

(*a*) Debit the receiver and credit the giver

(*b*) Debit what comes in and credit what goes out

(*c*) Debit expenses and losses and credit gains

(*d*) All of the above.

Q.9: How does profit made from normal business operations retained in business appear in the Balance Sheet.

(*a*) Under Capital

(*b*) Under Capital, Reserve and Surplus

(*c*) Under Cash in hand and at bank

(*d*) None of the above

Q.10: Where does the Net Profit appear in the Balance Sheet?

(*a*) Liabilities Side

(*b*) Assets side

(*c*) Either a or b

(*d*) None of these

(It is added in the capital or reserves on the liabilities side of the balance sheet)

Q.11: In double entry, the entry is balanced with a corresponding entry, which is called:

(*a*) Reverse entry

(*b*) Adjusting entry

(*c*) Contra entry

(*d*) Double entry

Q.12: For nominal accounts the fundamental rule of Debit and Credit is, Debit expenses and losses and Credit:

(*a*) The giver

(*b*) What goes out

(*c*) Incomes & gain

(*d*) None of the above

Q.13: In book keeping Capital account is a .... account?

(*a*) Nominal

(*b*) Real

(*c*) Personal

(*d*) Intangible

(Because Capital account is that of the proprietors' account, who is a person. Therefore, it is a Personal account)

Q.14: Where should a withdrawal of cash from business by the proprietor be credited to:

(*a*) Drawings

(*b*) Proprietors' account

(*c*) Capital account

(*d*) Cash account

Q.15: For nominal accounts, the fundamental rule of Debit and Credit is, Debit expenses and losses and Credit :

(*a*) The giver

(*b*) What goes out

(*c*) Incomes & Gains

(*d*) None of the above

Q.16: A person who owes money to the firm is called:

(*a*) Creditor

(*b*) Debtor

(*c*) Shareholders

(*d*) Owner

Q. 17: In Double entry system of Book Keeping every business transaction affects:

(*a*) Two accounts

(*b*) Two sides of the same account

(*c*) The same account on two different dates

(*d*) One personal and one real account

Q.18: Following is known as the book of prime entry :

(*a*) Journal

(*b*) Cash book

(*c*) Subsidiary books

(*d*) All of the above

Q.19: Double entry book-keeping refers to a system where :

(*a*) Each transaction is entered in the books by two persons to avoid frauds and mistakes

(*b*) At least two aspects of each transaction is recognized and recorded in accounts books

(*c*) Two sides of each account always tally

(*d*) Only transactions that are entered twice are recognized

Q.20: For a Real account, the rule for journalizing is:

(*a*) Debit the receiver credit the giver

(*b*) Debit what goes out credit what comes in

(*c*) Debit what comes in credit what goes out

(*d*) Debit Assets credit Liabilities

Q.21: In a transaction, the two accounts identified:

(*a*) should belong to only one type of account

(*b*) one of the accounts must belong to personal account

(*c*) must be necessarily of two types-real, nominal or personal

(*d*) may belong to any one or two or more types of accounts

Q.22: Express, whether the following statements are right or wrong:

(*a*) In real accounts, credit what comes in and debit what goes out (*b*) The accounting equation is Assets = Capital + Liabilities

(*c*) Accounting need to be maintained only if the business unit is subject to taxation

A.:(*a*) Wrong (*In real accounts the rule is Debit what comes in and credit what goes out)*

(*b*) Right

(*c*) Wrong (*Accounting is required to be maintained by all types of organizations for finding out reply to various financial matters, taxation is only one amongst them)*

Q.23: Commission received in advance is of the nature of:

(*a*) Real account

(*b*) Nominal account

(*c*) Personal account

(*d*) Intangible account

Q.24: Rebate on bills discounted account is of the nature of :

(*a*) Personal account

(*b*) Real account

(*c*) Nominal account

(*d*) Intangible account

Q.25: Patents right account is of the nature of :

(*a*) Nominal account

(*b*) Personal account

(*c*) Real account

(*d*) Intangible account

Q.26: Rent prepaid account is of the nature of

(*a*) Real account

(*b*) Personal account

(*c*) Nominal account

(*d*) Intangible account

Q.27: Salaries outstanding account belongs to the category of:

(*a*) Real account

(*b*) Personal account

(*c*) Nominal account

(*d*) Intangible account

Q.28: All losses and expenses are _________

(*a*) Debited

(*b*) Credited

(*c*) Either debited or credited

(*d*) Recorded in cash book

Q.29: The purchase of Machinery for the business is recorded in _________

(*a*) Purchase Register

(*b*) Journal

(*c*) Cash book

(*d*) Creditors' Register

ANSWERS					
1. (—)	2. (—)	3. (—)	4. (—)	5. (—)	6. (—)
7. (b)	8. (b)	9. (b)	10. (a)	11. (c)	12. (c)
13. (b)	14. (d)	15. (c)	16. (b)	17. (a)	18. (d)
19. (b)	20. (c)	21. (d)	22. (—)	23. (c)	24. (c)
25. (c)	26. (b)	27. (b)	28. (a)	29. (b)	

CHAPTER

9

JOURNAL

Q.1: Where should a withdrawal of Cash from business by the proprietor be credited to Drawings:

(*a*) Proprietor's a/c

(*b*) Capital a/c

(*c*) Cash a/c

(*d*) None of the above

Q.2: Goods worth Rs. 500 taken by the proprietor for personal use should be credited to:

(*a*) Sales a/c

(*b*) Proprietor's personal account

(*c*) Purchases a/c

(*d*) Expenses account

Q.3: The amount brought in by the proprietor in the business should be credited to:

(*a*) Proprietor's account

(*b*) Drawings account

(*c*) Capital Account

(*d*) Cash account

Q.4: The amount of Rs. 1,000 paid to Sindh Transport Co. to send Machine to us should be debited to:

(*a*) Sindh Transport Co.

(*b*) Freight A/c

(*c*) Machine A/c

(*d*) Cash A/c

Q.5: Mr. X starts business with stock. The journal entry for this transaction will be:

(*a*) Debit Cash a/c credit Stock a/c

(*b*) Debit Capital a/c credit Stock a/c

(*c*) Debit Stock a/c credit Cash a/c

(*d*) Debit Stock a/c credit Capital a/c

Q.6: Sold goods worth Rs. 50,000 to Mohan, on 45 days credit. The entry for this will be:

(*a*) Debit Mohan's a/c credit Sales a/c

(*b*) Debit 45 days credit a/c credit Sales a/c

(*c*) Debit goods a/c credit Sales a/c

(*d*) Debit Cash Receivable a/c credit Sales a/c

Q.7: Sold to Shyam goods worth Rs. 10,000 against cheque issued by him. The entry for this will be:

(*a*) Debit Bank a/c credit Shyam's a/c

(*b*) Debit Shyam's a/c credit Sales a/c

(*c*) Debit Bank a/c credit Sales a/c

(*d*) Debit Cheque received a/c credit Sales a/c

Q.8: Rs. 1,000 paid on carriage on purchases will be recorded in journal as:

(*a*) Debit Purchases Credit Carriage a/c

(*b*) Debit Carriage Credit Purchase a/c

(*c*) Debit Carriage Inward Credit Cash a/c

(*d*) Debit Purchases Credit Cash

Q.9: A Computer having a price tag of Rs. 30,000 was purchased at a discounted price of Rs. 28,000. This will be recorded as:

(*a*) Debit Office Equipment a/c Rs. 30,000, Credit Cash a/c Rs. 28,000, Credit discount Received Rs. 2,000

(*b*) Debit Office Equipment a/c Rs. 28,000, Credit Cash a/c Rs. 28,000.

(*c*) Debit Purchases a/c Rs. 30,000, Credit Cash a/c Rs. 28,000, Credit discount Received Rs. 2,000

(*d*) Debit Purchases a/c Rs. 28,000, Credit Cash a/c Rs. 28,000

Q.10: Paid on account Rs. 10,000 to Mahesh to whom we owe Rs. 12,000. The payment will be recorded as:

(*a*) Debit Mahesh a/c Rs. 10,000 Credit Cash a/c Rs. 10,000.

(*b*) Debit Mahesh a/c Rs. 12,000 Credit Cash a/c Rs. 10,000 Credit Discount a/c Rs. 2,000.

(*c*) Debit Mahesh a/c Rs. 12,000 Credit Cash a/c Rs. 10,000 Credit Commission a/c Rs. 2,000.

(*d*) Debit Mahesh a/c Rs. 10,000 Debit Discount 2,000 Credit Cash a/c Rs. 12,000.

Q.11: Of the goods purchased on Credit from Babu Lal, goods worth Rs. 5,000 were found unsuitable and returned to him. This will be accounted for as:

(*a*) Debit Babu Lal Credit Sales a/c

(*b*) Debit Sales Credit Purchases a/c

(*c*) Debit Babu Lal Credit Sales Return a/c

(*d*) Debit Babu Lal Credit Purchases Return a/c

Q.12: What is a Journal?

(*a*) Original entry

(*b*) Double entry

(*c*) Duplicate entry

(*d*) None of the above

ANSWERS					
1. (c)	2. (c)	3. (c)	4. (c)	5. (d)	6. (a)
7. (c)	8. (c)	9. (b)	10. (a)	11. (d)	12. (a)

CHAPTER

10

LEDGER POSTING & BALANCING

Ledger

Q.1: The ledger is the ________book of accounts where similar transactions relating to a particular person or property or revenue or expense are recorded.

A.: Principal

Q.2: A ledger is a bound book or register containing the various ________ connected with business.

a. Documents

b. Accounts

c. Records of meetings

d. None of the above

Q.3: The Ledger is the book of ------- entry

a. Original

b. Final

c. Every

d. Daily

Q.4: An account is a ________ record and systematic arrangement of transactions for a period affecting one person, one kind or property or one class of gains or expenses.

A.: Summarised

Q.5: The unit of classification of data within the ledger is the ____________

a. Transaction

b. Account

Ans. Account

Q.6: After posting from Journal, each account is balanced off

a. Right

b. Wrong

c. Depends on account

d. None of the above

Q.7: If the debit side of an account exceeds its credit side, the difference is called:

a. Debit balance

b. Credit balance

c. Depends on nature of account

d. None of the above

Q.8: The closing debit balance falls on the

a. Debit side

b. Credit side

c. Depends on nature of account

d. None of the above

Q.9: Salary paid in advance account has a

a. Debit balance

b. Credit balance

c. Nil balance

d. Either debit or credit balance

Q.10: Preliminary expenses account has

a. Debit balance

b. Credit balance

c. Intangible balance

d. Either debit or credit balance

Q.11: Provision for discount on debtors has

a. Debit balance

b. Credit balance

c. Either debit or credit balance

d. No balance

Q.12: Prepaid expenses are shown as

a. Debit

b. Credit

c. Either debit or credit

d. Intangibles

Q.13: The credit balance in the capital account is a

a. Liability

b. Asset

c. Revenue

d. None of these

ANSWERS					
1. (—)	2. (b)	3. (b)	4. (—)	5. (b)	6. (a)
7. (a)	8. (b)	9. (a)	10. (a)	11. (b)	12. (a)
13. (a)					

CHAPTER

11

MECHANICS OF COLUMNAR ACCOUNTING

Q.1: Cash book records

(*a.*) All cash receipts

(*b.*) All cash payments

(*c.*) All cash receipts and cash payments

(*d.*) All types of transactions

Q.2: ----- Book may be defined as the record of transactions concerning cash receipts and cash payments

a. Cash

b. Purchase

c. Sales

d. Ledger

Q.3: Cash book is a book of

a. Prime entry

b. Final Entry

c. Both of the above

d. None of the above

(It is a book of original entry because all cash transactions are first recorded in it, and thereafter, recorded from Cash Book to the various ledger accounts. For Cash account, it also works as a book of final entry, because after recording the transactions in the cash book, no separate cash account is required.)

Q.4: Cash book can also be sub-divided into many subsidiary books

a. Right

b. Wrong

Q.5: Cash book is an example of

a. General Journal

b. Special Journal

c. It is not a journal

d. Personal account

Double Column Cash Book

Q.6: Double column cash book records:

a. cash and credit transactions

b. cash and bank transactions

c. cash and discount transactions

d. cash and petty cash transactions

Q.7: Discount account should be balanced in the Cash Book

a. Right

b. Wrong

Q.8: Three Column Cash Book records

(*a*) Cash Transactions only

(*b*) Both Cash and Bank transactions excluding discounts

(*c*) Both Cash and Bank transactions including discounts

(*d*) None of the above

Q.9: Whenever a transaction relates to Cash and bank both, it is recorded on __________side(s) of the Cash Book

a. One

b. Both

c. Right

d. Left

Q.10: The three columns on each side of the three columnar Cash Book represent

(*a.*) Real and nominal accounts

(*b.*) Real and personal accounts

(*c.*) Real, Personal and Nominal accounts

(*d.*) Personal and nominal accounts

Q.11: The transactions in the bank column on the credit side of the three columnar cash book indicates:

a. Amount withdrawn from bank

b. Amount deposited into the bank

c. Both a & b above

d. None of the above

Q.12: In the multi-columnar cash book, each side is divided into as many amount columns as there are heads of regular receipts and payments

a. Right

b. Wrong

Q.13: State whether the following statements are true or false:

a. Cash account always show a debit balance

b. Cash book is a book of original entry

c. A cash book also serves the purpose of cash account.

d. Cheques received from the customers are recorded on the credit side of the columnar cash book.

e. Interest allowed by the bank will be entered on the debit side of the cash book in the cash column.

f. A bearer cheque received from a customer or paid to a supplier will always be entered in the cash column of the cash book.

g. Credit sales are recorded on the credit side of the cash book.

Ans. True: a, b, c.

False (d): Cheques received from the customer and deposited into the bank are recorded on the debit side in the Cash book in the bank deposits column.

False (e): Interest allowed by the bank is entered on the debit side in the bank deposits column.

False (f): Cheques received and issued are recorded only in the bank columns of the cash book.

False (g) Only cash transactions are recorded in Cash book. Credit sales are entered in the Sales book or in the Journal.

Petty Cash Book

Q.14: In every business, apart from big payments, a number of small payments have to be made. These payments should be recorded in:

a. the Journal

b. the cash book

c. the petty cash book

d. none of the above

Q.15: The petty cashier is handed over a small sum, called imprest, to meet the requirements of a given period

a. Right

b. Wrong

Q.16: The balance in the Petty Cash Book is

a. An expense

b. A profit

c. An Asset

d. A liability

Q.17: Amount paid to the petty cashier is called:

a. Advance amount

b. Loan amount

c. Imprest amount

d. Petty cash amount

Q.18: Petty Cash Book

a. Saves time of chief cashier

b. Saves labour for writing cash book and posting into ledger

c. Provides control over small payments

d. Convenience in preparing ledger accounts from the totals of individual heads

e. Avoids the recording of narration

f. Avoids posting of individual transactions

Q.19: Cash Discount is

a. The allowance to expedite cash receipts and payments within a specified period.

b. It is a loss for the firm receiving the payment and gain for the firm making the payment.

c. Discount allowed is entered on the debit side and discount earned on the credit side of cash book.

Q20: Fill in the blanks:

i. The debit side of cash book is called ________side and credit side is called ________side.

Ans. Receipts, Payments

ii. Cash column of cash book can never have a ________balance.

Ans. Credit

iii. The ______ balance in cash account should always be equal to the cash in cash box.

Ans. Debit or Closing

iv. Discount allowed by the creditor is recorded on the ______side of cash book.

Ans. Payment or credit

v. In case of an overdraft, the bank column of cash book will show a______balance.

Ans. Credit

ANSWERS					
1. (c)	2. (a)	3. (c)	4. (b)	5. (b)	6. (c)
7. (b)	8. (c)	9. (b)	10. (c)	11. (a)	12. (a)
13. (—)	14. (c)	15. (a)	16. (c)	17. (c)	18. (—)
19. (—)	20. (—)				

CHAPTER

12

SUBSIDIARY BOOKS

Q.1: Recording the transactions in the subsidiary books is the first step in the accounting cycle

a. Right

b. Wrong

Q.2: Subsidiary books are also called the books of original entry

a. Right

b. Wrong

Q.3: Trade Discount is:

a. allowed when the customer purchases goods above a certain quantity or above certain amount.

b. deducted from the total amount of the bill to arrive at the amount of purchase.

c. is not recorded in the ledger.

d. all the above

Q.4: The weekly or monthly total of the Purchase book is posted to the

a. Debit of the Purchases account

b. Debit of the Sales account

c. Credit of the Purchases account

d. Credit of the Creditors account

Q.5: In the purchase book the record is in respect of

a. Cash purchase of goods

b. Credit purchase of goods dealt in

c. All purchases of goods

d. Purchase of assets for the business

Q.6: The weekly or monthly total of the purchase book is

a. posted to the debit of the Purchases account

b. posted to the debit of the sales account

c. posted to the credit of the purchases account

d. none of the above

Q.7: Purchase book is an example of________journal

a. General

b. Special

c. Common

d. Cash

Q.8: Invoice Journal is used for recording_______purchases

a. Cash

b. Credit

c. Discount on

d. All

Q.9: The Sales book

a. is a part of the journal

b. is a part of the ledger

c. is a part of the Trading & Profit & Loss a/c

d. is a part of the balance sheet

Q.10: The total of the sales book is posted to the

a. credit of the sales account

b. credit of the purchases account

c. credit of the capital account

d. debit of the sales account

Q.11: The sale of business asset on credit is recorded in

a. Sales Journal

b. General Journal

c. Cash receipt in Cash Book

d. Nominal accounts

Q.12: Sales Journal is used for recording cash sales

a. Right

b. Wrong

(It is used to record only credit sales of goods dealt in by the trader.)

Q.13: Sales journal is also called ________book

a. Day

b. Invoice

c. Inventory

d. Stock

Sales Retur... or Return Inward Book

Q.14: The Sales Return Book Records

a. The return of goods to the suppliers

b. Return of anything purchased

c. Return of goods by the customers

d. Return of anything sold

Q.15: Return of goods from customer should be credited to

a. Sales return account

b. Customer account

c. Goods account

d. Purchases return account

Q.16: Sales Return journal is used to record the return of goods sold to customers on

a. Credit

b. Cash

c. Discount

d. Sample basis

Q.17: Total of sales return account is ________ to Retuns Inward account and the customers who have returned the goods are ________with the respective amounts.

Ans. Debited, Credited

Purchases Return Book or Return Outward Book

Q.18: Purchase return Journal is used for recording of goods purchased from suppliers against cash

a. Right

b. Wrong

Q.19: Total of Purchases return account is _______ to Retuns outward account and the Suppliers to whom the goods have been returned are _______with the respective amounts.

Ans. Credited, Debited

ANSWERS					
1. (a)	2. (a)	3. (d)	4. (a)	5. (b)	6. (a)
7. (b)	8. (b)	9. (a)	10. (a)	11. (b)	12. (b)
13. (b)	14. (d)	15. (b)	16. (a)	17. (—)	18. (b)
19. (—)					

MODULE

C

SPECIAL ACCOUNTS

CHAPTER 13

BANK RECONCILIATION STATEMENT

Introduction & Need

Q.1: Bank account is a :

a. Real account

b. Personal account

c. Nominal account

d. Intangible account

Q.2: When a cheque is deposited into Bank, the trader _____account and the Bank _____ account

Ans. Debits Bank, Credits the Customer

Q.3: When a cheque is issued for payment, the trader _____ account and the Bank _____ account

Ans. Credits Bank, Debits the Customer

Q.4: Entries for deposits of cheques into the Bank are made by the customer in the debit side of cash book

a. Immediately

b. On their clearing

c. At the time of reconciliation

d. After 7 days

Q.5: Entries for deposits of cheques into the Bank are made by the bank on the credit of customer account

a. Immediately

b. On their clearing/collection

c. After 7 days

d. after reconciliation

Q.6: Entries for issuance of cheques are made immediately by the customer to the credit of Cash Book, but the bank debits the customer account

a. Immediately

b. On presentation over counter

c. On presentation in clearing

d. On presentation on counter or in clearing

Q.7: ________ represents a copy of customer's account as it appears in the bank's ledger

Ans. Pass Book

Q.8: The dates of entries in the cash book and pass book will normally be

a. same

b. different

Q.9: At any point of time the balance shown by cash book and pass book are normally

a. the same

b. different

Q.10: Debit balance in the Cash Book means

a. Overdraft

b. Favourable Balance

c. None of the above

d. Balancing error

Q.11: Debit side of pass book means

a. Overdraft

b. Favourable Balance

c. None of the above

d. Balancing error

Q.12: When an entry is passed on credit side of pass book or on debit side of Cash book, the bank balance

a. Increases

b. Decreases

c. Has no effect

d. Can decrease or increase

Q.13: Undercasting of the credit side of Cash Book has the same effect as overcasting of the ___

a. Debit side of the pass book

b. Credit side of the pass book

c. There is no relevance between the two

d. Ledger account

Q.14: Cheques deposited and dishonoured is recorded on which side of the Cash Book

a. Debit

b. Credit

Q.15: Bank Reconciliation Statement is

a. Ledger account

b. Part of the Cash Book

c. A statement showing differences between Cash Book and Pass Book balances

Q.16: Bank Reconciliation Statement is prepared by

a. Businessman

b. Bank

c. Debtors

d. Creditors

Q.17: A Bank Reconciliation is prepared, so that the difference in the under noted balances is reconciled

a. the difference in the balance in the cash column and bank column of the Cash Book

b. the difference in the balance in the pass book at the beginning and at the end

c. the difference in the cash book and pass book balances as on a date

d. the difference in bank ledger and pass book

Q.18: The Pass book of an account holder is the copy of

a. the bank columns in the cash book of the account holder

b. the relevant account in the books of a bank

c. the cash column in the cash book of a customer

d. none of the above

Q.19: The pass book issued by a bank to its customer is

a. Extract from the journal of the bank

b. Copy of an account maintained in its ledger by the bank

c. Summary from the ledger of the bank

d. None of the above

Q.20: Interest on overdraft will appear in

a. Cash Book
b. Pass Book
c. Ledger
d. Journal

Q.21: A Bank Reconciliation Statement is

a. an account
b. also prepared by Bank
c. usually prepared at the end of the month
d. statement of book account

Q.22: Bank reconciliation statement is prepared to ascertain the causes of the difference between

a. The balance as per the bank column of the cash book and the balance as per pass book
b. The balance as per the cash column of the cash book and the balance as per pass book
c. Neither of the two
d. Both of the two

Q.23: Overdraft as per Cash Book means

a. Credit balance in the cash book
b. Credit balance in the bank column of the cash book
c. Neither of the two
d. Both of the two

Q.24: Debit balance as per pass book means

a. Balance
b. Overdraft
c. None of the two
d. Both of the two

Q.25: Normally, the items on the debit side of Cash Book are found on the ______ side of pass book, if both of them relate to same period

a. Debit
b. Credit

Q.26: Insurance premium paid by bank is ________by bank in pass book

a. Debited
b. Credited

Q.27: Direct deposits by customers is first recorded in

a. Cash book

b. Pass Book

c. Journal

d. Ledger

Q.28: Direct deposits by customers are recorded in cash book on

a. Debit side

b. Credit side

Q.29: Direct deposits by customers have a ________effect on the bank balance

a. Favourable

b. Unfavourable

Q.30: Normally pass book of a trader with no credit facility shows ________ balance

a. Debit

b. Credit

Q.31: Overdraft as per Cash book means

a. Debit balance

b. Credit balance

Causes of Difference

Q.32: Whenever there is a difference between the balance/overdraft shown by Pass Book and shown by Cash book, it may be due to

a. Debits in bank column of cash book but no credits in pass book *e.g.* Cheques deposited but not credited

b. Credits in the bank column of cash book but no debits in Pass book *e.g.* Cheques issued but not presented for payment

c. (Debits in pass book but no credits in the bank column cash book *e.g.* bank charges, interest on overdrafts, payments for standing instructions, dishonour of cheque deposited by the customer, errors by bank, etc.)

(Internal transfers of the bank affecting customer's A/c like credits in pass book but no debits in the bank column of the cash book *e.g.* Interest on savings balance, amount collected by bank towards interest or dividend, direct deposits into the customer's account, errors by bank, etc.)

d. All the above

Preparation of BRS

Q.33: What steps should be followed for the preparation of Bank Reconciliation Statement?

a. Entries appearing in the bank column of the cash book are compared with the entries on the opposite side of the Bank's pass book, provided both of them relate to the same period

b. The unticked entries in the Pass book/Cash book indicate the reasons for disagreement in their balances

(However, if the period for the same is different, say one is for January and other for February, then the ticked entries shall become the basis of disagreement between the closing balance of one with the opening of the other)

Where Favourable balance as per Cash book is given

Q.34: When favourable balance as per cash book is the starting point, wrong debit given by the Bank will be

a. Added

b. Deducted

Q.35: When balance as per Cash Book is the starting point, unpresented cheques are

a. Added

b. Subtracted

c. Not shown in cash book

d. Represented

When favourable balance as per pass book is given

Q.36: When balance as per pass book is given, cheques and drafts sent to bank but not collected will be

a. Added

b. Subtracted

c. Neither added nor subtracted

d. Sent for collection

When overdraft as per cash book is given

Q.37: When the overdraft as per cash book is the starting point, a cheque of Rs. 500 deposited into Bank but not recorded in Cash Book will be

a. Added by Rs. 500

b. Deducted by Rs. 500

c. Added by Rs. 1,000

d. None of the above

Q.38: Cheques issued but not presented is _______ in BRS, when started with overdraft as per cash book

a. Added

b. Subtracted

When overdraft as per pass book is given

Q.39: When overdraft as per pass book is the starting point, bank charges of Rs. 100 recorded twice in the cash book will be

a. Added Rs. 100

b. Added Rs. 200

c. Deducted Rs. 100

d. None of the above

Q.40: The credit balance of Rs. 1,000 in the bank column of the cash book was carried forward as its debit balance. When overdraft as per pass book is the starting point

a. Rs. 1,000 will be deducted

b. Rs. 1,000 will be added

c. Rs. 2,000 will be deducted

d. Rs. 2,000 will be added

Q.41: When payment side of the Cash Book is overcast by Rs. 100 and overdraft as per Pass Book is the starting point Rs. 100 will be

a. Added

b. Subtracted

Q.42: Cheques deposited but not cleared is _______ in BRS, when started with overdraft balance in pass book

a. Added

b. Deducted

Q.43: Whether the following statements are true or false

a. Bank Reconciliation Statement is an account

b. BRS is also prepared by bank

c. BRS is prepared to show causes of disagreement between two balances *d.* A credit balance in Pass Book indicates an excess of deposit over withdrawals

e. BRS is prepared by businessmen

f. Debit balance as per Cash Book means credit balance as per pass book

g. Cheque issued to party is recorded on receipt side of cash book

h. Interest and dividend collected by bank decreases bank balance

i. Direct deposits by customer increases bank balance

j. Direct payments by bank are recorded on withdrawal side of pass book

k. Bank charges and commission charged by bank are income of bank

l. Cash book and pass book balance never agree

m. Entry is recorded on deposit side of pass book for increase in bank balance

n. Overcasting the receipt side of cash book increases the bank balance in cash book

o. Usually BRS is prepared at the end of month

Ans. True: c, d, e, f, i, j, k, m, n, o.

False :

(*a*) BRS is a statement and not an account

(*b*) BRS is prepared only by the account holders to tally their cash book entries with the bank pass book. Bank is not supposed to prepare any BRS of its customers account

(*g*) Cheques issued to the party are recorded on the credit or payment side of cash book in the bank column

(*h*) Interest and dividend collected by bank increases bank balance

(*l*) Cash and bank balances should always agree, but due to certain reasons as explained they may not agree and to find out the reasons of disagreement, BRS is prepared

Adjusting the Cash Book Balance

Q.44: The trader incorporates the missing entries found in the BRS in the

a. Cash Book

b. Pass Book

c. Journal

d. Ledger

Q.45: Cash book is usually adjusted for

a. Payments made by bank as per standing instructions

b. Bank charges

c. Interest allowed by bank on deposits or charged by bank on overdraft

d. Direct receipt of interest or dividend by bank

e. Cheques dishonoured

f. Direct deposits by customers

g. Errors committed in Cash book

ANSWERS				
1. (b)	2. —	3. —	4. (a)	5. (b)
6. (d)	7. —	8. (b)	9. (b)	10. (b)
11. (a)	12. (a)	13. (a)	14. (b)	15. (c)
16. (a)	17. (c)	18. (b)	19. (b)	20. (b)
21. (c)	22. (a)	23. (a)	24. (b)	25. (b)
26. (a)	27. (b)	28. (a)	29. (a)	30. (b)
31. (b)	32. (d)	33. —	34. (b)	35. (a)
36. (a)	37. (b)	38. (b)	39. (a)	40. (c)
41. (a)	42. (b)	43. —	44. (a)	45. —

CHAPTER

14

TRIAL BALANCE

Purpose for the preparation of Trial Balance

Q.1: Trial Balance

a. is prepared every year

b. is prepared after preparing the Profit & Loss a/c

c. shows the profit earned by a firm during a period

d. checks the accuracy of posting the ledger accounts

Q.2: The arithmetic accuracy of the entries made in the books of account is verified by

a. Preparing the final accounts

b. Totalling the amount columns of the Journal

c. Balancing the ledgers

d. Preparing the Trial Balance

Q.3: The balances of the various accounts are put in a list-debit balances on the debit side and the credit balances on the credit side. The list so prepared is called a Trial Balance

a. Right

b. Wrong

Q.4: The total of debit side of the Trial Balance need not be equal to the total of its credit side

a. Right

b. Wrong

Q.5: Assets and expenses account show

a. Debit balances

b. Credit balances

Q.6: Incomes and Liabilities accounts show

a. Debit balances

b. Credit balances

Q.7: Drawings are shown in the_____ column of the Trial Balance

a. Debit

b. Credit

Q.8: Trial balance ensures ________ accuracy

(Arithmetical)

Q.9: Trial balance is prepared at the end of ________ year

(Accounting)

Q.10: Balances of liabilities are recorded on _______ side of the Trial Balance

(Credit)

Q.11: Trial balance is useful for locating ________

(Single sided errors)

Q.12: If the trial balance does not tally, difference of the trial balance is transferred to ________

(Suspense account)

Q.13: Expenses are recorded on _______ side of a trial balance

(Debit)

Q.14: Profits on sales of assets is shown on _____ of trial balance

(Credit side)

Q.15: A statement showing debit and credit balances of ledger accounts is ______

(Trial Balance)

Q.16: A trial balance is prepared as on a particular ______

(Date)

Q.17: A trial balance is a list of ________ balances

(Ledger)

Q. 18: _______ trial balance is not commonly used

(Gross)

Q. 19: Write a word, term or phrase which can substitute each of the following statements

i. The statement showing debit and credit balances of ledger accounts at the end of the year

Ans. *Trial Balance*

ii. Trial Balance in which the debit and credit total of each ledger account are shown in the two amount columns against the name of the account

Ans. *Gross Trial Balance*

iii. Trial balance in which only balance of each ledger account is shown against its name

Ans. *Net Trial Balance*

iv. Abstract or list showing the debit or credit balances of various accounts

Ans. *Trial Balance*

Q.20: State whether the following statements are true or false

i. Wrong balancing of an account will not affect the Trial Balance

Ans. False

(*If there is wrong balancing, the trial balance will not tally*)

ii. Trial balance does not ensure arithmetical accuracy

Ans. False

(*Trial balance is prepared mainly to check the arithmetical accuracy of accounts*)

iii. Trial balance is prepared at the end of the accounting year

Ans. True

iv. Preparation of a Trial Balance helps in locating accounting errors

Ans. True

v. If trial balance does not tally, there is no need to open suspense account

Ans. False

(*Whenever there is a difference in the Trial Balance, the amount is kept in a separate account called Suspense account. As and when the errors are located the suspense account is closed automatically*)

vi. *Debit balance* of ledger account is shown in debit column of the trial balance

Ans. True

vii. Closing balance appears in the Trial Balance

Ans. False

(Closing balance is included in the final accounts through an adjustment entry and its value is calculated by taking actual stock inventory multiplied by cost or market price whichever is low)

viii. Fixed deposits with bank shows debit balance

Ans. True

ix. Final accounts cannot be prepared until trial balance tallies

Ans. True

x. Net trial balance is more popular than gross trial balance

Ans. True

xi. Trial balance is prepared on a separate sheet of paper

Ans. True

xii. In preparation of gross trial balance, ledger account balances are extracted

Ans. False

(As the summations are only to be taken for the preparation of gross trial balance, there is no need to extract debit or credit balances of individual ledger accounts)

xiii. Deposits given are shown on the debit side of a trial balance

Ans. True

xiv. Trial balance is prepared after preparation of final accounts

Ans. False

(Trial balance is prepared prior to the preparation of final accounts.)

xv. Purchases are shown on the debit side of a Trial balance

Ans. True

xvi. Bank overdraft is shown on the debit side of a trial balance

Ans. False

(Bank overdraft is a liability and is shown as a credit balance in the Trial Balance)

xvii. Sales is shown on the debit side of a Trial Balance

Ans. False

(Sales represent income and therefore shown as a credit balance in the Trial Balance)

xviii. Balances of ledger accounts are posted to a trial balance

Ans. True

Q.21: Match the pairs

Sl. No.	*A*	*Sl. No.*	*B*	*Ans.*
1.	Trial balance	1.	Difference in trial balances	*1 & 5*
2.	Net Trial Balance	2.	Always shows debit balances	*2 & 6*
3.	Gross Trial Balance	3.	Always shows credit balances	*3 & 7*
4.	Suspense account	4.	Generally shows debit balances	*4 & 1*
5.	Real account	5.	Statement of balances of ledger a/cs	*5 & 2*
6.	Liabilities account	6.	Debit and credit balances	*6 & 3*
7.	Bank account	7.	Debit and credit totals	*7 & 4*

Functions of a Trial Balance

Q.22: Functions of a Trial Balance

a. To act as a device to check the arithmetical accuracy of the accounting process

b. To provide summary position of each account and accounts in general

c. To act as a starting point for preparation of Final accounts

d. All of the above

Q.23: Trial balance is

a. a list of debit and credit balances from individual ledger accounts, cash and bank balances

b. prepared to establish arithmetical accuracy of transactions recorded in the books of account

c. Prepared at the end of the year or as and when required as on a date

d. enables the trader to know his debtors (receivables) and creditors (payables)

e. facilitates preparation of final accounts

ANSWERS					
1. (d)	2. (d)	3. (a)	4. (b)	5. (a)	6. (b)
7. (a)	8. —	9. —	10. —	11. —	12. —
13. —	14. —	15. —	16. —	17. —	18. —
19. —	20. —	21. —	22. (d)	23. —	

CHAPTER

15

RECTIFICATION OF ERRORS

Q.1: Types of Errors

a. Errors can be classified into: Errors of Principle and Clerical errors

b. Clerical errors can be Errors of omission, errors of commission and compensating errors

c. Errors of omission can be of complete omission or partial omission

d. Errors can be single sided errors and double sided errors

e. Errors of Principle, Compensating errors and Errors of complete omission have no effect on Trial Balance

f. Clerical errors of partial omission and errors of commission are normally single sided errors and do affect the Trial Balance

Q.2: Errors that affect the trial balance

a. Omission of posting of an item from a subsidiary book

b. Posting a wrong amount to a ledger account

c. Posting an amount to a wrong side of the ledger account

d. Mistake in casting

e. Mistake in carry forward

f. Omission of an amount from ledger to Trial Balance

g. Balance of some account written to the wrong side in the Trial balance

h. Double posting to a ledger account

i. Wrong totalling of Trial Balance

j. Omitting to write cash and bank balances in the Trial Balance *k.* Omitting to post the totals of subsidiary books into thc lcdger

l. Omitting to write the totals of discount columns of Cash book in the Trial balance

Errors of Principle

Q.3: Errors arising from not observing the accounting principles correctly are called

a. Errors of Commission

b. Errors of Principle

c. Errors of Omission

d. Mathematical errors

Q.4: Error of principle involves an incorrect allocation of expenditure or receipt between Capital and Revenue

a. Right

b. Wrong

Q.5: On purchase of old furniture, the amount of Rs. 1,000 spent on its repairs should be debited to

a. The repairs a/c

b. Furniture a/c

c. Cash a/c

d. Charges a/c

Q.6: Rs. 2000 paid as wages for erecting a machine should be debited to

a. The wages a/c

b. Machinery a/c

c. Capital a/c

d. Charges a/c

Q.7: Wages paid for the erection of machine debited to wages a/c is

a. Error of Principle

b. Error of Commission

c. Error of Omission

d. Error of Mathematics

Q.8: Rs. 500 received from Umesh whose account was previously written off as bad debt should be credited to

a. Umesh's a/c

b. Bad Debts recovered a/c

c. Cash a/c

d. Charges a/c

Q.9: Purchase of office furniture for Rs. 2,000 has been debited to General Expenses a/c. It is

a. a clerical error

b. an error of principle

c. an error of omission

d. a mathematical error

Q.10: An asset was purchased for business. However, the amount was debited to Purchases account. This is an error of

a. Recording

b. Principle

c. Mathematics

d. Omission

Q.11: Cartage paid for the newly purchased Machinery, if debited to Cartage account will affect

a. Both the Cartage & Machinery Account

b. Only Machinery account

c. Only Cartage account

d. None of the accounts

Errors of Full Omission

Q.12: When a transaction is completely omitted to be recorded in the books, it will

a. affect the trial balance

b. will not affect the trial balance

Q.13: Omission of a transaction from a subsidiary record affects two accounts

a. Right

b. Wrong

Q.14: Sales to Mohan Rs. 123, were not recorded. This will affect

a. Only sales account

b. Only Mohan's account

c. Both the accounts

d. None of the accounts

Q.15: Purchases from Ram were not recorded. While rectifying this error, Ram's account will be ________ and Purchases account will be ________

a. Credited, Debited

b. Debited, Credited

Compensatory Errors

Q.16: Compensatory error is committed when posting is done to a wrong account, but on the correct side and with correct amount.

a. Right

b. Wrong

Q.17: Sales to Ram Rs. 500, have been debited to Shyam's account. This will be rectified by

a. Debiting Ram's account and crediting Shyam's account

b. Debiting Shyam's account and crediting Ram's account

c. Crediting both the accounts

d. Debiting both the accounts

Q.18: An amount of Rs. 5,000 paid to Mahinder against an acceptance was debited to Surinder's account. The rectification of this error will

a. Increase the net profit

b. Reduce the net profit

c. Have no effect on the net profit

d. Affect any purchase account

Clerical Errors

Q.19: The preparation of Trial balance helps in

a. Locating clerical errors

b. Locating errors of omission

c. Locating errors of principle

d. None of the above

Errors of partial omission

Q.20: Errors of part omission do not permit

a. Correct totalling of the Balance Sheet

b. Correct totalling of the Trial Balance

c. The trial balance to agree

d. Preparation of final accounts

Q.21: Sales to Mohan Rs. 123, posted to his account as Rs. 321 affect

a. Sales account

b. Mohan's account

c. Cash account

d. Profit and loss account

Q.22: Errors which affect one account can be

a. Errors of full omission

b. Errors of principle

c. Errors of posting

d. None of the above

Errors of Commission

Q.23: Errors of commission arise when any transaction is incorrectly recorded, either wholly or partially

a. Right

b. Wrong

Q.24: Errors of commission arise when

a. any transaction is incorrectly recorded, either wholly or partially

b. any transaction is left wholly or partially

c. any transaction is recorded in a fundamentally incorrect manner

d. all of the above

Q.25: Goods purchased from A for Rs. 5,000 were passed through Sales Book, the rectification of error will be

a. Purchases Debit Rs. 5,000, Sales Debit Rs. 5,000 and Credit A with Rs. 10,000.

b. Debit Purchase Rs. 5,000 and credit Sales Rs. 5,000.

c. Debit Purchase Rs. 5,000 and credit Ram Rs. 5,000.

d. None of the above

Q.26: Discount allowed Rs. 650 to Ramesh has been credited to his account as Rs. 560. The error will be rectified by

a. Crediting Ramesh by Rs. 90

b. Debiting Ramesh by Rs. 90

c. Debiting discount by Rs. 90

d. Crediting discount by Rs. 90

Q.27: Errors of carry forward affects two accounts

a. Right

b. Wrong

Q.28: The process of totalling the transactions at the end of the period is called casting

a. Right

b. Wrong

Q.29: Errors of casting affect personal accounts

a. Right

b. Wrong

Q.30: Wages paid Rs. 5,000 were posted to wages account as Rs. 500. To rectify this error, the wages account will be debited by Rs. 4,500

a. Right

b. Wrong

Q.31: Wages paid were not recorded in the Cash Book. The error affects only Cash account.

a. Right

b. Wrong

Q.32: In taking out a Trial Balance, it was found that it has an excess credit of Rs. 6,000. It means that the Suspense account had credit balance

a. Right

b. Wrong

Q.33: Sales book was undercast by Rs. 100. The rectification of this entry will decrease the gross profit by Rs. 100

a. Right

b. Wrong

Q.34: The error in the casting of Sales Book is

a. Error of Principle

b. Error of commission

c. Error of omission

d. None of the above

Q.35: Error of balancing affects

a. One

b. Two

Q.36: Error of casting in Bills Receivable book affects

a. B/R a/c

b. Debtors A/cs

c. Creditors a/c

d. Cash Book

Q.37: Error of posting affects

a. One

b. Two

Q.38: Sales of Rs. 720 to Mahesh posted to his account as Rs. 702. To rectify the error Rs. 18 will be

a. Credited to Mahesh's a/c

b. Debited to Mahesh's a/c

Q.39: An error may be located anytime

a. Immediately, after making the entry

b. After the entry is passed, but before prepairing the Trial balance

c. After the preparation of Trial balance

d. After the preparation of final accounts

Q.40: If an error is detected immediately after writing it, we may correct the error by

a. Overwriting the correct

b. Neatly crossing out the wrong entry and making the correct entry

c. None of the above

d. Both of the above

Q.41: One sided error when located before prepairing a Trial balance can be rectified by

a. Simply correcting the posting

b. Passing a rectifying Journal Entry

c. None of the above

d. Both of the above

Q.42: Double sided error when located before preparing a Trial balance can be rectified by

a. Simply correcting the posting

b. Passing a rectifying Journal Entry

c. None of the above

d. Both of the above

Q.43: What steps are required to find out the rectifying journal entry?

Ans.: *a.* first pass the correct entry

b. then write the wrong entry, which is already passed in the books

c. reverse the wrong entry

d. mix up the reversed wrong entry (step c) with the correct entry (step a) and the resultant entry will be the rectifying entry. In case of single sided errors, one account will be debited or credited and the similar amount shall be credited or debited to the suspense account, as the case may be

Effects of Errors and their rectification on Profit & Loss and Balance Sheet

Q.44: If an amount has been wrongly written on the debit side of a nominal account, it will _____ the profit, or______ the loss

Ans. Reduce, Increase

(Premium paid in advance is wrongly added in the premium paid)

Q.45: If an amount to be credited to a nominal account is omitted, the _______ will be reduced, or the _____ will be increased

Ans. Profit, Loss

(Amount spent on expansion of building, but wrongly entered in repairs account)

Q.46: An omission of an amount debitable to a nominal account will increase the _____ or reduce the _______

Ans. Profit, Loss

(Salary paid to a person is posted to his personal account)

Q.47: An amount creditable to a nominal account omitted, will _______ the profit and _____ the loss

Ans. Reduce, Increase

(Interest received on investments is omitted)

Q.48: If amount of profit increases or decreases on account of an error committed in nominal accounts, it affects ________ account in the Balance Sheet

Ans. Capital

Q.49: Errors in Nominal Accounts will also affect both Profit & Loss account and __________

Ans. Balance Sheet

Q.50: If errors are in personal accounts, it will affect ________.

Ans. Balance Sheet

(Increase in the amount of Debtors or Creditors are shown in Balance Sheet on the Assets or Liabilities sides respectively)

Q.51: *If any error is committed in real accounts, it will affect __________ only*

Ans. Balance Sheet

(Assets are shown in Balance Sheet and not in Profit & Loss account)

Q.52: An amount of Rs. 2,000, written off as bad, was received from X and was credited to X's personal account. The rectification of this error will

a. Increase the net profit by Rs. 2,000

b. Decrease the net profit by Rs. 2,000

c. Increase the net profit by Rs. 4,000

d. None of the above

Q.53: What will be the rectifying entries for the following and explain the effect of wrong entries on Trial Balance and Profit & Loss account and Balance Sheet of the business:

a. Sale of old furniture treated as sale of goods

Rectifying entry	*Effect on Trial Balance*	*Effect on profit*	*Effect on Balance Sheet*
Sale A/c.......................Dr. To Furniture A/c	No effect	Increase of profit	Increase of Capital Increase of Furniture

b. Receipt of amount from Ram credited to Shyam

Rectifying entry	*Effect on Trial Balance*	*Effect on profit*	*Effect on Balance Sheet*
Shyam......................Dr. To Ram	No effect	No effect	No effect

c. Goods bought from Mohan remained unrecorded so far

Rectifying entry	*Effect on Trial Balance*	*Effect on profit*	*Effect on Balance Sheet*
Purchases A/c............Dr. To Mohan	No effect	Increase of profit	Increase of capital Reduction of Creditors

d. Goods returned by Mahesh posted to his debit

Rectifying entry	*Effect on Trial Balance*	*Effect on profit*	*Effect on Balance Sheet*
Suspense A/c...................Dr. To Mahesh	Credit total short by double the amount	No effect	No effect

e. A return of Rs. 900 to Prashad posted as Rs. 90 in his account

Rectifying entry	*Effect on Trial Balance*	*Effect on profit*	*Effect on Balance Sheet*
Prashad A/c ....Dr. To Suspense A/c	Rs. 890 Rs. 890	Debit totals short by Rs. 890	No effect No effect

f. Rent of proprietors residence, debited to Rent account

Rectifying entry	*Effect on Trial Balance*	*Effect on profit*	*Effect on Balance Sheet*
Drawings A/c...............Dr. To Rent a/c	No effect	Profit is Reduced	Decrease in Capital Increase in Drawings

ANSWERS					
1. —	2. —	3. (b)	4. (a)	5. (b)	6. (b)
7. (a)	8. (b)	9. (b)	10. (b)	11. (a)	12. (b)
13. (a)	14. (c)	15. (a)	16. (a)	17. (a)	18. (c)
19. (a)	20. (c)	21. (b)	22. (c)	23. (a)	24. (c)
25. (a)	26. (a)	27. (b)	28. (a)	29. (b)	30. (a)
31. (b)	32. (b)	33. (b)	34. (b)	35. (a)	36. (a)
37. (a)	38. (b)	39. —	40. (b)	41. (a)	42. (b)
43. —	44. —	45. —	46. —	47. —	48. —
49. —	50. —	51. —	52. (a)	53. —	

CHAPTER 16

CAPITAL & REVENUE EXPENDITURE

Classification of expenses

Q.1: All expenses and receipts of revenue nature are shown in __________ and all expenses and receipts of Capital nature are taken to ____________

Ans.: Trading and Profit & Loss account, Balance Sheet.

Q.2: Whether an expenditure is of capital or revenue nature depend upon:

a. Nature of an expense

b. Effects on revenue earning capacity

c. Benefits of an expenditure

d. All of the above

Q.3: The nature of an expense may be

a. Recurring

b. Non-recurring

c. (a) or (b)

d. None of the above

Q.4: An expenditure which occurs very frequently is called:

a. Recurring expenditure

b. Non-recurring expenditure

c. Capital expenditure

d. Deferred revenue expenditure

Revenue Expenditure

Q.5: All recurring expenses are

a. Revenue expenses

b. Capital expenses

c. Deferred revenue expenses

d. Deferred capital expenses

Q.6: Payment for purchase of goods of Rs. 2000 is a revenue expenditure as

a. It is recurring

b. Amount involved is small

c. Both (*a*) and (*b*)

d. It is cash expenditure

Q.7: The expenses which help to generate income/revenue in the current year are

a. Revenue expenses

b. Capital expenses

c. Deferred revenue expenses

d. Current expenses

Q.8: If the benefit of an expenditure incurred is of short duration and its purpose is to earn income, it is

a. Revenue expenditure

b. Capital expenditure

c. Deferred revenue expenditure

d. Current expenditure

Q.9: Which of the following is a capital expenditure:

a. Expenses incurred to move the stock from one place to another

b. Renovation of the Cinema hall to convert it into PVR

c. Providing a new Tube fitting in the office

d. Repair of machinery

Q.10: An expenditure is revenue in nature when

a. It benefits the current period

b. It benefits the future period

c. It belongs to the previous period

d. It is of high value

Q.11: Cost of goods purchased for resale is an example of

a. Capital expenditure

b. Revenue expenditure

c. Deferred revenue expenditure

d. Deferred capital expenditure

Q.12: Rs. 5,000 spent on the replacement of worn out parts of the Machinery in use is charged to

a. Capital expenditure

b. Deferred revenue expenditure

c. Revenue expenditure

d. Deferred capital expenditure

Q.13: Expenses incurred in manufacturing products is:

a. Capital expenditure

b. Deferred revenue expenditure

c. Revenue expenditure

d. Deferred capital expenditure

Q.14: Cost of replacement of defective part of Machinery

a. Capital expenditure

b. Deferred revenue expenditure

c. Revenue expenditure

d. Deferred capital expenditure

Q.15: Expenditure for training employees for better running of the machinery

a. Revenue charge

b. Deferred revenue charge

c. Capital charge

d. Deferred capital charge

Q.16: Purchase of Machinery for sale

a. Capital expenditure

b. Deferred revenue expenditure

c. Revenue expenditure

d. Deferred capital expenditure

Q.17: Daily wages paid to an office peon

a. Revenue expense

b. Capital expense

c. Deferred revenue expenditure

d. Current expenditure

Q.18: Expenses incurred for the removal of stock from old godowns to new site

a. Revenue expense

b. Capital expense

c. Deferred revenue expense

d. Current expense

Q.19: The overhauling expenses of machines

a. Revenue expense

b. Capital expense

c. Deferred revenue expense

d. None of the above

Q.20: Labour welfare expenses

a. Revenue expense

b. Capital expense

c. Deferred revenue expense

d. Current expense

Q.21: Loss of goods due to fire Rs. 5,000 is a revenue expenditure as

a. It is recurring

b. Amount involved is small

c. Loss is arising out of business operations

d. None of the above

Capital Expenditure

Q.22: All non-recurring expenses are

a. Revenue expenses

b. Capital expenses

c. Deferred revenue expense

d. Deferred capital expense

Q.23: The expenditure which helps to generate revenue over more than one accounting period is:

a. Revenue expenditure

b. Capital expenditure

c. Deferred capital expenditure

d. None of the above

Q.24: The benefit of an expenditure incurred is of long duration and its purpose is to increase the earning capacity of the business, it is

a. Revenue expenditure

b. Capital expenditure

c. Deferred capital expenditure

d. None of the above

Q.25: Payment for purchase of car is a capital expenditure as

a. It is non-recurring

b. Benefit is of long duration

c. Increases earning capacity

d. All of the above

Q.26: Capital expenditure is that expenditure

a. The benefit of which is enjoyed over a long period

b. Which results in acquisition of assets or properties

c. Whose purpose is to increase the earning capacity of the business

d. Whose amount is usually large

e. Which is of non-recurring nature

f. Which is shown in the Balance Sheet

Q.27: Payment for purchase of AC is a Capital Expenditure as

a. It is non-recurring

b. Benefit is of long duration

c. Increases earning capacity

Q.28: Fixed assets are:

a. Kept in the business for use over a long period of time for earning income

b. Meant for resale

c. Meant for conversion into cash as quickly as possible

d. Always sold before their useful life end

Q.29: Which of the following is a Capital Expenditure

a. Rs. 12000 spent on repairs of Machine

b. Rs. 12000 spent on overhaul of machine purchased second hand

c. Rs. 12,000 spent on overhaul of machine already installed

d. Rs. 12,000 spent on purchase of goods

Q.30: Wages paid for installation of machinery is a capital expenditure as

a. It is non-recurring

b. It is necessary to put the asset in working condition

c. It is incidental to acquiring of new asset.

d. It is small

Q.31: An expenditure is capital in nature when

a. The receiver of the amount is going to treat it for the sale of fixed assets

b. It increases the quantity of fixed assets

c. It is paid as interest on capital

d. It affect capital

Q.32: Expenditure incurred in acquiring the Patents rights for the business is an example of

a. Capital expenditure

b. Deferred revenue expenditure

c. Revenue expenditure

d. None of the above

Q.33: Freight paid on the new Machine will be debited to

a. Machinery account

b. Freight account

c. Neither of the two

d. Either of the two

Q.34: Rs. 2,000 spent on the repairs before using the second hand machinery purchased recently is a

a. Revenue charge

b. Deferred revenue charge

c. Capital charge

d. Current charge

Q.35: Professional fees paid in connection with acquisition of leasehold premises

a. Capital expenditure

b. Deferred revenue expenditure

c. Revenue expenditure

d. Current expenditure

Q.36: Travelling expenses of directors for a trip abroad for purchasing a new Machinery.

a. Capital expenditure

b. Deferred revenue expenditure

c. Revenue expenditure

d. Current expenditure

Q.37: A petrol driven engine of a passenger bus is replaced by a diesel engine. It is

a. Capital expenditure

b. Deferred revenue expenditure

c. Revenue expenditure

d. Deferred capital expenditure

Deferred Revenue Expenditure

Q.38: If heavy revenue expenditure is incurred in one year, but the benefit of it may arise or accrue not in one year, but in the following two or more years, it is called

a. Capital expenditure

b. Deferred revenue expenditure

c. Revenue expenditure

d. Deferred capital expenditure

Q.39: Deferred expenditure is one which is basically a ________ expenditure, but charging of the expenditure to Profit & Loss account is deferred as the benefit of such expenditure is to remain with the organization for more than one year:

a. Revenue

b. Capital

c. Small

d. Big

Q.40: Which of the following is a deferred revenue expenditure:

a. Brokerage paid in connection of purchase of land

b. Expenses incurred to get the office Air-conditioned

c. Advertisement compaign to launch a new product

d. None of the above

Q.41: Discount allowed on issue of shares is an example of

a. Capital expenditure

b. Deferred revenue expenditure

c. Revenue expenditure

d. Deferred capital expenditure

Q.42: Preliminary expenses are an example of

a. Capital expenditure

b. Deferred revenue expenditure

c. Revenue expenditure

d. Deferred capital expenditure

Q.43: Legal expenses incurred in connection with issue of equity shares of the company

a. Capital expenditure

b. Deferred revenue expenditure

c. Revenue expenditure

d. Deferred capital expenditure

Q.44: Expenditure incurred in preparing a Project report

a. Capital expenditure

b. Deferred revenue expenditure

c. Revenue expenditure

d. Deferred capital expenditure

Q.45: Cost of Rs. 30,000 for dismantling, removing and reinstalling plant by a sugar mill incurred in connection with the removal of works to a more suitable locality

a. Capital expenditure

b. Deferred revenue expenditure

c. Revenue expenditure

d. Deferred capital expenditure

(*This expenditure has not resulted into acquiring of an asset, nor improved the earning capacity and the benefits for change of premises will be enjoyed over a long period.*)

Q.46: Cost of registration and documentation of a new formed company is a deferred revenue expenditure as

a. It is non-recurring

b. Benefit is not exhausted in one year

c. Increases earning capacity of the business.

d. None of the above

Revenue Receipts

Q.47: Those items of income which are received or accrued in the ordinary course of business and are recurring in nature are called

a. Revenue receipts
b. Capital receipts
c. Receipts
d. None of the above

Capital Receipts

Q.48: Capital receipts are those receipts, which

a. Do not recur
b. Are not arising through normal business activities
c. Are both (a) and (b)
d. None of them

Revenue & Capital Receipts

Q.49: Whether the following are capital receipts or revenue receipts

Sale of goods, Issue of fresh capital, Issue of debentures, Discount received, Commission received, Amount of Loan raised, Interest on deposits, Premium on shares.

Ans.

	Capital receipts		*Revenue receipts*
1.	Issue of fresh capital	1.	Sale of goods
2.	Issue of debenture	2.	Discount received
3.	Amount of loan raised	3.	Commission received
4.	Premium on shares	4.	Interest on deposits

Q.50: Furniture of the cost of Rs. 10,000, whose book value on date is 7,000 is sold for 11,000, what is the amount of capital and revenue receipt?

Ans.: Capital receipt: Rs. 7,000, book value to be reduced from asset.

Capital receipt: Rs. 1,000, excess of receipt over cost

Total capital receipt is Rs. 8,000

Revenue receipt: Rs. 3,000, difference between book value Rs. 7000 and cost Rs. 10,000.

Q.51: State, with reasons, whether following statements are true or false;

i. A revenue expenditure of one party may be capital receipt of the other party.

Ans. True. *e.g.* if a dealer in old cars purchases an old car, it is a revenue expenditure for the dealer, but capital receipt for the seller of the car.

ii. Receipts from sale of machinery is revenue receipt.

Ans. It is False in normal circumstances. It is a capital receipt because of sale of asset. However, if the machine is sold by a dealer of machines, it is a revenue receipt for him.

iii. The distinction between capital and revenue cannot be defined-it depends upon the facts and circumstances of each case.

Ans. It is true as is evidenced by the case given in point (ii) above.

iv. Legal expenses paid for purchase of land is a capital expenditure but legal charges paid in the ordinary course of business is a revenue expenditure.

Ans. It is true.

v. Wages paid in the ordinary course of business is a revenue expenditure but wages paid for erection of machinery is a capital expenditure.

Ans. It is true.

vi. Debentures receipts are revenue receipts.

Ans. It is false. Sale of Debentures is a capital receipt-these are non-recurring and do not arise in normal activities of the business. However for a stock broker, it will be a revenue receipt.

Alterations & Improvements

Q. 52: When an alteration is made to an existing asset like pulling down walls to make a room big or to put up partition walls, the expenditure is treated as:

a. Capital Expenditure

b. Revenue Expenditure

c. Deferred Revenue Expenditure

d. None of the above

Ans. (b), because there will be some benefit for some time.

Q.53: When there is a very big alteration in the building, *e.g.* an existing cinema hall is converted into a PVR, the expenditure is treated as

a. Capital Expenditure

b. Revenue Expenditure

c. Deferred Revenue Expenditure

d. Deferred Capital Expenditure

Q.54: Expenditure for making a few more exits in a Cinema Hall to comply with Government orders:

a. Capital Expenditure

b. Revenue Expenditure

c. Deferred Revenue Expenditure

d. None of the above

Ans. (c). This expenditure do not add to profit earning capacity.

Q.55: Developmental expenditure for developing a housing colony, or a tea garden, or for mines in the initial years is a

a. Capital Expenditure

b. Revenue Expenditure

c. Deferred Revenue Expenditure

d. None of the above

ANSWERS

1. —	2. (d)	3. (c)	4. (a)	5. (a)	6. (a)
7. (a)	8. (a)	9. (b)	10. (a)	11. (a)	12. (c)
13. (c)	14. (c)	15. (a)	16. (c)	17. (a)	18. (a)
19. (a)	20. (a)	21. (c)	22. (b)	23. (b)	24. (b)
25. (b)	26. —	27. (b)	28. (a)	29. (c)	30. (b)
31. (b)	32. (a)	33. (a)	34. (c)	35. (a)	36. (a)
37. (a)	38. (b)	39. (a)	40. (c)	41. (b)	42. (b)
43. (b)	44. (b)	45. (b)	46. (b)	47. (a)	48. (c)
49. —	50. —	51. —	52. —	53. (a)	54. —
55. (a)					

CHAPTER 17

FINAL ACCOUNTS

Q.1: The most important objective of accounting is to ascertain

a. The profit or loss made by the concern

b. Financial position of the concern

c. Both (a) and (b)

d. None of the above

Q.2: The final product of accounting process is

a. the trial balance

b. final accounts

c. management reports

d. auditors reports

Q.3: The objectives of accounting can be achieved by preparing the final accounts, which comprise of:

a. Profit & Loss Account & Balance Sheet

b. Cash book and ledger accounts

c. Bank reconciliation statement

d. None of the above.

Q.4: Summary of those accounts which affect the profit and loss of a business concern is called

a. Trial Balance

b. Final accounts

c. Income Statement

d. Balance Sheet

Income Statement

Q.5: The income statement shows either net profit or net loss for a particular accounting period

a. Right

b. Wrong

Q.6: A loss is an expense which does not bring any benefit to the concern.

a. Right

b. Wrong

Q.7: If the balance of an account on the debit side of the Trial Balance is such that the benefit out of it has already expired, it is treated as an expense

a. Right

b. Wrong

Q.8: The income statement has normally :

a. One part

b. Two parts.

Ans.: (b) *Income statement comprises of Trading and Profit & Loss Account. They have two parts-the first part is called Trading account which reveals gross profit or gross loss, and the second part is called Profit & Loss account to show net profit or net loss.*

Trading Account

Q.9: The Trading & Profit and Loss account are prepared

a. as on a particular date

b. as at the end of a particular period

c. every month

d. none of the above

Q.10: Trading account is prepared to know:

a. Total profit or loss

b. Gross profit or loss

c. Net profit or loss

d. None of the above

Q.11: Cost of goods sold = Purchases + Stock ______+ Direct Expenses - Stock at the end

a. In the beginning

b. At the end

c. Used

d. Issued

Q.12: Gross Profit + Purchases + Stock in the beginning + Direct Expenses - Stock at the end = ____

a. Sale

b. Cost of goods sold

c. Net profit

d. None of the above

Q.13: In a trading concern direct expenses include:

a. All expenses in bringing the goods to the godown of the firm and in making them ready for sale, like freight paid on purchases, cartage, octroi, custom duty, carriage inward, etc.

b. All expenses for sale and distribution of goods.

c. All operational and non-operational expenses on the business.

d. None of the above.

Q.14: In a manufacturing concern direct expenses include:

a. All expenses incurred for production of goods (like wages, power and fuel, Factory lighting, factory rent and rates) and all expenses incurred in bringing the goods to the godown of the firm and in making them ready for sale, like freight paid on purchases, cartage, octroi, custom duty, carriage inward, etc.

b. All expenses for sale and distribution of goods.

c. All operational and non-operational expenses on the business.

d. None of the above.

Q.15: The items of expenditure that will not appear in the trading account is

a. Wages account

b. Rent and rates

c. Carriage inward

d. Fuel & Power

Q.16: The balance in the trading account reveals

a. the gross profit

b. the net profit

c. the trading profit

d. the gross profit or gross loss

Q.17: The value of closing stock will appear in

a. Debit side of Trading account and Asset side in Balance Sheet

b. Credit side of Trading account and Asset side in Balance Sheet

c. Credit side of Trading account and debit side of Profit & Loss account

d. Credit side of Trading account and Liabilities side of Balance Sheet

Q.18: Trade discount allowed on the sales is shown

a. as an expense and debited to P & L account

b. is deducted from the sales and the net figure of sales is shown in the credit side of Trading account

c. is not deducted from the sales and the gross figure of sales is shown in the credit side of Trading account

d. in the balance sheet

Q.19: Sales - Cost of goods sold = Gross Profit

a. Right

b. Wrong

Q.20: The value of stock destroyed by fire will be credited to:

a. Trading A/c

b. P & L a/c

c. Insurance a/c

d. Balance sheet

Q.21: A claim of Rs. 4000 was accepted by the Insurance Co. in respect of stock worth Rs. 10,000 destroyed by fire. The amount of abnormal loss of Rs. 6000 will be debited to Abnormal Loss A/c and credited to:

a. Trading a/c

b. P & L A/c

c. Stocks a/c

b. Insurance a/c

Q.22: As on the date of preparation of the final accounts, the balances in Nominal accounts will be transferred to

a. Trading account

b. Profit & Loss account

c. Balance Sheet

d. Trading account and/or Profit & Loss account

Profit & Loss Account

Q.23: Profit & Loss account is prepared to know:

b. Total profit or loss

b. Gross profit or loss

c. Net profit or loss

d. None of the above

Q.24: Profit & Loss account shows:

a. financial position of the concern

b. the net profit earned

c. the gross profit earned

d. leverage of the concern

Q.25: Profit & Loss account starts with the gross profit or loss from trading account and then all the indirect expenses are debited in this account which are:

a. Administrative expenses

b. Selling & distribution expenses

c. Factory and manufacturing expenses

d. (a) and (b) above

Q.26: Administrative and office expenses include:

a. Office salaries

b. Establishment expenses

c. Office rent & taxes

d. Printing & Stationery

e. Postage & Telephone expenses

f. Electricity charges

g. Entertainment expenses

h. Conveyance expenses

i. Legal expenses & Audit fee

Q.27: Selling & Distribution expenses include:

a. Advertising

b. Commission

c. Discount

d. Packing expenses

e. Carriage outward

f. Freight on sales

g. Export duties

h. Insurance

i. Bad debts

Q.28: If profit is 25% of the sales, then it is

a. 25% of the cost price

b. 33.3% of the cost price

c. 20% of the cost price

d. None of the above

Q.29: If profit is 25% of the cost price, then it is

a. 25% of the sales price

b. 33.3% of the sales price

c. 20% of the sales price

d. None of the above

Q.30: The provision for bad debts is made by crediting

a. Profit & Loss account

b. Debtors account

c. Provision for bad debts account

d. Cash account

Q.31: Interest on capital is

a. Expenditure for the business

b. Expense for the business

c. Gain for the business

d. None of the above

Q.32: Interest on Drawings is

a. Expenditure for the business

b. Expense for the business

c. Gain for the business

d. None of the above

Q.33: The debts written off as bad, if recovered subsequently, are credited to debtors' account

a. Right

b. Wrong

Ans.: (b) *Bad debts already written off, but recovered afterwards are credited as income in the 'Bad Debts Recovered account'.*

Q.34: Depreciation account appearing in the Trial Balance is shown in the Profit & Loss account

a. Right

b. Wrong

Ans.: (a) *It means that the amount of depreciation has been adjusted from their respective assets. Therefore, the amount will be shown in the P & L account only to arrive at the correct profit.*

Q.35: Interest on advance payment of Income Tax is treated as __________ income and is added to the capital

a. Business

b. Private

c. Capital

d. All of the above

Q.36: The rental value of the building in which the factory workers have been housed owing to the nature of the employment will be debited to ________a/c

a. Trading A/c

b. P & L A/c

c. Building A/c

d. Rent A/c

Note: The gross profit shown by the Trading A/c is debited to trading account and credited to Profit & Loss account. After that all expenses and incomes, adjusted for outstanding and prepaid items (Discussed in the chapter on adjusting entries) are entered in Profit & Loss account. If the credit side of this account is bigger than the debit side, the difference is called net profit. It is debited to P & L A/c and credited to the Capital A/c. If the debit is bigger than credit, then it is a case of net loss, which is debited to Capital a/c and credited to P & L A/c. The P & L account is thus closed.

Balance Sheet

Q.37: A Balance Sheet is

a. An account

b. A statement

c. The final accounts

d. A statement of financial position

Q.38: How do profits made from normal operations retained in business appear in the Balance Sheet?

a. Under capital

b. Under capital, reserves & Surplus

c. Under Cash in hand, at Bank

d. Under current liabilities

Q.39: Goodwill is:

a. Current Asset

b. Fixed Asset

c. Intangible Asset

d. Tangible Asset

Q.40: Current liabilities are such obligations which are to be satisfied

a. Within one year

b. Within two years

c. Within three years

d. On demand

Q.41: Out of the following, the example of a current asset is

a. Surrender value of a life insurance policy

b. Discount on Debentures

c. Bills Receivable

d. Fixed deposits

Q.42: Purchase of an asset is called

a. an expense

b. an expenditure

c. a loss

Q.43: Stock is

a. included in the category of fixed assets

b. part of current assets

c. intangible asset

d. not an asset

Q.44: The balance appearing on the debit side of the Trial Balance as an expenditure is shown in the

a. Balance Sheet

b. Trading Account

c. Profit & Loss account
d. Suspense account

Q.45: Select the correct statement

a. The balance sheet represents an expansion of the equation as:
Assets= Liabilities + Capital
b. A has assets of Rs. 1,00,000 and Liabilities of Rs. 20,000. His capital would be Rs. 1,20,000.
c. If a firm borrows a sum of money, its capital is reduced
d. Assets - Original Capital introduced = Liabilities

Q.46: Income tax paid by the firm on the income of the proprietor is shown

a. shown on the debit side of Profit & Loss Account
b. added in the drawings of the proprietor
c. added in the capital of the proprietor
d. treated as revenue expense

Q.47: Wages paid on the erection of a new machinery should be debited to

a. Wages account
b. Cash account
c. Machinery account
d. Deferred revenue account

Q.48: Profit is shown as a Liability in the Balance Sheet because

a. It is the amount due to customers
b. It is amount received by exploiting the customers and is payable back to the society
c. It is the amount due to the owners
d. Income tax is to be paid out of it

Q.49: The Balance Sheet comprises of the items in the nature of

a. Real accounts only
b. Real and Personal accounts
c. Real, nominal and personal accounts
d. Nominal and personal accounts

Q.50: Rent of Rs. 5,000 received in advance will appear in final accounts as

a. Expenditure in P & L a/c and Asset in the Balance Sheet
b. Deduction from rent received in the credit side of P & L a/c and as Liability in the Balance Sheet

c. Deduction from rent received in the credit side of P & L a/c and as Asset in the Balance Sheet

d. Income in P & L a/c

Q.51: Gains from the sale or exchange of assets are not considered as revenue of the business.

a. Right

b. Wrong

(These are non-operational incomes, but will be considered as income of the business)

Q.52: Salary paid in advance is not an expense because it neither reduces assets nor increases liabilities

a. Right

b. Wrong

Ans.: (a) *Salary prepaid is deducted from the total amount paid for Salary during the year, and increases assets of the concern to that extent.*

Q.53: All liabilities which become due for payment in one year are classified as long term liabilities

a. Right

b. Wrong

Ans.: (b). *Liabilities payable in one year are classified as current liabilities.*

Q.54: The term current assets is used to designate Cash and other assets or resources which are reasonably expected to be realized or sold or consumed within one year

a. Right

b. Wrong

Q.55: The provision for bad debts is debited to Sundry Debtors account

a. Right

b. Wrong

Ans.: (b) *This provision is credited to Sundry debtors account*

Q.56: The provision for discount on creditors is often not provided in keeping with the principle of conservatism

a. Right

b. Wrong

Q.57: Stock at the end does not appear in the Trial Balance. In case it appears in the Trial Balance, the amount of purchases in the trial balance is reduced to that extent and closing stock is shown only in the balance sheet as asset

a. Right

b. Wrong

Q.58: If the Closing Stock appears in the Trial Balance, it is taken only to the ________

a. Trading a/c

b. Balance Sheet

c. Both *a* and *b*

d. None of the above

Q.59: Payment for the purchase of machinery is termed as:

a. Capital expenditure

b. Revenue expense

c. Deferred capital expenditure

d. None of the above

Q.60: Fixed assets are those which are acquired for

a. continuous use

b. not for sale

c. may be tangible

d. all the above

Q.61: Current assets are those which are:

a. kept temporarily for resale

b. for converting into cash

c. are cash or cash equivalent

d. all of the above

Q.62: Owners fund includes:

a. Capital less drawings of the owner

b. Undistributed profits

c. Reserves

d. Assets minus liabilities

Q.63: Mines, oil wells, and quarries which have a definite usefulness are called

a. Intangible assets

b. Wasting assets

c. Fictitious assets

d. None of the above

Q.64: Deferred expenditure is shown as an asset, which is in the shape of

a. Intangible assets

b. Wasting assets

c. Fictitious assets

d. None of the above

Q.65: The liabilities which are not shown in the balance sheet but are shown as a footnote are called:

a. Intangible liabilities

b. Fictitious liabilities

c. Contingent liabilities

d. All the above

Q.66: Liabilities in respect of bills discounted, Guarantee for a loan, disputed claims are all the examples of :

a. Intangible liabilities

b. Fictitious liabilities

c. Contingent liabilities

d. All the above

Q.67: The balance of the petty cash is :

a. an expense

b. an asset

c. an income

d. none of the above

Q.68: Fixed assets are

a. kept in the business for use over a long period for earning income

b. meant for resale

c. meant for conversion into cash as quickly as possible

d. purchased for capital gains

ANSWERS

1. (c)	2. (b)	3. (a)	4. (c)	5. (a)	6. (a)
7. (a)	8. —	9. (b)	10. (b)	11. (a)	12. (a)
13. (a)	14. (a)	15. (b)	16. (d)	17. (b)	18. (b)
19. (a)	20. (a)	21. (a)	22. (d)	23. (c)	24. (b)
25. (d)	26. —	27. —	28. (b)	29. (c)	30. (b)
31. (b)	32. (c)	33. —	34. —	35. (a)	36. (a)
37. (d)	38. (b)	39. (c)	40. (a)	41. (c)	42. (b)
43. (b)	44. (a)	45. (a)	46. (b)	47. (c)	48. (c)
49. (b)	50. (b)	51. (b)	52. —	53. —	54. (a)
55. —	56. (a)	57. (a)	58. (b)	59. (a)	60. (d)
61. (d)	62. (d)	63. (b)	64. (c)	65. (c)	66. (c)
67. (b)	68. (a)				

CHAPTER

18

CLOSING ENTRIES

Q.1: The purpose of maintaining the individual ledger accounts of expenses and income is to ascertain

a. Financial position of the business

b. Gross and net profit of the business

c. Amount of Debtors and Creditors

d. Amount of Capital

Q.2: To ascertain the profit or loss of the concern at the end of the year, business concerns prepare

a. Balance Sheet

b. Trial Balance

c. Trading and Profit & Loss account

d. Bank Reconciliation Statement

Q.3: Once the trading and Profit & Loss account is prepared, there is no need for the following balances to remain in the ledger

a. Assets & Liabilities account

b. Debtors & creditors account

c. Expenses and incomes

d. All of the above

Q.4: The journal entries passed for transferring the balances of Income & expenditure accounts are called:

a. Transfer entries

b. Adjustment entries

c. Rectifying entries

d. Closing entries

Q.5: Closing cntries are passed

a. for valuation of closing stock

b. for closing all ledger accounts

c. for closing all income & expenditure accounts

d. for balancing the accounts

Q.6: The items of expenses which show debit balance, appear as ______ item in the Trading or Profit & Loss account

a. Debit

b. Credit

Ans. (a)(*effect is the closure of the expenditure accounts*)

Q.7: The items of income which show credit balance, appear as ______ item in the Trading or Profit & Loss account

a. Debit

b. Credit

Ans. (b)(*effect is the closure of the income accounts*)

Q.8: For each item of transfer:

a. Separate journal entries are passed

b. Consolidated entries are passed

c. No journal entry is passed

d. None of the above

Q.9: The closing entry passed for transferring gross profit from Trading account to Profit & Loss account is:

a. Debit Trading a/c credit Profit & Loss A/c

b. Debit Trading a/c credit Gross Profit A/c

c. Debit Gross Profit a/c credit Profit & Loss A/c

d. Debit Profit & Loss A/c credit Trading a/c

Q.10: Closing entries refer to

a. Entries passed for valuation of closing stock

b. Entries passed at the end of a specified period to close all ledger accounts

c. Entries passed every day at the close of business for the day

d. Entries passed to close all income and expenditure accounts at the end of the period.

Q.11: The Principle of framing a Closing Entry in respect of Net Profit is to

a. Debit Trading a/c and credit Profit & Loss A/c

b. Debit Profit & Loss account and credit Capital account

c. Credit P & L a/c and debit Capital a/c

d. Debit Trading a/c and Credit Capital a/c

Q.12: Closing consolidated journal entries are normally passed for

a. Transfer of all manufacturing and purchase expense to the debit side of trading a/c

b. Transfer of Purchases and Sales return to the debit side of Trading a/c

c. Transfer of Sales and Purchases return to the credit side of Trading a/c

d. Transfer of closing stock to the credit of trading account by an adjustment entry

e. Transfer of Gross profit to the credit side of Profit & Loss a/c

f. Transfer of Gross loss to the debit side of Profit & Loss a/c

g. Transfer of all administrative, selling and financial expenses to the debit of P & L A/c

h. Transfer of all operational and non-operational incomes to the credit of P & L A/c

i. Transfer of Net profit to the credit of Capital a/c

j. Transfer of net loss to the debit of Capital a/c

ANSWERS					
1. (b)	2. (c)	3. (c)	4. (d)	5. (c)	6. —
7. —	8. (b)	9. (a)	10. (d)	11. (b)	12. —

CHAPTER 19

INVENTORY VALUATION

Need for Inventory valuation

Q.1: *The main objective of accounting is to determine profit.*

Profit = Sales - Cost of goods sold

Cost of goods sold = Opening Stock + Purchases - ***Closing Stock***

Therefore, valuation of closing stock is a must

a. True

b. False

Q.2: Closing Stock is brought into account by:

a. Debiting Trading a/c and Crediting Stock-in hand A/c

b. Crediting Trading a/c and Debiting Stock-in-hand A/c

c. Debiting P & L a/c and Crediting Stock-in hand A/c

d. Crediting P & L a/c and Debiting Stock-in-hand A/c

Q.3: The closing stock becomes opening stock for next period and the entry passed is:

a. Debiting Trading a/c and Crediting Opening Stock A/c

b. Crediting Trading a/c and Debiting Opening Stock A/c

c. Debiting P & L a/c and Crediting Opening Stock A/c

d. Crediting P & L a/c and Debiting Opening Stock

Q.4: Overvaluation of closing stock leads to

a. Inflation of current profits and deflation of profit of the succeeding period

b. Inflation of succeeding period profits and deflation of current profits

c. None of the above

d. Both (a) and (b)

Q.5: Undcrvaluation of closing stock leads to

a. Inflation of current profits and deflation of profit of the succeeding period

b. Inflation of succeeding period profits and deflation of current profits

c. None of the above

d. Both (a) and (b)

Meaning

Q.6: According to Accounting Standard 2 inventory means tangible property held

a. for sale in the ordinary course of business (finished goods)

b. in the process of production for such sale (work-in-process)

c. for production in the production of goods or services for sale (Raw materials)

d. all of above

Q.7: The inventory valuation is subjective because it depends on the Accounting policies followed by the accountant

a. True

b. False

Q.8: According to Accounting Standard 2 inventories are to be valued at lower of cost or net realisable value

a. True

b. False

Historical Cost

Q.9: Historical cost means:

a. Cost of purchase

b. Cost of conversion

c. Other costs incurred in normal course of business in bringing the inventories upto their present location and condition.

d. (a), (b) and (c) above

Q.10: Net realizable value is the estimated selling price - cost of completion - costs necessary to incur in order to make the sale.

a. True

b. False

Q.11: The test of objectivity and verifiability is satisfied by valuing stock at

a. historical price

b. current replacement price

c. net realizable value

d. average market price

Q.12: Historical cost concepts are reduced to net realizable value because of the accounting principle of

a. Consistency

b. Conservatism

c. Realisation

d. Materialism

Q.13: Historical cost is reduced to net realizable value due to the accounting convention of __________.

Ans. Conservatism

Q.14: The basis of inventory valuation adopted should not be changed frequently because it violates the accounting principle of

a. Consistency

b. Conservatism

c. Realisation

d. Materialism

Methods of Valuation

Q.15: Valuation of stock can be done by:

a. FIFO (First in First out) method

b. LIFO (Last in First out) method

c. Average cost method

d. Base Stock method

e. Adjusting selling price method

Q.16: In the FIFO method supplies are made from the godown for production at the price of the earliest stock on hand. The closing stock is valued at the

a. price paid for the latest lot

b. price paid for the earliest lot

c. current market price

d. average purchase price

Q.17: In the LIFO method supplies are made from the godown for production at the price of the latest on hand. The closing stock is valued at the

a. price paid for the latest lot

b. price paid for the earliest lot

c. current market price

d. average purchase price

Q.18: During inflation (period of rising prices), issue of material from the stores is charged to the products at the highest price under

a. FIFO method

b. LIFO method

c. Average cost method

d. Some other method

Q.19: During rising prices the ______ method will reflect

a. Lowest cost of material supplied and results in under pricing the products

b. Inventory is shown at the higher priced material.

c. Lock up of large amount of working capital.

d. More liability for payment of taxes

Ans. FIFO

Q.20: Under the simple average cost method, all the different prices are added together and then divided by the number of prices. The closing stock is valued at this price.

a. Right

b. Wrong

Q.21: Under the weighted average cost method, the total price paid is divided by the total quantity received. The closing stock is valued at this price.

a. Right

b. Wrong

Q.22: According to Accounting Standard 2 (Revised), where the goods are interchangeable, weighted average cost or First in First Out methods are permitted

a. Right

b. Wrong

Q.23: In retail business, widely followed method of inventory valuation is

a. FIFO

b. Weighted average

c. Adjusted selling price

c. LIFO

Q.24: Under the adjusted selling price method the cost of inventory is calculated by

a. Value of inventory is calculated at selling price.
b. Amount equal to the estimated gross margin of profit on this stock is deducted.
c. The net value is taken as the value of closing stock
d. (a), (b) and (c) are followed chronologically.

Q.25: The cost formulae recommended by Accounting Standard 2 for valuation of inventories are-

a. FIFO or Weighted average
b. Standard cost
c. LIFO or latest purchase price
d. Current market price

Q.26: Ascertaining value of stock from accounting record is known as

a. continuous stock taking
b. periodic inventory
c. perpetual inventory
d. stock audit

(Stock register is maintained which gives the stock figure at any point of time. It is possible for the management to provide for continuous stock taking. This method helps in finding out discrepancies in the stock, by comparing the actual quantity of individual items with the book balance)

Q.27: Ascertaining of value of stock at the end of the year by physically counting the stock is known as

a. continuous stock taking
b. periodic inventory
c. perpetual inventory
d. stock audit

(*Annual stock taking is taken and in order to finalise stock figures, the purchases and sales are normally suspended during the period of stock taking)*

Q.28: Closing Stock is valued at the historical cost or net realizable value, whichever is low

a. True
b. False

ANSWERS

1. (a)	2. (b)	3. (a)	4. (a)	5. (b)	6. (d)
7. (a)	8. (a)	9. (d)	10. (a)	11. (a)	12. (b)
13. —	14. (a)	15. —	16. (a)	17. (b)	18. (b)
19. —	20. (a)	21. (a)	22. (a)	23. (c)	24. (d)
25. (a)	26. (c)	27. (b)	28. (a)		

CHAPTER 20

ADJUSTING ENTRIES/SINGLE ENTRY SYSTEM

Need

Q.1: Final accounts are prepared every year on the basis of accounting year assumption.

a. True

b. False

Q.2: To arrive at the true and fair view of the business, it is desired that full account of the expenses and incomes of the year should be taken

a. True

b. False

Q.3: All such items which need to be brought into books of account at the time of preparing final accounts are called:

a. Adjusting entries

b. Closing entries

c. Rectifying entries

d. Suspense entries

Q.4: Some common adjustments required are with respect to :

a. Closing stock

b. Expenses due but not paid (Outstanding expenses)

c. Expenses paid in advance (Prepaid expenses)

d. Incomes due but not received (Accrued incomes)

e. Incomes not due but received (Unearned incomes)

f. Depreciation on asscts

g. Interest on Capital

h. Interest on Drawings

i. Interest on Loan

j. Bad debts to be written off

k. Provision for bad debts

l. Provision for discount on Debtors

m. Provision for discount on creditors

n. Losses on account of accidents

o. Commission payable on profit

p. Goods used by the proprietor

q. Goods distributed as Free Samples

Closing Stock

Q.5: All goods produced or purchased during the accounting year are not completely sold out by the end of the year. The goods which remain unsold at the end of the year are called

a. Finished goods

b. Closing Stock

c. Opening stock

d. Non-movable stock

Q.6 While making an entry in respect of Closing Stock, debit ______ and credit ______.

Ans.: Closing Stock, Trading A/c

Q.7: The closing stock is treated in the final accounts:

a. Credit side of Trading a/c and as an asset in the Balance Sheet as current asset

b. Debit side of Trading a/c and as an asset in the Balance Sheet as current asset

c. Credit side of P & L a/c and as an asset in the Balance Sheet as current asset

d. Debit side of P & L a/c and as a liability in the Balance Sheet as current asset

Q.8: If the amount of closing stock is given in the Trial balance, it means that its value is adjusted in the purchases and as such it is shown

a. on the credit side of trading a/c

b. on the assets side of balance

c. will not be shown anywhere

d. will be added in purchases

Expenses due but not paid (Outstanding expenses)

Q.9: The amount which has already been incurred but not yet paid is called

a. Outstanding expense

b. Accrued expense

c. Expenses due but not paid

d. By any one of the above names

Q.10: There is only one employee in a concern who is employed in the month of July at a monthly salary of Rs. 10,000. When the Trial Balance is made as at the end of March next year, the wages account shows a balance of Rs. 80,000. The adjustment to be made is:

a. To provide outstanding wages Rs. 10,000

b. To provide outstanding wages Rs. 40,000

c. No adjustment is required

d. To provide interest on wages unpaid at some stipulates rate

Q.11: Outstanding wages are shown as

a. an expense

b. a liability

c. an asset

d. an income

Q.12: The adjustment entry to be passed for wages outstanding as on the date of balance sheet is

a. Debit Wages a/c Credit Wages outstanding a/c

b. Debit Profit & Loss a/c Credit Wages outstanding a/c

c. Debit Wages a/c Credit Trading a/c

d. Debit Trading a/c Credit Wages outstanding a/c

Q.13: Outstanding rent is:

a. A real a/c

b. A Nominal A/c

c. A personal a/c without name

d. An Intangible a/c

Expenses paid in advance (Prepaid expenses)

Q.14: The benefit of the amount already spent is sometimes available in the next accounting period also. Such a portion of the expense concerned is called

a. prepaid expense

b. expense paid in advance

c. expense not due but paid

d. by any one of the above names

Q.15: Prepaid expenses are debited to prepaid expenses account and credited to _______account while making adjusting entry

a. Trading

b. Expenses

c. Suspense

d. Adjusting

Q.16: Insurance premium of Rs. 400 is paid on 1st July and the accounts are closed on 31st March. The benefit of the insurance policy will accrue up to 30th June next year. Therefore, the benefit for one quarter from 1st April to 30th June will be derived in the next accounting year.

a. Insurance prepaid account will be debited and Insurance Premium account will be credited for Rs. 100.

b. Unexpired insurance of Rs. 100 will be subtracted from the Insurance Premium in the profit & loss account.

c. Prepaid insurance will be shown on the asset side of Balance Sheet under current assets.

d. Next year the insurance prepaid account will be transferred to Insurance account.

Q.17: Insurance Policy was taken on July 1st for one year, paying a premium of Rs. 12,000. When the final accounts are prepared on Dec. 31st, the adjustment entry passed will be

a. Debit Insurance Credit Insurance Premium due a/c

b. Debit Insurance Credit Prepaid Insurance a/c

c. Debit Prepaid Insurance Credit Insurance a/c

d. Debit Prepaid Insurance Credit Profit & Loss a/c

Q.18: Prepaid rent is shown as

a. An asset

b. A Liability

c. An Expense

d. A suspense item

Incomes due but not received

Q.19: Those incomes which have been earned but not yet received in cash till the end of accounting period are called:

a. Accrued income

b. Outstanding income

c. Income due but not received

d. Any one of the above names

Q.20: As per the accrual accounting concept, the full income of the accounting period, both received and yet to be received, should be shown in the final accounts, otherwise the profit and assets will remain understated

a. True

b. False

Q.21: For the unexpired incomes:

a. Debit the accrued income A/c and credit the concerned income A/c.

b. Accrued income is added to the concerned income in the credit side of profit & loss a/c

c. Amount of accrued income will be shown on the assets side as a separate item under current assets

d. All the above actions are required to be completed

Q.22: Outstanding income is:

a. An asset

b. A liability

c. An expense

d. A suspense item

Incomes received in Advance :

Q.23: Amount received in respect of income during the year may pertain partially to the next year. This portion of amount received is called:

a. Income received in advance

b. Unearned income

c. Income not due but received

d. By any one of the above names

Q.24: The adjustment entry in respect of income received in advance account is Debit Income received in advance a/c, Credit Income a/c

a. Right

b. Wrong

(The correct entry will be to Debit the concerned income a/c and credit the concerned income received in advance A/c)

Q.25: Income received in advance is:

a. An asset

b. A liability

c. An expense

d. A suspense item

Depreciation on assets

Q.26: The value of assets keeps on reducing year after year because of usage and passage of time. This decrease in the value of assets is considered as an expense or loss and is debited to P & L A/c. Otherwise profits will remain overstated.

a. Right

b. Wrong

Q.27: While making the adjustment entry in respect of depreciation on Machinery, Depreciation on Machinery A/c is debited and __________account is credited

a. Profit & Loss A/c

b. Machinery A/c

c. Adjustment A/c

d. Suspense A/c

Q.28: Depreciation on the asset a/c is transferred to

a. Asset a/c

b. P & L a/c

c. Balance Sheet

d. Adjustment a/c

Q.29: If the depreciation is given in the Trial Balance, it means that depreciation is charged on the asset before the preparation of Trial Balance and the concerned asset is shown at its reduced value. In such a case

a. No further adjustment is necessary

b. Depreciation a/c will be transferred to the debit of P & L A/c *c.* Further adjustments are required

d. Both (a) and (b)

Interest on Capital

Q.30: According to Separate Entity Concept, the funds provided by the proprietor to the business become a liability and interest is to be paid to the proprietor.

a. Right

b. Wrong

Q.31: While making an adjustment entry in respect of interest on capital, we credit

a. Interest on capital account

b. Capital account

c. Profit & Loss account

d. Suspense account

Q.32: Interest on Capital account is an expense for the firm and is debited to P & L A/c

a. Right

b. Wrong

Interest on Drawings

Q.33: When the proprietor withdraws money for private use, the firm loses interest. Therefore, the proprietor may be debited with the interest on this amount.

a. Right

b. Wrong

Q.34: Calculation of interest on drawings depend on the amount and the date concerned. Normally it is assumed that the drawings were made evenly throughout the year, therefore interest should be charged for 6 months on the full amount.

a. Right

b. Wrong

Q.35: Interest on drawings is credited to P & L A/c and deducted from the capital

a. Right

b. Wrong

Interest on Loan

Q.36: Interest on loan is to be paid:

a. When there is profit to the firm

b. Whether there is profit or loss

Q.37: Interest outstanding A/c is debited and Interest a/c is credited for interest on loan

a. Right

b. Wrong

(The correct entry should be to debit Interest a/c and credit Interest outstanding A/c)

Q.38: There is a 10% Loan account for Rs. 10,000 taken on 1st July, 2005 and interest on loan paid is Rs. 300 in the trial balance as on 31st Dec. 2005. This will be responded by

a. Debiting Interest on loan A/c and crediting Loan a/c with Rs. 200

b. Debiting Profit & Loss a/c and Crediting Interest on Loan a/c with Rs. 200

c. Showing interest on loan in P&L a/c at Rs. 500 (Rs. 300 paid + Rs. 200 outstanding)

d. Adding the amount of Rs. 200 towards interest outstanding in the Loan a/c

(This is a case of implied adjustment)

Bad debts to be written off

Q.39: When some of the debtors fail to pay their dues partially or completely the amount is called bad debts and this is a likely loss.

a. Right

b. Wrong

Q.40: If bad debts appear as an adjustment outside the Trial Balance, then they are adjusted by debiting Bad Debts a/c and crediting

a. Debtors (by name) a/c

b. Provision for Bad debts a/c

c. Doubtful debts a/c

d. Bad debts a/c

(The sundry debtors are reduced and the bad debts are transferred to the debit of P & L A/c)

Q.41: If the bad debts incurred during the year appear in the Trial balance, it means that sundry debtors are shown after deducting the bad debts. Bad debts are shown only on the debit side of P & L A/c.

a. Right

b. Wrong

Q.42: If the amount written off in a bad debt is later on recovered wholly or partially, the entry will be

Cash or bank A/c...............Dr.

To Bad Debts recovered A/c

a. Right

b. Wrong

Provision for bad debts

Q.43: The flow of bad debts is not uniform. From the experience of the concern/ trade/industry, estimate of average level of bad debts likely to occur may be decided by the concern every year. The amount can be set aside every year from profits to meet bad debts as and when they arise. The amount set apart is known as provision for bad debts or Reserve for bad debts.

a. Right

b. Wrong

Q.44: The following balances are available in the Trial Balance:

Debtors. Rs. 35,000, Bad Debts Rs. 1,400, Provision for bad debts Rs. 2,800

It is required to maintain the provision for bad debts at 10% of the Debtors. The new provision will be required for

a. Rs. 3,500

b. Rs. 4,900

c. Rs. 2,100

d. Rs. 700

Q.45: When bad debts are given in the Trial Balance, provision is created on the entire balance of Sundry debtors. If bad debts are written off as an adjustment, the provision should be made on the sundry debtors after deducting bad debts.

Provision for discount on Debtors

Q.46: For prompt payment of dues, the debtors may be allowed cash discount, the provision for discount on debtors is calculated only on the good debts, i.e. on amount of Debtors

a. Before deducting the provision for doubtful debts

b. Left after deducting the bad debts written off and provision for doubtful debts

c. Before deducting the actual bad debts and the provision for doubtful debts

d. None of the above

Q.47: When there is provision or Reserve for discount on Debtors in the books, the discount allowed account is closed by transfer the balance to the

a. Profit & Loss A/c

b. Provision for discount on Debtors A/c

c. Bad debts A/c

d. Doubtful debts A/c

Provision for discount on creditors

Q.48: When the concern makes the prompt payments to its creditors, they receive cash discount from them. It is calculated as a certain percentage on creditors, depending upon the experience of the concern.

a. Right

b. Wrong

Q.49: The adjustment entry for provision for discount on creditors is:

a. Profit & Loss a/c.......................Dr.
To Provision for Discount on Creditors

b. Provision for Discount on Creditors...Dr.
To Profit & Loss a/c

c. Sundry Creditors..........................Dr.
To Provision for Sundry creditors

d. (c) & (b) together

(*The reserve for Discount on creditors will be deducted from Sundry creditors in the balance sheet and is carried forward to the next year*)

Note: The creation of this provision is against the concept of conservatism which takes into account the expected losses only and not expected gains. Therefore, it is usually avoided in practice.

Losses on account of accidents

Q.50: Losses because of fire, earthquakes or accidents may destroy stock; are fixed assets are called

a. Normal losses

b. Abnormal losses

c. Usual losses

d. Natural losses

Q.51: Journal entry for abnormal loss of a fixed asset is

a. Profit & Loss A/c..........................Dr.
To Asset A/c

b. Asset A/c ....Dr.
To Abnormal Loss A/c

c. (*i*) Abnormal Loss A/c...................... Dr.
To Asset A/c

(*ii*) Profit & Loss A/c...................Dr.
To Abnormal Loss A/c

d. None of the above

(This loss may be spread over two or three years)

Q.52: Journal entry for abnormal loss of Stock of goods is:

a. (*i*) Abnormal loss.............................Dr.
To Trading A/c (for stock of goods)

(*ii*) Profit & Loss A/c.......................Dr
To Abnormal loss A/c

b. Abnormal Loss A/c...........................Dr.
To Profit & Loss A/c

c. Profit & Loss A/c ....Dr.
To Abnormal Loss A/c

d. None of the above

(With a view to judge the trading operations of the business, it is desired to ascertain the gross profit which would have been earned in absence of the loss. Therefore, Trading account is credited in the beginning. However, ultimately the loss is transferred to P & L A/c)

Note: If the loss is insured against the risks and the insurance claim is passed, then the P & L A/c will be debited only with the difference of the amount of abnormal loss minus the claim passed. The entry will be passed as under:

Profit & Loss A/c ....Dr.

Insurance Company ....Dr. (For the amount of Insurance claim)

To Trading A/c

Commission payable on profit

Q.53: When the Manager is entitled to a commission on profits, it is calculated as a fixed percentage on the amount of profit and the entry is

Profit & Loss A/c.............................Dr.

To Commission Payable a/c

Commission payable is a liability for the concern.

a. Right

b. Wrong

Q.54: The commission may be paid on

a. The net profits before charging such commission

b. The net profits after charging such commission

c. Either (a) or (b)

d. Some other method

Q.55: A commission of 5% on net profits after charging such commission will be calculated as:

a. 5/105 of the amount of net profit

b. 5/100 of the amount of net profit

c. 5/95 of the amount of net profit

d. None of the above

Q.56: The manager is entitled to a commission @ 10% of profits after charging such commission. The net profit is Rs. 1,10,000. Therefore, the commission will be

a. Rs. 11,000

b. Rs. 10,000

c. Rs. 10,500

d. Rs. 11,500

Q.57: The manager is entitled to a commission @ 10% of profits before charging such commission. The net profit is Rs. 1,10,000. Therefore, the commission will be

a. Rs. 11,000

b. Rs. 10,000

c. Rs. 10,500

d. Rs. 11,500

Goods used by the proprietor

Q.58: The goods taken away by the proprietor from the business for his personal use should be credited to

a. Drawings account

b. Purchases account

c. Capital account

d. Charity account

Q.59: The proprietor has taken goods of the sale value of Rs. 10,000, whose purchase price is Rs. 8,000, this should be recorded as

a. Debit Capital a/c Credit Drawings a/c

b. Debit Drawings a/c Credit Sales a/c

c. Debit Purchases a/c Credit Sales a/c

d. Debit Drawings a/c Credit Purchases a/c

Goods distributed as Free Samples

Q.60: Goods given as charity/free samples are credited to

a. Charity/Advertisement account

b. Purchases account

c. Sales account

d. Samples account

Q.61: Of the goods purchased goods amounting to Rs. 1000 were distributed as free samples. This will be recorded as:

a. Debit Samples a/c and credit Sales a/c

b. The amount will be adjusted while valuing closing stock. No entry to be passed

c. Debit Advertisement A/c and credit purchases a/c

d. Debit Advertisement a/c and credit Free Samples a/c

Miscellaneous Adjustments

Q.62: Wages already paid for erection of a machinery will be recorded as:

a. Debit wages, credit Machinery

b. Debit Machinery, credit Wages

c. No adjustment required

d. Dr. Erection charges and credit P & L a/c

Q.63: Wages Rs. 5,000 paid for erection of Machinery is added to the Machinery account. The adjustment required is

a. Debit Wages and Credit Machinery account with Rs. 5000.

b. Debit Vendors account and credit Cash account

c. No adjustment is required

d. Debit Machinery and credit wages with Rs. 5,000.

Q.64: Sales includc Rs. 10,000 for sale on return basis, for which the consent of the customer is not received upto the date of finalization of accounts. The cost of such goods was Rs. 8,000. The adjustment entry for this will be:

a. Deduct Rs. 10,000 from sale and add it in stock

b. No adjustment required

c. Deduct Rs. 10,000 from sale and from Debtors and add Rs. 8000 in stock

d. Reverse the entry of sale

Q.65: The loss on sale of old machinery should be debited to

a. Profit & Loss account

b. Machinery account

c. Depreciation account

d. Deferred revenue account

Q.66: Goods purchased from Mohan for Rs. 10,000 were omitted to be accounted for, but included in the closing stock. The adjustments required are:

a. Remove the amount from Closing Stock

b. Add to Purchases and deduct from Closing Stock Rs. 10,000

c. Add to purchases

d. Add to purchases in Trading A/c and to Creditors in Balance Sheet

Q.67: Company has purchased the goods, but these are not yet received and are in transit. The adjustment entry is

a. Debit goods in transit A/c and credit Trading A/c

b. Debit the supplier and credit Purchases A/c

c. No adjustment required

d. Add the amount in the value of stock in hand.

Q.68: Statement of Affairs refers to which of the following, under Single Entry System

(*a*) Cash Book

(*b*) Profit and Loss Account

(*c*) Balance Sheet

(*d*) Trial Balance

Q.69: Under Single Entry System, Profit and Loss Account can be prepared by:

(*a*) Conversion Method

(*b*) Networth Method

(*c*) Both (a) and (b)

(*d*) None of the above

ANSWERS

1. (a)	2. (a)	3. (a)	4. —	5. (b)	6. —
7. (a)	8. (b)	9. (d)	10. (a)	11. (b)	12. (a)
13. (c)	14. (d)	15. (b)	16. (d)	17. (b)	18. (a)
19. (d)	20. (a)	21. (d)	22. (a)	23. (d)	24. (b)
25. (b)	26. (a)	27. (b)	28. (b)	29. (d)	30. (a)
31. (b)	32. (a)	33. (a)	34. (a)	35. (a)	36. (b)
37. (b)	38. —	39. (a)	40. (a)	41. (a)	42. (a)
43. (a)	44. (d)	45. —	46. (b)	47. (b)	48. (a)
49. (b)	50. (b)	51. (c)	52. (a)	53. (a)	54. (c)
55. (a)	56. (b)	57. (a)	58. (b)	59. (d)	60. (b)
61. (c)	62. (b)	63. (c)	64. (c)	65. (a)	66. (d)
67. (a)	68. (c)	69. (c)			

CHAPTER

21

DEPRECIATION ACCOUNTING/ RATIO ANALYSIS

Meaning

Q.1: Depreciation is the reduction in the value of ______

Ans. a fixed Asset

Q.2: Depreciation is charged on almost all fixed assets except land, because it has no finite economic life.

a. Right

b. Wrong

Q.3: Depreciation is the part of operating cost.

a. Right

b. Wrong

Q.4: Depreciation is to know the correct profit

a. Right

b. Wrong

Q.5: Depreciation is a fall in the value of an asset

a. Right

b. Wrong

Q.6: Depreciation is a reduction in the book value of

a. all fixed assets

b. all fixed assets excepting land

c. all fluctuating assets

d. both fixed and current assets

Q.7: Depreciation reduces the

a. book value of the asset
b. market value of the asset
c. realizable value of the asset
d. all the above

Q.8: Depreciation is a process of

a. Valuation of asset
b. Allocation of cost of the asset to the period of its life
c. Both a and b
d. Neither a nor b

Q.9: The term depreciation is used for

a. Tangible fixed assets
b. Wasting and fictitious assets
c. Amortisation of goodwill
d. Current assets

Q.10: Depreciation is:

a. a part of the operating cost
b. a reduction in the value of asset
c. gradual and continuous
d. on account of all the above

Causes

Q.11: Fall in market price is the main cause of depreciation

a. Right
b. Wrong

(Only current assets are affected by this fact. We talk of depreciation only on fixed assets)

Q.12: The main causes of depreciation are:

a. Wear and tear of asset due to its actual use
b. Efflux of time-fall in the value of asset even if it is not used
c. Obsolescence due to new inventions and technologies
d. All of the above

Q.13: Select the correct statement

a. Fall in the market price is the main cause of depreciation

b. The value of an Asset is reduced to Zero under WDV method of Depreciation

c. The expenditure on repairs and depreciation on assets are equal in every year under the Straight Line Method

d. Depreciation is provided to know the correct profit of the business

Q.14: Depreciation is charged on fixed assets:

a. when it is used in the business

b. when market value falls

c. annually, whether it is used or not

d. if it has a scrap value

Q.15: The extraction of natural resources like quarries, mines, etc. that reduce the availability of the quantity of the material is called its

a. Depreciation

b. Depletion

c. Amortisation

d. Obsolescence

Q.16: The decrease in the usefulness of the asset due to becoming out of date, old fashioned is called

a. Depreciation

b. Depletion

c. Amortisation

d. Obsolescence

Q.17: Writing off the proportionate value of the intangibles such as goodwill, copyright, patents, designs, etc. are called

a. Depreciation

b. Depletion

c. Amortisation

d. Obsolescence

Need

Q.18: Depreciation is charged to

a. Ascertain the profit or loss properly

b. To show the assets at their proper value

c. To retain funds out of profits for replacement of asset

d. All of the above

Q.19: Depreciation is provided to arrive at the profit earned by the business

a. Right

b. Wrong

Factors

Q.20: The following factors affect the rate of depreciation charged on a fixed asset

a. cost of the asset

b. estimated economic life of the asset

c. estimated residual or scrap value of the asset

d. all of the above

Accounting

Q.21: Depreciation is recorded in ______side of Profit & Loss A/c.

Ans. Debit

Q.22: For providing depreciation, Depreciation a/c is debited and the concerned Asset A/c or Provision for Depreciation A/c is credited

a. Right

b. Wrong

Q.23: When Depreciation A/c is debited and the concerned Asset A/c is credited,

a. Depreciation is shown on the debit side of P & L A/c

b. Asset appears at its reduced value in the Balance Sheet.

c. Both (a) & (b) above

d. Asset is shown at its original cost in the Balance Sheet

Q.24: When Depreciation A/c is debited and the Provision for Depreciation A/c is credited,

a. Depreciation is shown on the debit side of P & L A/c

b. Asset appears at its original value in the details column of the Balance Sheet

c. Accumulated Provision for depreciation is deducted from the value of the Asset.

d. The net value of the Asset is shown in the amount column of the balance sheet.

Q.25: The expression depreciation at 10% and 10% p.a. carry the same meaning

a. Right

b. Wrong

Methods

Q.26: Depreciation can be provided by any one of the following methods

(*i*) Straight Line Method

(*ii*) Diminishing balance method

(*iii*) Sinking Fund method

(*iv*) Insurance policy method

(*v*) Annuity method

(*vi*) Sum of digits method

(*vii*) Revaluation method

(*viii*) Depletion method

(*ix*) Machine hour rate method

Q.27: The most common methods of providing depreciation are:

a. Straight Line Method

b. Diminishing balance method

c. Sum of years' digits method

d. All the above

Straight Line Method

Q.28: Straight line method of providing depreciation is also known by the name of

a. Fixed Percentage on original cost method

b. Fixed Instalment method

c. (a) & (b) both above

d. Some other name also

Q.29: A fixed percentage of the original cost of the asset is charged as depreciation each and every year during the useful life of the asset under

a. Straight Line Method

b. Written Down Value Method

c. Sinking fund method

d. Sum of years' digits method

Q.30: When the rate of depreciation is given as 10% p.a.

a. the period for which the asset is used in the year concerned should be taken into account

b. depreciation is calculated for the full year

c. both *a* and *b*

d. neither *a* nor *b*

Q.31: When the rate of depreciation is given as 10%

a. the period for which the asset is used in the year concerned should be taken into account

b. depreciation is calculated for the full year irrespective of the date of purchase

c. both *a* and *b*

d. neither *a* nor *b*

Q.32: Under straight line method of depreciation

a. The rate of depreciation charged on the asset is the same all the year

b. The value of depreciation charged on the asset is the same for all the years.

c. Both the rate and value of depreciation charged on the asset is the same for all the years.

d. The value will be the same, but the rate will differ between different years.

Q.33: A machinery costing Rs. 1,00,000 is expected to have an economic life of 10 years. The installation cost is Rs. 10,000 and the machinery is expected to have a scrap value of Rs. 20,000 at the end of its economic life. On straight line method, the depreciation chargeable on the asset is:

a. Rs. 10,000

b. Rs. 11,000

c. Rs. 9,000

d. Rs. 13,000

Q.34: A machinery is purchased on 1st July, 2005 for Rs. 2,50,000. It is decided to charge depreciation on straight line method at 20% p.a. When the final accounts are prepared on 31st March, 2006, the depreciation that should be charged is:

a. Rs. 50,000

b. Rs. 25,000

c. Rs. 37,500

d. Rs. 35,000

Q.35: An equipment purchased is to be dcpreciated on fixed instalment system. The journal entry for charging depreciation is:

a. Depreciation A/c ....Dr.
To P & L A/c

b. P & L A/c ....Dr.
To Depreciation A/c

c. P & L A/c ....Dr.
To Equipment A/c

d. Depreciation A/c ....Dr.
To Equipment A/c

Q.36: Depreciation is provided to provide funds for repurchase of the asset after its economic life

a. True

b. False

Q.37: A company purchased a second-hand motor car for Rs. 80,000 and spent Rs. 35,000 on its overhauling. Depreciation is written off @ 10% on the original cost. After two years the car was found unsuitable and sold for Rs. 65,000. What is the amount of loss on sale of car?

a. Rs. 15,000

b. Rs. 27,000

c. Profit Rs. 1000

d. Rs. 50,000

Q.38: The expenditure on repairs and renewals and depreciation on assets are equal in every year under the straight line method of depreciation

a. Right

b. Wrong

(By the passage of time, work efficiency of assets decreases and repair expenses increase.In the initial years the depreciation will be more and repairs are less, and in later years the expenditure on repairs is high and less depreciation)

Q.39: The value of the asset is reduced to zero or the scrap value after the estimated life of the asset under

a. Straight line method of depreciation

b. Written down value method of depreciation

c. both *a* and *b*

d. neither *a* nor *b*

Written Down Value Method

Q.40: A fixed percentage is charged as depreciation on the diminishing value of the asset each year during the useful life of the asset under

b. Straight Line Method

b. Written Down Value Method

c. Sinking fund method

d. None of the above

Q.41: Depreciation is calculated on the diminishing value of the asset under__________.

Ans.: WDV Method

Q.42: The value of the asset is reduced to zero under the WDV method of depreciation

a. Right

b. Wrong

(In this method the value of asset can never be zero)

Q.43: A machinery purchased for Rs. 2,00,000 is to be depreciated at 20% on WDV method. Assuming the machinery is purchased on the first day of the year, the amount of depreciation for the third year will be:

a. Rs. 40,000

b. Rs. 32,000

c. Rs. 25,600

d. Rs. 20480

Q.44: A firm purchased a machinery for Rs. 5,00,000 on 1-1-2003, and wrote off depreciation @ 20% on diminishing value method. On 31st December, 2005 one fourth of the machinery was found unsuitable and disposed of for Rs. 56,000.

a. The loss on sale was Rs. 24,000 and Balance of Machinery A/c was Rs. 2,40,000

b. The loss on sale was Rs. 19,000 and Balance of Machinery A/c was Rs. 2,25,000

c. The loss on sale was Rs. 69,000 and Balance of Machinery A/c was Rs. 3,75,000

d. None of the above

Q.45: On an equipment purchased for Rs. 50,000, it is decided to charge depreciation @ 30%, the difference in the book value of the assets at the end of three years, assuming that the company is adopting (*i*) Straight line method, and (*ii*) Written down value method will be

a. Book value will be higher by Rs. 12,150 under WDV method

b. Book value will be higher by Rs. 12,150 under SLM method

c. Book value will be higher by Rs. 15,000 under WDV method

d. Book value will be higher by Rs. 15,000 under SLM method

(Under SLM it will be Rs. 5,000, but under WDV it will be Rs. 17,150)

Q.46: Interest on capital investment to acquire the asset is not considered in

a. Straight Line Method

b. Diminishing balance Method

c. Sinking fund method

d. All of the above

Q.47: Depreciation is deducted from the asset and no provision is made for the replacement of the asset under:

a. Straight Line Method

b. Diminishing balance Method

c. Sinking fund method

d. Both *a* nor *b*

Q.48: Once the depreciation is provided, it is desired that sufficient funds are available in the business to replace the asset. Ready cash is not available under the following methods:

a. Straight Line Method

b. Diminishing balance Method

c. Sinking fund method

d. Both *a* nor *b*

Sinking Fund Method

Q.49: The amount written off as depreciation should be kept aside and invested in readily salable securities

a. Right

b. Wrong

Q.50: The securities acquired and the old assets are sold at the time of replacement and a new asset is purchased under

a. Straight Line Method

b. Diminishing balance Method

c. Sinking fund method

d. Both *a* nor *b*

Q.51: The sinking fund investment earns interest, it is not necessary to provide full amount of depreciation

a. Right

b. Wrong

Q.52: Sinking fund is created and the fund amount is invested in securities every year along with the interest on the investments. At the time of replacement of asset, the securities are sold and the proceeds are used for replacement of the asset

a. Right

b. Wrong

Q.53: Under _________method of depreciation, the securities are sold and the proceeds are used for replacement of the asset.

Ans. Sinking Fund

The following steps and accounting entries are required under Sinking Fund Method

1. For purchase of Asset

   Debit: Asset A/c **Credit:** Bank A/c

2. Amount of depreciation is calculated with a reference to the Sinking fund table. The table gives the amounts to be invested annually to realize one rupee at the end of different years and at different rates of interest. Value of the asset is multiplied with the factor as per Sinking Fund Table and the amount of depreciation is arrived at.

3. The amount written off as depreciation is invested in outside securities to yield interest, and the interest earned thereon is reinvested.

For example if the cost of machine is Rs. 1,00,000. It is expected to have an economic life of 5 years and the investment yields 6% p.a.

(A reference to the Sinking Fund Table the factor applicable for 5 years at 6% rate is 0.177396. The annual depreciation would be Rs. 1,00,000 × 0.177396 or Rs. 17,739. 60). This amount will become Rs. 1,00,000 in 5 years @ 6% p.a. as under:

First year depreciation	Rs. **17,739.60**
Interest at the end of First year on 17,739.60	Rs. 1,064.37
Total investment at the beginning of 2nd year	*Rs. 18,803.97*
Second year depreciation	*Rs.* **17,739.60**
Interest on 18,803.97	*Rs. 1,128.24*
Total investment at the end of 2nd year	*Rs. 37,671.81*
Third year depreciation	*Rs.* **17,739.60**
Interest on 37,671.81	*Rs. 2,260.30*
Total investment at the end of 3rd year	*Rs. 57,671.71*

Fourth year depreciation	*Rs.* ***17,739.60***
Interest on 57,671.71	*Rs. 3,460.31*
Total investment at the end of 4th year	*Rs. 78,871.62*
Fifth year depreciation	*Rs.* ***17,739.60***
Interest on 78,871.62	*Rs. 4,732.30*
Total investment at the end of 5th year	*Rs. 1,01,343.52*

1. The annual depreciation is transferred to Sinking Fund A/c every year:

   Debit: Depreciation A/c **Credit:** Sinking Fund A/c
2. To the extent the amount of depreciation is written off, amount is invested in outside securities at the stipulated rate of interest and kept under Sinking Fund Investment A/c.

   Debit: Sinking Fund Investment A/c **Credit:** Bank A/c
3. Interest realized from the investments are again utilized and is invested in the Securities and kept under Sinking Fund Investment A/c.

   Debit: Bank A/c **Credit:** Interest on Sinking Fund Investment A/c

   Debit: Interest on Sinking Fund Investment A/c **Credit:** Sinking Fund A/c

   Debit: Sinking Fund Investment A/c **Credit**: Bank A/c
4. In the final year no fresh investment is made. Only the following entries are made:

   Debit: Depreciation A/c **Credit:** Sinking Fund A/c

   Debit: Bank A/c **Credit:** Interest on Sinking Fund Investment A/c

   Debit: Interest on Sinking Fund Investment A/c **Credit:** Sinking Fund A/c
5. For realization of investments

   Debit: Bank A/c **Credit:** Sinking Fund Investment A/c

   If the amount realized is the same as book value of the Sinking Fund Investment, this account is automatically closed.

   If the amount realized is more or less, there is a profit or loss on sale of investments, which is transferred to Depreciation Fund A/c.

9. The Asset account is closed by:

   Debit: Depreciation Fund A/c **Credit:** Asset A/c

10. The Depreciation fund account is closed by transferring any balance in it to the P & L A/c.

Q.54: Accounting Ratios help in :

(*a*) Inter firm comparison

(*b*) Intra firm comparison

(*c*) Comparison with industry norms

(*d*) All the above

Q.55: DSCR ratio is used in which of the following :

(*a*) Judging the margin of safety available before there is default in repaying the loan

(*b*) Judging whether the firm has borrowings disproportionate to its networth

(*c*) Judging the capacity of the firm to service the interest on debt

(*d*) All the above

Q.56: Which of the following is true

(*a*) Both EPS and PE ratio vary with the stock market price of company's share

(*b*) While calculating Debt/Equity ratio, fixed deposits from shareholders are taken as part of Debt

(*c*) While calculating Quick ratio, all current liabilities are not taken into account

(*d*) Debtor's Turnover ratio is higher if the company sells more goods on credit basis than on cash basis

Q.57: Which of the following is true

(*a*) Higher Debt/Equity ratio increase the profit margin of a company

(*b*) Debt/Equity ratio is an indicator of solvency of a company

(*c*) A high current ratio is always an indicator of the efficient management

(*d*) Depreciation is not an expense and should be excluded while calculating profitability ratios

ANSWERS					
1. —	2. (a)	3. (a)	4. (a)	5. (a)	6. (b)
7. (d)	8. (b)	9. (a)	10. (d)	11. (b)	12. (d)
13. (d)	14. (c)	15. (b)	16. (d)	17. (c)	18. (d)
19. (a)	20. (d)	21. —	22. (a)	23. (c)	24. (d)
25. (b)	26. —	27. (d)	28. (c)	29. (a)	30. (a)
31. (b)	32. (c)	33. (c)	34. (c)	35. (d)	36. (a)
37. (b)	38. (b)	39. (a)	40. (b)	41. —	42. (b)
43. (c)	44. (a)	45. (a)	46. (a)&(b)	47. (d)	48. (d)
49. (a)	50. (c)	51. (a)	52. (a)	53. —	54. (d)
55. (a)	56. (b)	57. (b)			

CHAPTER 22

BILL OF EXCHANGE

Q.1: When goods are sold on credit, seller becomes a _______ and buyer becomes a _________

Ans. Creditor, Debtor

Q.2: Bill of Exchange and Promissory notes are the documents called ________

Ans.: Instruments of credit/Negotiable Instruments

Bill of Exchange

Q.3: __________ draws a bill on _________

Ans. Creditor, Debtor

Q.4: A bill of exchange is a negotiable instrument

a. True

b. False

Q.5: Negotiable instruments can be _______from one person to another

Ans.: Transferred

Q.6: A bill of exchange must be in writing

a. True

b. False

Q.7: A bill of exchange is not to be dated

a. True

b. False

(It must be dated, because as per its definition it must be payable on a certain fixed future date and that is calculated with reference to the date when it is accepted or drawn)

Q.8: A bill of exchange contains an order for payment of a certain sum of _____ only

Ans.: money

Q.9: A Bill must be for a specified amount and specified period

a. True

b. False

Q.10: A bill of exchange must be signed by the ________

Ans.: Drawer/maker

Q.11: A bill of exchange must be accepted for payment by the party on whom the order is made, called the drawee.

a. True

b. False

Q.12: In ________ acceptance the drawee puts his signature across the face of the bill with or without the word "Accepted"

Ans.: General

Q.13: A bill of exchange has .... parties

a. Two

b. Three

c. Four

d. Five

(These three parties are-Drawer: who draws the bill. Drawee: on whom the bill is drawn. Payee: Who is going to receive the money. Sometimes, a drawer and payee may be the same)

Q.14: The party which is ordered to pay the amount is known as

a. Drawer

b. Acceptor

c. Payee

d. Drawee

Q.15: A bill of exchange may be drawn for payment in kind

a. True

b. False

(A bill contains an unconditional order to pay a certain sum of money and money only)

Q.16: A bill of exchange is a conditional order

a. True

b. False

(A bill of exchange contains an unconditional order)

Q.17: A bill may be payable to any person

a. True

b. False

(The money must be payable to a definite person or his order or to the bearer)

Q.18: A bill of exchange must be properly stamped

a. True

b. False

Q.19: Acceptance is voluntary for a bill of exchange

a. True

b. False

(Acceptance by debtor is necessary)

Q.20: Drawee is the maker of the bill

a. True

b. False

(Drawer is the maker of the bill, which is being accepted by the drawee)

Q.21: In general acceptance, the drawee agrees with some of the conditions of the bill

a. True

b. False

(A bill is an unconditional order to pay and a promissory note is an unconditional promise to pay)

Q.22: The advantages accruing from bill of exchange are:

a. Goods can be sold or purchased on credit without difficulty.

b. The firm allowing the credit can receive cash immediately because the bill can be got discounted.

c. It is easy to recover the amount legally, if the bill is dishonoured.

d. A bill can be used like cash, as it can be endorsed to other parties.

e. There is certainty of payment. Due to the fixed date of payment cash operations can be planned by both the parties.

f. The recovery of the debt is possible without reminding the debtor.

g. It is a convenient mode of remittance in foreign trade.

h. It is a legal document and a valid evidence of a debt.

Promissory Note

Q.23: Mere acknowledgement of a debt is not a promise

a. True

b. False

Q.24: There are two parties to a Promissory Note

a. True

b. False

(*The two parties to a Promissory Note are called the Maker, who makes the note and promises to make the payment and the Payee, who is to receive money.*)

Q.25: Debtor is the maker of a Promissory Note

a. True

b. False

Q.26: The maker of a Promissory Note must sign it

a. True

b. False

Q.27: A Promissory Note can be made payable to bearer

a. True

b. False

Types of Bills

From accounting point of view, bills of exchange are of two types:

(1) Trade bill - which is drawn and accepted for a genuine trade transaction

(2) Accommodation bill - which is drawn and accepted for mutual help.

Q.28: A bill of exchange which arises out of trading relationship of two parties is called as a Trade Bill

a. True

b. False

Q.29: There is no difference in appearance between Trade bill and accommodation bill

a. True

b. False

Due date of bills

Q.30: Every bill is payable on a certain fixed ________ or on demand

Ans.: Future date

Q.31: The date on which the bill is payable is called its ________

Ans.: Due date

Q.32: The due date is calculated after adding ________ to the actual period of the bill.

Ans.: Three days of grace

Q.33: If the due date falls on a public holiday, then it becomes due on the ________

Ans. Previous working day

Q.34: Three days are added for ascertaining the date of maturity. These are known as days of

a. Maturity

b. Grace

c. Payment

d. None of the above

Q.35: A draws on B three bills respectively on 29th, 30th and 31st January, 2006 for one month each. What will be the due date of payment in each case.

Ans. 3rd March, 2006

Q.36: A bill was drawn on 23rd Dec. 2005 for one month maturity. What will be its due date.

Ans.: 25th January, 2006

Q.37: A party who receives a bill of exchange has the option

a. To retain the bill till the date of maturity

b. To get the bill discounted from the bank

c. To endorse in favour of a creditor

d. To send the bill for collection.

Important terms used in Bills

Q.38: ________ is a person who draws a bill

Ans. Drawer

Q.39: ________ is a person on whom a bill is drawn

Ans. Drawee

Q.40: ________ is a person who is legally entitled to receive the amount of the bill on due date

Ans.: Holder

Q.41: _________ is a person who obtains the instrument for valuable consideration, becomes the holder before its maturity, and he had no cause to believe that any defect existed in the title of the person from whom he derived his title.

Ans. Holder in due course

Q.42: A __________ gets a good title even if the title of the transferor was defective.

Ans. Holder in due course

Q.43: ________ is a person who gives a promise

Ans.: Promissor

Q.44: ________ is a person in whose favour a promise is given

Ans.: Promisee

Q.45: _________ is a bill, which has no consideration and is drawn for the purpose of mutual help

Ans. Accommodation bill

Q.46: _________ means inability to pay the bills on due date

Ans.: Insolvency

Q.47: The amount received from the insolvent person's private estate is called ______

Ans.: Dividend

Q.48: The amount irrecoverable from the insolvent is called _____________

Ans. Bad debt

Q.49: Drawee is a person to whom the bill is endorsed

a. True

b. False

(The person to whom the bill is endorsed is known as Endorsee)

Q.50: Drawee after acceptance becomes acceptor

a. True

b. False

Q.51: Amount of the bill is to be paid to the payee

a. True

b. False

Honouring of the Bill

Q.52: When the drawee pays the amount of the bill on due date, the bill is said to be

a. Completed
b. Paid
c. Met
d. Honoured

Endorsement of a Bill

Q.53: Transfer of a bill to some other person is called

a. Transfer of the bill
b. Endorsement of the bill
c. Negotiation of the bill
d. Discounting the bill

Q.54: Instruments payable to bearer can be transferred or negotiated by

a. Endorsement & delivery
b. Mere delivery
c. Encashment
d. None of the above

Q.55: Instruments payable to order can be transferred or negotiated by

a. Endorsement & delivery
b. Mere delivery
c. Encashment
d. None of the above

Discounting of a Bill

Q.56: Before the due date of the bill, the holder may endorse the bill in favour of his banker and gets immediate cash from the banker. This is called

a. Transfer of the bill
b. Endorsement of the bill
c. Purchase of the bill
d. Discounting the bill

(From the bank point of view it is called B/D-bill discounted or B/P-bill purchased)

Q.57: A bill of exchange can be discounted with the ________

Ans.: Bank

Q.58: Discount on bill discounted is an ________ to bank and an ________ to the drawer.

Ans.: Income, Expense

Q.59: The bank is willing to discount a bill, because

a. In addition to the liability of the acceptor, the drawer and payee will also be liable.

b. An endorser is liable to all subsequent endorsees.

c. Both *a* and *b*

d. Neither *a* nor *b*

Q.60: The facility to get bill of exchange discounted puts them into the category of

a. Fixed assets

b. Intangible assets

c. Wasting assets

d. Current assets

Bill Sent for Collection

Q.61: When the bill is sent to bank for collection of the amount on behalf of the holder of the bill, it is called:

a. Negotiating the bill

b. Discouting the bill

c. Sale of the bill

d. Bill sent for collection

Accounting treatment

ACCOUNTING ENTRIES OF A BILL OF EXCHANGE

Transaction	*Books of Drawer*	*Books of Drawer*	*Books of Drawee*	*Books of Drawee*
	A/c Debited	*A/c Credited*	*A/c Debited*	*A/c Credited*
1. When goods are sold	Customer	Sales	Purchases	Supplier
2. When bill is drawn and accepted	B/R A/c	Customer	Supplier	B/P A/c
3. (*a*) When it is retained till maturity	No entry	No entry	No entry	No entry
(*b*) When it is discounted	Bank Discount	B/R A/c	No entry	No entry

Transaction	Books of Drawer	Books of Drawer	Books of Drawee	Books of Drawee
	A/c Debited	*A/c Credited*	*A/c Debited*	*A/c Credited*
(*c*) When it is endorsed	Creditor	B/R A/c	No entry	No entry
(*d*) When it is sent for collection	Bills sent for Collection	B/R A/c	No entry	No entry
On Maturity if the bill is met:				
4. (*a*) When it was retained till maturity	Cash	B/R A/c	B/P A/c	Cash or Bank
(*b*) When it was discounted	No entry	No entry	B/P A/c	Cash or Bank
(*c*) When it was endorsed	No entry	No entry	B/P A/c	Cash or Bank
(*d*) When it was sent for collection	Bank	BSC A/c	B/P A/c	Cash or Bank
On Maturity if it is dishonoured:				
5. (*a*) When it was retained till maturity	Acceptor	B/R A/c	B/P A/c	Drawer
(*b*) When it was discounted	Acceptor	Bank	B/P A/c	Drawer
(*c*) When it was endorsed	Acceptor	Creditor	B/P A/c	Drawer
(*d*) When it was sent for collection	Acceptor	BSC	B/P A/c	Drawer
On dishonour for noting charges				
6. (*a*) When it was retained till maturity	Acceptor	Cash A/c	Noting Charges	Drawer
(*b*) When it was discounted	Acceptor	Bank	Noting Charges	Drawer
(*c*)When it was endorsed	Acceptor	Creditor	Noting Charges	Drawer
(*d*) When it was sent for collection	Acceptor	Bank A/c	Noting Charges	Drawer
On renewal of the bill	As per Sl. 5	As per Sl. 5	As per Sl. 5	As per Sl. 5
7. (*a*) For cancellation of old B/R	Acceptor	Interest	Interest	Drawer
(*b*) For Interest Due	B/R a/c	Acceptor	Drawer	B/P A/c
(*c*) For new bill	Cash or Bank	B/R A/c	B/P A/c	Cash or Bank
8. On retiring the bill before due date	Rebate or discount			Rebate or discount
If the acceptor is declared insolvent	As per Sl. 5	As per Sl. 5	As per Sl. 5	As per Sl. 5
9. For Dishonour of old bill & For Noting Charges	As per Sl. 6 Acceptor	As per Sl. 6 B/R, Cash	As per Sl. 6 B/P, N. Charges	As per Sl. 6 Drawer

Transaction	*Books of Drawer*	*Books of Drawer*	*Books of Drawee*	*Books of Drawee*
	A/c Debited	*A/c Credited*	*A/c Debited*	*A/c Credited*
(*a*) When it was retained till maturity	Acceptor	Bank	B/P, N. Charges	Drawer
(*b*) When it was discounted	Acceptor	Creditor	B/P, N. Charges	Drawer
(*c*)When it was endorsed	Acceptor	BSC, Bank	B/P, N. Charges	Drawer
(*d*) When it was sent for collection	Bank	Acceptor	Drawer	Bank
10. For Partial amount realized from private estate of the insolvent	Bad debts			Contribu-tories

Q.62: For sale of goods on credit, the seller debits

a. Debtors A/c or Customers personal A/c

b. Creditors a/c

c. Sales A/c

d. Cash A/c

Q.63: At the time of drawing, accepting and receipt of the bill, the drawer credits customers a/c and debits

a. Debtor's account

b. Creditor's account

c. Bills Receivable account

d. Cash account

Q.64: When a bill is discharged, the acceptor debits

a. Creditors account

b. Cash account

c. Bills payable account

d. None of the above

Q.65: Drawee has the right to discount the bill

a. True

b. False

(Only the holder or the payee or the drawer can get the bill discounted)

Q.66: At the time of endorsement of a bill, the drawer credits

a. The drawee's account

b. The endorsee's account

c. Bills receivable account

d. None of the above

Q.67: When a bill is endorsed the drawee credits

a. Bills payable account

b. Drawee's account

c. No entry

d. Cash account

Dishonour of bill

Q.68: When on due date drawee of the bill is unable or refuses to make the payment of the bill, the bill is said to be ____________

Ans.: Dishonoured

Q.69: If a bill is dishonoured, when it is presented by the endorsee, the drawer will

a. Debit Endorsee's a/c

b. Debit Acceptor's account

c. Debit Bills Receivable account

d. Debit bank account

Q.70: An officer appointed by the Government to exercise the powers and functions relating to a protesting of negotiating instruments for dishonour is called

a. Protesting officer

b. Magistrate

c. Notary Public

d. Lawyer

Q.71: On dishonour of a bill, the holder in due course presents the bill to a Notary Public to record the facts of dishonour on the bill or on a paper attached to the bill, it is called

a. Dishonour

b. Noting

c. Noting charges

d. Protesting charges

Q.72: When a Bill of exchange or promissory note has been dishonoured for non-acceptance or non-payment, the holder may, within a reasonable period, cause such dishonour to be noted and certified by a notary public, such a certificate is called________

Ans. Protest

Q.73: Amount paid to notary public for recording the fact of dishonour is called_______

Ans. Noting Charges

Q.74: In the noting the evidence of dishonour is secured. This noting is done by recording

a. the fact of dishonour

b. the date of dishonour and the reason for dishonour

c. if the instrument has not been expressly dishonoured, then reasons as to why the holder wants to treat it as dishonoured

d. all of the above

Q.75: When noting charges on a dishonoured bill are paid by the bank , the drawee debits

a. Bank account

b. Noting Charges account

c. Drawer's account

d. Cash account

Renewal of bill

Q.76: When a drawee is unable to meet the bill on due date, and he requests the drawer to accept a part of the bill amount in cash and for the balance to draw on him a fresh bill together with interesr, it is called:

a. Dishonour of the bill

b. Retiring of the bill

c. Renewal of the bill

d. Honouring the bill

Retiring a bill under rebate

Q.77: The rebate on a bill shows that

a. it has been paid before the date of maturity

b. it has been paid after the date of maturity

c. it has been dishonoured

d. it will be paid shortly

Q.78: When a drawee pays the bill before the due date and asks for cash discount for early payment, it is called

a. Honouring the bill before maturity

b. Retiring the bill under rebate

c. Discounting the bill

d. Protesting the bill

Q.79: At the time of retirement of a bill, the acceptor debits

a. Bills payable account

b. Rebate account

c. Drawer's account

d. Bank account

Accomodation bills

Q.80: A bill drawn and accepted for mutual help is called Accommodation Bill.

a. True

b. False

Q.81: The purpose of Accommodation bill is to provide temporary finance.

a. True

b. False

Q.82: An Accommodation bill is ______ immediately after its acceptance.

Ans.: Discounted

Q.83: The Accommodation bill must be supported by R/R

a. True

b. False

(In Accommodation bill there is no sale or purchase of goods. Therefore, there is no Lorry receipt or railway receipt)

Q.84: Days of grace are not allowed in case of Accommodation bill

a. True

b. False

Q.85: An Accommodation bill must have consideration

a. True

b. False

(In Accommodation bill there is no sale or purchase and as such there is no consideration)

Q.86: There must be debtor-creditor relationship between the drawer and the drawee of an Accommodation bill

a. True

b. False

(Drawer of an Accommodation bill is not a creditor, and drawee is not a debtor)

Q.87: Proceeds of Accommodation bill are always shared equally by the drawer and the drawee

a. True

b. False

(Proceeds of Accommodation bill are shared by the parties in agreed ratio)

Q.88: Both the parties must accept an Accommodation bill.

a. True

b. False

(Only the drawee of the bill or bills accept the bill)

Q.89: The drawer has to bear the amount of discount on accommodation bill

a. True

b. False

(Discount in respect of Accommodation bill is shared by the parties in the same proportion in which they share the proceeds.)

Q.90: Accommodation bill is drawn and accepted without any consideration

a. True

b. False

Q91: Accommodation bill may be drawn

a. for the Accommodation of drawer only

b. for the Accommodation of Drawer and Drawee by drawing single bill

c. for the Accommodation of Drawer and Drawee by drawing bills on each other

d. any one of the above methods

Q.92: A Bill Receivable book is a part of

a. the journal

b. the ledger

c. the profit & loss a/c

d. None of the above

ANSWERS					
1. —	2. —	3. —	4. (a)	5. —	6. (a)
7. (b)	8. —	9. (a)	10. —	11. (a)	12. —
13. (b)	14. (d)	15. (b)	16. (b)	17. (b)	18. (a)
19. (b)	20. (b)	21. (b)	22. —	23. (a)	24. (a)
25. (a)	26. (a)	27. (b)	28. (a)	29. (a)	30. —
31. —	32. —	33. —	34. (b)	35. —	36. —
37. —	38. —	39. —	40. —	41. —	42. —
43. —	44. —	45. —	46. —	47. —	48. —
49. (b)	50. (a)	51. (a)	52. (c)&(d)	53. (c)	54. (b)
55. (a)	56. (d)	57. —	58. —	59. (a)	60. (d)
61. (d)	62. (a)	63. (c)	64. (a)	65. (b)	66. (c)
67. (c)	68. —	69. (b)	70. (c)	71. (b)	72. —
73. —	74. (d)	75. (b)	76. (c)	77. (a)	78. (b)
79. (a)	80. (a)	81. (a)	82. —	83. (b)	84. (a)
85. (b)	86. (b)	87. (b)	88. (b)	89. (b)	90. (a)
91. (d)	92. (a)				

CHAPTER

23

CONSIGNMENT ACCOUNTS

Consignment

Q.1: Consignment means:

a. to send

b. to sell

c. to dispatch

d. a packet

Q.2: Consignment accounts relate to accounts dealing with a situation where one firm sends goods to another firm on the basis that the goods will be sold on behalf of and at the risk of the former

a. Right

b. Wrong

Q.3: The party who sends the goods is called ________ or ___________

Ans.: Consignor, Principal

Q.4: The party to whom goods are sent is called ________ or __________

Ans. Consignee, Agent

Q.5: The possession of the goods remains with the ________, but the property in the ownership of the goods remains with the ____________

Ans.: The Consignee or the Agent, Consignor or the Principal

Q.6: Usually the consignee recovers all __________ by him on the consignment.

Ans. Expenses incurred

Q.7: It is usual that the consignee gives an __________ to the consignor in the form of cash, cheque or bill of exchange, which is adjusted against the sale proceeds of the goods.

Ans. Advance

Q.8: Consignment sale refers to an arrangement whereby

a. goods are consigned by ship

b. goods are held in trust by the buyer

c. goods are sent against orders

d. none of the above

Q.9: The relationship between the Consignor and Consignee is that of

a. Principal and Agent

b. Buyer and Seller

c. Debtor and Creditor

d. Barter and Bartee

Q.10: Consignment account is of the nature of

a. Personal account

b. Nominal account

c. Real account

d. None of the above

Q.11: 'Consignee' in a consignment is

a. the owner of the goods

b. agent of the consignor

c. buyer

d. buying agent

Proforma Invoice

Q.12: The consignor does not send an invoice to the consignee. He sends only a __________, a statement that looks like an invoice, but is really not one.

Ans. Proforma Invoice

Q.13: When the goods are sent by the consignor to the consignee, they are accompanied by

a. Proforma invoice

b. Commercial invoice

c. Account sales

d. Bank draft

Account Sales

Q.14: The details of sale under consignment sale is informed by the consignee to the consignor through

a. telegraphic information

b. account sales

c. commercial invoice

d. statement of account

Q.15: Periodically the consignee sends to the consignor a statement called Account sales. It contains:

a. the sales made by the consignee

b. the expenses incurred by the consignee on behalf of the consignor

c. commission earned by the consignee

d. balance due to the consignor

Commission to consignee

Q.16: For his work, the consignee receives a commission, calculated as a percentage of __________

Ans. Gross Sales

Q.17: The remuneration to the consignee is:

a. commission on cash sales

b. commission on credit sales

c. commission on goods sent on consignment

d. commission on total sales made by him under consignment

Del-credere commission

Q.18: For ordinary commission, the consignee is responsible for bad debts

a. Right

b. Wrong

(The agent is not responsible for any bad debts that may arise)

Q.19: If the agent is to be made responsible for debts, he is to be paid a commission called________-

Ans. *Del-credere* commission

Q.20: *Del-credere* commission is payable to the consignee

a. on cash sales only

b. on credit sales only

c. on all sales

d. only if no bad debts occur

Q.21: *Del-credere* commission is allowed to cover

a. Normal loss

b. Abnormal loss

c. Loss due to Bad debts

d. None of the above

Q.22: Where *del-credere* commission is paid:

a. the normal commission is not payable to the consignee

b. the amount of normal commission is reduced by the *del-credere* commission

c. the bad debts, if any occur, are borne by the consignor

d. the bad debts, if any occur, are borne by the consignee

Accounting

Q.23: Firms usually like to ascertain the profit or loss on _______ consignment separately.

Ans. Each

Q.24: To ascertain profit or loss on a particular consignment

(*i*) open the respective consignment account

(*ii*) put down the cost of goods and other expenses incurred or to be incurred on the debit side

(*iii*) enter the sale proceeds as also the cost of goods remaining unsold on the credit side

(*iv*) the difference between the total of two sides will reveal profit or loss.

(*v*) there is profit if the credit side is bigger.

a. Right

b. Wrong

ACCOUNTING ENTRIES OF CONSIGNMENT

Transaction	*Books of Consignor*	*Books of Consignor*	*Books of Consignee*	*Books of Consignee*
	A/c Debited	*A/c Credited*	*A/c Debited*	*A/c Credited*
1. When goods are sent	Consignment A/c	Goods sent on consignment A/c	No entry	No entry
2. Consignor incurs expenses	Consignment A/c	Cash/Bank a/c	No entry	No entry
3. Advance remittance by consignee	Cash/Bank/ BR A/c	Consignee	Consignor	Cash/Bank/ BP A/c
4. Goods returned by the consignee	Goods sent on Cons. A/c	Consignment a/c	No entry	No entry
5. Goods sold by the consignee	Consignee	Consignment a/c	Cash/Cons. Drs.	Consignor
6. Expenses incurred by consignee	Consignment A/c	Consignee	Consignor	Cash/Bank
7. Cash collected by consignee from consignment Debtors	No entry	No entry	Cash/Bank	Cons. Debtors
8. Bad debts from Con. Drs.				
a. No *del-credere* commission	Consignment A/c	Consignee	Consignor	Cons. Debtors
b. *Del-credere* commission allowed	No entry	No entry	Commission	Cons. Debtors
9. Goods are taken by the consignee	Consignee	Consignment a/c	Purchases	Consignor
10. Commission payable to consignee	Consignment A/c	Consignee	Consignor	Commission
11. Remittance from consignee	Cash/Bank/ BR A/c	Consignee	Consignor	Cash/Bank/ BP A/c
12. Stock with the consignee	Cons. Stock A/c	Consignment a/c	No entry	No entry
13. Normal loss of goods	Value of stock adjusted		No entry	No entry
14. Abnormal loss of goods	Abnormal Loss A/c	Consignment a/c	No entry	No entry
a. Amount recoverable from Insurance	Insurance Claim	Abnormal Loss	No entry	No entry
b. Irrecoverable loss	P & L A/c	Abnormal Loss	No entry	No entry
c. Claim is recovered by consignee	Consignee	Abnormal Loss	Cash/Bank	Consignor

Transaction	*Books of Consignor*	*Books of Consignor*	*Books of Consignee*	*Books of Consignee*
	A/c Debited	*A/c Credited*	*A/c Debited*	*A/c Credited*
15. *a.* For Profit on consignment	Consignment a/c	P & L A/c	No entry	No entry
b. For Loss on consignment	P & L A/c	Consignment a/c	No entry	No entry
16. Closing of goods sent on Consignment a/c	Goods sent on consignment A/c	Trading A/c	No entry	No entry

Q.25: When goods sent on consignment are sold by the consignee, the account to be debited in the books of consignor is:

a. Cash account

b. Consignment account

c. Consignee's personal account

d. None of the above

Q.26: When the consignee receives the goods from the consignor

a. Goods are debited to goods received on consignment account

b. No entry is to be passed

c. Credit consignor's personal account

d. None of the above

Consignment Stock

Q.27: The unsold stock is valued at

a. Original cost of the goods

b. Original cost plus non recurring (direct) expenses incurred by both consignor and consignee

c. Original cost plus non recurring (direct) expenses incurred only by the consignor

d. None of the above

Q.28: The principle followed in valuation of closing stock on consignment is

a. To include the expenses by the consignor only

b. Cost to the consignor plus proportionate expenses incurred till the goods reach the premises of the consignee

c. Cost plus proportionate non-recurring expenses incurred by the consignor

d. Cost plus proportionate non-recurring expenses incurred by the consignee

Q.29: Following expenses may be included in the value of stock

a. Packing

b. Freight

c. Cartage

d. Insurance in transit

e. Octroi

f. Import duty

Q.30: Expenses incurred after the goods have reached the consignee's godown are not treated as part of the cost of purchases for valuing consignment stock. These may include

a. Godown rent

b. Premises insurance

c. Insurance of stock/godown

d. Delivery charges

Note: If details of expenses are not available for valuing consignment stock- the expenses incurred by the consignor should be treated as part of cost, but those of the consignee should be ignored.

If the expected selling price of consignment stock is lower than the cost, the value put on stock should be expected net selling price only.

Normal loss

Q.31: Loss of stock is said to be normal when

a. It is because of leakage

b. It is unavoidable and natural

c. It is destroyed by fire

d. Both *a* and *b*

Q.32: While valuing the stock, the ________ loss is spread over the entire consignment

Ans. Normal

Q.33: If there is normal loss, the total cost plus expenses should be divided by the quantity available after the normal loss to ascertain the cost per unit for the purpose of valuing the stock

a. Right

b. Wrong

Abnormal loss

Q.34: A loss arising due to pilferage, theft, fire, etc. is

a. Normal

b. Abnormal

c. Total

d. None of the above

Q. 35: If the goods are lost in transit, abnormal loss is valued just like stock on hand.

a. right

b. wrong

(Under this case, consignees non-recurring expenses are not included. Only the proportionate direct expenses till the time the goods were lost in transit shall be included to value the abnormal loss)

Q.36: The abnormal loss on consignment is credited to

a. Consignment account

b. Consignees personal account

c. Profit & Loss account

d. No entry required

Q37: Abnormal loss of stock after adjusting the recovery and insurance claim is transferred to

a. Trading Account

b. Profit & Loss Account

c. Capital account

d. Balance sheet

Q38: The goods sent on consignment have been lost, but no insurance had been taken. The abnormal loss account should be closed by transferring to

a. Consignment A/c

b. Loss to the consignee A/c

c. Profit & Loss A/c

d. Trading A/c

Q.39: When there are normal losses and abnormal losses at the same time, the abnormal loss is calculated on

a. The original cost

b. The original cost plus non-recurring (direct) expenses duly reduced by the normal loss

c. The original cost plus non-recurring (direct) expenses

d. Market value

Goods sent at higher or invoice price

Q.40: A consignor may prepare the proforma invoice at a higher price, when he wants that

a. the consignee should have no knowledge of the cost of goods consigned

b. to keep the consignee in dark about the actual amount of profit earned.

c. (a) & (b) both

d. none of the above

Q.41: The excess amount, over the cost price is called _______

Ans. Loading

Q.42: When the goods under consignment are sent at invoice price:

a. the consignee will get higher commission

b. the goods will be invoiced at less than cost price

c. the goods will be sold only at the invoice price

d. the goods will be invoiced at the price higher than the cost price

Q.43: Where goods are sent under invoice price in a consignemt

a. the profit will be lower than that under goods sent on cost basis

b. the profit will be same as if sent on cost price

c. a profit or loss reconciliation statement will be prepared

d. stock reserve or stock suspense account is created to keep some stock in reserve

ACCOUNTING ENTRIES IN THE BOOKS OF THE CONSIGNOR WHEN GOODS ARE CONSIGNED AT INVOICE PRICE

Transaction	*Books of Consignor A/c Debited*	*Books of Consignor A/c Credited*
Consignment Stock at the beginning		
a. Consignment stock at invoice price	Consignment a/c	Consignment Stock a/c
b. To remove loading from opening stock	Cons. Stock Revenue A/c	Consignment a/c
Goods sent on consignment		
a. For goods sent at invoice price	Consignment a/c	Goods sent on consignment
b. For unloading the price factor	Goods sent on consignment	Consignment a/c

Transaction	*Books of Consignor A/c Debited*	*Books of Consignor A/c Credited*
Goods returned by the consignee		
a. Goods returned at invoice price	Goods sent on consignment	Consignment a/c
b. Unloading the effect	Consignment a/c	Goods sent on consignment
Consignment Stock at the end		
a. Consignment stock at invoice price	Consignment Stock a/c	Consignment a/c
b. For adjusting loading from closing stock	Consignment a/c	Cons. Stock Revenue A/c

Q.44: If the goods are lost in consignees' godown, abnormal loss is valued just like stock on hand.

a. right

b. wrong

ANSWERS					
1. (a)	2. (a)	3. —	4. —	5. —	6. —
7. —	8. (d)	9. (a)	10. (a)	11. (b)	12. —
13. (a)	14. (b)	15. —	16. —	17. (d)	18. (b)
19. —	20. (c)	21. (c)	22. (d)	23. —	24. (a)
25. (c)	26. (b)	27. (b)	28. (b)	29. —	30. —
31. (d)	32. —	33. (a)	34. (b)	35. (b)	36. (c)
37. (b)	38. (c)	39. (b)	40. (c)	41. —	42. (d)
43. (b)	44. (a)				

CHAPTER

24

JOINT VENTURE ACCOUNTS

Meaning

Q.1: A Joint venture is

a. a very short duration business

b. entered into by two or more persons jointly

c. to share profits or losses according to mutual agreement

d. all of the above

Q.2: In Joint Venture, the association of persons is of a

a. Permanent nature

b. Temporary nature

Q.3: Joint venture account is of the nature of

a. Nominal account

b. Personal account

c. Real account

d. Intangible account

Q.4: A debit balance in Joint Venture A/c indicates

a. Profit on Joint Venture

b. Loss on Joint venture

c. Amount receivable

d. Amount payable

Q.5: The persons entering into joint venture are called

a. Partners

b. Shareholders

c. Co-venturers

d. Owners

Q.6: The co-venturers

a. Enter into a contract with each other

b. Agree to contribute capital required to do the business

c. Agree to share profit or loss arising out of business

d. All of the above

Q.7: The co-venturers always share the profit equally

a. Right

b. Wrong

(Profits are to be shared in their agreed ratio. However, if there is no agreement between them on this issue, then profits and losses are shared equally by the co-venturers)

Q.8: They are required to share the expenses, incurred on the joint venture

a. Right

b. Wrong

Q.9: The Joint venture comes to an end as soon as the particular venture is over

a. Right

b. Wrong

Features

Q.10: The features of Joint venture agreement are:

a. It is an agreement between two or more persons

b. To carry on specific job

c. The agreement goes over as soon as the specific job is completed

d. All of the above

Joint Venture & Partnership

Q.11: Joint Venture is a restricted partnership

a. Right

b. Wrong

Q.12: Joint Venture may also be called as a

a. Temporary partnership

b. Restricted partnership

c. Permanent partnership

d. Sleeping partnership

Q.13: Liability of co-venturers is unlimited

a. True

b. False

(Partners have joint or several unlimited liability, while in Joint Venture it depends on the mode of contract)

Q.14: A Joint Venture differs from a partnership in the following respect

a. In a Joint Venture all the venturers contribute capital

b. A Joint Venture is for a specific task or venture

c. A Joint Venture is for a temporary period

d. Both (b) and (c) above

Q.15: Segregate the following features into Group A (Partnership) and Group B (Joint Venture)

a. Firm has a specific name.

b. Does not possess any common name

c. Continuing business

d. Temporary business

e. Co-venturers

f. Partners

g. Joint & several liability

h. Liability is based on the mode of contract

i. Only one separate account is maintained

j. Separate set of books are maintained

k. Accrual basis of accounting is followed

l. Cash basis of accounting is usually followed

m. Accounts are finalized at the end of the year

n. Accounts are finalized on completion of specific job

Ans:

Group A-Partnership	*Group B-Joint Venture*
a. Firm has a specific name	*b.* Does not possess any common name
c. Continuing business	*d.* Temporary business
f. Partners	*e.* Co-venturers

Group A-Partnership	*Group B-Joint Venture*
g. Joint & several liability	*h.* Liability is based on the mode of contract
j. Separate set of books are maintained	*i.* Only one separate account is maintained
k. Accrual basis of accounting is followed	*l.* Cash basis of accounting is usually followed
m. Accounts are finalized at the end of the year	*n.* Accounts are finalized on completion of specific job

Joint venture & Consignment

Q.16: The relationship between the co-venturers is that of Principal and an agent

a. True

b. False

(Co-venturers contribute capital, share profit or losses, they take part in the management. The agent gets commission for his work, and the principal or agent cannot take part in each other's business.)

Q.17: Segregate the following features into Group A (Consignment) and Group B (Joint Venture)

a. Capital and profits are shared in agreed ratio

b. (*i*) No contribution of capital

(*ii*) Not entitled to profit or loss

(*iii*) Only gets commission

c. Each one can take part in management

d. No one can take part in other's business

e. Governed by Partnership Act

f. Governed by law relating to agency

g. Relationship of Temporary partnership

h. Relationship of Principal and agent

Ans:

Group A-Consignment	*Group B-Joint Venture*
a. Capital and profits are shared in agreed ratio	*b.* (*i*) No contribution of capital (*ii*) Not entitled to profit or loss (*iii*) Only gets commission
c. Each one can take part in management	*d.* No one can take part in other's business
e. Governed by Partnership Act	*f.* Governed by law relating to agency
g. Relationship of Temporary partnership	*h.* Relationship of Principal and agent

Different methods of Joint Venture

Q.18: The different ways of maintaining the accounts of a joint venture are

i. All accounts to be kept by one of the co-venturer

ii. All accounts to be kept by all the co-venturers

iii. Accounts to be kept separately by opening a Joint Bank Account

iv. Each co-venturer recording only his own transactions by opening of joint venture Investment Account and to prepare Momorandum Joint Venture A/c

a. Right

b. Wrong

Accounting Treatment

I. When accounts are kept by one of the co-venturers

Transaction	*Books of Co-venturer*	*Books of Co-venturer*
	A/c Debited	*A/c Credited*
1. Amount received from other co-venturers	Cash/bank	Co-venturers
2. Purchase of goods for cash/incurring expenses	Joint Venture	Cash/Bank
3. Purchase of goods for credit	Joint Venture	Suppliers/Creditors
4. Supplying goods from his own stock	Joint Venture	Purchases
5. Goods supplied by the co-venturers	Joint Venture	Co-venturers
6. For cash sales of goods	Cash/Bank	Joint Venture
7. For goods sold on credit	J/V Customers/ Debtors	Joint Venture
8. For commission earned by him	Joint Venture	Commission
9. For commission earned by other co-venturers	Joint Venture	Co-venturers
10. For stock taken over by him	Purchases	Joint Venture
11. For stock taken over by co-venturers	Co-venturers	Joint Venture
12. For profit on Joint Venture	Joint Venture	P & L A/c (for his share) Co-venturers (others share)
13. On completion, final remittance to co-venturers	Co-venturers	Cash/Bank

(Under this method, one of the co-venturers is entrusted the whole job of maintaining accounts. Other co-venturers contribute their share of capital. The person so appointed is given commission for his work. He prepares a Joint venture

account and ascertains the profit or loss of the venture. The other co-venturers are paid the amount contributed by them adjusted for their share of profit or loss.)

Q.19: For profit on Joint Venture, Joint Venture account is debited. For his own share the co-venturer recording the transactions credits his P & L A/c, but for the share of other co-venturers, he credits their personal account with him

a. Right

b. Wrong

Q.20: When expenses are incurred or goods are purchased for the Joint Venture, the account to be debited is

a. Purchases account

b. Joint Venture account

c. Venturers' Capital account

d. Bank account

Q.21: When the venturer recording transactions brings goods into Joint Venture, then these are credited to

a. Joint Venture account

b. Purchases account

c. Neither of the two

d. Either of the two

II. When all accounts are kept by all the co-venturers

Transaction	*Books of Co-venturer A/c Debited*	*Books of Co-venturer A/c Credited*
1. Amount received from other co-venturers	Cash/Bank	Co-venturers
2. Purchase of goods for cash/incurring expenses	Joint Venture	Cash/Bank
3. Purchase of goods for credit	Joint Venture	Suppliers/Creditors
4. Supplying goods from his own stock	Joint Venture	Sales
5. Goods supplied by the co-venturers	Joint Venture	Co-venturers
6. For cash sales of goods	Cash/Bank	Joint Venture
7. For goods sold on credit	J/V Customers/ Debtors	Joint Venture
8. For commission earned by him	Joint Venture	Commission
9. For commission earned by other co-venturers	Joint Venture	Co-venturers
10. For stock taken over by him	Purchases	Joint Venture
11. For stock taken over by co-venturers	Co-venturers	Joint Venture

Transaction	*Books of Co-venturer A/c Debited*	*Books of Co-venturer A/c Credited*
12. For profit on Joint Venture	Joint Venture	P & L A/c (for his share) Co-venturers (others share)
13. For final settlement with co-venturers		
a. for remitting the amount due to co-venturers	Co-venturers	Cash/Bank
b. for receiving the amount due from co-venturers	Cash/Bank	Co-venturers

(All the co-venturers keep the accounts relating to the Joint Venture. Each of them opens the accounts of other co-venturers and Joint Venture account. At the end of the venture, accounts are reconciled by them and settled.)

Q.22: When the record of transactions relating to Joint Venture is made in the books of one party, then the Co-venturer recording the transactions records his share of investment by

a. Debiting cash account

b. Crediting his personal account

c. No entry is made

d. Debiting bank account

III. When accounts are kept separately by opening a Joint Bank Account

Transaction	*Separate books of Joint-venture A/c Debited*	*Separate books of Joint-venture A/c Credited*
1. For the amount contributed by the co-venturers	Joint Bank A/c	Co-venturers
2. *a.* For purchase of goods on cash/incurring expenses	Joint Venture	Joint Bank A/c
b. For Purchase or expenses by co-venturers	Joint Venture	Co-venturers
3. For purchase of goods on credit	Joint Venture	Supplier's A/c
4. For cash sale	Joint Bank A/c	Joint Venture
5. For credit sales	Customer's	Joint Venture
6. For stock taken over by the co-venturers	Co-venturers	Joint Venture
7. *a.* If there is profit on Joint Venture	Joint Venture	Co-venturers (Profit sharing)
b. If there is loss on Joint Venture	Co-venturers (Profit sharing)	Joint Venture
8. For settlement of the accounts of co-venturers	Co-venturers	Joint Bank A/c

(Joint Bank A/c, Joint Venture A/c and individual co-venturers accounts are maintained separately. Each co-venturer contributes and it is deposited into Joint Bank A/c. Expenses of the joint venture are met from Joint Bank A/c as well as by co-venturers from their personal resources. After the venture is complete, profit or loss is calculated from the Joint Venture A/c, which is transferred to co-venturers a/c and final settlement is made, which automatically closes Joint Bank A/c.)

Q.23: When co-venturers decide to maintain a separate set of accounts, they open a

a. Fixed deposit A/c in the bank
b. Current account in the name of one of the co-venturers
c. Joint Bank a/c
d. Bank A/c payable to either or survivor

Q.24: When separate set of books are kept for keeping the accounts of Joint Venture, then

a. Memorandum Joint Venture Account is prepared
b. Transactions take the form of ordinary accounting system
c. Only Joint Venture and Personal accounts of the co-venturers are maintained
d. Joint Venture, Co-venturers and Joint Bank accounts are opened

IV. When each co-venturer keeps a record of his transactions separately and profit is calculated by preparing Memorandum Joint Venture A/c

Transaction	*Books of Joint-venture*	*Books of Joint-venture*
	A/c Debited	*A/c Credited*
1. For goods purchased by him	Joint Venture with B Investment A/c	Cash/Bank/Suppliers'
2. For expenses incurred by him	Joint Venture with B Investment A/c	Cash/Bank
3. For goods sold by him	Cash/Bank/Customers	Joint Venture with B Investment A/c
Profit is arrived at by preparing	**Memorandum Joint Venture A/c**	
4. *a.* for his share of profit	Joint Venture with B Investment A/c	P & L A/c
b. for his share of loss	P & L A/c	Joint Venture with B Investment A/c
5. For settlement with co-venturers		
a. Amount payable	Joint Venture with B Investment A/c	B (Other co-venturer)
b. Amount receivable	B (Other co-venturer)	Joint Venture with B Investment A/c

(Each co-venturer opens a Joint Venture Investment Account and keeps a record of all the transactions relating to him in this account. Costs and expenses incurred by himself (not the other party), goods purchased by him on account of Joint Venture are debited to this a/c. This account is credited by sale proceeds received by him on account of joint venture. On completion of Joint Venture, a Memorandum Joint Venture A/c is made in which the amount paid and received by each of the co-venturer are included. This account shows the collective result of income/expenditure relating to Joint Venture. The balance of this account represents the amount of profit or loss on the Joint Venture. After ascertaining the profit or loss, each of the co-venturer records his share in the Joint Venture Investment A/c maintained by him.

Note: All the co-venturers prepare Memorandum Joint Venture A/c with them separately after receiving details from other co-venturers. This account does not form part of the double entry system. It is a nominal account disclosing profit or loss on entire Joint Venture.

Joint Venture Investment A/c is treated as a personal account, indicating the amount

Q.25: In Joint Venture, Profit or loss is ascertained by putting down all costs and expenses on one side and all proceeds and income on the other in a separate account called

a. Memorandum Joint Venture A/c

b. Profit & Loss A/c

c. Income & expenditure A/c

d. Revenue and expenses A/c

Q.26: There will be profit on Joint Venture, if the _____ side is bigger and loss if ______ side is bigger.

Ans. Credit, Debit

Q.27: Match the pairs

Group A	*Group B*	*Answer*
a. Joint Venture	*i.* Personal	a & ii
b. Co-venturers a/c	*ii.* Nominal	b & i
c. Goods supplied on Joint Venture	*iii.* Real	c & iii
d. Joint bank a/c	*iv.* Joint Venture	d & viii
e. Credit balance in Joint Venture A/c	*v.* Profit on Joint Venture	e & v
f. Separate set of books	*vi.* Joint Bank A/c	f & vi
g. Unsold stock taken by co-venturers	*vii.* Credit Joint Venture	g & vii
h. Particular partnership	*viii.* Personal	h & iv

ANSWERS					
1. (d)	2. (b)	3. (a)	4. (b)	5. (c)	6. (d)
7. (b)	8. (a)	9. (a)	10. (d)	11. (a)	12. (a)or(b)
13. (b)	14. (d)	15. —	16. (b)	17. —	18. (a)
19. (a)	20. (b)	21. (b)	22. (c)	23. (c)	24. (d)
25. (a)	26. —	27. (c)			

CHAPTER

25

ACCOUNTS OF LEASING COMPANIES

Meaning

Q.1: Leasing is a contract

a. Between two parties known as lessor and lessee,

b. Whereby the owner of the Asset (Lessor) transfers his right to use to some other party (Lessee)

c. On payment of a rent periodically

d. All of the above

Q.2: The owner of an Asset under a lease agreement is called

a. Landlord

b. Tenant

c. Lessor

d. Lessee

Q.3: The user of the Asset under a lease agreement is called

a. Landlord

b. Tenant

c. Lessor

d. Lessee

Q.4: In a lease agreement there are

a. Two Parties

b. Three Parties

c. Four Parties

d. Any number of parties

Q.5: In a lease agreement the ownership of the Asset remains with the

a. Lessor

b. Lessee

Q.6: Leasing agreement is usually for a specific period

a. Right

b. Wrong

(Normally this agreement is for 5 years)

Q.7: On the expiry of a lease agreement, it can be:

a. Renewed

b. Terminated

c. Asset may be purchased by the lessee

d. Any of the above depending upon the terms of the contract

Advantages to Lessor

Q.8: Manufacturers of high cost capital goods may find it difficult to expand their sales if they insist in selling their products on outright ownership basis

a. True

b. False

Q.9: Manufacturers of Plant & Machinery with high prices find it easy to expand their sales if they sell their products on

a. Out-right ownership basis

b. Hire-purchase basis

c. Instalments basis

d. None of the above

Q.10: For the growth of capital goods industry, the manufacturers of such goods have benefited immensely by adopting

a. Leasing arrangements

b. Selling the goods on consignments

c. Selling the capital goods by hire-purchase methods

d. Offering Monthly equated instalments

Q.11: If a manufacturer of capital goods sells them

i. He is getting huge profits in one go

ii. He has to pay very high taxes under higher slabs of income tax

a. True

b. False

Q.12: Manufacturer or dealer of high cost capital goods

a. can save income tax, if he lease the assets instead of selling them, because the lease rent is received over a specific period and profits are distributed over a longer period, which may help him in reducing his overall tax liability. He may be assessed under a lower slab also.

b. cannot save his tax liability. He will have to pay the same amount of income tax, whether he sells the product or lease it out.

c. neither *a* nor *b* is true

d. either *a* or *b* can be true

Q.13: Leasing is beneficial to lessor as it helps him in

a. Expanding his business

b. Tax planning

c. Reduction in capital investment

d. (a) & (b) above

Advantages to Lessee

Q.14: Entrepreneurs with less financial capacity with a vision to start ventures requiring huge capital investment may

a. Borrow the funds on interest from banks and purchase such assets

b. Purchase such assets on hire purchase/instalments

c. Take the assets on lease and save huge interest burden on funds

d. Do all the above

Q.15: With the fast developing technology, there is always a risk of obsolescence of an asset in a short period of time. An entrepreneur can eliminate this risk

a. By taking an insurance policy against the risk

b. To take an asset on lease

c. Both *a* and *b*

d. Neither *a* nor *b*

(Risk is to be borne by the owner. Under the lease agreement, the lessee is not the owner. Therefore, he has not to bear this risk. On expiry of the lease period, he can always have an option to take on lease another asset with advanced technology.)

Q.16: Taking an asset on lease helps a lessee to increase his borrowing capacity because:

i. If he purchases capital goods with borrowed funds, the asset will be shown on Assets and Bank loan on Liabilities side of his Balance Sheet. This will reduce his further borrowing capacity.

ii. If he takes the asset on lease, no loan or asset will be shown in the balance sheet. The entrepreneurs borrowing capacity increases with no past borrowings.

iii. The lessee can borrow more funds from the financial institutions without much difficulty.

a. True

b. False

Q.17: The tax liability of the lessee is reduced because

i. Lease rent paid or payable is treated as a revenue expense

ii. It will reduce the taxable profit of the lessee every year

a. True

b. False

Q.18: Taking an asset on lease is beneficial to lessee as it helps him in

a. Reducing his capital investment as he has to pay only the rent of the asset

b. Eliminates the risk of obsolescence due to technology advancement

c. Increases his borrowing capacity

d. Reduces his tax liability

e. By keeping the capital investment at lower level, he can avoid the application of the provisions of MRTP Act

f. Lesser dependence on financial institutions and banks reduces their interference in the day to day management of the organization.

Disadvantages or Limitations to Lessee

Q.19: Lease rent is quite high because the lessor has to cover

a. Interest on capital investment on the asset or cost of finance on borrowed funds

b. Cost of depreciation

c. Risk factor on account of loss of obsolescence due to change of technology

d. Administrative and legal expenses for entering into a lease deed

Q.20: If the lessor has acquired the leased asset by borrowing funds against the hypothecation of the said asset, any default on the part of the lessor may affect the operations of the lessee

a. Right

b. Wrong

Q.21: Leased assets are not eligible for

a. Capital subsidies for projects in backward areas

b. Moratorium period. (Not attractive for projects with long gestation period)

c. Protection of warranties as available if the asset is purchased

d. Lease rents are payable inspite of loss, destruction or defects in the leased assets

Types of Lease

Capital Lease or Finance Lease

Q.22: Features of a Capital lease are:

i. Most popular type of lease.

ii. By nature it is for a very long term-generally for the entire economic life of the asset

iii. Cost of the asset and interest there on are recovered by the lessor during the primary period of the lease, which is normally 5 years.

iv. Lease deed is non-cancellable during primary period.

v. Risks of under utilization and/or obsolescence are born by lessee.

vi. The total amount of fixed lease rents is much higher than the cost of equipment.

vii. During the secondary period, lease is generally continued on a nominal rent.

a. Right

b. Wrong

Accounting Treatment of Capital Lease

Q.23: When the lessor calculates annual lease rent to be charged from the lessee he recovers

i. Financial income (return on funds blocked in the asset)

ii. Annual lease charges

a. Right

b. Wrong

(Annual lease rent = Finance income for that year + Annual lease charges, or Annual lease charges = Annual lease rent - Finance income for that year)

Q.24: The Total Finance Income = The total annual lease rent for all the years

\+ Residual value of leased asset

— Cost or fair value of the leased asset at the beginning of the term

a. Right

b. Wrong

Q.25: Total Finance Income is allocated over each year of the lease term by

a. Sum of the digits method

b. Straight line method

c. (a) or (b)

d. (a) & (b)

Q.26: The sum of digits method is regarded as a reasonable approximation to the actuarial method

a. Right

b. Wrong

Q.27: The allocation of total finance income is made under the sum of digits method in the same ratio as number of years outstanding bears to the sum of the digits of the years of lease term

a. Right

b. Wrong

Q.28: Allocating total finance income of Rs. 30,000 over the lease period of 4 years by sum of the digits method results in

a. 1st year Rs. 12,000, 2nd year Rs. 9,000, 3rd year Rs. 6,000 and 4th year Rs. 3,000

b. 1st year Rs. 3,000, 2nd year Rs. 6,000, 3rd year Rs. 9,000 and 4th year Rs. 12,000

c. 1st year Rs. 7,500, 2nd year Rs. 7,500, 3rd year Rs. 7,500 and 4th year Rs. 7,500

d. None of the above

(Sum of digits of 1 to 4 years is 1+2+3+4 = 10

1st year 30,000×4/10=12,000; 2nd year 30,000×3/10=9,000; 3rd year 30,000× 2/10 = 6,000; 4th year 30,000×1/10 = 3,000)

Q.29: The total finance income is equally allocated over all the years under

a. Sum of the digits method

b. Straight line method

c. (a) or (b)

d. (a) & (b)

Q.30: Allocating total finance income of Rs. 30,000 over the lease period of 4 years by Straight line method results in

a. 1st year Rs. 12,000, 2nd year Rs. 9,000, 3rd year Rs. 6,000 and 4th year Rs. 3,000

b. 1st year Rs. 3,000, 2nd year Rs. 6,000, 3rd year Rs. 9,000 and 4th year Rs. 12,000

c. 1st year Rs. 7,500, 2nd year Rs. 7,500, 3rd year Rs. 7,500 and 4th year Rs. 7,500

d. None of the above

Note: Once the total finance income is appropriated over each year, then
Annual lease charges = Annual lease rent - Finance income allocated for that year
This is again bifurcated into two elements
Annual lease charge = Statutory Depreciation + Lease Equalisation charges

ACCOUNTING ENTRIES IN THE BOOKS OF LESSOR

Transaction	*Books of Lessor*	*Books of Lessor*
	A/c Debited	*A/c Credited*
1. For the statutory depreciation	Depreciation a/c P & L A/c	Leased Asset A/c Depreciation a/c
2. For Lease equalisation charges: If lease charges		
a. exceed the depreciation amount	Lease Equalisation A/c	Lease Terminal Adjustment
b. are less than the depreciation amount	Lease Terminal Adjustment	Lease Equalisation A/c
Lease Equalisation is deducted or added in the Annual Lease Rent in the credit side of P & L A/c Lease Terminal Adjustment A/c is carried forward and shown in the Balance sheet If credit balance under current liabilities and if debit balance under current assets In the last year of the lease, the credit balance in the Lease Terminal Adjustment is deducted from the WDV of the leased asset		
3. *a.* For payment of Commission to agent and payment of legal fees	Commission A/c Legal fee A/c	Cash/Bank A/c
b. Transferring the expenses to P & L A/c	P & L A/c	Commission A/c Legal fee A/c
4. *a.* For receiving the service charges and management fee	Cash/Bank A/c	Service charges A/c Management Fee A/c
b. Transferring the income to P & L A/c	Service charges A/c Management Fee A/c	P & L A/c

Note: Asset given on lease under Finance or capital lease is to be disclosed as Assets given on Lease under the head Fixed Assets in the Balance Sheet. Depreciation at the statutory rate is allowed on the asset and it is shown at its written down value.

ACCOUNTING ENTRIES IN THE BOOKS OF LESSEE

Transaction	*Books of Lessee A/c Debited*	*Books of Lessee A/c Credited*
1.*a.* For payment of annual lease rent	Lease Rent	Bank A/c
b. Transferring to P & L A/c	P & L A/c	Lease Rent
2.*a.* If lump sum is paid for acquiring the leasehold property	Leasehold property	Bank A/c
b. Amount is written off equally every year over the period of the term	P & L A/c	Leasehold property
3.*a.* If lump sum is paid as prepaid lease rent	Leasehold A/c	Bank A/c
b. For the amount of annual lease rent	Annual lease Rent	Leasehold A/c
c. Transferring to P & L A/c	P & L A/c	Annual lease Rent

Operating Lease

Q.31: Features of an operating lease are:

i. It is normally for a short period-may be from a day to about 3 years

ii. Lease is usually cancelable

iii. Period of lease has no link with the economic life of the asset

iv. This type of lease is very common for Computers, Vehicles, Telephones, etc.

(*a*) Right

(*b*) Wrong

Q.32: A lease which does not secure for the lessor, the recovery of his capital outlay (original cost of the asset leased) plus a return on the funds invested during the lease term is called

a. Capital lease

b. Operational lease

c. Service lease

d. Leveraged lease

ACCOUNTING ENTRIES IN THE BOOKS OF LESSOR

Transaction	*Books of Lessor*	*Books of Lessor*
	A/c Debited	*A/c Credited*
1. *a.* **If the operating lease is for less than a year**	Bank A/c	Lease Rent A/c
b. For transferring to P & L A/c	Lease Rent A/c	P & L A/c
2. *a* **If the operating lease is for more than a year, but the lease rent is fixed**	Bank A/c	Lease Rent A/c
b. For transferring to P & L A/c	Lease Rent A/c	P & L A/c
3. *a.* **If the lease rent is received in advance**	Bank A/c	Advance Lease Rent A/c
b. To account for the current year rent	Advance Lease Rent A/c	Lease Rent A/c
c. Transferring current rent to P & L A/c	Lease Rent A/c	P & L A/c
4. *a.* For incurring expenses to maintain the asset	Expenses	Bank A/c
b. For transferring to P & L A/c	P & L A/c	Expenses
5. *a.* For charging Depreciation on leased asset	Depreciation A/c	Asset (on Lease) A/c
b. For transferring to P & L A/c	P & L A/c	Depreciation A/c
6 **If the total lease rent is receivable in various instalments:**		
a. In the first year of lease, entry with the total lease rent receivable	Lessee's A/c	Lease Rent Suspense A/c
b. To account for the current years lease rent	Lease Rent Suspense A/c	Lease Rent A/c
c. For receiving the lease rent	Bank A/c	Lessee's A/c

Note: The leased asset is treated by the lessor as fixed asset. It is depreciated in the usual manner and is shown at its WDV in the Balance Sheet.

ACCOUNTING ENTRIES IN THE BOOKS OF LESSEE

Transaction	*Books of Lessee*	*Books of Lessee*
	A/c Debited	*A/c Credited*
1. *a* For payment of annual lease rent	Lease Rent	Bank A/c
b. Transferring to P & L A/c	P & L A/c	Lease Rent A/c
2. *a.* For the total lease rent due	Lease rent suspense A/c	Lessors' A/c
b. For the current years lease rent payable	Lease Rent A/c	Lease rent suspense A/c
c. For payment of current years instalment	Lessors' A/c	Bank A/c
d. Transferring to P & L A/c	P & L A/c	Lease Rent A/c

Note: Credit balance in the lessor's account will appear as a liability in the Balance Sheet.

Service Lease

Q.33: Service lease is offered by manufacturers or dealers of capital goods like Machinery, Air-conditioners, Washing machines, etc. to cover

i. Cost of maintenance and servicing the asset
ii. It is for a short period, say 1 year
iv. Lease payment covers the cost of maintenance & service only with or without parts
v. It does not cover the cost of capital outlay

Leveraged Lease

Q.34: In a leveraged lease agreement, there are

a. Two Parties
b. Three Parties
c. Four Parties
d. Any number of parties

(The three parties are the Lessor, the Lessee and the Financier to the lessor)

Q.35: In order to lease assets involving huge capital outlay (in crores of rupees), the leasing companies or lessors take funds from financiers. When a business uses low cost funds as compared to their profits, their aim is to maximize their profits. This is called

a. Using of Financial Leverage
b. Borrowing low cost funds
c. Bridging arrangement
d. Double leasing

Q.36: When the lessor (leasing companies) use borrowed funds to finance their leasing activities, it is called:

a. Factoring
b. Leasing
c. Advancing
d. Leveraged lease

Miscellaneous Problems

Q.37: Leasing is a tool of tax planning

a. Right
b. Wrong

Q. 38: Under a leasing agreement, risk of obsolescence is to be borne by the lessee

a. Right
b. Wrong

(With the fast developing technology, the owner of an asset has to bear the risk of his asset becoming obsolete or outdated. Since lessee is not the owner of the asset, he does not have to bear this risk)

Q.39: Lease rent paid by lessee is not an expense

a. Right

b. Wrong

(Lease rent is an expense for the lessee and income for the lessor, which is transferred to their P & L A/c at the end of the accounting period)

Q.40: Lessor can claim depreciation on leased assets

a. Right

b. Wrong

Q.41: In an Operative Lease, period of lease is much less compared to the economic life of the asset

a. Right

b. Wrong

Q.42: Which of the following items can be covered under Operating lease

a. Machinery

b. Telephone

c. Computer

d. Airconditioner

Q.43: Which of the following items can be covered under Service lease

a. Machinery

b. Telephone

c. Computer

d. Airconditioner

ANSWERS					
1. (d)	2. (c)	3. (d)	4. (a)	5. (a)	6. (a)
7. (d)	8. (a)	9. (d)	10. (a)	11. (a)	12. (a)
13. (d)	14. (c)	15. (b)	16. (a)	17. (a)	18. —
19. —	20. (a)	21. —	22. (a)	23. (a)	24. (a)
25. (c)	26. (a)	27. (a)	28. (a)	29. (b)	30. (c)
31. (a)	32. (b)	33. —	34. (b)	35. (a)	36. (d)
37. (a)	38. (b)	39. (b)	40. (a)	41. (a)	42. (b)&(c)
43. (a)&(d)					

CHAPTER

26

ACCOUNTS OF HIRE PURCHASE/ INSTALMENT - PURCHASE COMPANIES

Hire Purchase - Meaning

Q.1: A buyer purchases the goods but pays the price of the goods not in one but in various instalments under

a. Leasing

b. Hire Purchase

c. Instalments

d. (b) & (c) above

Q.2: Under ________, the buyer takes possession of the goods and enjoys them as if he is the sole owner of the goods, although the price of the goods is not fully paid

a. Leasing

b. Hire Purchase

c. Instalments

d. (b) & (c) above

Q.3: Under the Hire Purchase agreement, the term 'Hirer' means

a. the Hire Purchase Vendor

b. the Hire Purchaser

c. the landlord

d. the tenant

Q.4: Under the Hire Purchase agreement, the seller or the owner is called

a. the Hire Purchase Vendor

b. the buyer

c. the landlord

d. the tenant

Hire Purchase Agreement

Q.5: An hire purchase agreement must be in writing and should contain

i. Description of the goods

ii. Hire purchase price of the goods

iii. Cash price

iv. Date on which agreement commences

v. Interest to be charged

vi. Number of instalments and amount of each instalment

vii. The dates on which the instalments are payable

viii. The place where the instalments are payable

a. Right

b. Wrong

Q.6: The hire purchase price consists of

a. Cash price

b. Interest for delayed payments

c. Risk element of non-payment by hirer

d. Administrative cost

Q.7: Under hire purchase a certain amount is paid immediately at the time of signing the agreement. This amount paid is called

a. Advance payment

b. Cash payment

c. Down payment

d. Instalment payment

Pricing and Interest under Hire Purchase

Q.8: The Interest on hire purchase transaction is charged at the agreed rate, for the entire period during which the instalment is spread.

a. flatly on the cash price - down payment.

b. on the reducing balance after each instalment

c. either *a* or *b*

d. neither *a* nor *b*

Q.9: The effective rate of interest charged under hire purchase is higher than the agreed rate of interest

a. Right

b. Wrong

Q.10: The price of a product under hire purchase is higher than its cash price. The difference is on account of interest.

i. Cash price represents the value of the asset and is a capital expenditure

ii. The interest is a revenue expenditure to be charged to P & L A/c

a. Right

b. Wrong

Q.11: Which one of the statements relating to hire purchase price is wrong

a. Hire purchase price is higher than the cash price

b. The difference between the hire purchase price and cash price is the hire/interest charges

c. Hire purchase price is equal to the down payment plus the sum of all instalments

d. Hire purchase price includes interest on diminishing balance method

Q.12: The cash price of a Scooter is Rs. 25,000. It is offered on hire purchase with the following terms:

Down payment Rs. 5,000, balance in equated 24 instalments with interest at 10%.

The amount of monthly equated instalment (MEI) will be:

a. Rs. 1,250

b. Rs. 1,000

c. Rs. 867

d. Rs. 867 plus interest on amount outstanding

(Cash price Rs. 25,000 - Cash down payment Rs. 5,000= Rs. 20,000 plus interest @ 10% for 2 years Rs. 4,000. Therefore Hire Purchase price is Rs. 29,000 - Cash down payment Rs. 5,000, means a net payment of Rs. 24,000 payable in 24 monthly instalments of Rs. 1,000 each)

Q.13: An air-conditioner whose cash price is Rs. 40,000 is sold under hire purchase, the terms being :

Down Payment Rs. 10,000, balance in 3 annual instalments of Rs. 12,000 each.

In the books of the hirer, interest will be apportioned for three years as:

a. Rs. 2,000 each year

b. Rs. 1,000, Rs. 2,000 and Rs. 3,000 for first, second and third year, respectively

c. Rs. 3,000, Rs. 2,000 and Rs. 1,000 for first, second and third year, respectively

d. Rs. 6,000, Rs. 4,000 and Rs. 2,000 for first, second and third year, respectively

(If the effective rate of interest on hire purchase is not given, the interest is apportioned for the years on the basis of the hire purchase price outstanding at the beginning of each year.

Total payment under Hire Purchase: 10,000 + 12,000 × 3	*Rs. 46,000*
Cash price	*Rs. 40,000*
Interest	*Rs. 6,000*

No. of instalments due at the beginning of first year = 3

No. of instalments due at the beginning of second year = 2

No. of instalments due at the beginning of third year = 1

Interest will be apportioned for the three years in the ratio of 3:2:1.

Interest for the first year is Rs. 6,000 × 3/6=Rs. 3,000

Interest for the second year is Rs. 6,000 × 2/6=Rs. 2,000

Interest for the third year is Rs. 6,000 × 1/6=Rs. 1,000)

Transfer of Ownership

Q.14: Under hire purchase, the ownership of property is transferred to the buyer on:

a. Payment of advance money

b. Signing of purchase agreement

c. Payment of first instalment

d. Payment of last instalment

Q.15: Under the hire purchase, the buyer has a right to dispose of goods in any manner he likes

a. Right

b. Wrong

(The buyer under hire purchase cannot dispose of the goods as ownership has not passed on to him)

Q.16: Loss of goods has to be borne by the buyer under the hire purchase agreement

a. Right

b. Wrong

(Loss of goods has to be borne by the seller provided the buyer has taken reasonable care of the goods)

Default & Repossession

Q.17: If the Hire-purchaser defaults in payments of the instalments, the remedy available to the Vendor is

a. repossess the asset and recover the balance of the cash price from the hire purchaser

b. repossess the asset, treating the instalment received as hire charges

c. repossess the asset and refund the excess amount received to the purchaser

d. sue the purchaser for the amount due

Q.18: Goods repossessed account is opened by:

a. the Vendor to transfer the balance in the defaulted purchaser's a/c

b. the purchaser when the asset is purchased again from the vendor after settling the dues

c. the vendor to transfer the amount already received from the purchaser

d. the purchaser to transfer his dues to the vendor

Q.19: When the hire vendor repossesses the asset due to default, the purchaser should

a. seek court injection

b. claim all the monies paid by him

c. transfer the balance in the vendor's account along with up to date interest in the asset account

d. withdraw depreciation charged on the asset during the previous year

Q.20: A hire vendor repossessed a machine when the balance due to the hirer account was Rs. 30,000. The interest up to date of repossession was Rs. 5,000. Repairs undertaken on machine were Rs. 2,000. The machine is ultimately sold for Rs. 28,000. The vendor should transfer to P & L A/c:

a. Rs. 4,000 as loss

b. Rs. 5,000 as profit

c. Rs. 1,000 as profit

d. Rs. 9,000 as loss

Termination of Contract

Q.21: The hirer has a right to terminate the agreement at any time after giving notice to the hire vendor

a. of 7 days

b. of 10 days

c. of 14 days

d. of 21 days

Depreciation

Q.22: On the machinery acquired under hire purchase, for the first year, the buyer is entitled to

a. Depreciation on the down payment made

b. Depreciation on the total price under hire purchase

c. Depreciation on the cash price

d. No depreciation

Q.23: The depreciation on the asset purchased under hire-purchase is charged on

a. The hire purchase price

b. The cash price

c. The hire purchase price or the cash price whichever is higher

d. None of the above

Accounting Treatment of Hire Purchase

ACCOUNTING ENTRIES IN THE BOOKS OF BUYER (Hirer)

Transaction	*Books of Buyer A/c Debited*	*Books of Buyer A/c Credited*
1. On purchase of the asset-with cash price	Asset	Hire Vendor
2. For making down payment	Hire Vendor	Bank A/c
At the end of every year:		
3. For interest due	Interest A/c	Hire Vendor
4. For payment of instalment	Hire Vendor	Bank A/c
5. For depreciation on the asset	Depreciation A/c	Asset A/c
6. For closing interest & depreciation A/c	Profit & Loss A/c	Depreciation A/c Interest A/c
7. If there is default in payment and the vendor takes back the asset	Hire Vendor A/c Profit & Loss A/c	Asset A/c

ACCOUNTING ENTRIES IN THE BOOKS OF SELLER (Hire-vendor)

Transaction	*Books of Hire vendor*	*Books of Hire vendor*
	A/c Debited	*A/c Credited*
1. On sale of the asset-with cash price	Hire Purchaser A/c	Sales A/c
2. For down payment received	Bank A/c	Hire Purchaser A/c
At the end of every year:		
3. For interest due	Hire Purchaser A/c	Interest A/c
4. For instalment received	Bank A/c	Hire Purchaser A/c
5. For closing interest A/c	Interest A/c	Profit & Loss A/c
6. If there is default in payment and the vendor takes back the asset	Goods repossessed A/c	Hire Purchaser A/c
7. For repairs on goods repossessed	Goods repossessed A/c	Cash A/c
8. For sale of repossessed goods Customer A/c	Cash/Bank/ repossessed A/c	Goods
9. a. If there is profit on this sale	Goods repossessed A/c	P & L A/c
b. If there is loss on this sale	P & L A/c	Goods repossessed A/c

Q.24: Cash paid at the time of Hire Purchase transaction is debited by the purchaser of goods to

a. Asset account

b. Purchases account

c. Hire Vendor account

d. Cash account

Q.25: The amount of Interest under hire purchase transaction is credited by the buyer to

a. Interest account

b. Vendor account

c. Asset account

d. Cash account

Q.26: When the goods are repossessed by the vendor, the balance in the asset account is transferred to

a. Hire vendors' account

b. Goods repossessed account

c. Profit & Loss account

d. None of the above

Q.27: When the buyer debits the assets with total cash price at the signing of the contract, the asset account shows balance

a. Equivalent to total cash price

b. Equivalent to total Hire purchase price

c. Neither of the two

d. Either of the two

Q.28: Sonia pays Rs. 12,000 as instalment towards car purchased on hire purchase by her from Vipul Motors. Instalment comprises Rs. 2,000 interest and Rs. 10,000 principal. To record the transaction, Sonia will pass the accounting entry:

a. Hire Purchase A/c ....Dr. 12,000
    To Car A/c 12,000

b. Interest A/c ....Dr. 2,000
    To Vipul Motors A/c 2,000

c. Vipul Motors A/c ....Dr. 12,000
    To Bank A/c 12,000

d. Both (b) & (c) above

Q.29: Maruti Udyog sells on hire purchase to Ramsingh a passenger van. The cash price of the van is Rs. 3,25,000. The terms of the hire purchase sale make down payment of Rs. 1,00,000, balance in five annual instalments of Rs. 60,000 each. On the date of sale, the accounting entry made by Maruti Udyog is:

a. Ram Singh ....Dr. 4,00,000
    To Sales A/c 4,00,000

b. Ram Singh ....Dr. 3,25,000
    To Sales A/c 3,25,000

c. Bank A/c...................Dr. 1,00,000
    To Ram Singh 1,00,000

d. (b) & (c) above

Instalment Purchase

Q.30: Under instalment purchase system, the property in the asset passes to the buyer

a. When the sale is effected

b. When substantial instalments are paid

c. When the final instalment is paid and the property is conveyed through a separate deed

d. When the final instalment is paid

Q.31: From the time of sale, till the last instalment is paid, the seller remains an unpaid vendor

a. Right

b. Wrong

Q.32: A buyer of a Motor Car under instalment purchase system has defaulted in the payment of the third annual instalment. The recourse to the seller is

a. Repossess the car

b. Sue the buyer for balance due

c. Repossess the car after due notice

d. Approach the recovery agents

(Since the vendor under instalment purchase is not the owner, for default in payment of instalment by the purchaser, he cannot repossess the goods. He can only sue the buyer for non payment)

Q.33: The buyer has an option to terminate the contract and return the goods under instalments purchase

a. Right

b. Wrong

(The buyer has no right to terminate the contract in between, but should make payment under instalments as committed. If he fails, the seller can sue him for breach of contract)

Q.34: Under the instalments purchase, the buyer has a right to dispose of goods in any manner he likes

a. Right

b. Wrong

(The buyer is the sole owner of the goods)

Q.35: Loss of goods has to be borne by the buyer under the instalments agreement

a. Right

b. Wrong

(The buyer is the sole owner of the goods)

Accounting Treatment of Instalment Sale

ACCOUNTING ENTRIES IN THE BOOKS OF BUYER

Transaction	*Books of Buyer*	*Books of Buyer*
	A/c Debited	*A/c Credited*
1. On purchase of the asset	Asset A/c (with cash price) Interest Suspense A/c	Vendor's (with total price)
2. For making down payment	Vendor's	Bank A/c
At the end of every year:		
3. For interest due to vendor	Interest A/c	Interest Suspense A/c
4. For payment of instalment	Vendor's	Bank A/c
5. For depreciation on the asset	Depreciation A/c	Asset A/c
6. For closing interest & depreciation A/c	Profit & Loss A/c	Depreciation A/c Interest A/c

ACCOUNTING ENTRIES IN THE BOOKS OF SELLER

Transaction	*Books of Vendor*	*Books of Vendor*
	A/c Debited	*A/c Credited*
1. On sale of the asset	Purchaser's (total price)	Sales A/c (with cash price) Interest Suspense A/c
2. For down payment received	Bank A/c	Purchaser's A/c
At the end of every year:		
3. For interest due	Interest Suspense A/c	Interest A/c
4. For instalment received	Bank A/c	Purchaser's A/c
5. For closing interest A/c	Interest A/c	Profit & Loss A/c

Q.36: A machinery with a cash price of Rs. 3,00,000 is acquired under instalment purchase, Rs. 1,00,000 paid as advance and the balance payable in 3 annual instalments of Rs. 80,000 each. The entries to be made in the books of the seller on sale are:

a. Purchaser's A/c ....Dr. 3,40,000
    To Sales A/c 3,40,000

b. Purchasers's A/c.......................Dr. 3,40,000
    To Sales A/c 3,00,000
    To Interest Suspense A/c 40,000

c. Bank A/c..............................Dr. 1,00,000
    To Purchaser's A/c 1,00,000

d. Both (b) & (c) above

Q.37: Under the Instalment Purchase system, the balance in the interest suspense account, in the books of the buyer, is shown on the

a. Debit side of Profit & Loss account

b. Liabilities side of the Balance Sheet

c. Assets side of the Balance sheet

d. Credit side of profit & loss account

ANSWERS

1. (d)	2. (d)	3. (b)	4. (a)	5. (a)	6. —
7. (c)	8. (a)	9. (a)	10. (a)	11. (d)	12. (b)
13. (c)	14. (d)	15. (b)	16. (b)	17. (b)	18. (a)
19. (c)	20. (d)	21. (c)	22. (c)	23. (b)	24. (c)
25. (b)	26. (a)	27. (a)	28. (d)	29. (d)	30. (a)
31. (a)	32. (b)	33. (b)	34. (a)	35. (a)	36. (d)
37. (b)					

CHAPTER

27

ACCOUNTS OF NON-TRADING CONCERNS

Meaning of Non-Trading Organisations:

Q.1: Which of the following are engaged in rendering services and their aim is not to make profit:

a. Educational Institutions

b. Sports club

c. Public Hospitals

d. All of the above

Q.2: Organizations not engaged in Trading activities are called __________

Ans. Non-trading organizations

Q.3: For rendering services to the public, these organizations collect moneys by way of

i. Membership and Entrance Fee

ii. Tuition Fee

iii. Subscriptions

iv. Donations

v. Legacies

vi. Grants

a. Right

b. Wrong

Need for maintaining Accounts

Q.4: It is necessary to maintain books of account by Non-trading organizations, to enable them

a. to know the result of their activities at the year end
b. to know whether their income during the year was enough to meet their expenses
c. to have proper control over the collections made
d. to reduce the possibility of misappropriation of funds
e. to submit their accounts to Government agencies, municipal authorities, public trusts, etc.
f. to get grants from the Government authorities on the basis of their accounts
g. to fulfil the requirements of specific Acts, which require the submission of accounts by them in a particular form

Q.5: To record their day-to-day transactions, they maintain the following books of account:

a. Cash Book
b. General ledger
c. Journal
d. Membership & Subscriptions Register
e. Donations Register
f. Assets & Properties Register
g. Other registers as per their specific requirements

Q.6: The following financial statement is not prepared by a non-trading concern

a. Receipt and Payment account
b. Income & Expenditure Account
c. Profit & Loss Account
d. Balance Sheet

(Receipts & Payments Account, Income & Expenditure Account and Balance Sheet are prepared by the non-trading organizations as their final accounts)

Receipts & Payments Account

Q.7: The Receipt and Payment account

a. Shows date-wise details of cash receipts and cash payments
b. Shows the summary of cash receipts and cash payments for the period

c. Is prepared on accrual basis

d. Is just like the Profit & Loss account of a non-trading concern

Q.8: Receipts & Payments account prepared by a non-trading concern

a. provides summary of the cash transactions of the concern

b. is equivalent to Trading a/c prepared by a trading concern

c. is outside the double entry system

d. is prepared on accrual basis

Q.9: Receipts and Payments account is

a. Real account

b. Personal account

c. Nominal account

d. Intangible account

Q.10: The receipts and payments account records receipts and payments of

a. Capital nature only

b. Revenue nature only

c. Both capital and revenue nature

d. Either *a* or *b*

Q.11: Receipts in Receipts & Payments account means

a. Income

b. Expense

c. Asset

d. Liability

Q.12: Payment in Receipts & Payments account means

a. Income

b. Expense

c. Asset

d. Liability

Income & Expenditure Account

Q.13: Income & Expenditure account is prepared on the basis of

a. Mercantile system of accounting

b. Cash system of accounting

c. Hybrid system of accounting

d. None of the above

Q.14: The Income & Expenditure account begins with

a. Debit balance

b. Credit balance

c. No balance

d. Either *a* or *b*

Q.15: The debit balance in the Income & Expenditure account indicates

a. the excess of income over expenditure

b. the excess of expenditure over income

c. the excess of cash receipts over cash payments

d. none of the above

Q.16: If the income earned by non-trading concern in a year exceeds its expenses, the excess is:

a. known as surplus, being excess of income over expenditure

b. divided among members in equal ratio

c. divided among members in proportion of their voting rights

d. transferred to the State Government

Q.17: Subscriptions for the current year received during the current year are to be

a. Credited to Receipts and Payments account

b. Debited to Income and Expenditure account

c. Credited to Income and Expenditure account

d. None of the above

Q.18: The debit balance in the Income & expenditure account indicates

a. The excess of Income over expenditure

b. The excess of Expenditure over Income

c. The excess of Cash receipts over cash payments

d. None of the above

Balance Sheet

Q.19: Subscriptions received in advance by a club are shown

a. On the credit side of Income & Expenditure Account

b. On the Assets side of the Balance Sheet

c. On the liabilities side of the Balance Sheet

d. None of the above

Q.20: Specific donations appearing on the receipts side of the Receipts and Payments account are to be carried to

a. Income & Expenditure account as income
b. Assets side of the Balance Sheet
c. Liabilities side of the Balance Sheet
d. None of the above

Q.21: Expenses of a club, in respect of which there appears a Fund, will be shown by way of

a. Deductions from the respective fund on the liabilities side of the Balance Sheet
b. Expenditure on the debit side of Profit & Loss account
c. Expenditure on the debit side of Income & Expenditure account
d. None of the above

Opening Balance Sheet

Q.22: The difference between assets side and liabilities side of the opening balance sheet represents

a. Excess of income over expenditure
b. Cash & Bank balance
c. Capital fund
d. None of the above

Q.23: Opening balances of capital fund, special funds and assets are transferred to

a. Income & expenditure account of the current year
b. Receipts & Payments account of the current year
c. The closing balance sheet except cash & bank balance, outstanding/prepaid expenses/incomes.
d. None of the above

Q.24: Outstanding incomes appearing in the opening balance sheet are compared with the actual receipts as per Receipts & payments a/c. If the opening balance is more than the actual receipts, the difference means:

a. Income for the previous year is still outstanding and is shown in the closing balance sheet as an asset
b. Income for the previous year is totally adjusted.
c. The difference is shown as a liability in the closing balance sheet
d. None of the above

Closing Balance Sheet

Q.25: For the preparation of the closing balance sheet, steps taken are

i. Transfer the opening balances of assets and liabilities from the opening balance sheet in the details column.

ii. Adjust the current year transactions to the respective of assets and liabilities

iii. Take down the closing balances in the outer column.

iv. Add the surplus or deduct the deficit from the opening capital fund as arrived at from the balance of Income & expenditure account

a. True

b. False

Accounting Treatment

Q.26: Steps to be taken for preparing final accounts from Receipts & Payments account are :

1. Transfer opening cash & bank balances to the opening balance sheet
   a. If the balance is shown on receipts side, it will appear as asset.
   b. If the balance is shown on payments side, it means overdraft and will appear as liability.
2. Transfer all revenue receipts pertaining to the current year on the income side of income & expenditure Account
   a. Deduct previous year receipts and future collections from the actual receipts.
   b. Add any amount receivable for the current period in the actual receipts.
   c. Any amount received in respect of previous year be shown in the opening balance sheet as income outstanding on the assets side
   d. Any amount received in respect of the next year be shown in the closing balance sheet as income received in advance on the liabilities side
3. Transfer all capital receipts to the closing Balance Sheet
   a. Receipts for specific purpose on the liabilities side as specific fund for that purpose
   b. Receipts on account of sale of fixed assets should be divided into two parts:
      (*i*) Reduce their book value from the concerned asset
      (*ii*) Profit or loss on sale in Income & expenditure A/c

4. Transfer all revenue payments pertaining to the current year on the expenditure side of Income & expenditure Account
   a. Deduct previous year payments and future payments from the actual payments.
   b. Add any amount payable for the current period in the actual payments.
   c. Any amount paid in respect of previous year be shown in the opening balance sheet as expense outstanding on the liabilities side
   d. Any amount paid in respect of the next year be shown in the closing balance sheet as expenses paid in advance on the assets side.
5. Transfer all capital payments to the assets side of closing Balance Sheet
6. Closing cash and bank balances on payment side will appear on the assets side of the closing balance sheet.
   a. True
   b. False

Q.27: While preparing final accounts of non-trading concern, all revenue receipts and expenditures are recorded in

a. Receipts & Payments A/c
b. Revenues & Expenses A/c
c. Profit & Loss A/c
d. Income & expenditure A/c

Q.28: In case of non-trading concerns
Outstanding incomes shall be

a. added to the respective income account and shown in the balance sheet on the assets side as Income receivable a/c
b. deducted from the respective income account and shown in the balance sheet on the liabilities side as Income outstanding a/c
c. either *a* or *b*
d. neither *a* nor *b*

Q.29: Incomes received in advance shall be:

a. added to the respective income account and shown in the balance sheet on the assets side as Income prepaid a/c
b. deducted from the concerned income item and shown in the balance sheet on the liabilities side as Income received in advance a/c
c. either *a* or *b*
d. neither *a* nor *b*

Q.30: Outstanding expenses shall be

a. added to the respective expense account and shown in the balance sheet on the liabilities side as outstanding expenses A/c

b. deducted from the respective expense account and shown in the balance sheet on the assets side as Expenses due but not paid a/c

c. either *a* or *b*

d. neither *a* nor *b*

Q.31: Prepaid expenses shall be:

a. added to the respective expense account and shown in the balance sheet on the liabilities side as Expenses prepaid a/c

b. deducted from the concerned expense item and shown in the balance sheet on the asset side as Prepaid Expenses a/c

c. either *a* or *b*

d. neither *a* nor *b*

Q.32: Depreciation on Assets shall be:

a. shown on the debit side of Income & expenditure A/c and the value of the respective asset shall be reduced to that extent.

b. shown on the credit side of Income & expenditure A/c and the value of the respective asset shall be reduced to that extent.

c. either *a* or *b*

d. neither *a* nor *b*

Q.33: Which of the following items should not be entered in the receipts and payments account of a club

a. Subscriptions received

b. Sale of Machinery

c. Loss on sale of old furniture

d. None of the above

Q.34: In the case of non-trading concerns, the following item is normally treated as capital receipt and is shown on the liabilities side in the closing balance sheet:

a. Entrance fee

b. Donations for general purpose

c. Life Membership fee

d. Receipts from sale of sports material

Q.35: In the case of non-trading concerns, the following item is normally treated as revenue receipt and is shown on the credit side Income & Expenditure A/c

a. Subscriptions by members

b. Donations for specific purpose

c. Legacies

d. Sale of fixed assets

Q.36: The debit side of Receipts & Payments account shows subscription at Rs. 6,000 while the credit side of Income and expenditure account shows subscriptions at Rs. 7,500. It implies:

a. Subscriptions outstanding at the end of the year Rs. 1,500

b. Subscriptions received in advance as at the end of the period Rs. 1,500

c. Subscriptions received in advance during the last year Rs. 1,500

d. Subscriptions due as at the end of the last year Rs. 1,500

Q.37: Subscriptions received at the beginning and end of the year are Rs. 2,000 and Rs. 3,000 respectively. Income and expenditure accounts show subscriptions at Rs. 20,000. The amount shown in the Receipts & Payments account under subscription account

a. Rs. 19,000

b. Rs. 23,000

c. Rs. 22,000

d. Rs. 21,000

(Income for the current year as per Income & Expenditure A/c	*Rs. 20,000*
Add: Amount received in advance for next year	*Rs. 3,000*
Total	*Rs. 23,000*
Less: Amount received in the previous year for the current year	*Rs. 2,000*
Actual amount received in the current year	*Rs. 21,000)*

Q.38: A club has 1000 members each paying membership fee of Rs. 100. During the year 850 members have paid their subscription. 50 members have paid the current year subscription during the previous year. 100 members have paid their subscription in advance. The Income and expenditure account will show subscription as

a. Rs. 8500

b. Rs. 9000

c. Rs. 10,000

d. Rs. 11,000

Q.39: Receipts and payments account shows receipts on account of subscription as Rs. 2,000. Further information says that subscriptions outstanding for the current year are Rs. 500 and subscriptions received in advance are Rs. 200. The amount to be shown in the Income & Expenditure account will be

a. Rs. 2,000

b. Rs. 2300

c. Rs. 2500

d. Rs. 2100

Q.40: What amount will be debited in the income & expenditure account during the year 2005 from the following particulars:

i.	Amount paid for stationery as per receipts & payments A/c	Rs. 10,800
ii.	Stock of stationery on 1st Jan. 2005	Rs. 3,000
iii.	Stock of stationery on 31st Dec. 2005	Rs. 500
iv.	Creditors for stationery on 1st Jan. 2005	Rs. 2,000
v.	Creditors for stationery on 31st Dec. 2005	Rs. 1,300
vi.	Advance payment for stationery as on 1st Jan. 2005	Rs. 200

Value of stationery consumed is

a. Rs. 10,800

b. Rs. 12,800

c. Rs. 13,300

d. Rs. 13,500

(Amount paid for stationery during the year		Rs. 10,800
Add: Advance paid in the previous year for the current year		Rs. 200
Add: Opening stock consumed during the year		Rs. 3,000
Add: Credit purchases during the year Creditors on 31st Dec.		Rs. 1,300
Total		Rs. 15,300
Less: Closing stock	Rs. 500	
Less: Payment for Creditors for previous year	Rs. 2,000	Rs. 2,500
Cost of stationery consumed =		*Rs. 12,800)*

Q.41: What amount will be credited in the income & expenditure account during the year 2005 from the following particulars:

i.	Subscriptions received during the year	Rs. 28,680
ii.	Subscriptions outstanding as on 1.1.2005	Rs. 2,400

iii. Subscriptions outstanding as on 31.12.2005 Rs. 3,000

iv. Subscriptions received in advance as on 1.1.2005 Rs. 1,800

v. Subscriptions received in advance as on 31.12.2005 Rs. 1,080

Amount of subscriptions for the current year is

a. Rs. 30,000

b. Rs. 33,480

c. Rs. 29,280

d. Rs. 29,400

(Amount received during the year		*Rs. 28,680*
Add: Outstanding for the current year		*Rs. 3,000*
Add: Amount received in previous year for the current year		*Rs. 1,800*
Total		*Rs. 33,480*
Less: Received for previous year outstanding	*Rs. 2,400*	
Less: Received in advance for next year	*Rs. 1,080*	*Rs. 3,480*
Amount of subscriptions for the current year		*Rs. 30,000)*

Accounting treatment of Special Items

Q.42: Lumpsum amount of fee received, instead of receiving it periodically is called ________

Ans.: Life membership fees

Q.43: At the time of admission of new members to a club/institution is called ________

Ans.: Entrance Fee

Q.44: Entrance fees received by Chelmsford Club during the year is Rs. 40,000. It is decided to capitalize 40% of the entrance fees received. In the final accounts, the treatment will be as under:

a. In the Income & Expenditure A/c credit Rs. 40,000.

b. In the Income & Expenditure A/c credit Rs. 16,000 and in Balance Sheet on Liabilities side Capital Reserve Rs. 24,000.

c. In the Income & Expenditure A/c credit Rs. 24,000 and in Balance Sheet on Liabilities side Reserve Fund Rs. 16,000

d. In the Income & Expenditure A/c credit Rs. 24,000 and in Balance Sheet on Liabilities side additions to Capital Fund Rs. 16,000

Q.45: In case of non-trading concerns, the term legacy refers to:

a. bad debts carried forward from previous year

b. legal endowments

c. amounts passed on by courts when public donate in favour of the concern

d. assets acquired by the concern on the death of a person, as per the terms of his will

Q.46: Amount received from the legal representatives as per the will of the deceased person is called ____________

Ans. Legacies

Q.47: Amount received by way of a gift is called________

Ans. Donation

Q.48: Amount paid to the person who is not employee of the organization ________

Ans. Honorarium

Q.49: Subscriptions account is of the nature of

a. Real account

b. Personal account

c. Nominal account

d. Intangible account

Q.50: Amount received towards endowment fund is

a. Revenue receipt

b. Capital receipt

c. Deferred revenue receipt

d. Deferred capital receipt

Q.51: Membership fees is a non-recurring receipt and is accounted for by

a. Credited to Income & Expenditure account

b. Shown on the Liabilities side of the Balance Sheet as a separate fund or added to Capital Fund

c. Shown on the Assets side of the Balance Sheet

d. None of the above

Q.52: Legacies debited to Receipts & Payments account are

a. Credited to Income & Expenditure account

b. Shown on the Liabilities side of the Balance Sheet

c. Shown on the Assets side of the Balance Sheet

d. None of the above

Q.53: Donations received for a specific purpose, say for building fund are

a. Credited to Income & Expenditure account

b. Shown on the Liabilities side of the Balance Sheet

c. Shown on the Assets side of the Balance Sheet

d. None of the above

Q.54: Donations received as routine revenue item are

a. Credited to Income & Expenditure account

b. Shown on the Liabilities side of the Balance Sheet

c. Shown on the Assets side of the Balance Sheet

d. None of the above

Q.55: Entrance fees received by a club

a. If collected only once in the life time are called _______

b. If collected every year are called _______

Ans.: (a) Capital Receipts and are taken to the liabilities side in the Balance Sheet

(b) Revenue receipts and are taken to Income side in the Income & Expenditure A/c

Q.56: Government grants received

a. for maintenance is taken as _________

b. for specific purpose is taken as _________

Ans. (a) Income and credited to the Income & Expenditure A/c

(b) Specific fund and shown in the liabilities side of Balance Sheet.

Q.57: While preparing the final accounts of non-trading concern, when a special fund exists, the expenses relating to it should be treated as follows:

a. the expenses should be debited to Income & Expenditure A/c and the special fund shown as liability on balance sheet

b. the expenses should be debited to Income & Expenditure A/c and the special fund credited to Income & Expenditure A/c

c. the expenses should be debited to Income & Expenditure A/c and the special fund shown in Receipts & Payments A/c

d. the expenses should be shown as deduction from the special fund in the balance sheet

Q.58: If any special fund is created like Building fund, Endowment Fund, Charity Fund, etc., all incomes and expenses pertaining to that fund are

a. shown in the Income & Expenditure A/c

b. adjusted against the fund in the liabilities side of balance sheet *c.* not shown anywhere

d. both *a* and *b*

Q.59: Opening and closing stocks of Stationery, Bats & Balls, Crockery & cutlery, etc. are shown in the

a. Opening and closing balance sheets, respectively

b. Income & expenditure account-the difference between the two to be assumed as the items consumed during the year

c. Are not shown anywhere

d. both *a* and *b*

Q.60: Receipts on account of sale of fixed assets are shown on the debit side of receipt and payment account and then

a. book value of the assets sold is deducted from the value of the specific asset on the Assets side of balance sheet.

b. if sale proceeds are more than the book value, excess amount being profit on sale of asset is shown on the credit side of Income & Expenditure A/c

c. if sale proceeds are less than the book value, short amount being loss on sale of asset is shown on the debit side of Income & expenditure A/c

d. all the above are true

Q.61: Any profit on sale of old Furniture of a Cricket Club will be taken to

a. Income & Expenditure account

b. Cash account

c. Profit & Loss account

d. None of the above

Q.62: Purchase of sports material is shown on the payments side of Receipt & Payments A/c and then

a. taken as revenue expenditure and shown on the debit side of Income & expenditure A/c

b. taken as capital expenditure and shown on the assets side of Balance Sheet.

c. both *a* and *b*

d. neither *a* nor *b*

Q.63: Sale of old bats and balls, etc. is a regular transaction of recurring nature is debited in the Receipts & payments A/c and is taken

a. as deduction from the value of sports material in the balance sheet

b. on the credit side of Income & expenditure account

c. on the liabilities side of the balance sheet

d. none of the above

Q.64: Match the pairs

Group A	*Group B*	*Answer*
A. Receipts & Payments A/c	1. No intention of earning profit	A & 4
B. Income & Expenditure A/c	2. Excess of expenditure over income	B & 3
C. Deficit	3. Income & expenditure for the year	C & 2
D. Non-trading organisation	4. Actual receipts & payments in cash	D & 1

ANSWERS					
1. (d)	2. —	3. (a)	4. —	5. —	6. (c)
7. (b)	8. (a)	9. (a)	10. (c)	11. (a) & (d)	12. (b) &(c)
13. (a)	14. (c)	15. (b)	16. (a)	17. (c)	18. (b)
19. (c)	20. (c)	21. —	22. (c)	23. (c)	24. (a)
25. (a)	26. (a)	27. (d)	28. (a)	29. (b)	30. (a)
31. (b)	32. (a)	33. (c)	34. (c)	35. (a)	36. (d)
37. (d)	38. (c)	39. (b)	40. (b)	41. (a)	42. —
43. —	44. (d)	45. (d)	46. —	47. —	48. —
49. (c)	50. (b)	51. (b)	52. (b)	53. (b)	54. (a)
55. —	56. —	57. (d)	58. (b)	59. (a)	60. (d)
61. (a)	62. (b)	63. (b)	64. —		

MODULE

D

FINAL ACCOUNTS

CHAPTER

28

BALANCE SHEET EQUATION OR ACCOUNTING EQUATION (ASSETS=LIABILITIES)

Meaning

Q.1: The Balance sheet represents an expansion of the equation

a. Assets = Liabilities

b. Assets = Liabilities + Capital

c. Assets = Creditors + Capital + Reserves & Surplus

d. Assets = Creditors + Net worth

Q.2: Balance sheet equation is

a. Liabilities = Asset - Capital

b. Capital = Assets - Liabilities

c. Assets = Equities

d. All of the above

Q.3: Assets - Original Capital = Liabilites

a. True

b. False

Q.4: Rehman has assets of Rs. 10,000 and liabilities of Rs. 5,000. His capital therefore would be Rs. 15,000

a. True

b. False

Q.5: Assets will be equal to liabilities, if there are no liabilities of the business.

a. True

b. False

Q.6: If a firm borrows money, its capital would be reduced.

a. True

b. False

(When amount is borrowed it adds to the outside liabilities and assets. It has no effect on the Capital of the firm)

Accounting Terminology

Q.7: The amount which the owner of business has invested in the firm and can claim from the firm is called

a. Claims

b. Investments

c. Loans

d. Capital

Q.8: The amount which the firm owes to outsiders is called

a. Loans

b. Claims

c. Liabilities

d. Deposits

Q.9: The liabilities which are payable after a long term are called

a. Secured loans

b. Unsecured loans

c. Term liabilities

d. Fixed liabilities

Q.10: Current liabilities are those liabilities which are payable in near future, generally

a. Within a day

b. Within a month

c. Within six months

d. Within one year

Q.11: Things of value owned are called

a. Goodwill

b. Assets

c. Fixed assets

d. Current assets

Q.12: Assets which are purchased for the purpose of operating the business but not for resale are called:

a. Operating Assets

b. Current Assets

c. Fixed assets

d. Tangible assets

Q.13: Assets which are kept for short term for converting into cash or for resale are called:

a. Operating Assets

b. Current Assets

c. Liquid assets

d. Tangible assets

Q.14: The amount which, as a result of operations, is added to the capital, is called

a. Revenue

b. Net profit

c. Drawings

d. Sales-Cost of goods sold

Q.15: The amount spent in order to produce and sell the goods and services which produce the Revenue is called

a. Revenue

b. Expense

c. Assets

d. Investments

Q.16: The difference between income and expense, if income is more is called

a. Net Revenue

b. Profit

c. Surplus

d. All of the above

Q.17: A person who owes money to the firm on account of credit sales of goods is, in accounting language, called

a. Creditor

b. Customer

c. Debtor

d. Depositor

Q.18: A person to whom money is owed by the firm on account of credit purchase of goods is, in accounting language, called

a. Creditor

b. Customer

c. Debtor

d. Depositor

Computation of Balance Sheet Equation

Q.19: Find the missing figure on the basis of accounting equation

a. Assets Rs. 20,000, Liabilities Rs. 15,000

b. Liabilities Rs. 5,000, Capital Rs. 10,000

c. Assets Rs. 10,000, Capital Rs. 8,000

Ans. (a) 5,000, (b) 15,000, (c) Rs. 2,000

Q.20: The liabilities of a firm are Rs. 3,000, the Capital of the proprietor is Rs. 7,000. The total assets are

a. Rs. 7,000

b. Rs. 10,000

c. Rs. 4,000

d. Rs. 3,000

Q.21: The assets of a business are worth Rs. 50,000 and its capital is Rs. 35,000. Its liabilities on that date shall be:

a. Rs. 85,000

b. Rs. 15,000

c. Rs. 35,000

d. Rs. 50,000

Q.22: If capital of business is Rs. 20,000 and liabilities are Rs. 5,000, (Loss Rs. 7,000), the amount of total assets is

a. Rs. 15,000

b. Rs. 18,000

c. Rs. 8,000

d. Rs. 22,000

Q.23: If total assets of a business are Rs. 1,30,000 and net worth is Rs. 80,000, (Profit Rs. 10,000), the amount of creditors will be:

a. Rs. 20,000

b. Rs. 40,000

c. Rs. 50,000

d. Rs. 60,000

Q.24: Ram commenced his business on 1st January, 2005 with a capital of Rs. 30,000. On 31st December, 2005, his assets were worth Rs. 50,000, and Liabilities Rs. 10,000. His profit was

a. Rs. 10,000

b. Rs. 20,000

c. Rs. 40,000

d. Rs. 70,000

Q.25: Calculate the (a) Owner's equity and (b) Total Liabilities

(*i*) Opening capital Rs. 60,000

(*ii*) Creditors Rs. 50,000

(*iii*) Revenue Rs. 70,000

(*iv*) Expenses Rs. 65,000

Ans. (a) Rs. 65,000 (b) Rs. 1,15,000

Q.26: Calculate the (a) Capital and (b) Profit

Initial Capital Rs. 50,000

Assets at the end Rs. 65,000

Liabilities at the end Rs. 6,000

Ans. (a) Rs. 59,000 (b) Rs. 9,000

Q.27: Calculate the (a) Capital and (b) Profit

Initial Capital Rs. 50,000

Assets at the end Rs. 65,000

Liabilities at the end Rs. 6,000

Additional capital invested Rs. 5,000

Drawings Rs. 2,000

Ans.(a) Rs. 59,000 (b) Rs. 6,000

Q.28: Calculate the (a) Capital and (b) Profit

Initial Capital Rs. 50,000

Assets at the end Rs. 65,000

Liabilities at the end Rs. 6,000

Drawings Rs. 3,000

Ans. (a) Rs. 59,000 (b) 12,000

Effects of transactions on Balance Sheet Equation

Q.29: A had a capital of Rs. 75,000. He had also goods amounting to Rs. 15,000 which he had purchased on credit and the payment had not been made. The value of the total assets of the business is :

a. Rs. 90,000
b. Rs. 60,000
c. Rs. 75,000
d. Cannot be calculated

Q.30: A had a capital of Rs. 75,000. He had also goods amounting to Rs. 15,000 which he had purchased on credit and the payment had not been made. After a period of one month, he came to know that he had suffered a loss of Rs. 1,700. He withdrew Rs. 800 for personal use. His capital and the value of the assets of the business

Match the correct pairs

Capital	*Assets*
a. Rs. 92,500	*i.* Rs. 87,500
b. Rs. 90,000	*ii.* Rs. 92,500
c. Rs. 72,500	*iii.* Rs. 72,500
d. Rs. 87,500	*iv.* Rs. 90,000

Ans. (c) & (i) or Capital Rs. 72,500, Assets Rs. 87,500

Q.31: Mahesh started business on 1st Jan. 2005 with a capital of Rs. 25,000 and a loan of Rs. 12,500 borrowed from Ramesh. On 31st December his assets were Rs. 50,000. His capital as on 31st Dec. and profit or loss made during the year were:

Match the correct pairs

Capital	*Profit*
a. Rs. 37,500	*i.* Rs. 25,000
b. Rs. 50,000	*ii.* Rs. 12,500
c. Rs. 12,500	*iii.* Rs. 37,500
d. Rs. 87,500	*iv.* Rs, 50,000

(Ans. (a) & (ii) or Capital Rs. 37,500 and Profit Rs. 12,500)

Q.32: A started a business with a capital of Rs. 10,000 and he borrowed Rs. 3,000 from a friend. He earned a profit of Rs. 5,000 and withdrew Cash Rs. 4,000 for private use. What was his capital at the end of the year?

Rs. 17,000

a. Rs. 22,000

b. Rs. 11,000

c. Rs. 14,000

d. Rs. 19,000

Q.33: Mahender started a business with Rs. 15,000. During the year he made a profit of Rs. 3,000. He owes Rs. 2,500 to suppliers of goods. What are the total assets of the business?

a. Rs. 18,000

b. Rs. 20,500

c. Rs. 15,500

d. Rs. 14,500

Q.34: On 31st December, the total assets and external liabilities were Rs. 2,00,000 and Rs. 6,000, respectively. During the year, the proprietor had introduced capital of Rs. 20,000 and withdrew Rs. 12,000 for personal use. He made a profit of Rs. 20,000 during the year. Calculate his opening capital as on 1st Jan.

a. Rs. 1,94,000

b. Rs. 2,22,000

c. Rs. 1,66,000

d. Rs. 1,82,000

ANSWERS

1. —	2. (d)	3. (b)	4. (b)	5. (a)	6. (b)
7. (d)	8. (c)	9. (c)	10. (d)	11. (c)	12. (c)
13. (b)	14. (b)	15. (b)	16. (d)	17. (c)	18. (a)
19. —	20. (b)	21. (b)	22. (b)	23. (b)	24. (a)
25. —	26. —	27. —	28. —	29. (a)	30. —
31. —	32. (c)	33. (b)	34. (c)		

CHAPTER

29

FUNDAMENTALS OF PARTNERSHIP ACCOUNTS

Meaning of Partnership

Q.1: Partnership is defined under Sec. ____ of Indian ________ Act of ______.

Match the correct columns

Section	*Act*	*Year*
a. 2	*i.* Contract	A. 1932
b. 4	*ii.* Companies	B. 1947
c. 5	*iii.* Partnership	C. 1956

Ans. (b), (iii), (A) or Section 4 of Indian Partnership Act of 1932

Q.2: The important features of partnership are

a. It is a relationship between persons

b. There should be minimum two persons to form a partnership

c. It is the result of an agreement

d. The partnership agreement may be written or oral

e. The agreement is to share the profits of the business

f. There must be a lawful business

g. The business must be carried on by any one of them acting for all or by more than one, or by all of the partners

Q.3: The persons who have entered into partnership with one another are individually called

a. Shareholders

b. Co-venturers

c. Agents

d. Partners

Q.4: The persons who have entered into partnership with one another are collectively called

a. Proprietorship

b. Partnership

c. Joint venture

d. Firm

Q.5: Partnership is a separate legal entity

a. True

b. False

(It is the firm which has a separate legal entity for its activities/operations and subsequent accounting treatment. Partnership reflects only a relation between persons, called partners)

Q.6: There should be at least two persons to form a partnership

a. True

b. False

Q.7: In partnership, profits of the partnership have to be shared by all, though loss may be borne by only one or few partners or all the partners

a. True

b. False

Q.8: According to the Indian Partnership Act, there is no maximum limit of partners in the partnership

a. True

b. False

(The maximum limit of partners is not given in the Partnership Act. However, according to Companies Act the maximum number of partners is 10 in case of banking business and 20 in case of other business operations)

Q.9: There can be a partnership firm consisting of professionals up to 50 partners

a. True

b. False

(The Companies (Amendment) Bill, 2003 permits formation of partnership of 50 partners. An association of persons of more than the said limit is an illegal association)

Partnership Deed

Q.10: The relations among the partners are governed by mutual agreement. This agreement is known as

a. Lease deed
b. MoU (Memorandum of Understanding)
c. Partnership Agreement
d. Partnership deed

(To avoid disputes later on, this partnership deed should be comprehensive and be properly stamped)

Q.11: It is compulsory to get the Partnership deed registered

a. True
b. False

(The partnership deed may or may not be registered)

Q.12: In the absence of agreement on the point, certain provisions of Partnership law are applicable. One such provision is given wrongly here

a. No interest is payable on capital
b. No interest is payable on drawings
c. A partner is entitled to a salary
d. Interest on loan from partners is payable @ 6% p.a.

(Partners are not entitled for any salary or other remuneration, unless agreed)

Q.13: Following details should be incorporated in the Partnership deed as different clauses:

1. Name and business of the partnership firm
2. Commencement and duration of the business
3. Amount of capital to be contributed by each of the partner
4. Rate of interest to be allowed/charged to each of partner on his
   (*a*) Capital
   (*b*) His loan to the firm
   (*c*) His drawings
5. Profit sharing ratio for disposal of profits
6. Amount to be allowed as drawings and the timings of such drawings
7. Whether any partner will be allowed a salary
8. Any variations in the mutual rights and duties of partners
9. Method by which goodwill is to be calculated on the admission, retirement or death of a partner

10. Procedure by which a partner may be admitted or retired, and the method of payment of dues
11. Basis of the determination of the executors if any one of them is deceased and the method of payment
12. Treatment of losses arising out of the insolvency of a partner. Whether Garner vs. Murray rule will be applicable to them or not.
13. Procedure to be followed for settlement of disputes among partners
14. Preparation of accounts and their audit.

Q.14: If the Partnership deed is silent on certain points, then in such a case, the relevant provisions of the Partnership Act will apply

a. True

b. False

Q.15: If on any point the partnership deed contains a clause

a. Partnership Act clause on the matter will hold good

b. Partnership deed clause on the matter will hold good

c. None of the above

d. All of the above

Profit & Loss Adjustment or Appropriation Account

Q.16: In a partnership firm, the P&L adjustment account is prepared to:

a. Distribute profit among partners

b. Provide interest on capital and drawings

c. Make adjustments for interest, profits, taxation, etc.

d. Provide for taxation

Q.17: Format of P&L Adjustment A/c is as under:

Dr. Cr.

Particulars	Amount	Particulars	Amount
To P & L A/c *(for net loss brought forward)* To Interest on capital of partners To Partner's Salary To Commission to partners To Provision for taxation To Balance transferred to: Partners Capital/Current A/cs *(if there is profit)*		By P & L A/c *(for net profit brought forward)* By Interest on Drawings of partners By Balance transferred to: Partners Capital/Current A/cs *(if there is loss)*	

a. Right

b. Wrong

Partnership Capital

Q.18: The original capital invested by the partners remains unaltered unless additional capital is invested or the capital is withdrawn by mutual agreement. Another account called either drawings or current account will appear side by side with capital account for each partner under the

a. Fixed Capital Method

b. Fluctuating capital method

c. Current capital method

d. Adjustable capital method

Q.19: All transactions relating to the amount of capital contributed, drawings, interest on capital and drawings, salary or commission, share of profit or loss are passed through the capital accounts of the partners under:

a. Fixed Capital Method

b. Fluctuating capital method

c. Current capital method

d. Adjusting capital method

Fixed Capital Method

Q.20: Under the fluctuating capital method, two accounts are maintained for each partner, *viz.* Current account and Capital account

a. True

b. False

(Under the fixed capital method, two accounts are maintained for each partner, viz. Current account and Capital account.)

Q.21: The current accounts of individual partners are maintained

a. When fluctuating capital accounts are maintained

b. When fixed capital accounts are maintained

c. When bank accounts are opened in the names of partners

d. When the concerned partners has no capital contribution

Q.22: If the partnership firm is following the Fluctuating capital account method, salary payable to a partner is credited to Partners' account

a. True

b. False

(Current account of partners are opened only when fixed capital account method is adopted.)

Fluctuating Capital Method

Q.23: Under the fixed capital method, all the transactions are recorded in the capital account only

a. True

b. False

(Under the Fluctuating capital method, all the transactions are recorded in the capital account only).

Q.24: If the Partnership deed does not mention any method of maintaining capital accounts, then the ________ capital account method has to be followed

a. Fixed

b. Fluctuating

c. Adjusting

d. Current

Interest on Capital invested by partners

Q.25: The Partnership deed provides for payment of interest on capital @ 10% p.a. The firm has two partners A and B with capital of Rs. 1,00,000 and Rs. 20,000 respectively. The profit for the year before charging interest on capital is Rs. 5,000. The interest on capital payable to the partners is

a. Rs. 4,000 to A and Rs. 1,000 to B,

b. Rs. 5,000 to A and nil to B,

c. Rs. 10,000 to A and Rs. 2,000 to B and the resultant net loss will be shared between partners in their profit sharing ratio,

d. No interest on capital is payable since profits are insufficient,

(Interest on capital is an appropriation on profit and not a charge on profit)

Drawings by Partners

Q.26: Drawings made by partners are never entered in the Profit & Loss Appropriation A/c

a. True

b. False

(Drawings are a reduction in the amount of capital of the partners and has no effect on the profit or loss of the business concern).

Interest on Drawings by Partners

Q.27: One of the following statements is not true. Identify it:

a. Interest on drawings is not charged if the firm makes insufficient profits

b. Interest on drawings is debited to the capital account of the concerned partner

c. Profit & Loss Appropriation account is used for making adjustments regarding interest on capital and drawings

d. Where current accounts of partners are maintained, interest on drawings is debited to these accounts

Q.28: During the financial year, a partner withdraws

Rs. 30,000 on 1st July

Rs. 20,000 on 1st October, and

Rs. 10,000 on 1st January.

Interest on drawings is payable at 10 % p.a.

When the final accounts are prepared on 31st March, the interest on drawings amount to

a. Rs. 6,000

b. Rs. 4,000

c. Rs. 5,400

d. Rs. 3,500

(Interest on 30,000 for 9 months from 1st July to 31st March @ 10% Rs. 2,250

Interest on 20,000 for 6 months from 1st Oct. to 31st March @ 10% Rs. 1,000

Interest on 10,000 for 3 months from 1st Jan to 31st March @ 10% Rs. 250)

Q.29: A is drawing Rs. 15,000 regularly on the 16th of every month. He will have to pay interest in a year on Rs. 1,80,000 (at the given rate) for a total period of

a. 12 months

b. 6 months

c. 6.5 months

d. 5.5 months

Q.30: During a particular financial year, a partner withdraws Rs. 3,000 at the beginning of each month. If the interest on drawings is chargeable at 12%, the interest will amount to

a. Rs. 1,500

b. Rs. 360

c. Rs. 300

d. Rs. 2,340

(He will have to pay interest in a year on Rs. 36,000 @ 12% for 6.5 months)

Interest on Loan from partners

Q.31: In the absence of any partnership deed or where a deed is silent in respect of the entitlement of a partner for any interest on loans given by him to the firm, he will be given

a. No interest on his loan as he is one of the owners and his amount will be treated as his capital

b. He is entitled on interest on loan at the bank rate

c. He will get interest at the market rate

d. He is entitled for interest on loan @ 6% p.a.

Q.32: Interest on loan is payable to a partner

a. Only when the firm makes sufficient profits

b. At a fixed rate of 6%

c. Only when other partners agree

d. At the agreed rate irrespective of the fact that the firm makes profit or not

Q.33: Interest on Loan from a partner is closed by transfer to:

a. Profit & Loss account

b. Profit & Loss appropriation account

c. Capital accounts of the concerned partners

d. Drawings accounts of the concerned partners

(Interest on loan is a charge on profit.)

Goodwill

Q.34: Goodwill is normally due to:

a. Favourable Location

b. Nature of business

c. Licences and quotas with the business

d. Possibility of competition

e. Better customer service

f. Efficient advertisement

g. Possession of patent rights and trade marks

h. Efficiency and Personal skill/reputation of the management

i. Better products

Q.35: Old firms must have goodwill account in their books of account

a. True

b. False

(Goodwill is the value of the good name of the firm, which attracts more customers and helps it to earn more profits. It is an intangible asset built up slowly by the owners of the business over a period of time and is normally not recorded in the books of account- although it has a realizable value and can be bought and sold in the market)

Q.36: Is the value of an established business over and above the value represented by its tangible assets

a. Tangible value

b. Secret Reserve

c. Goodwill

d. Super Value

Q.37: Is the value attached to the super profit earning capacity of business arising from its wide connections, reputation and long standing in the business

a. Reputed value

b. Super value

c. Created value

d. Goodwill

Q.38: Is the value of reputation of a firm in respect of profits expected in future over and above the normal rate of profits

a. Reputed value

b. Super value

c. Created value

d. Goodwill

Q.39: Select the correct statement

a. If the Partnership deed does not mention any method of maintaining capital accounts, then the fixed capital account method has to be followed

b. While calculating average profit of previous years, loss incurred in any year should be ignored

c. The share which the new partner is entitled is called the sacrificing ratio *d.* Adjustment for goodwill can be made privately by the partners without passing any entries in the books of account

Methods of Valuation

Average Profit Method

Q.40: When the profits of the past few years are averaged and adjusted for any expected change in future, it is called

a. Average Profit Method

b. Super profit method

c. Annuity based method

d. Capitalisation method

Q.41: While calculating average profit of previous years loss incurred in one of those years is to be ignored

a. True

b. False

(While calculating the average profits, the correct method is to total up all the profits earned during the period under reference, deduct the amount of losses incurred in any one or more years and then the net total is to be divided by the number of years taken into consideration.)

Q.42: It was decided by a firm to value their goodwill at 2 years purchase of 3 years average profits. The profits during the previous three years were:

1st year Rs. 40,000

2nd year Rs. 38,000

3rd year Rs. 54,000

The value of goodwill will be

a. Rs. 1,32,000

b. Rs. 44,000

c. Rs. 88,000

d. Rs. 1,98,000

(The total profits are Rs. 1,32,000, Average profits are 1,32,000/3=Rs. 44,000 and its two years purchase value is Rs. 44,000 × 2 = Rs. 88,000)

Super Profit Method

Q.43: Super profit means, excess profit that can be earned by a firm over and above the normal profit usually earned by similar firms under similar circumstances

a. True

b. False

Q.44: Super profit can be calculated by the following steps:

1. Identify the total capital employed by the Partnership firm
2. Identify the average profit earned by the partnership firm based on past few years figures
3. Determine the normal rate of return prevailing in the industry or locality for the similar firms
4. Apply normal rate of return on capital employed to arrive at normal profit
5. Deduct normal profit from the average profit of the firm. If the average profit of the firm is more than the normal profit, there exists super profit

   a. Right

   b. Wrong

Q.45: Goodwill under the super profit method is calculated by

a. Multiplying the average profits by certain number of years

b. Multiplying the amount of super profits by certain number of years depending upon the expectation about the maintenance of such profits in future

c. Average profits are calculated by assigning appropriate weights and the weighted average profit is multiplied by certain number of years

d. None of the above

Q.46: It was decided by a firm to calculate goodwill at 3 years purchase of average of super profits. The firm has an investment of Rs. 1,00,000 over which the expected rate of return is 10%.

Profits for the last four years were Rs. 15,000, Rs. 13,000, Rs. 18,000 and Rs. 16,000 respectively

a. Rs. 16,500

b. Rs. 46,500

c. Rs. 22,000

d. Rs. 18,150

(Total of 4 years profits is Rs. 62,000, while the expected return for 4 years is Rs. 40,000, therefore super profits for 4 years are Rs. 22,000. Average super profits are Rs. 22,000/4 = Rs. 5,500 and three times of this is = Rs. 16,500)

Capitalisation of Profit Method

Q.47: When value of whole business is determined and to it the normal rate of return is applied and the amount so calculated is compared with the capital employed in the business, this method of valuing goodwill is called

a. Super Profit Method
b. Capitalization Method
c. Average profit method
d. Annuity based method

Q.48: Goodwill on capitalization basis can be calculated by the following steps:

1. Determine the normal rate of return
2. Find the average profits of the firm
3. Find out the total capital employed by the same firm
4. Find the normal value of business by dividing Average profits into normal rate of return
5. Take the difference of normal value of business and the capital employed
6. This will be the value of goodwill of the firm

    a. Right
    b. Wrong

ANSWERS					
1. —	2. —	3. (d)	4. (d)	5. (b)	6. (a)
7. (a)	8. (a)	9. (a)	10. (d)	11. (b)	12. (c)
13. —	14. (a)	15. (b)	16. (c)	17. (a)	18. (a)
19. (b)	20. (b)	21. (b)	22. (b)	23. (b)	24. (b)
25. (d)	26. (a)	27. (a)	28. (d)	29. (b)	30. (d)
31. (d)	32. (d)	33. (a)	34. —	35. (b)	36. (c)
37. (d)	38. (d)	39. (d)	40. (a)	41. (b)	42. (c)
43. (a)	44. (a)	45. (b)	46. (a)	47. (b)	48. (a)

CHAPTER

30

ADMISSION OF A PARTNER

Q.1: Joining of a new person into an existing partnership as a partner is called

a. Enrolment of a partner

b. Registration of a partner

c. Entry of a partner

d. Admission of a partner

Q.2: The following adjustments are made in the accounts of a partnership when a new partner is admitted

a. Changes in profit sharing proportions

b. Valuation of goodwill

c. Distribution of accumulated profits and reserves by existing partners

d. Revaluation of assets and liabilities

e. Restructuring of capitals

f. Preparation of a new balance sheet

Changes in profit sharing proportions

Q.3: The profit of a business is usually taken to be "one" and share of each partner in the profit is called

a. His ratio

b. His proportion

c. His share

d. His right

(e.g. ¼, ¼ and ½)

Q.4: When the division of profit is denoted by integers and not by fractions, it is called

a. Ratio
b. Proportion
c. Fraction
d. All of the above

(e.g. 1 : 1 : 2)

Q.5: The share which the new partner is entitled to is called the

a. Gaining ratio
b. Sacrificing ratio
c. Old ratio
d. New ratio

Q.6: A and B are partners sharing profits in the ratio of 3 : 2. C is admitted for 1/3rd share. The new ratio is

a. 2 : 1 : 1
b. 1/3, 1/3, 1/3
c. 3 : 2 : 1
d. 6 : 4 : 5

(A, and B were sharing one full share in the proportion of 3/5th and 2/5th. C has taken away 1/3rd share out of the total one share. The left over for A and B is 1 - 1/3=2/3rd. Therefore A will now get 3/5th of 2/3rd which is = 6/15. B will get 2/5th of 2/3rd, which is = 4/15. The new proportion are A 6/15, B 4/15 and C 1/3 or 5/15)

Q.7: A, B and C are partners sharing profits in the ratio of 2 : 2 : 1. D is admitted for 2/5th share. The new ratio is

a. 2 : 2 : 1 : 2
b. 4 : 4 : 2 : 4
c. 6 : 6 : 3 : 10
d. 2 : 2 : 1 : 5

(A, B and C were sharing one full share in the proportion of 2/5th, 2/5th and 1/5th. D has taken away 2/5th share out of the total one share. The left over for A, B and C is 1 - 2/5 =3/5th. Therefore A will now get 2/5th of 3/5th which is = 6/25. B will get 2/5th of 3/5th, which is = 6/25.C will get 1/5th of 3/5th which is = 3/25. The new proportion are A 6/25, B 6/25, C 3/25 and D 2/5th or 10/25.)

Q.8: A and B are partners sharing profits in equal ratio. C is admitted as third partner with1/3rd share, which he acquires equally from A and B. The new profit sharing ratio/proportion is:

a. 1 : 1 : 1

b. 3 : 2 : 1

c. 1 : 2 : 3

d. 1/6, 1/6, 1/3

(A : B=1/2,1/2.C's share is 1/3 acquired ½ of 1/3 i.e. 1/6th from A and same from B. Therefore A's new share is 1/2 -1/6=2/6 or 1/3, same is B's share and C's share is 1/6 + 1/6= 2/6 or 1/3rd. Therefore, the new share is 1/3, 1/3, 1/3 or 1: 1: 1.)

Q.9: A and B are partners sharing profits in the ratio of 2 : 1. C is admitted into partnership for 1/4th share which he acquires 1/6 from A and 1/12 from B. The new profit sharing ratio will be

a. 2 : 1 : 1

b. 1/3, 1/3, 1/3

c. 5/8, 1/8, 1/4

d. 1 : 1 : 2

(A:B=2/3,1/3. A sacrifices 1/6. Therefore his new proportion is 2/3-1/6=3/6. B sacrifices 1/12. Therefore his new proportion is 1/3-1/12=3/12. C's share is 1/6 + 1/12= 3/12. The new proportions are 3/6, 3/12 and 3/12 for A, B and C, respectively. The new ratio is 6:3:3 or 2:1:1)

Q.10: A and B were sharing profits in the proportion of 3/8 and 5/8. They admit C with 1/2 share. The sacrifice made by A and B in the ratio of 1 : 3. The new profit sharing ratio is

a. 1 : 2 : 1

b. 2 : 1 : 1

c. 1 : 1 : 2

d. 3 : 8 : 2

(A : B = 3/8, 5/8. C is admitted for 1/2. A Sacrifices 1/4th of 1/2 i.e. 1/8th, and B sacrifices 3/4th of ½ i.e. 3/8th. A's new share is 3/8 - 1/8 = 2/8. B's new share is 5/8 - 3/8 = 2/8 and C's share is 1/2 or 4/8. The new proportion is 2/8, 2/8 and 4/8 or 2 :2: 4 or 1: 1: 2)

Q.11: A and B were sharing profits in the proportion of 5 : 4. They admit C. A is sacrificing 2/3 of his share and B sacrificing 1/3 of his share. The new ratio will be:

a. 10 : 4 : 14

b. 5 : 8 : 14

c. 8 : 5 : 14

d. 3/9, 2/9, 4/9

(A : B=5/9 and 4/9.A sacrifices 2/3 of 5/9= 10/27. B sacrifices 1/3 of 4/9= 4/27. New proportions are A=5/9 or 15/27-10/27= 5/27. B= 4/9 or 12/27-4/27= 8/27 and C= 10/27+ 4/27= 14/27. New ratio is 5 : 8 : 14.)

Q.12: A and B sharing profits in the ratio of 3 : 2. They admit C into partnership, after which the profit sharing ratio is changed to 4 : 3 : 2. The sacrifice/gain in profit sharing by A and B is:

a. Sacrificing ratio 3 : 7

b. Gaining ratio 3 : 7

c. Sacrificing ratio 7 : 3

d. Gaining ratio 7 : 3

(A's old share is 3/5 and new share is 4/9. Therefore he sacrifices 3/5 - 4/9 = 7/45

B's old share is 2/5 and new share is 3/9. Therefore he sacrifices 2/5 - 3/9=3/45

C's gaining is 2/9 which should be equal to A's sacrifice of 7/45 + B's sacrifice of 3/45)

Valuation of goodwill

Accounting Treatment of goodwill on admission of a partner

Transaction	Books of the Firm	Books of the Firm
	A/c Debited	A/c Credited
1.When the new partner pays the goodwill privately	No entry	No entry
2. When the new partner brings in his share of goodwill and cash brought in as goodwill is retained in the business	Cash/Bank A/c Goodwill	Goodwill Old Partners Capital A/c *(in sacrificing ratio)*
3. When the new partner brings in his share of goodwill and cash brought in as goodwill is withdrawn by the old partners	Cash/Bank A/c Goodwill Old Partners Capital A/c	Goodwill Old Partners Capital A/c Cash/Bank A/c
4. When the new partner does not bring cash for goodwill and goodwill is raised by the old partners and is shown as an asset in the Balance Sheet	Goodwill	Old Partners Capital A/c *(in old profit sharing ratio)*
5. When the new partner does not bring cash for goodwill and goodwill is raised and written off immediately	Goodwill All Partners Capital A/c (including new partner-*in new profit sharing ratio)*	Old Partners Capital A/c *(in old profit sharing ratio)* Goodwill
6. When the new partner does not bring cash for goodwill, and no goodwill account appears in the books. If it is decided to record new partners share without raising goodwill	New Partners Capital A/c (for New Partners share only)	Old Partners Capital A/c *(in their sacrificing ratio)*
7. When goodwill appears in the books at its full value	No entry	No Entry
8. When goodwill appears in the books, but the present value of the goodwill is more than that, goodwill is raised only for the difference in these two values	Goodwill	Old Partners Capital A/c *(in old profit sharing ratio)*
9. When goodwill appears in the books, but the present value of the goodwill is less than that, goodwill is written off reduced to that extent i.e. for the difference in these two values	Old Partners Capital A/c *(in old profit sharing ratio)*	Goodwill
10. When the incoming partner acquires his share from a particular partner only, the goodwill is transferred only to the sacrificing partner.	*New Partner Capital A/c*	Sacrificing Partners Capital A/c

Q.13: A joins B as a partner bringing in Rs. 1,00,000 as capital and Rs. 40,000 as goodwill. What will be the journal entry, if goodwill is to be retained in the business;

a. Cash A/c.................................... Dr. 1,40,000
To A's Capital 1,00,000
To Goodwill A/c 40,000

b. (*i*) Cash A/c............................ Dr. 1,40,000
To A's Capital 1,00,000
To Goodwill A/c 40,000
(*ii*) Goodwill A/c .... Dr. 40,000
To B's Capital 40,000

c. Cash A/c.................................... Dr. 1,40,000
To A's Capital 1,00,000
To B's Capital 40,000

d. (*i*) Cash A/c............................ Dr. 1,40,000
To A's Capital 1,40,000
(*ii*) A's Capital........................... Dr. 40,000
To Goodwill A/c 40,000

Q.14: C the newly admitted partner, brings Rs. 60,000 as goodwill which has been properly accounted for in the books. A and B, the old partners, desire to withdraw this amount. Their old profit sharing ratio was 2 : 1 and their sacrificing ratio was 3 : 2. Journal entry required to effect the withdrawal is :

a. Goodwill A/c................................Dr. 60,000
To A 40,000
To B 20,000

b. A...Dr. 40,000
B...Dr. 20,000
To Cash 60,000

c. A...Dr. 36,000
B...Dr. 24,000
To Cash 60,000

d. A...Dr. 40,000
B...Dr. 20,000
To Goodwill 60,000

(Goodwill being the reward for sacrifice, the old partners will share the cash brought in by the new partner towards goodwill in their sacrificing ratio)

Q.15: A and B sharing profits in the ratio of 3 : 1, admit C as a partner with 1/4th share which he acquires equally from the old partners. On admission the goodwill of the firm was valued at Rs. 4,00,000. The journal entry to raise the goodwill of the firm is:

a. Goodwill A/c................................Dr. 4,00,000
To A 2,00,000
To B 2,00,000

b. Goodwill A/c................................Dr. 1,00,000
To A 50,000
To B 50,000

c. Goodwill A/c................................Dr. 4,00,000
To A 3,00,000
To B 1,00,000

d. C's A/c................................Dr. 1,00,000
To A 50,000
To B 50,000

(Goodwill will be raised for the full amount. It being the reward for sacrifice, the old partners will share it in their sacrificing ratio)

Distribution of accumulated profits and reserves by existing partners

Q.16: At the time of admission, if there is any reserve or reserve fund account or balance of P & L A/c, they are

a. not affected

b. transferred to old partner's capital accounts in their old profit sharing ratio

c. transferred to old partner's capital accounts in their Sacrificing ratio

d. transferred to all partner's capital accounts in their new profit sharing ratio

Q.17: On the day C is admitted into partnership of A and B, a balance sheet is prepared which shows a reserve fund of Rs. 1,20,000 on the liabilities side. A and B were sharing profits in the ratio of 2 : 3 and the new profit sharing ratio agreed after the admission is 2 : 3 : 4

a. Reserve fund should be transferred to Revaluation A/c

b. Reserve fund should be transferred to General Reserve Account

c. Reserve fund should be credited to the Capitals of A & B in their old ratio of 2 : 3

d. Reserve fund should be credited to the Capitals of A, B and C in the old ratio of 2 : 3 : 4

Revaluation of assets and liabilities

Q.18: At the time of admission of a partner into an existing partnership firm, the profits on revaluation will arise when:

a. Increase in value of assets is less than the increase in the value of liabilities.

b. Net Increase in value of assets is higher than the net increase in the value of liabilities.

c. Decrease in value of assets is lesser than the increase in the value of liabilities.

d. Decrease in value of assets is higher than the increase in the value of liabilities.

Q.19: On admission of a new partner, the profit/loss on revaluation of assets and liabilities should be treated thus:

a. Profit/loss should be transferred to old partners in their Capital ratio

b. Profit/loss should be transferred to old partners in their Sacrificing ratio

c. Profit/loss should be transferred to old partners in their old Profit sharing ratio

d. Profit/loss should be transferred to all the partners in their new Profit sharing ratio

(When a new partner is admitted, he acquires the ownership rights of the assets and also makes himself responsible for the firm's liabilities. It, therefore, becomes necessary to scrutinize the balance sheet carefully so that new partner should not get any benefit from the appreciation in the value of assets or reduction in the value of liabilities, nor he should suffer because of any decrease in the value of assets or increase of liabilities. Therefore, on the date of admission, the assets and liabilities of the firm are revalued and its profit or loss is transferred to the old partners capital accounts in their old profit sharing ratio)

Restructuring of capitals

Q.20: When the capital of the new partner is fixed on the basis of the combined capital of old partners, it requires following steps:

1. Post all entries relating to old partner's capital accounts and arrive at the closing balances.
2. The combined capital represents the capital for the share held by old partners i.e. One *minus* proportion of new partner.
3. Based on the balance of old partner's capital and their share, calculate the capital for full one share of profits.

4. On this basis calculate the share of new partner.

   a. Right

   b. Wrong

Q.21: When the capital of the old partners is fixed on the basis of capital brought in by the new partner, it requires following steps:

1. Post all entries relating to all partner's capital accounts and arrive at the closing balances.
2. Based on the balance of new partner's capital and his share, calculate the capital for full one share of profits.
3. Calculate the balances that each old partner should hold keeping in view the total amount of capital multiplied with his proportion.

The capital accounts of old partners may show debit or credit balances. If debit balance, it shows the amount to be brought in by that partner. If it shows credit balance, the excess amount may either be paid back to him or may be transferred to his current account.

a. Right

b. Wrong

Q.22: A and B are Partners and C joins them as a partner with a share of 1/3rd in profits. The capital accounts of A and B show a credit balance of Rs. 1,00,000 and Rs. 2,00,000, respectively. The revaluation account prepared on the event of admission showed revaluation profit of Rs. 90,000. It was decided that C should bring in his capital in proportion to his share of profits. The capital to be brought in by him is:

a. Rs. 1,00,000

b. Rs. 1,30,000

c. Rs. 1,95,000

d. The capital to be brought in cannot be determined in the absence of information about the old profit sharing ratio

(The total capital of the firm is Rs. 3,90,000 i.e. 1,00,000 + 2,00,000 + 90,000. This is the amount for 2/3rd remaining share of A and B i.e. 1 - 1/3 of C. Therefore the total capital of the firm will be 3,90,000 × 3/2 = 5,85,000. C is to bring 1/3rd of the total capital which comes to Rs. 1,95,000.)

Q.23: On admission of C into the partnership, it was decided to re-align the capitals of the old partners A and B. It is found that on this basis, the capital of B is in excess by Rs. 20,000.

a. The excess should continue, since only deficits can be adjusted

b. The excess should be transferred to the current account of B

c. Excess should be transferred to the loan account of B carrying interest @ 6% p.a.

d. The partner should withdraw the excess, otherwise the amount will be forfeited by the firm

Preparation of a new balance sheet

Q.24: After the admission of a partner and the revaluation of assets and liabilities, the assets and liabilities are recorded in the new balance sheet

a. at the old figures

b. at the revalued figures

c. at lower of old and revalued figures

d. at market prices

Q.25: After the admission of a partner and the revaluation of assets and liabilities, if the Memorandum Revaluation Account is prepared, the assets and liabilities are recorded in the new balance sheet

a. At the old figures

b. At the revalued figures

c. Except certain changes in the capital accounts of partners all other assets and liabilities will be shown at old figures

d. at market value

(When a memorandum revaluation account is prepared, firstly the effect of changes in the value of assets and liabilities is transferred to the old partners capital accounts in their old ratio. Simultaneously, the entries are reversed and the balance is transferred to all the partners, including the new, in their new profit sharing ratio. This nullifies the effect of changes in the value of assets and liabilities of the firm and the capitals of the partners are adjusted.)

ANSWERS					
1. (d)	2. —	3. (b)	4. (a)	5. (a)	6. (d)
7. (c)	8. (a)	9. (a)	10. (c)	11. (b)	12. (c)
13. (b)	14. (c)	15. (a)	16. (b)	17. (c)	18. (b)
19. (c)	20. (a)	21. (a)	22. (c)	23. (b)	24. (b)
25. (c)					

CHAPTER

31

RETIREMENT/DEATH OF A PARTNER

Retirement of a Partner

Q.1: ______ of a partner means that a partner breaks off his relations with all other partners and withdraws himself from the firm.

Ans. Retirement

Q.2: The following is expected to be done when a partner retires from a firm:

a. Goodwill of the firm is valued and the share of the retiring partner is credited to his capital account

b. Assets and liabilities of the firm are revalued and the retiring partners share of the resultant profit or loss is adjusted in his capital account

c. His share of reserves and undistributed profit is credited to his capital account

d. The amount due to the retiring partner is either paid off immediately or is transferred to his loan account which will be settled according to arrangement

New Profit sharing ratio of continuing partners

Q.3: New profit sharing proportion of continuing partners is equal to

a. Old share plus acquired share

b. Old share minus sacrificing proportion

c. The old share without any change

d. None of the above

Q.4: When one partner retires and nothing is mentioned about the new ratio between the remaining partners

a. the mutual profit sharing ratio of the remaining partners will not change *b.* the outgoing partners share is added to the previous shares in their capital ratio

c. the profit sharing ratio will remain same amongst the continuing partners, but their proportions will change.

d. none of the above

Q.5: When the remaining partners purchase the share of retiring partner in some specified portions

a. this specified portion should be added to their previous portion

b. the mutual profit sharing ratio of the remaining partners will not change

c. the profit sharing ratio will remain same amongst the continuing partners, but their proportions will change

d. the outgoing partner's share is added to the previous shares in their capital ratio

Q.6: A, B and C are partners sharing profit in the ratio of 6 : 5 : 3. A retires from partnership. In the absence of any specific agreement, B and C will share future profits in the ratio of

a. 1 : 1

b. 6 : 5

c. 5 : 3

d. in capital ratio

(If gaining ratio is not given, it is assumed that the continuing partners will share in their original profit sharing ratio among them. Their proportions will however change)

Q.7: A, B and C are partners sharing profit in the ratio of 4 : 5 : 2. B retires from partnership. In the absence of any specific agreement, A and C will share future profits in the ratio of

a. 1 : 2

b. 2 : 1

c. 5 : 2

d. 4 : 5

(The original ratio between them is 4 : 2 i.e. 2 : 1)

Q.8: A, B and C are partners sharing profit in the ratio of 1/2, 1/3, and 1/6. C retires from partnership. In the absence of any specific agreement, A and B will share future profits in the ratio of:

a. 1/2, 1/3

b. 2 : 3

c. 3 : 2

d. 1/3, ½

(The original proportions are 1/2, 1/3 and 1/6 or the ratio was 3 : 2: 1. When C retires, the ratio will remain 3 : 2)

Q.9: A, B and C are partners sharing profit in the ratio of 5 : 4 : 2. C retires and his share is taken up by A and B equally. The new profit sharing ratio is:

a. 4 : 3

b. 5 : 4

c. 3 : 2

d. 6 : 5

(C is sacrificing his 2/11 share, which is taken over equally by A and B, i.e. 2/22 each. A will now get 5/11+2/22=12/22 and B will get 4/11+2/22=10/22. New ratio is 12 : 10 or 6 : 5)

Gaining Ratio

Q.10: On retirement of a partner, the additional share in the profits by the continuing partners is called

a. Sacrificing ratio

b. Gaining ratio

c. Old ratio

d. New Ratio

Q.11: Gaining ratio is calculated by:

a. New ratio - old ratio

b. New proportion - old proportion

c. Old ratio - new ratio

d. Old proportion - new proportion

Q.12: A, B and C are partners sharing profit in the ratio of 2 : 1 : 1. B retires. A and B continue with a new profit sharing ratio of 3 : 2. The gaining ratio is:

a. 3 : 2

b. 2 : 3

c. 1 : 1

d. 1 : 2

(A is getting 3/5 instead of 2/4 i.e. excess of 2/20 and B is getting 2/5 in place of 1/4 i.e. gaining of 3/20. Thus the gaining ratio is 2 : 3)

Q.13: A, B and C are partners sharing in the ratio of 4 :5 :2. B retires. The gaining ratio of A and C is

a. 2 : 1
b. 1 : 2
c. 5 : 2
d. 4 : 5

Goodwill

Accounting treatment of goodwill

ACCOUNTING TREATMENT OF GOODWILL ON RETIREMENT OF A PARTNER

Transaction	Books of the Firm A/c Debited	Books of the Firm A/c Credited
When Goodwill appears in the books:		
1.When the book value and the present value of goodwill are same	No Entry	No entry
2. If the book value of goodwill is less than the present value, goodwill will be raised to that extent	Goodwill	All partners capital A/cs (*in their old ratio*)
3. If the book value of goodwill is more than the present value, goodwill will be written off that extent	All partners capital A/cs (*in their old ratio*)	Goodwill
When Goodwill does not appear in the books:		
1. It is raised for its full value	Goodwill	All partners capital A/cs (*in their old ratio*)
2. If goodwill is not retained in the books, but immediately written off	Remaining partners capital (*in their new ratio*)	Goodwill
3.a. When goodwill is raised with the retiring partners' share	Goodwill	Retiring partners capital (*his share of goodwill*)
b. Goodwill is written off or	Remaining partners capital (*in their gaining ratio*)	Goodwill
Single entry may be passed	Remaining partners capital (*in their gaining ratio*)	Retiring partners capital (*his share of goodwill*)

Q.14: When a partner retires from the firm, the adjustment of capital accounts to be done for goodwill is:

a. Debit all partners capital accounts with proportionate value of goodwill in old profit sharing ratio and credit the capital accounts of the continuing partners in the new profit sharing ratio.

b. Credit all partners' capital accounts with proportionate value of goodwill in old profit sharing ratio and debit the capital accounts of the continuing partners in the new profit sharing ratio.

c. Debit revaluation account and credit the retiring partners capital account with his share of goodwill

d. No adjustment is required

Q.15: A, B and C are in partnership sharing profits in the ratio of 2 : 3 : 4. B retires from the partnership and the goodwill is raised to the extent of Rs. 9,000 and written off immediately. The balances in the capital accounts of the three partners are Rs. 40,000, Rs. 30,000 and Rs. 35,000, respectively. After the adjustment of goodwill, the balances in the capital accounts of the continuing partners will be:

a. A Rs. 42,000, C Rs. 39,000

b. A Rs. 40,000, C Rs. 35,000

c. A Rs. 39,000, C Rs. 33,000

d. A Rs. 37,000, C Rs. 31,000

(When the goodwill is raised in the old ratio A, B and C gets Rs. 2,000, Rs. 3,000 and Rs. 4,000, respectively. When it is written off in the new ratio of 2 : 4, A's and C's accounts are debited with Rs. 3,000 and 6,000, respectively. Thus A's new capital is Rs. 40,000+Rs. 2,000 - Rs. 3,000= 39,000. B's Capital Account shows Rs. 30,000 + Rs. 3,000=Rs. 33,000 and C's a/c is Rs. 35,000+ Rs. 4,000 - Rs. 6,000=Rs. 33,000.)

Q.16: A, B and C are in partnership sharing profits in the ratio of 5 : 4 : 3. The balances in the capital accounts of the three partners are Rs. 30,000, Rs. 40,000 and Rs. 50,000 respectively. A retires from partnership and his share of goodwill is reckoned at Rs. 14,000. A single journal entry that can be passed to give effect to the adjustment for goodwill is

		Dr.	Cr.
a.	Goodwill a/c..........................	Dr. 14,000	
	To A's Capital a/c		14,000
b.	A's Capital a/c	Dr. 14,000	
	To Goodwill		14,000
c.	Goodwill a/c..........................	Dr. 33,600	
	To A's Capital a/c		14,000
	To B's Capital a/c		11,200
	To C's Capital a/c		8,400

d. B's Capital a/c .... Dr. 8,000
C's Capital a/c 6,000
To A's Capital a/c 14,000

Adjustments for Reserves & Surplus

Q.17: Which one of the statements relating to adjustment for reserves and surplus, when a partner retires from a partnership is wrong:

a. The balances in the reserves and surplus can be transferred to the capital accounts of all partners in their profit sharing ratio

b. Only the share of the retiring partner in the reserves and surplus can be transferred to his capital, and the balance carried in the balance sheet.

c. When the balances in the reserves and surplus is transferred to the capital accounts of all partners in their profit sharing ratio, they will not appear in the Balance sheet.

d. Reserves and surplus account is closed by transfer to the revaluation account.

Revaluation of Assets and Liabilities

Q.18: A revaluation account is prepared on the date of retirement or death of a partner. This account is prepared when

a. The assets and liabilities are revalued to bring them to their current market value.

b. The assets and liabilities are revalued on retirement of a partner, but they are required to be shown in the balance sheet at their original values

c. A partner retires from the firm and a new partner simultaneously admitted

d. There is one partner left in the business, due to the retirement of other partner

Q.19: The following is expected to be done when revaluation account is prepared at the time of retirement of a partner

a. Increase in the value of assets and decrease in the value of liabilities are credited to the revaluation account.

b. Decrease in the value of assets and increase in the value of liabilities are debited to the revaluation account.

c. The profit on revaluation is transferred or credited to all partners in the old profit sharing ratio.

d. After all adjustments the assets and liabilities will appear in the balance sheet at their current values.

Memorandum Revaluation Account

Q.20: Memorandum revaluation account is prepared in partnership when:

a. The assets are revalued to bring them to their current market value

b. The assets and liabilities are revalued on retirement of a partner, but they are required to be shown in the balance sheet at their original values

c. A partner retires from the firm and a new partner simultaneously admitted

d. There is one partner left in the business, due to the retirement of other partner

Q.21: The following is expected to be done when a memorandum revaluation account is prepared at the time of retirement of a partner

a. Increase in the value of assets and decrease in the value of liabilities are credited to the memorandum revaluation account.

b. The profit on revaluation is transferred or credited to all partners in the old profit sharing ratio at the first stage.

c. The profit on revaluation is recovered or debited to the capital of continuing partners in the new profit sharing ratio in the second stage.

d. After all adjustments the assets and liabilities will appear in the balance sheet at their original values.

Payment to Retiring Partner

Q.22: Which one of the following statements relating to retiring partner in settlement is wrong:

a. he is paid in cash, debiting his capital account and crediting bank account

b. if the balance in bank is not sufficient to pay off the retiring partner, the amount unpaid may be credited to his loan account carrying no interest.

c. if the liability to the retiring partner is taken over by continuing partner, the retiring partners' capital account is debited and the continuing partners'(who has taken over this liability) account is credited

d. a part of the dues to the partner may be paid in cash and the balance may be taken over by a partner

Death of a Partner

Q.23 : On the death of a partner the executors or representatives of the deceased partner are entitled to the following benefits:

a. The amount standing to the credit of deceased partners' capital a/c

b. His share in the goodwill of the firm

c. His share of profits earned from the beginning of the year to the date of death

d. His share of profits on revaluation of assets and liabilities. His share of the loss, if any, shall be deducted

e. His share of undistributed profit or reserves

f. Interest on capital, salary or commission, etc. if provided in partnership deed.

g. His share of the proceeds of the joint life policy.

Q.24: In partnership with four partners, one of the partners meets with an untimely death. The effect of the death on the partnership is:

a. There is no effect since the surviving partners will continue the partnership

b. The firm has to be closed

c. The share of the deceased will vest with his legal heirs, who will become partners in his place

d. The partnership is dissolved, but the surviving partners can continue the business

Q.25: The adjustment, that is carried out on the death of a partner, but not on the retirement of a partner is:

a. Valuation of goodwill

b. Revaluation of Assets & Liabilities

c. Ascertainment of up-to-date profit or loss

d. Transfer of accumulated reserves

Q.26: The deceased partners cannot be given share in the profits till his death

a. True

b. False

(If the death takes place in the middle of accounting period, the deceased partner is entitled to his share in profit or loss upto the date of his death. The amount can be determined by)

(i) *preparing final accounts up to the date of death, or*

(ii) *an estimated share in profit or loss is determined on the basis of*

(a) *preceding year*

(b) *on the basis of sales up to the date of death and calculating profit on the basis of the percentage of profit earned in the previous year*

(c) *on the basis of the time*

(d) *on the basis of the average of the two*

Q.27: On the death of a partner, the profit up to the date of death is calculated on the basis of

a. Time

b. Sales

c. Time or sales whichever is higher

d. Time or sales as agreed by partners or as given in the partnership deed.

Q.28: Which one of the following statements relating to adjustment in accounts on the death of a partner is wrong

a. The profit due to the deceased partner is credited to his capital account to the debit of Profit & Loss suspense account

b. Balance payable to the deceased partner is transferred to the account of his executors

c. Profit & Loss suspense account cannot appear in the balance sheet

d. The Profit & Loss suspense account is closed by transferring its balance to Profit & Loss account of next year

Joint Life Policy

Q.29: The premium on a joint life policy is taken by a partnership firm on the lives of its partners is

a. payable by the partners from their own resources

b. payable by the firm to the debit of their drawings accounts

c. payable by the firm, treating it as an expenditure of the firm

d. payable by the firm to the debit of their capital accounts

Q.30: Where a Joint Life Policy is taken by a firm, and it is decided to treat it as an asset, the JLP a/c will be shown in the Balance Sheet at the

a. Value of Premium paid

b. Value of Premium paid plus bonus declared

c. Face value of the policy

d. Surrender value of the policy

Q.31: ABCD Associates, a partnership firm, had taken a joint life policy for Rs. 3,00,000. D, a partner, dies and the policy amount is received from the LIC. The premium so far paid is Rs. 60,000.

a. Rs. 3,00,000 is payable to the executors of D

b. Rs. 2,40,000 is payable to the executors of D

c. Rs. 3,00,000 should be credited to the capital accounts of all the partners, including D in their old profit sharing ratio

d. Rs. 2,40,000 should be credited to the capital accounts of all the partners, including D in their old profit sharing ratio

ANSWERS					
1. —	2. —	3. (a)	4. (a)&(c)	5. (a)	6. (c)
7. (b)	8. (c)	9. (c)	10. (b)	11. (b)	12. (b)
13. —	14. (b)	15. (c)	16. (d)	17. (d)	18. (a)
19. —	20. (b)	21. —	22. (b)	23. —	24. (d)
25. (c)	26. (b)	27. (d)	28. (c)	29. (c)	30. (d)
31. (c)					

CHAPTER 32

SLEEPING/QUASI-PARTNERSHIP

Sleeping Partner

Q.1: A partner who invests capital in a business for getting share in the profits of the firm, but not interested in day to day working of the partnership is called

a. Semi-partner

b. Dummy partner

c. Quasi partner

d. Sleeping partner

Q.2: A partner who invests capital in a business for getting share in the profits of the firm, and is also interested in day to day working of the partnership is called

a. Working-partner

b. Active partner

c. Busy partner

d. Effective partner.

Q.3: A sleeping partner is not responsible to the third parties for the acts and omissions of the partnership.

a. True

b. False

(Law makes no difference between a sleeping partner and a working partner. A sleeping partner will be equally responsible to the third parties for all acts or omissions of a working partner)

Quasi or Nominal Partner

Q.4: Sometimes, some prominent persons lend their names to a firm in order to allow the firm to enjoy their goodwill in furtherance of its business. Such persons are known as

a. Sleeping partners
b. Quasi partner
c. Nominal partner
d. Dummy partner

Q.5: A quasi partner is in fact

a. a partner in the firm
b. not a partner in the firm
c. partner to a limited extent
d. partner without liability

Q.6: If a person keeps quiet, inspite of being fully aware of the fact that his name is utilized as a partner

a. legally he is not liable to third parties
b. he is liable to third parties
c. law estops him from disclaiming his status as partner to third parties
d. (b) & (c) above

ANSWERS					
1. (d)	2. (a) or (b)	3. (b)	4. (b) or (c)	5. (b)	6. (d)

CHAPTER 33

COMPANY ACCOUNTS (ISSUE OF SHARES)

Meaning

Q.1: Select the incorrect statement:

a. A company is an association of persons

b. The persons contribute money or money's worth to a common stock

c. They use the money for a common purpose

d. The liability of the members is unlimited

(The liability of the members of the joint stock company is limited to the face value of shares held by them)

Q.2: Select the incorrect statement:

a. A company is a registered body of individuals

b. It is an artificial person created by law

c. A company has a perpetual succession

d. The members of the company participate in the management of the company

(Even though the shareholders are true owners, they do not participate in the management of the company. They elect their representatives called Board of Directors.)

Q.3: Select the incorrect statement:

a. The liability of the members of the joint stock company is limited to the face value of shares held by them

b. Even though the shareholders are true owners, they do not participate in the management of the company.

c. The shares of a company are freely transferable.

d. A company has no legal status. Shareholders are liable for the acts of the company.

(A company has an independent legal status, as such, the shareholders are not liable for the acts of the company)

Q.4: A member of a company may bind the company by his actions and the shareholder of a company is liable for the acts of the company.

a. True

b. False

(Legal existence of a company is different from that of its members)

Q.5: The company may file a suit in its own name and suits may be filed against the company

a. True

b. False

Q.6: Select the correct statement

a. Shares are not freely transferable in a Pvt. Ltd. Co.

b. The maximum number of members is 50 in case of a public company

c. Shareholders liability is unlimited in a Public company

d. The minimum number of members to form a partnership firm is 7

Q.7: The objects of a company are given in the

a. Articles of Association

b. Prospectus

c. Memorandum of association

d. Objects of association

Q.8: For the floatation of a public company at least _____ members are required

a. 2

b. 5

c. 7

d. 11

Q.9: The allotment of shares should be completed within ......days of the issue of prospectus

a. 90

b. 120

c. 150

d. 180

Types of Companies

Q.10: Companies cannot be classified on the basis of their

a. Incorporation

b. Ownership

c. Liability

d. Capital

Q.11: On the basis of incorporation, a company cannot be divided into

a. Statutory company

b. Chartered company

c. Holding company

d. Registered company

Q.12: On the basis of ownership, a company cannot be divided into

a. Private company

b. Public company

c. Statutory company

d. Government company

Q.13: On the basis of liability, a company cannot be divided into

a. Company limited by activities

b. Company limited by shares

c. Company limited by guarantee

d. Company with unlimited liability

Q.14: A ....Company puts restrictions on the transfer of its shares

a. Public limited company

b. Statutory company

c. Private company

d. Holding company

Partnership and Limited Liability Company

Q.15: The formation of a Limited company is easier than the formation of a Partnership firm

a. Right

b. Wrong

(The formation of a limited company is difficult because too many legal formalities are involved)

Q.16: Registration of a partnership firm as well as that of a company are compulsory

a. True

b. False

(Registration of a partnership firm is not compulsory)

Q.17: Select the incorrect statement

a. A firm can be formed with a minimum of 2 members

b. A private company can be formed with a minimum of 2 members

c. A private company can be formed with a minimum of 7 persons

d. A public company can be formed with a minimum of 7 persons

Q.18: Select the incorrect statement

a. A firm can be formed with a Maximum number of 10 members for banking business

b. A firm can be formed with a Maximum number of 20 members for other business.

c. A Private company can be formed with a Maximum number of 50 persons.

d. A public company can be formed with a Maximum number of 1000 persons.

(There is no restriction on maximum number of members in case of a public company)

Q.19: Select the incorrect statement

a. Liability of partners of a firm is unlimited

b. Liability of shareholders is usually limited to the face value of the shares held by them.

c. In partnership, the ownership rest with the partners and management with the managers

d. In a company there is a separation of ownership and management

(In partnership ownership and management both rests with partners. The property of the firm is owned by the partners themselves)

Q.20: Select the incorrect statement

a. A partnership does not have a perpetual existence

b. A limited company enjoys perpetual existence. Death or insolvency of any shareholder does not affect existence of the company.

c. A share in the partnership can be transferred without the consent of other partners

d. The shares of a company are freely transferable

(A share in the partnership cannot be transferred without the consent of other partners)

Classes of Share Capital

Q.21: Select the incorrect statement

a. Share capital can be of two types-Equity and Preference

b. Preference share capital can be of three types-Cumulative, redeemable, participating

c. Preference shares enjoys the preferential right as to the payment of (i) dividend at a fixed rate and (ii) the return of capital on winding up of the company

d. Preference shares are a part of equity shares

(Preference shares are a part of total share capital. Preference shares have some preferential rights. Equity share capital is that part of share capital which is not preference share capital)

Q.22: Select the incorrect statement

a. Dividend is declared out of profits. If there is no profit or inadequate profit, dividend is not declared

b. In case of cumulative preference shares, if dividend is not declared, the amount of fixed dividend is carried over to the next year. In subsequent years when the company makes profits, arrear of preference dividend are paid first before any payment to equity shareholders.

c. Redeemable preference shares are those preference shares which can be redeemed.

d. Preference shares are participating and non-cumulative, unless expressly stated otherwise.

(Preference shares are non-participating and cumulative, unless expressly stated otherwise.)

Q.23: Select the incorrect statement

a. Share capital can be classified as Authorised, Issued, Subscribed, Called up and paid up capital.

b. Authorised capital is stated in the Memorandum of Association. This is the amount up to which the company can raise the capital

c. Paid up capital is the amount which has actually been paid by the share holders.

d. Called up capital is that part of issued capital which has been actually subscribed by the public.

(That part of issued capital which has been actually subscribed by the public is called Subscribed Capital. It can be less than the or at the most equal to issued capital)

Q.24: Select the incorrect statement

a. Issued Capital is that capital which is issued. Its maximum limit is the authorized capital. It may be issued to the public or partly to vendors against purchase consideration

b. Subscribed capital is that part of issued capital which has been actually subscribed by the public.

c. Called up capital is the amount which the company has asked the shareholders to pay.

d. Paid up capital is the amount which has actually been paid by the share holders.

Ans. All are correct

Q.25: State the order in which the following terms in respect of share capital are listed:

i. Paid up capital

ii. Calls in advance

iii. Subscribed capital

iv. Authorised capital

v. Issued capital

a. iv, v, iii, ii,i

b. v, iv, iii, i, iii

c. iv, v, iii, i, ii

d. None of the above

Issue of Shares

Q.26: Select the incorrect statement

a. The total applications received may be for a larger number of shares than what the company issued.

b. In case of over-subscription, the company cannot issue more shares than what it has offered through its prospectus.

c. If the minimum subscription is not received, the company cannot allot the shares.

d. In case of under subscription, shares can be issued at discount

Q.27: In a public issue of shares, the following are responsible

i. Regional Stock Exchange

ii. Lead Merchant Banker

iii. Registrar to the issue

a. Right

b. Wrong

Q.28: When the shares are over-subscribed the fair basis of allotment is finalized in accordance with the following guidelines

i. Applicants are categorized according to number of shares applied for

ii. Total number of shares to be allotted to each category as a whole is arrived at on a proportionate basis.

iii. The amount received on the rejected applications is refunded.

iv. The excess amount received, on applications accepted on pro-rata basis, is refunded or adjusted towards future calls on shares

a. Right

b. Wrong

Issue of Shares - at par

Q.29: When share applications are received

i. Application monies are deposited into Bank

ii. Application money does not become a part of share capital, until shares are allotted.

iii. Application money is temporarily kept under 'Share Application account'

a. Right

b. Wrong

Accounting Treatment on Issue of Shares by a Company

Transaction	Books of the Company	Books of the Company
	A/c Debited	A/c Credited
1. Receipt of application money	Bank	Share application
2. On allotment:		
a. for transfer of share application money to share capital.	Share application	Share capital a/c
b. for refund of amount on rejected applications		Bank a/c

Transaction	Books of the Company	Books of the Company
	A/c Debited	A/c Credited
c. for utilizing the amount towards allotment		Share allotment a/c
d. for utilizing the amount towards calls		Calls in advance
3. To make the allotment due	Share allotment a/c	Share capital a/c
4. For receiving the amount of allotment money	Bank a/c	Share allotment a/c
5. To make the calls due	Share ....Call a/c	Share capital a/c
6. For receiving the amount of calls money	Bank a/c Calls in advance a/c	Share ....Call a/c
7. When shares are issued for exchange of assets	Assets a/c	Share capital a/c

Accounting Treatment on purchase of a running business by a company

Transaction	Books of the Company	Books of the Company
	A/c Debited	A/c Credited
1. For purchase of business at a certain agreed price	Business Purchase	Vendors
2. For assets and liabilities taken over at agreed price *(if credit exceeds debits-put the difference in Goodwill a/c and if debit exceeds credit-put the difference in Capital Reserve a/c)*	Assets A/c	Liabilities A/c Business purchase A/c
3. For discharging the payment by cheque/ shares/debentures	Vendors	Bank/Share capital/ Debentures a/c

Q.30: Money received in advance from shareholders before it is actually called up is

a. Debited in calls in arrears A/c

b. Credited in calls in arrears A/c

c. Debited in calls in advance A/c

d. Credited in calls in advance A/c

Issue of Shares - at Premium

Q.31: Select the incorrect statement

a. When shares are issued at higher price than their face value, they are said to be issued at premium.

b. The company act does not prohibit the issue of shares at a premium.

c. Amount of premium is decided by the Board of directors as per guidelines issued by SEBI.

d. Premium amount can be utilized for any purpose.

Q.32: Premium amount can be utilized for the following purposes

i. Buy back of shares

ii. Issue of fully paid bonus shares

iii. Writing off preliminary expenses and discount or commission on issue of shares or debentures

iv. Paying premium on redemption of preference shares or debentures.

a. Right

b. Wrong

Accounting Treatment for issue of shares at a premium

Transaction	Books of the Company	Books of the Company
	A/c Debited	A/c Credited
When premium is received with application		
1.On receiving application money		
2. For transferring the application money	Bank A/c	Share Application A/c
	Share Application A/c	Share Capital
When premium is received with allotment money;	Share Premium A/c	
1. For making allotment due	Share Allotment A/c	Share Capital Share Premium A/c
2. On receipt of amount	Bank A/c	Share Allotment A/c
When premium is received with calls;		
1. For making call due	Share Allotment A/c	Share Capital Share Premium A/c
2. On receipt of amount	Bank A/c	Share Allotment A/c

Issue of Shares - at Discount

Q.33: Points to note :—

a. Normally shares are not issued at discount.

b. If the shares are to be issued at a discount, they should be of the same class which have already been issued

c. It should be authorized by members by passing resolution in the General meeting

d. Sanction should be obtained from Company Law Board

e. Shares must be issued within 2 months or within extended time from the date of sanction.

f. Rate of discount must be specified

g. Rate of discount should not exceed 10% of the face value of shares

h. Shares issued must be of the same class which have already been issued

(A company cannot issue shares at a discount within one year from the date it commenced its business)

Accounting Treatment for issue of shares at a discount

Transaction	**Books of the Company**	**Books of the Company**
	A/c Debited	**A/c Credited**
1. On receiving application money	Bank A/c	Share Application A/c
2. For transferring the application money	Share Application A/c	Share Capital
3. For making allotment due	Share Allotment A/c Discount on issue of shares	Share Capital
2. On receipt of amount	Bank A/c	Share Allotment A/c
When premium is received with calls;		
1. For making call due	Share Allotment A/c	Share Capital Share Premium A/c
2. On receipt of amount	Bank A/c	Share Allotment A/c

Issue of Sweat Equity Shares

Q.34: Sweat shares means

i. Equity shares issued by the company to employees or directors

(*a*) at a discount, or

(*b*) for consideration other than cash

- for providing know how
- making available right in the nature of intellectual property rights
- value additions

ii. shares should be of the same class which have already been issued

iii. it should be authorized by members by passing resolution in the General meeting

iv. it should be issued in accordance with the regulations made by the SEBI

a. Right

b. Wrong

Issue of Shares under ESOS

Q.35: Under Employees Stock Option Scheme, the company grants option to an employee

i. to apply for shares at a pre-determined price

ii. the right to be exercised during a specified period

iii. listed companies have to follow SEBI guidelines for ESOS

a. right

b. wrong

Forfeiture of shares

Q.36: Forfeiture means cancellation of the name of defaulting shareholder from the register of members and the amounts already paid by him are forfeited. The shares can be forfeited

i. When a shareholder does not pay dues

ii. On continuous default company sends him a final notice that if he does not pay his dues within 14 days, the Board can pass a resolution to forfeit his shares.

iii. The amount paid by the member is not to be returned to him

a. True

b. False

Q.37: Select the correct statement:

a. Share premium amount can be distributed as dividend amongst the shareholders

b. A company can issue shares at a discount in its very first year of working

c. If calls on shares are not received, company can forfeit these shares

d. Capital Redemption Reserve can be utilized for payment of dividend.

Accounting Treatment for forfeiture of shares

Transaction	A/c Debited Books of the Company A/c Debited	A/c Credited Books of the Company A/c Credited
1. For recording calls in arrears	Calls in arrears A/c	.....Call A/c
2. On forfeiture of shares issued at par	Share Capital A/c (Amount called up)	Calls in arrears (Unpaid amount) Share forfeiture (Amount received)

Transaction	A/c Debited Books of the Company A/c Debited	A/c Credited Books of the Company A/c Credited
3. On forfeiture of shares issued at premium *a.* If share premium is due on shares to be forfeited	Share Capital A/c (Amount called up) Share Premium A/c (Premium due)	Calls in arrears (Unpaid amount) Share forfeiture (Amount received)
4. On forfeiture of shares issued at a discount	Share Capital A/c (Amount called up)	Share forfeiture (Amount received) Calls in arrears (Unpaid amount) Discount on issue of shares

Q.38: Indicate the alternative which you consider to be correct:

On a hundred rupee share, Rs. 80 have been called up. On forfeiture, the amount to be debited to share capital account will be:

a. Rs. 100
b. Rs. 80
c. Rs. 50
d. Rs. 20

Q.39: Indicate the alternative which you consider to be correct:

If a Rs. 10 share has been issued at a premium of Rs. 2, on which the whole of the amount has been called up, has been forfeited for non payment of Rs. 4, the share capital account will be debited by

a. Rs. 12
b. Rs. 10
c. Rs. 8
d. Rs. 6

Q.40: Indicate the alternative which you consider to be correct:

If a share of Rs. 10 issued at a premium of Re. 1, on which Rs. 9 (including premium) have been called and Rs. 7 (including premium) paid is forfeited. The capital account should be debited by

a. Rs. 10
b. Rs. 9
c. Rs. 8
d. Rs. 7

Reissue of Forfeited Shares

Q.41: Forfeited shares can be re issued by the company at any time. There is, however, restriction with regard to price at which they can be re-issued.

i. Such shares cannot be reissued at a price which is lower than the amount in arrears.

ii. If the total amount received on re-issue of forfeited shares (Reissue amount +forfeited amount) exceeds the face value of the share, the excess amount is transferred to capital reserve.

a. Right

b. Wrong

Accounting Treatment for re-issue of forfeiture of shares

Transaction	**Books of the Company**	**Books of the Company**
	A/c Debited	**A/c Credited**
1. For re-issuing the forfeited shares	Bank A/c (Actual amount received) Share Forfeiture A/c (Discount allowed on re-issue)	Share Capital (Amount called up and credited to Share capital on the forfeited shares)
2. For transferring profit on re-issue of forfeited shares	Share Forfeiture A/c	Capital Reserve A/c

Q.42: When all forfeited shares are not issued

i. Only proportionate amount of forfeited shares account relating to that part which has been re-issued can be utilized towards discount to be given to the new shareholders

ii. Any balance left from this proportionate amount will be treated as net gain on re-issue of shares. This amount is transferred to capital reserve account.

iii. The amount relating to that part of forfeited shares, which have not yet been reissued, will be left in the share forfeiture account.

iv. The balance in share forfeiture account is utilized for allowing discount as and when such shares are re-issued.

v. The amount of shares forfeited will be shown on the liabilities side of the balance sheet

a. Right

b. Wrong

Issue of Bonus Shares

Q.43: Bonus shares are normally issued to the company's, existing shareholders without any consideration under the following circumstances

i. Company possesses large reserves as a result of its policy not to distribute whole of its profits

ii. Profits are accumulated by the company to meet unforeseen contingencies

iii. It is deemed desirable to give the benefit of these huge reserves to the existing shareholders

a. Right

b. Wrong

Q.44: Select the incorrect statement

The capitalization of profits by bonus issue may be done in the ways given below;

a. Issuing cheques for the amount of bonus to each existing shareholder

b. Making partly paid up shares into fully paid shares

c. Issue of fully paid bonus shares, without consideration

d. Reserves are reduced and capital is increased

Non-voting Shares

Q.45: Select the incorrect statement

Issue of non-voting shares have been authorized by

a. Indian Companies Act, 1956

b. Draft Companies Bill, 1997

c. Companies Amendment Act, 1999

d. Companies cannot issue non-voting shares

Q.46: Share capital of a company consists of

i. Equity Shares with voting rights

ii. Equity shares without voting rights

iii. Preference shares

iv. Deferred shares

a. All the four

b. (i) & (iii)

c. (i), (ii) and (iii)

d. (ii) & (iii)

Q.47: The main object of permitting the companies to issue non-voting equity shares is

a. to enable them to raise resources without losing management control

b. to provide a measure to the management to tap a class of investors who are interested in higher dividend against absence of voting rights.

c. to avoid election and objections in general body meetings

d. (i) and (ii) above

Q.48: Shares without voting rights can be issued only by a public company limited by shares when

(*i*) Authorised by the Articles of association of the company

(*ii*) Approved by existing shareholders in their General body meeting by passing

(*iii*) A special resolution is to be passed stating therein

(*a*) The price at which the shares can be issued

(*b*) The higher rate of dividend which these shares shall carry

(*iv*) Such shareholders are entitled to all rights and bonus shares, but no voting rights

(*v*) Only 25% of the paid up capital of the company can be issued as non-voting equity shares

(*vi*) No company is permitted to convert its existing shares with voting rights into shares without voting rights.

a. True

b. False

ANSWERS					
1. (d)	2. (d)	3. (d)	4. (b)	5. (a)	6. (a)
7. (c)	8. (c)	9. (b)	10. (d)	11. (c)	12. (c)
13. (a)	14. (c)	15. (b)	16. (b)	17. (c)	18. (d)
19. (c)	20. (c)	21. (d)	22. (d)	23. (d)	24. —
25. (c)	26. (d)	27. (a)	28. (a)	29. (a)	30. (d)
31. (d)	32. (a)	33. —	34. (a)	35. (a)	36. (a)
37. (c)	38. (b)	39. (b)	40. (c)	41. (a)	42. (a)
43. (a)	44. (a)	45. (b)	46. (c)	47. (d)	48. (a)

CHAPTER

34

FINAL ACCOUNTS OF COMPANIES

Need and Legal Requirement

Q. 1: Final accounts of a limited company consist of

a. Receipts & Payment account, Income & Expenditure account and Balance Sheet.

b. Profit & Loss Account and Statement of affairs

c. Schedules of Debtors, Creditors, Assets and Liabilities

d. Profit & Loss account and Balance Sheet

Q. 2: Trading account need not be prepared separately but can be included in

a. Manufacuring Account

b. Consignment Account

c. Profit & Loss Account

d. The form of a separate schedule

Q. 3: Companies Act provides the form of Balance Sheet under Part I of Schedule VI of Section

a. 209

b. 210

c. 211

d. 2

Q. 4: Preparation of final accounts by a limited company is

a. optional

b. compulsory

c. not required

d. made compulsory under law

(Under Companies Act, 1956

(i) *section 209 makes it compulsory for a company to keep certain books of accounts*

(ii) *section 210 governs the preparation of the final accounts, and*

(iii) *section 211 requires that the Balance Sheet and Profit & Loss account of the company should exhibit a true and fair view of the affairs and profit or loss of the company*

(iv) *section 211 Schedule VI Part I gives a format for the preparation of Balance Sheet*

(v) *section 211 Schedule VI Part II gives requirements for the preparation of P & L A/c)*

Form of Balance Sheet

Q. 5: A balance sheet of a limited company can be prepared

a. Horizontally

b. Vertically

c. By any of the alternative

d. By some other method

Q. 6: The balance sheet of a company is having

a. 4 columns

b. 2 columns

c. 6 columns

d. 8 columns

(*The balance is divided mainly into two parts-Liabilities and Assets. Each part is sub-divided into three columns to show figures for the previous year, figures for the current year along with the Liabilities/Assets)*

Q. 7: As per Schedule VI Part I

a. the Liabilities are taken below Assets

b. the Assets are taken below Liabilities

c. the assets and liabilities are shown side by side

d. some other method of presentation is followed

Q. 8: The Liabilities of a company are arranged in the following order

I. Share Capital

II. Reserves and Surplus

III. Secured Loans

IV. Unsecured loans

V. Current Liabilities & Provisions

(*A*) Current Liabilities

(*B*) Provisions

(*C*) Other Provisions

Q. 9: Re-arrange the following sequence under the liabilities side of Balance Sheet

I. Share Capital

II. Unsecured loans

III. Secured Loans

IV. Reserves and Surplus

V. Current Liabilities & Provisions

A. Current Liabilities

B. Provisions

C. Other Provisions

a. *I, IV, III, II, V*

b. *V, II, III, IV, I*

c. *I, III, II, IV, V*

d. *I, IV, II, III, V*

Q. 10: The Assets side of the Balance Sheet shows the following sequence:

I. Fixed Assets

II. Investments

III. Current Assets, Loans and Advances

(A) Current Assets

(B) Loans & Advances

IV. Miscellaneous Expenditure

V. Profit & Loss account (Debit balance, if any)

Q. 11: Re-arrange the following sequence under the liabilities side of Balance Sheet

I. Fixed Assets

II. Current Assets, Loans and Advances

a. Current Assets

b. Loans & Advances

III. Investments

IV. Miscellaneous Expenditure

a. I, IV, III, II

b. I, III, II, IV

c. IV, II, III, I

d. I, III, IV, II

Share Capital

Q.12: Share Capital of a company is required to be shown as under:

I. Share Capital :

Authorised:

...........Shares of Rs. ...... each

Issued

...........Shares of Rs. ...... each

Subscribed

...........Shares of Rs. ...... each

Called up

...........Shares of Rs. ...... per share called up

Less: Unpaid calls

Add: Forfeited Shares

Paid up Capital

Q. 13: With regard to Share Capital, the company should specifically state:

1. Details of Authorised, Issued, Subscribed, Called-up and Paid up capitals
2. Details of number of shares and face value of each share
3. Amount called up on each share
4. Classes of shares-Preference or Equity with or without voting rights
5. Shares allotted as fully paid for consideration other than cash
6. Shares issued as bonus shares and source

Reserves and Surplus

Q.14: Reserves and Surplus is required to be shown as under:

II. Reserves and Surplus

1. Capital Reserve

2. Capital redemption Reserve
3. Share Premium Account
4. Other reserves

   Less: Debit balance in P & L A/c, if any
5. Surplus (Balance in the P & L appropriation A/c)
6. Proposed additions to reserves
7. Sinking funds

Q.15: Re-arrange the following sequence under the liabilities side of Balance Sheet

Reserves and Surplus

1. Capital Reserve
2. Sinking funds
3. Surplus (Balance in the P & L appropriation A/c)
4. Proposed additions to reserves
5. Capital redemption Reserve
6. Share Premium Account
7. Other reserves

   Less: Debit balance in P & L A/c, if any

   a. 1, 5, 6, 7, 3, 4, 2

   b. 2,4,3,7,6,5,1

   c. 1,6,3,2,5,7,4

   d. 5,7,4,1,6,3,2

Secured Loans

Q.16: Secured Loans are to be shown as under:

III. Secured Loans

1. Debentures
2. Loans and advances from banks
3. Loans and advances from Subsidiaries
4. Other Loans and advances

Q. 17: Re-arrange the following sequence under the liabilities side of Balance Sheet

Secured Loans

1. Debentures
2. Loans and advances from Subsidiaries

3. Other Loans and advances
4. Loans and advances from banks
    a. 1,2,3,4
    b. 1,4,2,3
    c. 4,3,2,1
    d. 3,2,4,1

Unsecured loans

Q. 18: Unsecured loans are to be shown under the following sequence:

IV Unsecured loans

1. Fixed deposits
2. Loans and advances from subsidiaries
3. Short term loans & Advances
    (*a*) From Banks
    (*b*) From Others
4. Other loans and advances
    (*a*) From Banks
    (*b*) From Others

Q. 19: Re-arrange the following sequence under the liabilities side of Balance Sheet

Unsecured loans

1. Short term loans & Advances
    a. From Banks
    b. From Others
2. Other loans and advances
    (*a.*) From Banks
    (*b*) From Others
3. Loans and advances from subsidiaries
4. Fixed deposits
    a. 4, 3, 1, 2
    b. 2,1,3,4
    c. 1,2,3,4
    d. 4,1,2,3

Current Liabilities & Provisions

Q. 20: Current Liabilities are to be shown as under:

V. Current Liabilities & Provisions

(A) Current Liabilities

1. Acceptances
2. Sundry Creditors
3. Subsidiary companies
4. Advance payment and unexpired discounts
5. Unclaimed dividends
6. Other liabilities (if any)
7. Interest accrued but not due on loans

Q.21: Re-arrange the following sequence under the liabilities side of Balance Sheet

Current Liabilities

1. Advance payment and unexpired discounts
2. Other liabilities (if any)
3. Interest accrued but not due on loans
4. Subsidiary companies
5. Acceptances
6. Unclaimed dividends
7. Sundry Creditors

a. 5, 7, 4, 1, 6, 2, 3

b. 3, 2, 6, 1, 4, 5, 7

c. 5, 7, 1, 4, 2, 6, 3

d. 1, 2, 4, 3, 6, 5, 7

Q. 22: Re-arrange the following sequence under the liabilities side of Balance Sheet

V. Current Liabilities & Provisions

(B) Provisions

1. Provision for taxation
2. Provision for Proposed dividend
3. Provision for contingencies
4. Provision for Provident Fund Scheme
5. Provision for Insurance, Pensions and similar staff benefit schemes

Q. 23: Re-arrange the following sequence under the liabilities side of Balance Sheet

Provisions

1. Provision for Provident Fund Scheme
2. Provision for Insurance, Pensions and similar staff benefit schemes
3. Provision for Proposed dividend
4. Provision for contingencies
5. Provision for taxation

   a. 5, 3, 4, 1, 2
   b. 2, 1, 4, 3, 5
   c. 5, 4, 3, 2, 1
   d. 1, 2, 3, 4, 5

Fixed Assets

Q. 24: Fixed Assets are to be shown as under:

I. Fixed Assets

1. Goodwill
2. Land
3. Buildings
4. Leaseholds
5. Railway sidings
6. Plant & Machinery
7. Furniture & fittings
8. Development of property
9. Patents, trade marks & designs
10. Live stock
11. Vehicles, etc.

Q. 25: Re-arrange the following sequence under the Assets side of Balance Sheet

Fixed Assets

1. Buildings
2. Land
3. Leaseholds
4. Plant & Machinery
5. Furniture & fittings

6. Development of property
7. Goodwill
8. Patents, trade marks & designs
9. Livestock
10. Vehicles, etc.
11. Railway sidings

    a. 10, 9, 8, 6, 5, 4, 11, 3, 1, 2, 7
    b. 1, 2, 3, 4, 7, 5, 6, 8, 9, 10, 11
    c. 1, 2, 3, 4, 5, 7, 6, 10, 11, 8, 9
    d. 7, 2, 1, 3, 11, 4, 5, 6, 8, 9, 10

Q. 26: The fixed assets must be

1. Classified and distinguished
2. The following details are required to be shown separately:
    (*i*) original cost,
    (*ii*) additions during the year,
    (*iii*) deductions therefrom during the year,
    (*iv*) total depreciation written off or provided up to the end of the year

Investments

Q. 27: Investments are to be shown as under:

Investments

1. Investments in Government or trust securities
2. Investment in shares, Debentures or bonds
3. Investment in immovable properties
4. Investment in the capital of partnership firms
5. Balance of unutilised monies raised by issues

Q.28: The following must be clearly stated with regard to Investments:

1. Nature of Investments
2. Mode of valuation (Cost or market value)
3. Classification of Investments

Current Assets Loans & Advances

Q. 29: Current Assets are to be shown as under

Current Assets, Loans & Advances

A. Current Assets

1. Interest accrued on investments
2. Stores and spare parts
3. Loose tools
4. Stock in trade
5. Sundry Debtors
6. Cash in hand
7. Bank balances
   (*a*) With scheduled banks
   (*b*) With others

Q.30: Re-arrange the following sequence under the Assets side of Balance Sheet

Current Assets

1. Cash in hand
2. Bank Balances
   (*a*) With scheduled banks
   (*b*) With others
3. Stock in trade
4. Sundry Debtors
5. Interest accrued on investments
6. Stores and spare parts
7. Loose tools

   a. 5, 6, 7, 3, 4, 1, 2
   b. 2, 1, 4, 3, 7, 6, 5
   c. 1, 2, 3, 4, 5, 6, 7
   d. 4, 3, 2, 1, 5, 6, 7

Q. 31: In respect of Sundry Debtors following details are to be shown:

1. Debts considered good and in respect of which the company is fully secured
2. Debts considered good for which the company holds no security other than personal security of debtors
3. Debts considered doubtful or bad

Q.32: In respect of balance at the bank, the following particulars should be given:

1. Balance with scheduled bank on current accounts, call accounts and deposit accounts
2. Balance with other banks-which are not scheduled banks

Q. 33: Loans and advances are shown in the following sequence on the assets side of the balance sheet

Loans & Advances

1. Advances and loans
2. Bills of Exchange
3. Advances receivable in cash or kind or for value to be received
4. Balances on current accounts
5. Balances with Customs, Port trust, etc. (where payable on demand)

Q. 34: Re-arrange the following sequence under the Assets side of Balance Sheet

1. Bills of Exchange
2. Balances on current accounts
3. Balances with Customs, Port trust, etc.
4. Advances and loans
5. Advances receivable in cash or kind or for value to be received

   a. 4, 1, 5, 2, 3
   b. 3, 2, 5, 1, 4
   c. 1, 2, 3, 4, 5
   d. 2, 1, 4, 3, 5

Miscellaneous Expenditure

Q. 35: Miscellaneous expenditure is shown in the following sequence on the assets side of the balance sheet:

1. Preliminary expenses
2. Expenses including commission or brokerage on underwriting or subscription of shares or debentures
3. Discount allowed on issue of shares or debentures
4. Interest paid out of capital during construction
5. Development expenditure not adjusted
6. Other items

Contingent Liabilities

Q. 36: Match the following pairs in columns A & B:

Column A	Column B	Answer
1. Fixed assets	A. Partly paid up shares held as investments	1 D
2. Current Liabilities	B. Debentures	2-E
3. Secured loans	C.Deposits from public	3-B
4. Unsecured loans	D. Goodwill	4-C
5. Contingent liability	E. Sundry creditors	5-A

Q. 37: Match the following pairs in columns A & B:

Column A	Column B	Answer
1.Proposed dividend	A.Provisions	1-D
2. Unclaimed dividend	B.Reserves & Surplus	2-E
3. Provision for taxation	C.Share Capital	3-A
4. Share premium	D.Provisions	4-B
5. Forfeited Shares account	E.Current Liability	5-C
6. P & L A/c (Cr. Balance)	F.Reserves & Surplus	6-F

Q. 38: Match the following pairs in columns A & B:

Column A	Column B	Answer
1.Work in Progress	A. Miscellaneous expenditure	1-E
2. Government Bonds	B. Loans & Advances	2-D
3. Goodwill	C. Fixed Assets	3-C
4. Prepaid Insurance	D. Investments	4-B
5. Discount on issue of shares	E. Current Assets	5-A

Q. 39: Match the following pairs in columns A & B:

Column A	Column B	Answer
1. Bills Receivable	A. Contingent liability	1-I
2. Loose tools	B. Provisions	2- H
3. Unclaimed dividend	C. Current Liabilities	3-G
4. Preliminary expenses	D. Reserves & Surplus	4-F
5. Forfeited Shares Account	E. Share Capital	5-E
6. Share premium account	F. Miscellaneous Expenditure	6-D
7. Unclaimed dividend	G. Liabilities	7-C
8. Proposed dividend	H. Current Assets	8-B
9. Arrears of fixed cumulative dividend	I. Loans & advances	9-A

Q. 40: Re-arrange the following heads of Assets side of Balance Sheet

i. Miscellaneous expenditure

ii. Loans & advances

iii. Fixed assets

iv. Investments

v. Current Assets

a. (i), (ii), (v), (iv), (iii)

b. (iii), (iv), (v), (ii), (i)

c. (iii), (iv), (v), (ii), (i)

d. The arrangement is in order

Legal requirements as to Profit & Loss account

Q. 41: There are four groups of guidelines to prepare Profit & Loss account as per part II of Schedule VI under section 211 of Indian Companies Act, 1956

1. General
2. Income
3. Expenditure
4. Quantitative and other information

Q. 42: As per the general instructions for the preparation of Profit & Loss account of a company, following are the guidelines.

Point out the incorrect statement

a. It should clearly disclose the results of the activities of the company

b. Every material information should be disclosed

c. The corresponding figures of previous year for all the items are also to be disclosed

d. Every item of expenditure and income should be shown separately.

(As per the guidelines various items of income and expenses in the account should be grouped under the most convenient heads)

Q. 43: As per the general instructions for the preparation of Profit & Loss account of a company, following are the guidelines.

Point out the incorrect statement

a. It should clearly disclose the profit before taxation, provision for tax and profit after tax.

b. It should clearly disclose all the appropriations made out of profits and the amount of surplus carried forward to next year

c. Adjustments regarding incomes and expenses pertaining to the previous year may be ignored.

d. Any change in accounting system should be clearly disclosed with full information and its effect on the profit or loss of the company.

(Adjustments regarding the incomes and expenses pertaining to the previous year should be clearly shown in the appropriation part of the P & L A/c)

Income

Q. 44: As per the instructions on Income while preparing the Profit & Loss account of a company, following are the guidelines.

Point out the incorrect statement

a. It should disclose the aggregate amount of sales as well as sales in respect of each class of goods in which the company deals

b. In case the company provide services, then gross income derived from rendering services

c. Income derived from trade and other investments

d. Profit and loss on sale of fixed assets or investments are not to be shown,

(Profit & Loss on sale of fixed assets or investments or any other exceptional or non-recurring transactions is also required to be exhibited.)

Expenditure

Q. 45: As per the instructions on Expenditure while preparing the Profit & Loss account of a company, following are the guidelines

Point out the incorrect statement

a. Item-wise break up of raw material consumed

b. Opening and closing value of work in progress

c. Closing stock of finished goods

d. Opening stock of finished goods is not shown.

(Both opening and closing stock of goods are required to be shown)

Q. 46: As per the instructions on Expenditure while preparing the Profit & Loss account of a company, following are the guidelines

Point out the incorrect statement

a. Remuneration paid to managing director/directors

b. Commission paid to directors, sole selling and other agents

c. Discount or brokerage

d. Depreciation charged. If depreciation is not provided on any asset, it may be ignored.

Q. 47: Income tax assessment for the previous year is completed and a demand notice has been served for Rs. 40,000. Other related items in trial balance are

Advance income tax Debit Rs. 35,000

Provision for income tax Credit Rs. 42,000

The adjusting entry will be

		Dr.	Cr.
a.	Provision for income tax a/c........................Dr.	42,000	
	To Advance tax		35,000
	To Tax payable		5,000
	To P & L appropriation A/c		2,000
b.	Income Tax ....Dr.	40,000	
	To advance tax		35,000
	To tax payable		5,000
c.	Provision for Income Tax.......................Dr.	42,000	
	Tax demanded .... Dr.	40,000	
	To advance Tax		35,000
	To tax payable		47,000
d.	None of the above		

(Provision for income tax and advance income tax accounts are closed.

Rs. 5,000, tax payable is shown under current liabilities

Rs. 2,000 is shown on the credit of P & L appropriation account as an excess provision)

Q. 48: Income tax assessment for the previous year is completed and a demand notice has been served for Rs. 40,000. Other related items in trial balance are

Advance income tax Debit Rs. 42,000

Provision for income tax Credit Rs. 38,000

		Dr.	Cr.
a.	Provision for income tax a/c........................Dr.	38,000	
	P & L appropriation A/c...........................Dr.	2,000	
	Income tax refund due............................Dr.	2,000	
	To Advance tax		42,000

b.	Income Tax ....Dr.	40,000	
	Income tax Refund..............................Dr.	2,000	
	To advance tax		42,000
c.	Provision for Income Tax.......................Dr.	42,000	
	Tax demanded .... Dr.	40,000	
	To advance Tax		42,000
	To tax payable		40,000
d.	None of the above		

(*Here Rs. 2000 is recoverable from Income Tax department, whereas provision for income tax is less by Rs. 2,000. Thus provision for income tax and advance tax accounts are closed. Income tax refund due shall appear in the assets side of Balance Sheet under the head Loans & Advances and short provision for income tax is debited to Income tax provision account*).

ANSWERS					
1. (d)	2. (c)	3. (c)	4. (d)	5. (c)	6. (c)
7. (b)	8. —	9. (a)	10. —	11. (b)	12. —
13. —	14. —	15. (a)	16. —	17. (b)	18. —
19. (a)	20. —	21. (a)	22. —	23. (a)	24. —
25. (d)	26. —	27. —	28. —	29. —	30. (a)
31. —	32. —	33. —	34. (a)	35. —	36. —
37. —	38. —	39. —	40. (c)	41. —	42. (d)
43. (c)	44. (d)	45. (d)	46. (d)	47. (a)	48. (a)

CHAPTER

35

FINAL ACCOUNTS OF BANKING COMPANIES

1. Introduction

Q1. What is true about a Banking Company?

(*a*) A company that carries on the business of Banking in India.

(*b*) It is generally governed by the Provisions of the Companies Act, 1956.

(*c*) It is specifically governed by the Banking Regulation Act.

(*d*) All of these

Q2. The Banking Regulation Act came into force on:

(*a*) 15th August,1947

(*b*) 26th January,1950

(*c*) 16th March,1949

(*d*) 14th April,1980

Q3. The Major institutions that are carrying on business of banking in India are:

(*a*) Nationalised Banks

(*b*) State Bank of India and their associates

(*c*) Foreign Banks having branches in India

(*d*) Co-operative Banks

(*e*) Rural Banks

(*f*) Private Sector Banks

2. Definitions and Functions of a bank

Q4. Main functions of modern commercial Banks are:

(*a*) Accepting money on deposits.

(*b*) Facilities to depositors for making payments by cheques.

(*c*) Granting of loans and advances.

(*d*) Dealing in securities on its own account or on behalf of customer.

(*e*) Opening letters of credit and issuing Guarantees

(*f*) Dealing in Foreign Exchange

(*g*) Transferring money from one place to another in the form of Demand Draft, Telegraphic Transfers, Traveller's Cheques and bills.

(*h*) Acting as Trustees and Executors.

(*i*) Dealing in Merchant Banking

Q5. As a function of Bank, "Banks can accept deposit from public for the purpose of lending or investment and deposits are repayable on demand or otherwise by cheques, draft, order or otherwise". This has been defined in:

(*a*) Section 2 of BR Act, 1949

(*b*) Section 10 of RBI Act, 1934

(*c*) Section 5 of BR Act,1949

(*d*) Section 6 of RBI Act, 1934

Q6. Section 6 of Banking Regulation Act defines:

(*a*) Basic functions of Banking companies.

(*b*) Certain classes of business, which are incidental to the business of banking which are permitted to be engaged in by the Banking Companies.

(*c*) The business activities in which Banking Companies are prohibited to be engaged.

(*d*) All of these

Q7. As per section 8 of BR Act, banks:

(*a*) Can be engaged in buying, selling or dealing in goods.

(*b*) Prohibited from buying, selling or dealing in goods.

(*c*) Prohibited from buying, selling or dealing in goods except in connection with the realization of a security held by it or in connection with the business of collections or negotiating bills of exchange.

(*d*) Banks can sell or purchase property.

3. Requirements of Banking Companies as to Accounts and Audit

1. Preparation of Financial Statements and Accounting Date

Q8. Guidelines regarding preparation of Financial Statements and Accounting Date for banking companies has been mentioned in:

(*a*) Section 30 of BR Act.

(*b*) Section 30 of Companies Act

(*c*) Schedule VI annexed to Companies Act

(*d*) Section 29 of BR Act, 1934

Q9. The format of Balance Sheet and Profit and Loss account in which the accounts of Banks should be presented are given in:

(*a*) Schedule VI annexed to Companies Act.

(*b*) Schedule II annexed to RBI Act

(*c*) Third Schedule annexed to BR Act.

(*d*) Section 211 of Companies Act

Q10. Which of the following are true for accounts of Banking Companies?

(*a*) Balance sheet is to be prepared on Form A (Proforma Balance Sheet).

(*b*) Profit and Loss Account is to be prepared on Form B (Proforma Profit and Loss Account).

(*c*) Accounts of the Banking companies shall be closed on 31st March every year.

(*d*) All of these

2. Audit

Q11. As per section 30 of Banking Regulation Act,1949:

(*a*) Bank accounts must be audited by a person, duly qualified by law in force to be an auditor of companies.

(*b*) Banking company may appoint, reappoint or remove any such auditor without any reference to Reserve Bank of India.

(*c*) Banking company is required to obtain prior approval from Reserve Bank of India before appointing, re-appointing or removing any auditor.

(*d*) a & c

3. Submission of Accounts

Q.12 As per sections 31 and 32 of Banking Regulation Act,1949, three copies of Balance Sheet and Profit and Loss Account prepared under section 29 and Auditor's report under section 30 must be submitted to RBI:

(*a*) Within one month from the end of the period to which they refer.

(*b*) Within six months from the end of the period to which they refer.

(*c*) Within three months from the end of the period to which they refer.

(*d*) Within twelve months from the end of the period to which they refer.

Q13. The period for submission of Balance Sheet and Profit and Loss Account to RBI by the banks can be extended by RBI for further period up to:

(*a*) One month

(*b*) One year

(*c*) Six months

(*d*) Three months

4. Publication of Accounts

Q14. Rules regarding publication of accounts of banks has been prescribed in:

(*a*) Rule 16 of Banking Regulating (Companies) Rules,1949

(*b*) Rule 20 of Banking Regulation Act,1949

(*c*) Rule 15 of Banking Regulating (Companies) Rules,1949

(*d*) Rule 30 of Banking Regulation Act,1949

Q15. As per Banking Regulating (Companies) Rules,1949:

(*a*) Bank's Accounts and Auditor's report shall be published in a Newspaper circulating at a place where the Banking Company has its principal office within 6 months from the end of the period to which they relate.

(*b*) Bank's Accounts and Auditor's report shall be published in Newspapers circulating at all big Metropolitan cities within 6 months from the end of the period to which they relate.

(*c*) Bank's Accounts and Auditor's report shall be published in a Newspaper circulating at a place where the Banking Company has its principal office within 3 months from the end of the period to which they relate.

(*d*) Bank's Accounts and Auditor's report shall be published in Newspapers circulating at all big Metropolitan cities within 3 months from the end of the period to which they relate.

5.Banker's Book

Q16. 'Bankers' Books' have been defined in:

(*a*) Sec. 2(3) of Banking Regulation Act,1949

(*b*) Sec. 2(3) of Reserve Bank of India Act,1934

(*c*) Sec. 2(3) of Banking Companies Act,1956

(*d*) Sec. 2(3) of Bankers' Books Evidence Act, 1891

Q17. Bankers' Books include:

(*a*) Ledgers

(*b*) Day Books

(*c*) Cash Books

(*d*) Account Books

(*e*) All other records used in the ordinary business of a bank

Q18. Fill in the blanks:

In Slip system of posting, all cash receipts and payments are recorded in cashier's cash books and then the pay in slips, cheques and withdrawals slips are entered first in the accounts of —— and after that the ——— is written.

(*a*) Customers, General ledger

(*b*) Banker, General ledger

(*c*) Customers, Day Book

(*d*) Customer, Cash Book

Concept:

Various Ledger Books and Other Books:

Ledger Books	Other Books
1. Current Accounts Ledger	1. Clearing Register
2. FD Accounts Ledger	2. Securities Register
3. RD Accounts Ledger	3. Draft Register
4. Loan Ledger	4. Bills for collection Register
5. Investment Ledger	5. Safe Deposit Vault Register
6. Bills discounted and Purchase Ledger	6. Dishonored Cheques Register Letter of Credit Register

4. Preparation and Presentation of Financial Statements of Banks

Q19. The revised format of Form A for Balance Sheet and revised format of Form B for Profit and Loss Account for bankers is effective from:

(*a*) 31st March, 1992

(*b*) 1st April, 1991

(*c*) 31st December, 1992

(*d*) 1st April, 1993

1. Preparation of Balance Sheet:

Format of Balance Sheet:

Third Schedule: Form 'A'

Form of Balance Sheet

Balance Sheet as on 31st March,............

Capital and Liabilities	Schedule	Rs.
Capital	1	....
Reserves and Surplus	2	....
Deposits	3	....
Borrowings	4	....
Other Liabilities and Provisions	5	....
Total		....

Assets	Schedule No.	Rs.
Cash and Balance with RBI	6	....
Balance with Banks and Money at call and Short Notice	7	....
Investments	8	....
Advances	9	....
Fixed Assets	10	....
Other Assets	11	....
Total		
Contingent Liabilities	12	....

Q20. Relate the following items of Capital and Liabilities with respective schedules of Balance Sheet (Form A):

Deposits, Other Liabilities and Provisions, Capital, Borrowings, Reserves and Surplus.

(*a*) 1,2,3,4,5,

(*b*) 2,5,3,4,1

(*c*) 3,5,1,4,2

(*d*) 5,3,4,1,2

Q21. Relate the following items of Assets with respective schedules of Balance Sheet (Form A):

Fixed Assets, cash and Balance with RBI, Balances with Banks and Money at Call and short notice, Investments, other Assets, Advances, Contingent Liabilities.

(*a*) 8,9,10,11,12,6,7

(*b*) 10,6,7,8,11,9,12

(*c*) 7,9,12,11,8,6,10

(*d*) 9,10,6,7,11,12,8

Q22. The various items in schedule-1 (Capital) in Balance Sheet (Form A) includes:

(*a*) For Nationalised Banks-Capital

(*b*) For Banks incorporated outside India- Start up capital as prescribed by RBI + Amount of deposit kept with RBI under section 11(2) of BR Act,1949.

(*c*) For other Banks- (*i*) Authorised Capital (…shares of Rs. ...each)

(*ii*) Issued Capital —do-

(*iii*) Subscribed Capital —do—

(*iv*) Called-up Capital —do—

(*v*) Less call unpaid + Add Forfeited Shares

(*d*) All of these

Q23. The various items in schedule-2 (Reserve and Surplus) in Balance Sheet(Form A) includes:

(*a*) Statutory Reserves (Opening Balance + Additions and Deductions during the year).

(*b*) Capital Reserves (————————— do——————————————————————).

(*c*) Share Premium (—————————— do——————————————————————).

(*d*) Revenue and other Reserves (————————— do——————————————).

(*e*) Balance in Profit and Loss Account.

Q24. The various items in schedule-3 (Deposits) in Balance Sheet (Form A) includes:

(*a*) (I) Demand Deposits— (i) From Banks, (ii) From Others.

(II) Savings Bank Deposits

(III) Term Deposits - (i) From Banks, (ii) From Others

(IV) Total (I + II + III)

(*b*) (I) Deposits of Branches in India

(II) Deposits of Branches Outside India

(*c*) All of these

(*d*) None of these

Q25. The various items in schedule-4 (Borrowings) in Balance Sheet (Form A) includes:

(*a*) Borrowings in India (Reserve Bank of India +Other Banks +Other Institutions and agencies)

(*b*) Borrowings outside India

(*c*) All of the above

(*d*) None of the above

Q26. The various items in schedule-5 (other Liabilities and Provisions) in Balance Sheet (Form A) includes:

(*a*) Bills Payable

(*b*) Inter-office Adjustments (net)

(*c*) Interest Accrued

(*d*) All of the above

Q27. The various items in schedule-6 (Cash and Balances with RBI) in Balance Sheet (Form A) includes:

(*a*) Cash in Hand (including foreign currency notes)

(*b*) Balances with RBI in (Current Account, other Accounts)

(*c*) Total (a + b)

(*d*) None of the above

Q28. The various items in schedule-7 (Balance with Banks & Money at call and short notice) in Balance Sheet (Form A) includes:

(*a*) In India:

(*i*) Balance with banks (in Current Accounts + in Other Deposit Accounts)

(*ii*) Money at Call and Short Notice (With Banks + With other Institutions)

Total (i + ii)

(*b*) Outside India:

(*i*) In Current Accounts

(*ii*) In other Deposit Accounts

(*iii*) Money at Call and Short Notice

Total (i + ii + iii)

(*c*) Grand Total (a + b)

(*d*) None of these

Q29. The various items in schedule-8 (Investments) in Balance Sheet (Form A) includes:

(*a*) Investments in India in:

(*i*) Government Securities

(*ii*) Other Approved Securities

(*iii*) Shares

(*iv*) Debentures and Bonds

(*v*) Subsidiaries and/or Joint Ventures

(*vi*) Others (to be specified)

Total:

(*b*) Investments outside India in:

(*i*) Govt. Securities (including Local Authorities)

(*ii*) Subsidiaries and/or Joint Ventures abroad

(*iii*) Other Investment (to be specified)

Total:

(*c*) Grand Total (a and b)

(*d*) None of these

Q30. The various items in schedule-9 (Advances) in Balance Sheet (Form A) includes:

(*a*) (*i*) Bills Discounted and Purchased

(*ii*) Cash Credits, Overdrafts and Loans Payable on Demand

(*iii*) Term Loans

Total:

(*b*) (*i*) Secured by Tangible Assets

(*ii*) Covered by Bank/Government Guarantees

(*iii*) Unsecured

Total:

(*c*) I. Advances in India:

(*i*) Priority Sectors

(*ii*) Public Sector

(*iii*) Banks

(*iv*) Others

Total:

II. Advances Outside India:

(*i*) Due from Banks

(*ii*) Due from Others (Bills Purchased and Discounted, Syndicated Loans, Others)

Total:

Grand Total (I and II)

(*d*) All of these (but fig. in balance sheet is either a, or b, or c)

Q31. The various items in schedule-10 (Fixed Assets) in Balance Sheet (Form A) includes:

(*a*) Premises :

At cost as on 31st March of the preceding year

Additions during the year

Deductions during the year

Depreciation to date

(*b*) Other Fixed Assets (including Furniture and Fixture)

At cost on 31st March of the preceding year

Additions during the year

Deductions during the year

Depreciation to date

(*c*) Total (a + b)

(*d*) None of these

Q32. The various items in schedule-11(Other Assets) in Balance Sheet (Form A) includes:

(*a*) Inter-Office Adjustments

(*b*) Interest Accrued

(*c*) Tax Paid in Advance/Tax Deducted at source

(*d*) Stationery and Stamps

(*e*) Non-banking Assets acquired in satisfaction of claims

(*f*) Others (any unadjusted balance of loss, when the loss exceeds the aggregate of Capital, Reserves and Surplus)

Q33. The various items in schedule-12 (Contingent Liabilities) in Balance Sheet (Form A) includes:

(*a*) Claims against the Bank not acknowledged as debts

(*b*) Liability for partly paid investments

(*c*) Liability on account of Outstanding Forward Exchange Contracts

(*d*) Guarantees given on behalf of constituents;

  (*i*) In India

  (*ii*) Outside India

(*e*) Acceptances, Endorsements and other Obligations

(*f*) Other items for which the Bank is contingently liable

2.Comments on Balance Sheet Items

Schedule 1 Capital

Q34. In Schedule1 (Capital):

(*a*) Contribution from Government, if any, for participation in World Bank Project should also be shown.

(*b*) For other Banks (Indian), where necessary items can be combined under one head like, 'Issued and Subscribed Capital'.

(*c*) Any changes made in any item during the year, should be explained in the notes.

(*d*) All of these

Schedule 2 Reserve and Surplus

Q35. State whether 'yes' or 'no':

(*a*) Reserves created in terms section 17 or any other section of BR Act must be separately disclosed. (yes/no)

(*b*) 'Capital Reserve' shall include any amount regarded as free for distribution through P&L Account. (yes/no)

(*c*) Surplus on revaluation should not be treated as Capital Reserve. (yes/no)

(*d*) Surplus on translation of the financial statements of foreign branches is not a revaluation reserve. (yes/no)

Ans. (a) yes (b) no (c) no (d) yes

Q36. State whether 'yes' or 'no':

(*a*) Premium on issue of share capital should be separately shown. (yes/no)

(*b*) 'Revenue Reserve' mean any reserve other than Capital Reserve and would include all reserves, other than those separately classified. (yes/no)

(*c*) 'Reserve' shall include any amount written off or retained for providing for depreciation, renewals or diminution in value of assets or retained for providing for any known liability. (yes/no)

(*d*) In Balance of profit, loss may be shown as deduction. (yes/no)

Ans. (a) yes (b) yes (c) no (d) yes

Schedule 3 Deposits

Q37. State whether 'yes' or 'no':

(*a*) Demand deposits from others include, Bank deposits repayable on demand.

Also includes demand deposits of non-bank sectors, credit balance in overdrafts, CC accounts, deposits, payable at call, overdue deposits, inoperative current accounts, matured time deposits and cash certificates, certificates of deposits. (yes/no)

(*b*) Does not include deposits in inoperative savings bank accounts. (yes/no)

(*c*) Term deposits from others include all types of deposits of the non-bank sector repayable after a specified term. It also includes fixed deposits, cumulative and recurring deposits, cash certificates, certificates of deposits, annuity deposits, deposits mobilized under various schemes, ordinary staff deposits, foreign currency non-resident deposits accounts. (yes/no)

Ans. (a) yes (b) no (c) yes

Q38. State whether 'yes' or 'no':

(*a*) Interest payable on deposits which is accrued but not due should be shown under other liabilities. (yes/no)

(*b*) Matured time deposits and cash certificates should not be treated as demand deposits. (yes/no)

(*c*) Deposits under special schemes, not payable on demand should be included under term deposits but on maturity for payment, those should be shown under demand deposits. (yes/no)

(*d*) Deposits from banks will include deposits from the banking system in India, Co-operative banks, Foreign banks which may or may not have a presence in India. (yes/no)

Ans. (a) no (b) no (c) yes (d) yes

Schedule 4 Borrowings

Q39. State whether 'yes' or 'no':

(*a*) Borrowings in India include, borrowings/refinance obtained from RBI, from Commercial Banks including co-operative Banks, and from IDBI, EXIM Bank, NABARD and other institutions, agencies (including liability against participation Certificates, if any). (yes/no)

(*b*) Borrowings outside India includes borrowings from Indian branches abroad and borrowings of foreign branches. (yes/no)

(*c*) Inter-office transactions should be shown as borrowings. (yes/no)

(*d*) Funds raised by foreign branches should be classified as 'Deposits', 'Borrowings' depending upon the documentation. (yes/no)

(*e*) Refinance obtained by Banks from RBI and various Institutions are brought under the head 'Borrowing'; therefore, advances will be shown at the gross amount on the asset side. (yes/no)

Ans. (a) yes (b) yes (c) no (d) yes (e) yes

Schedule 5 Other liabilities and Provisions

Q40. State whether 'yes' or 'no':

(*a*) If any instrument for remittance of funds like, drafts, cheques, telegraphic transfers, pay orders etc. remains uncashed on the day of preparation of final accounts, those should be shown under the heading "Bills Payable". (yes/no)

(*b*) In case there is difference on account of incomplete recording of transactions between two branches or between a branch and Head office and the difference shows credit balance, it should be shown under the head Inter Office (or branch) adjustments (net).To be noted that only net portion is to be shown of inter-office accounts, inland as well as foreign. (yes/no)

(*c*) It includes interest accrued but not due on deposits and borrowings. (yes/no)

(*d*) The head Others (including Provisions) include, Net provision for income tax and other taxes like interest tax (less advance payment, Tax deducted at source, etc.), surplus in aggregate in provisions for bad debt provision account, surplus in aggregate in provisions for depreciation in securities, contingency funds which are not disclosed as reserves but actually are in the nature of reserves, proposed dividend/transfer to Government, other liabilities which are not disclosed under any of the major heads such as unclaimed dividend provisions and funds kept for specific purposes, unexpired discount, outstanding charges like rent, conveyance etc. Deposits like staff security deposits, margin deposits etc., where the repayment is not free, should also be included. (yes/no)

Ans. (a) yes (b) yes (c) yes (d) yes

Note:

1. For arriving at the net balance of inter-office adjustments all connected inter-office accounts should be aggregated and the net balance only will be shown, representing mostly items in transit and unadjusted items.

2. The interest accruing on all deposits, whether the payment is due or not, should be treated as liability.

3. It is proposed to show only pure deposits under this head 'Deposits' and hence, all surplus provisions for bad and doubtful debts, contingency funds, secret reserves, etc., which are not netted off against the relative assets, should be brought under the head 'Others'(including Provisions).

Schedule 6 Cash and Balance with the Reserve Bank of India

Q41. Cash and Balance with the Reserve Bank of India includes:

(*a*) Cash in hand including foreign currency notes.

(*b*) Balance with RBI in current account and in other accounts.

(*c*) It includes cash in hand including foreign currency notes and also of foreign branches in case of banks having such branches.

(*d*) All of these

Schedule 7: Balances with other Banks and Money at Call and Short Notice

Q42. Balances with other Banks and Money at Call and Short Notice includes:

(*a*) Balances with Banks in India including Co-operative Banks, in current accounts and in other Deposit accounts shown separately.

(*b*) Money at call and short notice with banks and other institutions. It represents loans given by one bank to other for a short period. Call loans are repayable at any time the banker recalls while short notice advances are repayable within short notice say, 24 hours to maximum period of two weeks. It also includes deposits repayable within 15 days notice lent in the inter-bank call money market.

(*c*) Balances in current accounts and deposit accounts outside India which includes balances held by foreign branches and branches of Indian Banks outside India.

(*d*) Money at call and short notice in foreign countries.

Schedule 8 Investment

Q43. Investment in India includes:

(*a*) Central and State Government securities and govt. treasury bills shown at the book value. Difference between the book value and market value should be mentioned in notes.

(*b*) Other than Government securities which are treated as approved securities as per BR Act,1949.

(*c*) Investments in shares, debentures and bonds of companies and corporations not included above.

(*d*) Investments in Subsidiaries/Joint Ventures (including RRBs)

(*e*) Residual investments, if any, like Gold, commercial paper and instruments in the nature of share/debentures/bonds.

Q44. Investment outside India includes:

(*a*) All foreign government securities including securities issued by local authorities.

(*b*) Investments made in the share capital of subsidiaries floated outside India and/or joint ventures abroad.

(*c*) All other investments made outside India.

(*d*) All of the above

Schedule 9 Advances:

Q45. State whether 'True' or 'False':

(*a*) In discounting of bills, net amount after deducting the amount of discount is credited to the account of the customer. Such discount may be with or without any additional security from the debtor.(True/False)

(*b*) Cash Credit is an arrangement where borrower is allowed to borrow money up to a certain limit from the Banker against security of stocks hypothecated or pledged with the bank. (True/False)

(*c*) In cash credit facility the borrower is required to borrow at once the whole amount of the cash credit limit and start paying interest on that.(True/False)

Ans. (a) True (b) True (c) False

Q46. State whether 'True' or 'False':

(*a*) In overdrafts, the customer is allowed to overdraw in his current account with or without security as temporary accommodation, where, he is required to pay interest on the actual amount used by him. (True/False)

(*b*) A loan is a kind of advance where a lump sum payment is made to the borrower or credited to his deposit account as advance with or without security. Repayments are made in instalments or at the expiry of a period. Interest is paid on the whole advance from the beginning whether the amount advanced is used by the borrower or not. Money once repaid cannot be drawn again unless fresh sanction is given by the bank.(True/False)

(*c*) Term Loans are usually for a fixed term usually not exceeding one year and demand loan is payable on demand usually for a period exceeding a year. (True/False)

Ans. (a) True (b) True (c) False

Q47. State whether 'True' or 'False':

(*a*) Under the heading "Covered by Bank/Government guarantee", advances in India and outside India, to the extent those are covered by guarantees of Indian and Foreign Governments, Indian and Foreign Banks, DICGC, ECGC are to be included. (True/False)

(*b*) Under the heading "Advances in India (Priority Sectors; Public Sectors; Banks and others)", Priority Sector will include advances to Priority Sectors as per RBI classifications. (True/False)

(*c*) Advances to Central and State Governments and other Government undertakings including Government companies and corporations which are, according to the statutes, to be treated public sector companies are to be included in the category 'Public Sector'. (True/False)

(*d*) Advances to Banking sector including co-operative banks will come under the head 'Banks' and the remaining advances under the head 'Others' will include non-priority advances to the Private, Joint and Co-operative sectors. (True/False)

(*e*) The gross amount of advances including refinance and rediscounts but excluding provisions made to the satisfaction of auditors should be shown as advances and Consortium advances would be shown net of shares from other participating banks/institutions. (True/False)

Ans. (a) True (b) True (c) True (d) True (e) True

Schedule 10 Fixed Assets

Q48. As regards the Fixed Assets (True/False):

(*a*) Premises wholly or partly owned by the Banking company for the purpose of business including residential premises should be shown against 'Premises'. (True/False)

(*b*) In the case of premises and other Fixed assets, the previous balance, additions thereto and deductions therefrom during the year as also the total depreciation written off should be shown. (True/False) (*c*) Where sums have been written off on reduction of capital or revaluation of assets, every balance sheet after the first balance sheet subsequent to the reduction or revaluation should show the revised figures for a period of five years with the date and amount of revision made. (True/False)

(*d*) Under the head "Other Fixed Assets" (including Furniture and Fixtures), Motor vehicles and all other fixed assets other than premises but including furniture and fixtures should be shown. (True/False)

Ans. (a) True (b) True (c) True (d) True

Schedule 11 Other Assets

Q49. Under the heading "Other Assets"(True/False):

(*a*) For arriving at the net balance of inter-office accounts, Inland as well as foreign, accounts should be aggregated and the net balance, if in debit, only should be shown representing mostly items in transit and unadjusted items. (True/False):

(*b*) Interest accrued but not due on investment and advances and interest due but not collected on investments will be the main components of the item, "Interest Accrued". But only such interest as can be realized in the ordinary course should be shown. (True/False):

(*c*) Under the head, "Tax paid in advance/deducted at source", the amount of tax deducted at source on securities, advance tax paid, etc., the extent that these items are not set off against relative tax provisions should be shown. (True/False):

Ans. (a) True (b) True (c) True

Q50. Under the heading "Other Assets" (True/False):

(*a*) Under the heading, "Stationery and Stamps", only exceptional items of expenditure on stationery like bulk purchase of security paper, loose leaf or other ledger, etc., which are shown as quasi-asset to be written off over a period of time should be shown. The value should be on a realistic basis and cost escalation should not be taken into account, as these items are for internal use. (True/False):

(*b*) "Non-banking assets acquired in satisfaction of claims" would include immovable properties/tangible assets acquired in satisfaction of claims. (True/False):

(*c*) "Others" will include items like claims which have not been met, for instance, clearing items, debit items representing additions to assets or reduction in liabilities which have not been adjusted for technical reasons, want of particulars, etc., advances given to staff by a bank as employer and not as a banker, etc. Items which are in the nature of expenses, which are pending adjustments, should be provided for and the provisions netted against this item so that only realizable value is shown under this head. Accrued income other than interest may also be included here. (True/False):

Ans. (a) True (b) True (c) True

Schedule 12 Contingent Liabilities

Q51. Under the heading, "Contingent Liabilities" (True/False):

(*a*) "Acceptances, Endorsements and other obligations" would include Letters of Credit and bills accepted by the bank on behalf of customers, if some of these obligations remain undisbursed at the end of the accounting year. (True/False)

(*b*) "Other items for which the Bank is Contingently liable" would include, arrears of cumulative dividends, bills rediscounted under underwriting contracts, estimated amount of contracts remaining to be executed on capital account and not provided for, etc. (True/False)

(*c*) At the end of the accounting period, the amount of bills yet to be collected is ascertained from the bills for collection register and to be shown here. (True/False)

(*d*) In case certain persons are required to make compulsory deposits with a bank as per income tax, excise tax rules, etc., these deposits have been received by the concerned bank on behalf of concerned authority and may be included in the category of Demand deposits and shown in the balance sheet accordingly. (True/False)

Ans. (a) True (b) True (c) True (d) True

General Instructions for compilation

Q52. The general instructions for compilation of Balance sheet and Profit and Loss account include:

(*a*) The format of Balance Sheet and Profit and Loss account covers all items likely to appear in these statements, but in case a Bank does not have any particular item to report, it may be omitted from the formats.

(*b*) Corresponding comparative figures for the previous year are to be disclosed as indicated in the formats. The words 'Current year' and 'Previous year' used in the formats are only to indicate the order of presentation and may not appear in the accounts.

(*c*) Figures should be rounded off to the nearest thousand rupees.

(*d*) All of these

5. Accounting Treatment of Specific Items

Q53. Which of the following are true:

(*a*) With effect from April 1, 1991, the amount of bad debts and provision for bad debts has to be charged under the heading "Provision & Contingencies" in the Profit and Loss Account. In the Balance Sheet, the advances are shown after deducting both, bad debts and provision for bad debts.

(*b*) With effect from 1-4-1991, the amount of provision for taxation has to be charged to the Profit and Loss Account under the heading "Provision & Contingencies". In the Balance Sheet it will be shown under the heading "Other Liabilities & Provisions", on the liabilities side.

(*c*) If adjustment has to be done after preparation of the trial balance in respect of rebate on bills discounted in respect of the unearned discount relating to the next period, the amount of such rebate will be deducted from the total discount in the Profit and Loss Account and will also appear as a liability in the balance sheet.

(*d*) All of the above

6. Preparation of Profit and Loss Account

Concept:

Format of Profit and Loss Account:

Third Schedule: Form 'B'

Form of Profit and Loss Account

Profit and Loss Account for the year ended 31st March,............

		Schedule Number	Year Ended
I.	**Income:**		
	Interest Earned	**13**	....
	Other Income	**14**	....
II.	**Expenditure**		
	Interest Expended	**15**	....
	Operating Expenses	**16**	....
	Provisions and Contingencies	....	....
	Total		
III.	**Profit/Loss:**		
	Net Profit/(Loss) of the year		....
	Total		....

	Schedule Number	Year Ended
IV. Appropriations:		
Transfer to Statutory Reserves		....
Transfer to Other Reserves		....
Transfer to Government Proposed Dividend		....
Balance Carried over to Balance Sheet		....
Total		....

Q54. Relate the following items with the various schedules of Profit & Loss Account (Form 'B'):

Operating Expenses, Other Income, Interest Earned, Interest expended:

(*a*) 13,14,15,16

(*b*) 14,15,13,16

(*c*) 16,14,13,15

(*d*) 15,14,13,16

Q55. The various items in Schedule 13 (Interest Earned) of Profit and Loss Account (Form B) includes:

(*a*) Interest/Discount on Advances/Bills

(*b*) Income on Investments

(*c*) Interest on balances with RBI and other inter-bank funds

(*d*) Others

Total

Q56. The various items in Schedule 14 (Other Incomes) of Profit and Loss Account (Form B) includes:

(*a*) Commission, Exchange and Brokerage

(*b*) Profit on Sale of Investments

Less: Loss on sale of investments

(*c*) Profit on Revaluation of Investments

Less: Loss on Revaluation of Investments

(*d*) Profit on Sale of Land/Building and other Assets

Less: Loss on sale of Land, Building & Other assets

(*e*) Profit on Exchange Transactions

Less: Loss on Exchange Transactions

(*f*) Income earned by way of dividends, etc., from subsidiaries, companies and/ or joint ventures abroad/in India (*g*) Misc. Income

Total

Note: Under items (b) to (e) loss figures to be shown in brackets.

Q57. The various items in Schedule 15 (Interest Expended) of Profit and Loss Account (Form B) includes:

(*a*) Interest on deposits

(*b*) Interest on RBI/Inter-Bank Borrowings

(*c*) Others

Total

(*d*) All of the above

Q58. The various items in Schedule 16 (Operating Expenses) of Profit and Loss Account (Form B) includes:

(*a*) Payments to and Provisions for Employees

(*b*) Rent, Taxes and Lighting

(*c*) Printing and Stationery

(*d*) Advertisement and Publicity

(*e*) Depreciation on Bank's property

(*f*) Director's fees, Allowances and Expenses

(*g*) Auditor's fees and expenses (Including Branch Auditors)

(*h*) Law Charges

(*i*) Postages, Telegrams, Telephones, etc.

(*j*) Repairs and Maintenance

(*k*) Insurance

(*l*) Other Expenditure

Total

Note: Corresponding figures for the immediately preceding financial year should be shown in separate columns.

7. Comments on Profit and Loss Account Items

Schedule 13 Interest Earned

Q59. Interest Earned (schedule 13) includes:

(*a*) Interest/discount on Advances/bills: includes interest and discount on all types of loans and advances like Cash Credit, demand loans, overdrafts, export loans, term loans, domestic and foreign bills purchased and discounted (including those rediscounted), overdue interest and also interest subsidy, if any, relating to such advances/bills.

(*b*) Income on investments: Includes all income derived from the investment portfolio by way of interest and dividend.

(*c*) Interest on Balances with RBI and other inter-bank funds: includes interest on balances with Reserve Bank and other banks, call loans, money market placements, etc.

(*d*) Others: Includes any other interest/discount income not included in the above heads.

Schedule 14 Other Incomes

Q60. Other Incomes (schedule 14) includes:

(*a*) Commission, Exchange and Brokerage: includes all remuneration on services such as commission on collection, commission/exchange on remittances and transfers, commission on letters of credit, letting out of lockers, guarantees, commission on Government business, commission on the other permitted agency business including consultancy and other services, brokerage etc., on securities excluding foreign exchange income.

(*b*) Profit on sale of investments less loss on sale of investments.

(*c*) Profit on revaluation of investments less loss on revaluation of investments.

(*d*) Profit on sale of Land, buildings and other assets less loss on sale of land, buildings and other assets. It also includes profit/loss on sale of securities, furniture, land and buildings, motor vehicle, gold, silver, etc. (only net position to be shown and net loss should be shown as deduction).

(*e*) Profit on Exchange transaction less loss on Exchange transaction. It includes profit/loss on dealing in Foreign Exchange, all income earned by way of foreign exchange, commission and charges on foreign exchange transactions excluding interest which will be shown under interest. (only net position to be shown and net loss should be shown as deduction.

(*f*) Income earned by way of dividends, etc., from subsidiaries, companies, joint ventures abroad/in India.

(*g*) Miscellaneous Income: Includes recoveries from constituents for Godown rents, income from bank properties, security charges, insurance etc., and any other miscellaneous income. In case any item under this head exceeds one percent of the total income, particulars may be given in the notes.

Schedule 15 Interest Expenses

Q61. Interest Expenses (schedule 15) includes;

(*a*) Interest on deposits: Includes interest paid on all types of deposits from banks and other institutions.

(*b*) Interest on RBI/Inter-bank borrowings: Include discounts/interest on all borrowings and refinance from RBI and other banks.

(*c*) Others: Includes discount/interest on all borrowings/refinance, penal interest paid, etc.

(*d*) All of the above

Schedule 16 Operating Expenses

Q62. Operating Expenses (schedule 16) includes:

(*a*) Payments to and provisions for employees: Includes staff salaries/wages, allowances, bonus, other staff benefits like provident fund, pension, gratuity, leave fare concessions, staff welfare medical allowance to staff.

(*b*) Rent, Taxes and lighting: Includes rent paid by the banks on buildings and other municipal and other taxes paid excluding income tax and interest tax, electricity and other similar charges and levies. House rent allowance and other similar payments to staff should appear under the head "Payment to and provisions for employees".

(*c*) Printing and stationery: Includes books and forms of stationery used by the bank and other printing charges which are not incurred by way of publicity expenditure.

(*d*) Advertisement and publicity: Includes expenditure incurred by the bank for advertisement and publicity purposes including printing charges of publicity matter.

(*e*) Depreciation on bank's property: Includes depreciation on bank's own property, motor cars and other vehicles, furniture, electric fittings, vaults, lifts, leasehold properties, non-banking assets, etc.

(*f*) Directors' fees, allowances and expenses: Includes sitting fees and all other items of expenditure incurred on behalf of directors. The daily allowance, hotel charges, conveyance charges, etc., which though in the nature of reimbursement of expenses incurred may be included under this head. Similar expenses of local committee members may be included under this head.

(*g*) Auditors' fees and expenses (Including branch auditors' fees and expenses): Includes the fees paid to the statutory auditors and branch auditors for professional services rendered and all expenses for performing their duties, even though they may be in the nature of reimbursement of expenses. If external auditors have been appointed by bank themselves for internal inspection and audits and other services, the expenses incurred in that context including fees may not be included under this head but shown under 'Other expenditure'.

(*h*) Law charges: includes all legal expenses and reimbursement of expenses incurred in connection with legal services.

(*i*) Postage, telegrams, telephones, etc.: Includes all postage charges like stamps, telegram, telephones, teleprinters, etc.

(*j*) Repairs and Maintenance: Includes repairs to bank's property, their maintenance charges.

(*k*) Insurance: Includes insurance charges on bank's property, insurance premium paid to DICGC, etc., to the extent they are not recovered from the concerned parties.

(*l*) Other expenditures; Includes all expenses other than those not included in any of the other heads like, license fees, donations, subscriptions to papers, periodicals, entertainment expenses, travel expenses, etc. In case any particular item under this head exceeds one percent of the total income, particulars may be given in the notes.

Provisions and Contingencies

Q63. The Provisions and Contingencies include:

(*a*) Provisions made for bad and doubtful debts

(*b*) Provisions for taxation

(*c*) Provision for diminution in the value of investments

(*d*) All of the above

8. Important Items of Balance Sheet

Balance Sheet: Asset Side

Q64. Which of the following are true about 'Money At Call and Short Notice'?

(*a*) It relates to inter-bank transactions

(*b*) Banks having short supply of money borrow from banks having surplus money.

(*c*) Money is borrowed usually for 1 to 14 days.

(*d*) All of these

Q65. Which of the followings are true about 'Advances'?

(*a*) It includes Loans, Cash Credit and Overdraft

(*b*) Cash Credit is an arrangement where banks agree to lend money to borrowers up to a fixed limit against Hypothecation or Pledge of securities. However the borrower need not avail of the whole amount in one go.

(*c*) Overdraft is an arrangement where customer is permitted to overdraw money in his current account up to a certain limit against securities like, L.I.C. Policy, FDRs, National Saving Certificates, Quoted shares, etc.

(*d*) All of the above

Q66. Which of the following are true about 'Bills receivable being Bills for collection as per contra'?

(*a*) It is a contra item in the Balance Sheet.

(*b*) 'Bills received being bills for collection' account denotes the amounts receivable and is shown on assets side of the balance sheet.

(*c*) 'Bills for collection being Bills receivable' account denotes the amount payable to the customer and is shown in the liabilities side of the balance sheet.

(*d*) All of the above

Q67. Which of the following are true about 'Acceptance Endorsements and other Obligations'?

(*a*) It represents liabilities, which the bank assumes on behalf of its customers.

(*b*) The various ways in which a bank may accommodate its customers are, opening of L/C, accepting bills on behalf of customers, making endorsements on Promissory Note prepared by customers, issuing Letter of Guarantee.

(*c*) The bank obtains Counter Guarantee from its customers to meet the third party liabilities.

(*d*) All of the above

Q68. Which of the following are true about 'Acceptance Endorsements and other Obligations'?

(*a*) It creates contra item in balance sheet.

(*b*) The account 'Constituents' liability for acceptances, endorsements or other obligations' appears in the asset side of the balance sheet.

(*c*) The account 'Acceptances, Endorsements and other Obligations' appears in the liabilities side of the balance sheet.

(*d*) All of the above

Q69. Which of the following are true about, 'Non-Banking Assets?

(*a*) This relates to assets, which are not acquired by the banks, but against security of which Loan is given.

(*b*) In case of non-payment of loan amount such securities are taken in possession for recovery.

(*c*) Profit or loss on disposal of such assets are disclosed separately in the Profit and Loss account.

(*d*) All of the above

Q70. Which of the following are true?

(*a*) Gold appears under 'Investment' and silver appears under 'other assets'.

(*b*) Lockers or Safe deposit Vaults are assets included under Furniture.

(*c*) Transactions that take place between the branches or a branch and Head office are recorded in the books of the branch or head office where the transaction take place.

(*d*) All of the above

Q71. Which of the following are true?

(*a*) In absence of advice or non-completion of the transactions, some of such transactions remains unrecorded, because of which some balances are left in branch account in the head office books, which is known as 'Branch adjustment account'.

(*b*) The debit balance is shown in the liabilities side and the credit balance is shown in the assets side of the balance sheet.

(*c*) All of the above

(*d*) None of the above

Balance Sheet: Liabilities side

Q72. Which of the following are true:

(*a*) Under the head 'Share capital', authorized, subscribed, issued and paid up capital are shown separately. Calls in arrears are reduced from paid-up capital and forfeited shares amount is added to it.

(*b*) Every banking company incorporated in India shall before declaring a dividend, transfer a sum equal to 20% of net profit of each year to a reserve fund.

(*c*) The amounts lying in 'Deposits and other accounts 'are the amounts lying to the credit of customers' accounts. Fixed deposits are payable on a fixed period, whereas Current and Savings account balances are payable on demand.

(*d*) All of the above

9. Disclosure Requirements of Banks to be added as Notes to Accounts (Schedule 17)

Q73. Banking companies are required to make additional disclosures in Schedule 17 on 'Notes on Accounts' regarding:

(*a*) Movement on provisions held towards NPA (excluding provision on Standard Assets).

(*b*) Movement of provisions held towards depreciation on investments.

(*c*) Both of the above

(*d*) None of the above

Asset Classification, Income Recognition and Provisioning Norms

Q74. State whether 'True' or 'False':

(*a*) An advance which remains 'out of order' for 60 days is a non-performing asset.

(*b*) An advance which remains out of order for 90 days is NPA.

(*c*) In term loan, if interest/instalment remain overdue for more than 180 days, it is NPA.

Ans. (a) False (90 days) (b) True (c) True

Q75. State whether 'True' or 'False':

(*a*) In a cash Credit/Overdraft account, if outstanding amount remains over and above sanctioned limit/Drawing Power for more than 90 days, it is not NPA.

(*b*) In Bills Purchased/discounted account, if bills remain overdue and unpaid for 90 days it is NPA.

(*c*) If in an account, outstanding amount is less than Drawing Power, but there is no credit in the account or the credit is less than the debit on account of interest, during preceding 90 days as on the date of balance sheet, it is NPA.

Ans. (a) False (it is NPA) (b) True (c) True.

Q76. State whether 'True' or 'False':

(*a*) The income from performing asset is recognized on accrual basis and interest income from non-performing assets is recognized on cash basis. In case interest on NPA is already recognized in the books on accrual basis, the same should be adjusted by making provision for income recorded but not received on NPA.

(*b*) The provisioning requirement for Standard Asset is 10%.

(*c*) A sub-standard asset is that, which has remained NPA for a period not exceeding 18 months.

(*d*) A doubtful asset is that which remained NPA for a period exceeding 18 months.

Ans. (a) True (b) False (0.25%) (c) True (d) True

Q77. State whether 'True' or 'False':

(*a*) A standard asset is that which is a performing asset with just normal risk attached to it.

(*b*) The provisioning requirement for sub-standard asset is 0.25%.

(*c*) The provisioning requirement for doubtful asset is:

For unsecured portion—100%,

For secured portion, doubtful up to 1 year————25%

——do——————, doubtful from 1 to 3 years——30%

—— do——————, doubtful more than 3 years——50%

(*d*) The provisioning requirement for Loss Asset is 100% of total outstanding.

Ans. (a) True (b) false (10%) (c) False (doubtful up to 1 year 20%) (d) True

Investment Classification

Q78. Investment by banks include;

(*a*) Government Securities

(*b*) Debentures and Bonds

(*c*) Subsidiaries/Joint Ventures

(*d*) All of these

Q79. Which of the following are SLR securities for Banks:

(*a*) Shares

(*b*) Approved securities

(*c*) Government securities

(*d*) b & c

Q80. As per new guidelines SLR and non-SLR securities are to be divided into categories:

(*a*) Held to maturity

(*b*) Available for sale

(*c*) Held for trading

(*d*) All of the above

Q81. State whether 'True' or 'False':

(*a*) The investment under 'Held to maturity' is like, 'Old permanent Category' and should not exceed 25% of bank's total investment.

(*b*) The Banks have no freedom to decide on extent of holding under, 'Available for Sale' and 'Held for trading' category.

(*c*) The securities held for trading are to be sold within 90 days.

(*d*) The profit and loss on securities, 'Held to Maturity' is ultimately transferred to Capital Reserve account and need not be marked to market.

(*e*) The profit/loss on sale of investments in 'Available for sale' and 'Held for trading' securities is taken to Profit and Loss account and are marked to market.

Ans. (a) True (b) False (c) True (d) True (e) True

Q82. "Balancing of Books" in a bank refers to

(*a*) Preparation of trial balance half yearly

(*b*) Preparation of final balance sheet

(*c*) Preparation of trial balance of personal ledgers, periodically, to agree with General Ledger accounts

(*d*) None of the above

Q83. In a bank, the amount of advance, given to an employee, is debited to which account?

(*a*) Profit and loss account

(*b*) Sundry expenses account

(*c*) Suspense account

(*d*) Travelling expenses account

ANSWERS					
1. (d)	2. (c)	3. —	4. —	5. (c)	6. (b)
7. (c)	8. (d)	9. (c)	10. (d)	11. (d)	12. (c)
13. (d)	14. (c)	15. (a)	16. (d)	17. —	18. (c)
19. (b)	20. (c)	21. (b)	22. (d)	23. —	24. (c)
25. (c)	26. (d)	27. (c)	28. (c)	29. (c)	30. (d)
31. (c)	32. —	33. —	34. (d)	35. —	36. —
37. —	38. —	39. —	40. —	41. (d)	42. —
43. —	44. (d)	45. —	46. —	47. —	48. —
49. —	50. —	51. —	52. (d)	53. (d)	54. (c)
55. —	56. —	57. (d)	58. —	59. —	60. —
61. (d)	62. —	63. (d)	64. (d)	65. (d)	66. (d)
67. (d)	68. (d)	69. (d)	70. (d)	71. (c)	72. (d)
73. (c)	74. —	75. —	76. —	77. —	78. (d)
79. (d)	80. (d)	81. —	82. (c)	83. (c)	

CHAPTER

36

ACCOUNTING IN A COMPUTERIZED ENVIRONMENT

Meaning of Computerised Accounting

Q1. Computerised Accounting is a system that uses a computer and performs the functions of:

(*a*) Capturing business transactions in the form of accounting entries.

(*b*) Using accounting entries to prepare financial statements.

(*c*) Preparing financial statements on the basis of Accounting Standards.

(*d*) All of the above

Q2. The physical components of which a computer is made of is known as:

(*a*) Software

(*b*) Hardware

(*c*) Program

(*d*) Information

Q3. The instructions fed to the computer to process data is known as:

(*a*) Software

(*b*) Hardware

(*c*) Program

(*d*) Information

Q4. A computer has components like, printer, video monitor, keyboard, disk drive which are known as:

(*a*) Computer accessories

(*b*) Computer programs
(*c*) Computer peripherals
(*d*) Computer network

Q5. The accounting system in a computer runs as per set of instructions called software programs. The professional who develops such software programs is known as:

(*a*) Hardware specialist
(*b*) Network specialist
(*c*) Programmer
(*d*) Computer specialist

Q6. An accounting software developed for running in computer may be written in which of the programming languages:

(*a*) COBOL
(*b*) FOXPRO
(*c*) UNIX
(*d*) All of these

Q7. Computers can be classified as:

(*a*) Analog computer
(*b*) Digital computer
(*c*) Hybrid computer
(*d*) All of these

Q8. Computerized accounting softwares are run on:

(*a*) Analog computers
(*b*) Digital computers
(*c*) Hybrid computers
(*d*) All of these

Q9. Analog computers are mostly used for:

(*a*) Running accounting softwares
(*b*) Running simulation of guided missile system
(*c*) Using in scientific and mechanical fields
(*d*) All of these

Features of Computerised Accounting

Q10. The main features of computerized accounting are:

(*a*) Speed
(*b*) Accuracy
(*c*) Generation of reports
(*d*) All of these

Q11. How it is economical to use computerized accounting:

(*a*) Human labour has become more costly.
(*b*) In manual accounting same work will require engagement of more people.
(*c*) In computerized accounting more work can be done employing few people.
(*d*) All of these

Q12. How a multiple user computer system is beneficial:

(*a*) A multiple user system connects several computers through LAN or WAN.
(*b*) More than one person can share the work of data feeding simultaneously.
(*c*) Each user can handle particular segment of a transaction.
(*d*) All of these

Terms used in computerized accounting

Q13. Data means:

(*a*) Facts
(*b*) Observations
(*c*) Assumptions
(*d*) All of these

Q14. For accounting entries related to preparation of sales invoices which are the Data:

(*a*) Price
(*b*) Date of sales
(*c*) Sales tax
(*d*) All of the above

Q15. Fill in the blank:

Record consists of a —— of Data items that relates to an object of data processing:

(*a*) Result

(*b*) Program
(*c*) Group
(*d*) Software

Q16. Compilation of related data records maintained in some pre-arranged order is known as:

(*a*) Data base
(*b*) Data file
(*c*) Data mart
(*d*) Data group

Q17. Fill in the blank:

A computer system implies various ——— that process data and give output.

(*a*) Computers
(*b*) Files
(*c*) Components
(*d*) All of these

Q18. For a computerized accounting system the system means:

(*a*) Software programs
(*b*) Computer peripherals
(*c*) Data
(*d*) a & b

Difference between computerized and manual accounting

Q19. In what ways the computerized and manual accounting are different from each other?

(*a*) Visibility of data and its treatment can be clearly seen in a manual system, whereas in a computerized environment, neither the data is visible when it is stored nor the manipulation of the data is visible. So, there is concern for integrity of data and risk of manipulation. Various frauds in this area have made people aware of such complexity.

(*b*) In a manual system the scope of generating various reports and statements are limited because of complexity and cost. In a computerized environment, various reports and statements and reports related to various fields can easily be prepared from the basic data with less complexity and less cost.

(*c*) A computerized accounting system may be used even by those who do not have much knowledge of accounting, whereas in a manual environment it is only the experts in accounting system can do the specialized works.

(*d*) All of these

Advantages and disadvantages of computerized accounting

Q20. Which of the following are the advantages of computerized accounting system?

(*a*) Accuracy, high speed and low cost

(*b*) Generation of various reports from the same accounting data.

(*c*) Error-free accounting.

(*d*) All of these

Q21. What are the disadvantages of computerized accounting?

(*a*) Requirement of special program and professionals.

(*b*) Requirement of qualified operators.

(*c*) Costly computer peripherals and stationery.

(*d*) All of these

Functions performed by computerized accounting softwares available in the market

Q22. Some of the accounting softwares available in the market are:

(*a*) Tally 4, 4.5, 5, 5.4, 6.3

(*b*) Windows 2000

(*c*) Quick FA

(*d*) a & c

Q23. MEFCOMP is:

(*a*) Operating system software

(*b*) Accounting software

(*c*) Manufacturing software

(*d*) Designing software

Q24. Some of the functions that can be performed by majority of accounting softwares are:

(*a*) Maintenance of statutory books.

(*b*) Currency conversion

(*c*) Report generation

(*d*) All of these

Q25. Which of the following functions can be performed by accounting softwares?

(*a*) Valuation of closing stock of materials and stores.

(*b*) Maintenance of widespread branches and head office and consolidation of financial statements.

(*c*) Entity-wise profit estimation helping management in planning.

(*d*) All of these

Computerisation - Scope and Experiences in banking

Q26. Which are the functions of banks that has been influenced by computerization:

(*a*) Computerised Banking operations

(*b*) Computerised accounting

(*c*) Centralised Banking

(*d*) All of these

Q27. Total Branch Computerisation is a:

(*a*) Real time off-line banking

(*b*) Unreal time on-line banking

(*c*) Real-time on-line banking

(*d*) Really on-line banking

Q28. In real time on-line banking:

(*a*) Transactions are entered through the terminal and recorded immediately but updations are done later on.

(*b*) Transactions are entered through the terminal and recorded immediately but authentication, verification and updations are done later on.

(*c*) Transactions are entered through the terminal and then it is recorded, verified, authenticated and corresponding updations are reflected instantly.

(*d*) None of these

Q29. Which of the following are true:

(*a*) In computerized accounting, for all accounting entries, physical voucher is a must.

(*b*) In computerized accounting, for all big accounting entries, physical voucher is a must as a safeguard.

(*c*) In computerized accounting, for accounting entries, in most cases vouchers are not prepared and transactions are recorded on the system only.

(*d*) None of these

Q30. In lending activity of banks which activities can be computerized for ease and quickness:

(*a*) Interest charging

(*b*) Monitoring of disbursement

(*c*) Repayment schedule

(*d*) All of these

Q31. RTGS has facilitated:

(*a*) Interest calculation

(*b*) Cash payment

(*c*) Transfer of funds

(*d*) All of these

Q32. In what ways centralized banking can offer facilities to the customers:

(*a*) Customers of any branch can deposit money in any other connected branch at his convenience for credit to his account.

(*b*) Customers of any branch can withdraw money from any other connected branch at his convenience to the debit of his account.

(*c*) Customers can make enquiries about his account from any connected branch of the bank.

(*d*) All of these

Q33. ATMs are capable of:

(*a*) Accepting cash/cheques

(*b*) Disbursing cash

(*c*) Making inter-bank transfer

(*d*) All of these

Internet and World Wide Web - influences on Banking

Q34. Fill in the blank:

Internet is a network of ——————.

(*a*) Computers

(*b*) Terminals

(*c*) Organisations

(*d*) Networks

Q35. The abbreviation WWW stands for:

(*a*) World Wide Web

(*b*) World Without Web

(*c*) World With Web

(*d*) World Who's Who

Q36. Hypertext is a method by which:

(*a*) Certain texts are selected

(*b*) Certain texts are highlighted

(*c*) Certain texts are activated

(*d*) None of these

Q37. Hyperlinks allow the users to:

(*a*) Select documents

(*b*) List documents

(*c*) Navigate through documents

(*d*) None of these

Q38. Internet Explorer, Netscape Navigator and Mosaic are:

(*a*) Operating system softwares

(*b*) Utility softwares

(*c*) Data base softwares

(*d*) Browser softwares

Q39. A browser software helps the users to:

(*a*) Navigate through documents

(*b*) Navigate through Internet

(*c*) Navigate through directories

(*d*) All of these

Q40. Home page is the:

(*a*) Index page of any organisation

(*b*) It contains links to further information

(*c*) Page of home office of an organisation

(*d*) a & b

Q41. E-mail feature of Internet:

(*a*) Is most widely used feature.

(*b*) It is a means of sending message through Internet.

(*c*) It can send message to definite addresses.

(*d*) All of these

Q42. E-Commerce means:

(*a*) Electronic Commerce

(*b*) Buying and selling on the web

(*c*) Way of enabling business over net.

(*d*) All of these

Q43. Security as well as secrecy is very important for Electronic Commerce, because transactions are mostly done through:

(*a*) Cash

(*b*) Computers

(*c*) Credit cards

(*d*) All of these

Q44. Which of the following are the facilities of modern banking?

(*a*) Customer becomes customer of entire bank rather than of one branch.

(*b*) It allows immediate transfer of funds.

(*c*) It gives convenience of home-banking.

(*d*) All of the above.

Q45. The 'Home Page' of any organisation helps in:

(*a*) Keeping the details of products and services on the net for reference of customers.

(*b*) Responding to immediate queries of customers.

(*c*) Making online sell, purchase and payment.

(*d*) All of these

Q46. Fill in the blanks from the options given at the end:

(*a*) A.U.D.I.T.O.R is a ———— software.

(*b*) Tailor made means made as per ————.

(*c*) In computerized accounting system standing instructions of customers are carried out ————

(*d*) A computer virus is a ——— computer software.

(*e*) WAN is ——— area network.

Options: 1. Automatically 2. Wide 3. Requirement 4. Cash Basis 5. Mischievous

Ans. (*a*) 4

(*b*) 3

(*c*) 1

(*d*) 5

(*e*) 2

Q47. In a computerised bank, we should practice the following:

(*a*) Change our password at least once a month

(*b*) Not share our password with anyone under any circumstances

(*c*) Not allow anyone to use our computer

(*d*) None of the above

Q48. For the core banking system of a large Bank, which of the following statements is true

(*a*) Each branch has its own server connected directly to servers of other branches

(*b*) There is only one powerful server at centralised data centre.

(*c*) Each branch has a server connected to the server at centralised data centre

(*d*) None of the above

ANSWERS					
1. (d)	2. (b)	3. (a)	4. (c)	5. (c)	6. (d)
7. (d)	8. (b)	9. (c)	10. (d)	11. (d)	12. (d)
13. (d)	14. (d)	15. (c)	16. (b)	17. (c)	18. (d)
19. (d)	20. (d)	21. (d)	22. (d)	23. (b)	24. (d)
25. (d)	26. (d)	27. (c)	28. (c)	29. (c)	30. (d)
31. (c)	32. (d)	33. (d)	34. (d)	35. (a)	36. (b)
37. (c)	38. (d)	39. (b)	40. (d)	41. (d)	42. (d)
43. (c)	44. (d)	45. (d)	47. (a)	48. (c)	

PAPER 3

LEGAL & REGULATORY ASPECTS OF BANKING OPERATIONS

CONTENTS

PAPER - 3

QUESTIONS - 1

Answer all the questions:

1. The contract of indemnity has ......parties
   - *a.* 2
   - *b.* 3
   - *c.* 4
   - *d.* 5
2. Identify the odd item (in respect of private Ltd. company)
   - *a.* Memorandum of Association
   - *b.* Certificate of Incorporation
   - *c.* Common Seal
   - *d.* Certificate of Commencement of Business.
3. A minor is not competent to contract, but he/she
   - *a.* can become partner in a partnership firm
   - *b.* can become partner as a special case
   - *c.* cannot be a partner, but may be admitted to share losses
   - *d.* cannot be a partner, but may be admitted to share benefits, with the consent of all the partners
4. Every Bank Guarantee contains
   - *a.* Validity Period
   - *b.* Claim period
   - *c.* Both a & b
   - *d.* Neither a nor b
5. Partner has implied authority to enter into partnership on behalf of the firm.
   - *a.* with other partnership firm

b. under special circumstances only

c. he/she does not have the implied authority

d. he/she can enter according to his/her will

6. A person employed by and acting under the control of the original agent is called :—

a. another agent

b. sub-agent

c. broker

d. none

7. To create an agency

a. there has to be a consideration

b. no consideration is necessary

c. understanding is enough

d. none of the above

8. Under the Banking Ombudsman scheme an arbitrator is separately appointed by

a. Banking ombudsman himself/herself

b. RBI

c. GOI-MOF

d. GOI-Law Ministry

9. Under the SARFAESI Act who has the power to condone delay in filling of the particulars :—

a. an Arbitrator

b. Registrar

c. Central Registrar

d. Registrar of Assurances

10. The owner of a financial asset acquired by a securitisation company is called

a. purchaser

b. seller

c. originator

d. vendor

11. If a Civil Court has already given a decree then the recovery certificate can be issued by

a. any different court

b. at the request of any of the parties

c. DRT only

d. none of the above

12. A bank agreement contains a provision to convert hypothecation into pledge. The said agreement is called

a. hypothecation agreement

b. pledge agreement

c. both

d. none of the above

13. When no rate of interest is specified in the negotiable instrument, interest due thereon shall be calculated at the rate of .... % pa

a. bank rate

b. PLR rate

c. 6

d. discretion of the bank

e. none of the above

14. The Irrevocable LC imposes an absolute obligation on the banker to

a. honour its commitment

b. ignore its commitment

c. take its own time.

d. all of the above

15. RRBs were set up in 1975

a. Under the Regional Rural Banks Ordinance,1975

b. The Ordinance was later replaced by the Regional Rural Banks Act,1976

c. Both are correct

d. Both are wrong

16. Deferred payment guarantee constitutes an undertaking on the part of the bank to honour/ensure to

a. make timely payment

b. defer payment

c. wait or keep the matter pending indefinitely

d. none of the above

17. If the beneficiary is a Municipal Corporation then, they can suc thc bank within

a. 3 years

b. 30 years
c. Any period without invocation of the guarantee
d. Any period after 30 years after invoking the guarantee in time

18. Indemnifier is
a. a person to whom promise is given
b. a person who makes the promise
c. both
d. neither a nor b

19. The SARFAESI Act is applicable to secured creditors only to enforce the securities criteria
a. without the intervention of Court or Tribunal
b. after taking permission of the Court or Tribunal
c. in case of assets on which charge is registered
d. none of the above

20. Non-registration of a business organisation or concern would not deter from carrying on the business as a
a. proprietorship concern
b. private limited company
c. public limited company
d. partnership firm

21. In this type of mortgage, possession of mortgaged property is normally given to the mortgagee.
a. simple
b. english
c. conditional sale
d. equitable

22. The limitation period for filing suit for foreclosure of mortgage is
a. 3 years
b. 30 years
c. 12 years
d. none

23. A & D are having a joint SB a/c. Operative instructions jointly. One of the signatures is forged
a. a collecting banker is not affected

b. a paying banker will get protection

c. paying banker will not get protection

d. none

24. Asset Reconstruction company has to get registration from

a. RBI

b. its own bank

c. both

d. none

25. After using the securitisation measures a bank can proceed further in

a. the Civil Court

b. DRT

c. both as the case may be

d. none

26. Securitisation or SARFAESI Act is not applicable to assets

a. in possession of the creditor

b. charge on which is in favour of the creditor

c. both a and b

d. none of the above

27. A certified copy of any entry in a banker's book shall in all legal proceedings be received as ....

a. final evidence

b. primary evidence

c. absolute evidence

d. *prima facie* evidence

28. A proposal as defined in the Indian Contract Act, on acceptance, becomes

a. proposal only

b. promise

c. agreement

d. contract

29. If there is no provision in the contract between the partners for the duration of the partnership, such partnership is known as

a. particular partnership

b. partnership for a duration

c. partnership at will

d. none

30. A person cannot be a director of more than ... companies (excluding a private company)

a. 2

b. 3

c. 50

d. 15

31. Foreign exchange - bringing it to India and selling it to an authorised person in India in exchange for rupees is known as

a. inward remittance

b. exchange transaction

c. repatriation to India

d. all

32. Any terms of the ....of Association can be altered by a special resolution and no approvals are required from the Company Law Board or Registrar of companies

a. memorandum

b. articles

c. both a & b

d. none of a & b

33. A director of the private limited company (who has started the same) has died. Then

a. the company has to be dissolved.

b. it can continue

c. it can continue only with the consent of other Promoter Directors.

d. none of the above

34. A claim to any debt (other than a debt secured by mortgage, hypothecation or pledge) is called :

a. lien

b. acknowledgement

c. actionable claim

d. none of the above

35. A further credit issued in favour of the beneficiary's supplier on the basis of LC in favour of the beneficiary is known as

a. revolving credit

b. revocable

c. red clause

d. back to back

36. As per provisions of UCPDC 600, in the absence of any indication in the LC it will be deemed to be ......

a. revocable LC

b. irrevocable LC

c. none

d. all

37. After conduct of audit of co-operative banks, RBI will

a. Supply a copy of the report to the State Co-operative bank

b. Not provide a copy of the report

c. Provide to the Registrar a copy of the report

d. None of the above

38. Whether the year mentioned in the following Act is correct. If not then which one is not correct

a. Reserve Bank of India Act, 1934

b. The Banking Regulation Act,1959

c. The Partnership Act,1932

d. The Companies Act,1956

39. As per the Bankers' Books Evidence Act, 1891, books include

a. day books

b. cash books

c. magnetic tape

d. all

40. The Banker's Books Evidence Act,1891 is not applicable in the State of

a. Tamilnadu

b. Maharashtra

c. Karnataka

d. Jammu and Kashmir

41. The Sale of Goods Act, 1930 does not cover

a. bonds

b. shares

c. grass

d. all

42. An aggrieved person against the order passed by the District Consumer Forum may prefer an appeal to the State Commission within a period of ..... days from the date of order.

a. 15

b. 30

c. 45

d. 60

43. For filing a complaint before a District Forum the limitation period prescribed is ...... from the date of cause of action :—

a. 90 days

b. 1 year

c. 2 years

d. 3 years

44. Delivery of goods by one person to another for some purpose is

a. hypothecation

b. mortgage

c. pledge

d. bailment

45. The title in goods remains with the seller and passes on to the buyer only on fulfilment of conditions stipulated in the

a. sale agreement

b. agreement to sell

c. both

d. none

46. A minor has been admitted to the benefits of the partnership firm. Unfortunately he/she dies.

a. the firm has to be dissolved

b. the firm may continue

c. since he/she is not a partner there is no need to take notice of his/her death, partnership can continue

d. none of the above

47. **A Government Company is one in which not less than 51% of the paid-up capital is held by :—**

a. The Central Government

b. Any State Government or Governments

c. Partly by the Central Government and partly by State Government

d. All

48. **A bank has lent Rs. 5 lakhs to a Pvt. Ltd. company to purchase a pick up van, therefore the bank's charge**

a. has to be registered with RTO/ROC

b. need not be registered with ROC

c. registration is optional

d. none of the above

49. **A person holding not less than 10% of the paid up equity capital of securitisation company or reconstruction company is called.**

a. Donor

b. Donee

c. Proposer

d. Sponsor

50. **A reconstruction company has to have owned funds not less than**

a. Rs. 25 lakh

b. Rs. 50 lakh

c. Rs. 1 crore

d. Rs. 2 crore

51. **Borrower under the securitisation process is known as**

a. Obligor

b. Obligee

c. Borrower only

d. None

52. **Which of the following Acts is social welfare benefit oriented legislation?**

a. Contract Act

b. Sale of Goods Act

c. Limitation Act

d. None

53. An agreement in which a party to the agreement has the option to treat the agreement as void is called :

 a. contract
 b. valid agreement
 c. void agreement
 d. voidable agreement

54. The liability of the surety is co-extensive delete with that of the principal-debtor but the action should first be taken against

 a. principal debtor
 b. assets of the principal debtors
 c. all remedies against principal debtor
 d. surety only

55. Which statement is not correct ?

 a. A partner of an unregistered firm can enforce by way of a suit any rights available to him/her
 b. A private Ltd. company should have Articles of Association
 c. A minor cannot be a partner
 d. Assignment is applicable to actionable claims

56. Which of the following is a public document ?

 a. Articles of Association
 b. Resolution
 c. Internal communication of the company
 d. None

57. Qualification shares are to be held by

 a. Shareholder
 b. Government
 c. Banker
 d. None

58. A lease hold property where lease deed permits transfer by lessee

 a. Can be mortgaged
 b. Cannot be mortgaged
 c. Only lien can be noted
 d. Documents can be pledged

59. A member of the company has a right to
   a. receive copies of annual accounts
   b. to apply to the CLB to call Annual General Meeting
   c. transfer shares
   d. all

60. The famous phrase Buyer Beware is known as :
   a. Contract
   b. Seller's caution
   c. Caveat Emptor
   d. Warranty

61. A stipulation collateral to the main purpose of the contract
   a. Warranty
   b. Guarantee
   c. Condition
   d. All

62. Under SARFAESI Act, a notice to the borrower should be given calling upon him to discharge his full liabilities within a period of
   a. 15 days
   b. 30 days
   c. 60 days
   d. 90 days

63. The Trustee of Muslim Wakf is called Mutawali
   a. True
   b. False
   c. Trustee
   d. None

64. A minor has been supplied necessaries. If a bank has lent money to this minor to meet expenses for purchasing necessaries of life then bank can recover the money from
   a. the minor
   b. only from the estate of the minor
   c. both
   d. none

65. Book debts are to be
   a. hypothecated
   b. assigned
   c. pledged
   d. all
66. As per Sec. 176 of the Contract Act .... in respect of Pledge
   a. notice need not be given
   b. a reasonable notice to be given
   c. before sale of pledged goods
   d. b & c
67. Verification of crossing is the responsibility of
   a. collecting banker
   b. paying banker
   c. both
   d. none
68. A payment in due course is discussed in
   a. Contract Act
   b. Bankers' Book Evidence Act
   c. RBI Act
   d. None
69. A bank guarantee (once issued) cannot be cancelled by
   a. the principal debtor
   b. beneficiary
   c. banker
   d. none
70. Under LC, the liability to make payment by a bank is
   a. important
   b. obligatory
   c. primary
   d. secondary
71. A banker can issue a bank guarantee keeping
   a. specific amount in the guarantee
   b. specific period in the guarantee

c. a or b only

d. a & b above

72. Letter of Credit where in addition to advance payment, the beneficiary is entitled to payment of storage charges is called

a. LC

b. red clause credit

c. yellow clause credit

d. green clause credit

73. The State Bank of India Act was amended to divide capital into shares of

a. Rs. 10

b. Rs. 5

c. Rs. 25

d. Rs. 100

74. In case of liquidation of a banking company, a person who has made the claim within 1 month of service of notice

a. will get the preference

b. will have to wait along with other creditors

c. first liquidator has to settle the claims of SB a/c holders

d. none

75. Who may constitute an Advisory Council under Board for Financial Supervision to tender advice from time to time to the Board.

a. President

b. Vice President

c. Governor of RBI

d. Executive Director

76. Non-scheduled banks have to submit return before ....th day of every month regarding their cash reserves.

a. 10

b. 15

c. 20

d. 25

77. Return of unclaimed deposits is to be filed within

a. 30 days

b. 1 month

c. 3 months

d. none

78. A paid instrument :—

a. can be given to the drawer

b. bank should charge

c. without charges

d. a &c

79. The Banking Ombudsman scheme will cover :

a. non-payment of deposits

b. non-observation of RBI directives, if any, applicable to rate of interest on deposits

c. non-adherence of prescribed working hours by branches

d. all

80. Average daily balance with respect to CRR means

a. average closing balance

b. for 1 month

c. for a fortnight

d. a & c

81. Regulating the distribution and direction of bank credit to particular sensitive commodities in the economy in accordance with broad national priorities is

a. An RBI directive

b. Selective credit control

c. RBI control

d. None

82. For the cash reserves to be maintained, the rate of interest payable is determined by the

a. Government

b. IBA

c. RBI

d. Committee formed for this purpose

83. A return to RBI to be prepared on a Friday which happens to be a public holiday; then the return has to be prepared at the close of the :

a. next working day

b. previous working day

c. same day

d. none

84. If penalty is imposed by RBI for a default in maintaining CRR balance by a Scheduled bank the amount of penalty has to be paid within a period of .... days of the notice demanding payment

a. 14

b. 20

c. 25

d. 30

85. In case of an acquired bank the shareholders :

a. have a right to get compensation

b. do not have a right to get compensation

c. rights will be decided by the Banking Department

d. none

86. For State Bank of India the Chairman is appointed for a period not exceeding ...... years and eligible for reappointment

a. 2

b. 3

c. 4

d. 5

87. The majority of the issued share capital of the SBI subsidiary banks are held by

a. RBI

b. Respective Subsidiary banks

c. SBI

d. Government

88. A person who, for a consideration, becomes the possessor of a bill is known as

a. holder in due course

b. drawee in case of need

c. payee

d. none

89. A banker becomes a holder for value of a bill when he/she
   a. collects on behalf of a customer
   b. discounts
   c. collects on behalf of another banker
   d. all

90. For RRB the sponsor bank holds ...% of issued capital
   a. 15
   e. 35
   c. 50
   d. 100

91. Subsidiary banks have to close and balance their accounts annually as on 31st December
   a. yes
   b. no
   c. or any other date decided by RBI
   d. any date fixed by the Central Government

92. Management of a RRB is
   a. by the Sponsor bank
   b. by the State Government
   c. by RBI
   d. Board of Directors

93. A drawer's signature has been forged. In another case the endorser's signature is forged. Then, a paying bank will get
   a. protection in both the cases
   b. will not get protection in both
   c. will get protection for drawer's signature and not endorser's
   d. will not get for drawer's signature and get for endorser's

94. A banking company is required to transfer not less than 20% of its profits to reserve fund subject to the condition
   a. after declaring dividend
   b. before declaring dividend
   c. no such condition
   d. at bank's discretion

95. A co-operative bank is functioning in Maharashtra only. It can register itself in...

a. New Delhi

b. Maharashtra

c. any where in India

d. none

96. Identify the odd item (In case of Registration of charge)

a. goodwill

b. calls made but not paid

c. book debts

d. pledge

97. When a company closes a loan a charge registered with the Registrar of Companies has to be ...

a. re-registered

b. modified

c. cancelled

d. satisfied

98. Which statement in respect of the Debts Recovery Tribunal is not correct ?

a. Debt Recovery Tribunal consists of only one person

b. Head of the DRT is known as Presiding Officer

c. Appointment of DRT is done by the State Government

d. Appointment of DRT is done by issuing notification

99. A public Ltd. company requires the previous approval of ...... to give any loan to its directors

a. RBI

b. State Government

c. Central Government

d. No such approval required

QUESTIONS - 2

1. Section 24(2A) of Banking Regulation Act requires banks to maintain liquid assets to the extent of ... per cent of Demand and Time liabilities
   a. 3%
   b. 10%
   c. 15%
   d. 25%
2. Preservation of the old records by the banks is governed by the rules framed by
   a. Boards of the respective Banks
   b. State Government
   c. Central Government
   d. Registrar of Companies
3. Board for Financial Supervision of banks is headed by a Chairman who is the
   a. Governor, Reserve Bank
   b. Deputy Governor, Reserve Bank
   c. Finance Minister
   d. Banking Ombudsman
4. Violation of Warranty gives rise to
   a. Claim of damages
   b. Reject Goods
   c. No liability to pay anything
   d. Take free delivery of the goods
5. "Corporate Veil" is often in respect of a company acting as a legal person which in effect is
   a. a curtain for the men behind the scene

b. those who run the show

c. in the name of the company

d. all the above

6. The loss under indemnity should be due to the act of

a. a party giving indemnity

b. any third party

c. both should have committed the act

d. a & b

7. The person to whom the promise is made under an indemnity is called

a. indemnified

b. indemnifier

c. indemnity holder

d. all these

8. In a contract of indemnity there is/are ... party/parties.

a. 1

b. 2

c. 3

d. any number

9. In a contract of guarantee there is/are ....party/parties.

a. 1

b. 2

c. 3

d. any number

10. When a banker issues a duplicate FDR after obtaining an indemnity, the banker can recover

a. loss suffered under FDR

b. costs incurred

c. claim damages

d. all these

11. Bank Guarantees (BG) issued in lieu of cash deposit or earnest money for customers are called

a. financial guarantee

b. performance guarantee

c. DPG

d. statutory guarantee

12. If the beneficiary under BG is the Government, the limitation period to enforce the claim is

a. 3 years

b. 12 years

c. 21 years

d. 30 years

13. BG assuring a third party that the customer will honour the contract entered into and in case of failure, the bank will compensate the third party up to the agreed amount is called

a. financial guarantee

b. performance guarantee

c. DPG

d. statutory guarantee

14. BG is called the

a. life line of international commerce

b. life blood of international commerce

c. life line of inter-bank settlements

d. life blood of inter-bank settlements

15. BG issued guaranteeing payment of instalments spread over a period of time is called

a. financial guarantee

b. performance guarantee

c. DPG

d. statutory guarantee

16. BG issued favouring Courts, Customs, etc. guaranteeing payment by customers is called

a. financial guarantee

b. performance guarantee

c. DPG

d. statutory guarantee

17. Letter of Credit covers payment against

a. demand bills

b. usance bills
c. either a or b
d. no payment at any point of time, but only undertaking

18. Letter of Credit is also known as
a. Line of Credit
b. Buyer's credit
c. Supplier's Credit
d. None of the above

19. Letter of credit is a ...... instrument
a. negotiable
b. quasi negotiable
c. not negotiable
d. avalised instrument

20. LC is opened at the request of
a. issuing bank
b. applicant
c. beneficiary
d. confirming bank

21. LC issuing bank is also called
a. importer's bank or opening bank
b. advising bank or confirming bank
c. negotiation or nominated bank
d. reimbursement bank

22. The right to receive payment under LC or the right to draw bills under LC is vested with
a. opener of LC
b. issuing bank
c. beneficiary
d. all the above

23. Advising bank's responsibility is
a. to inform issuing bank as to whom to issue LC
b. to advise buyer the dispatch of documents by seller
c. inform beneficiary/seller about LC
d. none of these

24. Advising bank is also called ... bank
   a. Confirming
   b. Notifying
   c. Reimbursing
   d. None

25. Negotiating bank is the bank which
   a. negotiates the contract of sale between seller and buyer
   b. makes payment of bills drawn by seller and accepts documents
   c. guarantees payment by issuing bank
   d. none of these

26. When the LC specifies the bank that is to negotiate the bills drawn under the LC, then the bank is also called ... bank
   a. confirming
   b. reimbursing
   c. nominated
   d. none

27. The confirming bank is
   a. the issuing bank when it confirms issue of LC
   b. the negotiating bank when it confirms the negotiation of the bills
   c. the advising bank when it confirms the LC
   d. none of these

28. When the confirming bank confirms the credit, it
   a. does not take any liability
   b. undertakes on its part the liability under the LC
   c. undertakes to make timely delivery of the documents and bills to the buyer or his bank
   d. none

29. Reimbursing bank is the bank
   a. that reimburses the seller
   b. that reimburses the negotiating/paying/confirming bank
   c. that reimburses the buyer on the goods being found defective
   d. none

30. A revocable LC is one which can be amended or cancelled by ..... without prior notice

a. any or all parties to LC

b. the beneficiary

c. the issuing bank

d. all these

31. An irrevocable LC is one which cannot be amended or cancelled, without the consent of

a. the applicant

b. the issuing bank & confirming bank

c. the beneficiary

d. none of these

32. In a back-to-back credit, there will be

a. 1 bank only

b. 2 banks

c. 3 banks

d. none of the above

33. Bill of exchange under LC can also be called

a. bill

b. draft

c. bill of lading

d. a or b

34. Documents of title to goods mean

a. Bill of lading

b. Airway bill

c. Railway Receipt

d. a and c only

35. If a LC permits transfer of LC

a. it is not permissible as per UCPDC

b. it can be transferred only once

c. it can be transferred maximum three times only

d. it can be transferred any number of times

36. As per UCPDC, in a LC transaction all the parties deal only in

a. documents

b. goods

c. services

d. all these

37. As per UCPDC, in the absence of any indication in LC, such LC is

a. revocable

b. irrevocable

c. a or b as agreed to by parties

d. a or b as agreed to by banks

38. As per UCPDC, the issuing bank can return the discrepant documents under the LC within

a. 7 Banking days

b. 5 Banking days

c. 10 Banking days

d. 15 Banking days

39. When documents are tendered under LC, the negotiating bank should

a. ensure that the documents are genuine

b. take sufficient care to scrutinize

c. take reasonable care to scrutinize

d. should accept documents as tendered

40. The beneficiary under the LC can present the documents

a. only to the negotiating bank

b. direct to the opening bank

c. only to advising bank

d. either a or b

41. If the LC prohibits trans-shipment, but BL contains a printed clause providing for trans-shipment under certain circumstances

a. banks should refuse the documents

b. banks will accept the documents

c. banks will accept the documents if LC is confirmed

d. banks will accept the documents under protest

42. As per UCPDC, the invoice should be

a. proforma invoice

b. commercial invoice duly signed

c. commercial invoice signed or unsigned

d. any of the above

43. Where the LC provides maximum quantity for shipment, a tolerance of .... % is allowed.

a. 10%

b. 15%

c. 5%

d. 20%

44. UCP 600 is made operative under LC by way of

a. international law

b. commercial law

c. by contract by parties

d. all the above

45. In DPG, the guarantee is to ensure

a. delivery of goods

b. payment of instalments

c. payment of interest

d. all the above

46. The common feature between a promissory note and a bill of exchange is

a. both contain unconditional undertaking

b. both are in writing

c. both are payable always on Demand

d. all these

47. The number of parties in a bill of exchange is/are

a. one

b. two

c. three

d. four

48. "Corresponding new banks" is the term used for the banks constituted under

a. Banking Companies Acquisition & Transfer of Undertakings Act, 1970

b. New generation banking companies registered under Companies Act

c. A new bank formed by amalgamation of two banking companies

d. None of the above

49. For co-operative banks deposit insurance is available under DICGC
   a. not deposits but advances
   b. only deposits up to certain limit
   c. not for co-operative banks
   d. none

50. Obtaining of counter guarantee, while issuing guarantee is optional.
   a. yes
   b. it is required without which bank cannot hold the beneficiary responsible
   c. it is essential to proceed against the principal
   d. none of the above

51. Banks seeking licenses from RBI for opening branches are required to apply
   a. separately for each and ever branch
   b. in a consolidated mode at monthly frequencies
   c. in a consolidated mode at quarterly frequencies
   d. in a consolidated mode at yearly frequencies

52. Local area banks are those which operate
   a in a specific locality in a metropolis
   b. in a single city/town
   c. in a couple of districts which are contiguous
   d. none of the above

53. Banks are not permitted to carry out, as per existing rules, which of the following activities :—
   a. commodity trading
   b. capital market activities
   c. investment advising activities
   d. none of the above

54. Under the current guidelines of RBI, the percentage of independent directors in a public sector bank to total number of directors, is
   a. 25%
   b. 50%
   c. 33%
   d. none of the above

55. RBI pays interest to banks on the cash balances held by the latter under the CRR guidelines at

a. 3%

b. 6%

c. bank rate

d. 0%

56. Risk based supervision by RBI gives more emphasis on the

a. systems and controls of a bank to identify, measure and manage risks

b. analysis of the individual transactions in a bank during their on line audit of banks

c. market information

d. a and b

57. When RBI initiates amalgamation of a bank with another, subsequent to keeping the banking operations in a moratorium, the scheme will be considered to be final only after

a. RBI approves the plan of amalgamation

b. Central Government approves the plan

c. State Government where the affected bank is registered approves the plan

d. None of the above

58. In a nationalized bank the number of directors from the shareholders can be a maximum of

a. 2

b. 3

c. 4

d. 5

59. The contract for which a performance guarantee was issued by a bank was suspended by a statutory authority. Since there was a default by the contractor, the beneficiary invoked the guarantee. The bank is

a. not liable under the guarantee since purpose for which the guarantee was issued was suspended

b. not liable since the stoppage was beyond the principal party on whose behalf the guarantee was issued

c. bank is liable since the guarantee is independent of the underlying commercial transaction

d. a and b

60. When a L.C is marked without recourse, the recourse is not available against
   a. opener of L.C.
   b. beneficiary of L.C.
   c. negotiating bank
   d. none of the above
61. Bill of Lading marked "received for shipment" are
   a. generally acceptable
   b. generally not acceptable
   c. not acceptable since there is no certainty as to the date of starting of the commencement of journey
   d. none of the above
62. In a cash credit facility secured by hypothecation of stocks,
   a. the bank retains possession
   b. customer retains possession and title
   c. bank retain title and charge
   d. none of the above
63. When banks advance against security of a life policy, the assignment in favour of the bank is done
   a. on the policy itself
   b. by a separate document which requires stamping
   c. by a separate communication by the insurance company acknowledging the bank's charge
   d. b and c
64. Banks do not lend against deposits with other banks because
   a. of their own policy
   b. due to RBI restrictions
   c. not easily enforceable even if lien is acknowledged by the other bank
   d. none of the above
65. Lok Adalats are organized by legal services committees of Taluks, High Courts and Supreme Court in addition to
   a. state authority
   b. district authority
   c. both of the above
   d. none of a or b

66. Lok adalats can take up any civil dispute
   a. provided both parties agree for a compromise
   b. even if one party disputes reference to the Lok Adalat
   c. only if permitted by the High Court
   d. none of the above

67. The monetary limit of civil disputes that can be addressed by Lok Adalat is
   a. Rs. 10 lakhs
   b. Rs. 20 lakhs
   c. Rs. 25 lakhs
   d. Rs. 50 lakhs

68. The grievance redressal mechanism of a consumer forum is
   a. available to all consumers of goods and services
   b. available to all except those who purchase goods for resale.
   c. available to even loan customers against non-sanction of loans
   d. none of the above

69. The order made by a district, state or a central consumer forum is
   a. recoverable like any civil decree
   b. like revenue dues by concerned District collector
   c. only by other district officials and not collector
   d. by the state police

70. Current guidelines on Anti Money Laundering Act require banks to submit information about suspicious transactions to Central Government but
   a. do not disclose this information to the customer
   b. disclose this to the customer since we have a confidentiality agreement with him
   c. do not disclose but stop the transactions in the account
   d. 'b' above and also advise him that the account remains frozen till cleared by the Central Government.

QUESTIONS - 3 (CASES & CASE-LETS)

1. There is a fixed deposit of Rs. 1,00,000 in the name of Mr. A & B. A is requesting for a loan of Rs. 50,000 on the security of the fixed deposit. B (12 years old) is a minor son of A and A is signing as the guardian of the minor. Which one of the following additional document is required?

   a. Birth Certificate giving the date of birth.

   b. School certificate that B is a student.

   c. Declaration by A that the loan will be used for minor's benefit.

   d. Declaration by the minor himself that he has no objection to the loan taken by the father.

2. Mr. Shekhar has approached the bank for an emergency loan of Rs. 50,000 immediately. He is offering the following securities. Please select the most appropriate one among them to grant immediate finance :

   a. Same bank's deposit of Rs. 75,000

   b. Post Office National Savings Certificates (NSCs) of Rs. 1,00,000

   c. Life Insurance Policies of the Face Value Rs. 5,00,000

   d. His flat valued at Rs. 25,00,000

3. Assuming that the bank is going to create charge on all the securities, state whether the following is true or false :

   a. In respect of a deposit the bank will have hypothecation.

   b. In respect of NSCs the bank will have pledge.

   c. In respect of LIC policies the bank will have mortgage.

   d. In respect of the Flat the bank will have an agreement to mortgage.

4. Mr. Shankar has a loan account fully overdue with a balance of Rs. 32,000 and also a Savings Bank account in the same bank that shows a credit balance of Rs. 60,000. He is not responding to the bank's due notices to repay. Which among the following will be the best course available to the bank.

a. contact personally and obtain a cheque drawn on the Savings Account, in favour of the bank

b. issue a Vakil Notice and threaten legal action if not paid forthwith

c. file a suit in the court of law to teach him a lesson

d. exercise banker's lien and set off on the Savings account balance and close the loan account

5. In the above case, instead of Shankar having a Savings Account with our bank, he has an account with another bank with a fixed deposit of Rs. 60,000 in that bank. The other day when he called on the manager, inadvertently he left on the manager's table an envelope that contained the FD receipt of the other bank. The bank can

a. exercise its lien on the receipt and get the proceeds to close the loan.

b. cannot exercise the lien as the receipt has not come in the normal course of banking business, say for collection.

c. lien cannot be exercised on some other bank's receipt.

d. lien can be exercised only with consent of Mr. Shankar.

6. "A" has an overdue loan with a balance of Rs. 27,000. There is also a Recurring Deposit with a balance of Rs. 60,000 in the name of Mr. & Mrs. A repayable to Either or Survivor. The Bank can

a. exercise the lien

b. cannot exercise the lien because the liability and assets are not in the same right and capacity

c. 50% of the deposit can be deemed to belong to "A" and the bank can adjust the dues even without the lien

d. approach a Court of law and obtain their permission to adjust

7. A jewel loan of Rs. 6,000 was granted on the pledge of ornaments valued at Rs.10,000 The borrower could not repay even after three years and so the bank sold the ornaments by public auction. After adjusting the dues there was a surplus of Rs. 2,000. The surplus should be treated by the bank as

a. profit to the bank.

b. borrower's property to be handed over with a proper account.

c. an incentive to be given to the bank staff for recovery of loans.

d. a credit to some other overdue borrowing account to reduce NPAs.

8. Pyarelal is a SB Account holder for last several years. He has approached the bank manager with his life policy of the face value of Rs.1,00,000 with a premium paid of Rs.10,000 to grant him the maximum permissible loan. Select among the following the basis for granting the loan.

a. Face value of Rs.1,00,000

b. Premium Paid Rs.10,000

c. Surrender Value of the policy to be ascertained from the Insurance Company

d. Surrender value plus accrued bonus

9. State true or false in the above case

a. A bank never grants loans against life policies

b. The mode of charging security is assignment

c. The bank will have its name included as a Nominee when a loan is granted.

10. During the course of weeks prior to Diwali, the following business enterprises have approached the bank for 'advances against book debts'. Which one among them is suitable for sanctioning the finance?

a. proprietary concern

b. partnership firm

c. joint Hindu family

d. limited liability company

11. Laxmi & Co. a partnership firm is dealing in timber. However, they approach the bank, for a loan of Rs. 5,00,000 to acquire gold coins and keep with the bank as a security till the prices go up and then sell and make profits. They are not in jewellery business but ask for the loan with a profit motive. They feel gold is an extremely good and safe security and the bank can very well sanction without any hesitation.

The Manager however is not inclined to sanction and has jotted down the following reasons of which he/she wants to select the most appropriate one and convey. The appropriate reason is

a. The bank does not have a night watchman.

b. The bank does not deal in gold.

c. The purpose of the advance is unproductive.

d. Only jewellery merchants can avail loans against gold.

12. Mr. Shyamsunder, the Chief Accountant of a Private limited company drawing a handsome salary is asking for a loan of Rs. 50,000 against the shares of Rs.1,25,000 of his company. The company has the account with the bank in which there is always substantial balance. The audited balance sheet of the Private Limited Company also reveals that the company is financially very sound. The bank can

a. cannot sanction the loan because the shares cannot be sold in the market in the case of an eventuality.

b. can buy the shares and hold for Reserve purposes.

c. sanction the loan because the audited statements reveal financial soundness.

d. obtain Registrar of Companies' permission and then sanction the loan.

13. A loan of Rs.10,00,000 was granted to a small scale industrialist against the hypothecation of machinery of Rs.15,00,000. The industry is closed and the loan is fully overdue. Owing to the change in the technology the machinery has become a junk with a scrap value of Rs. 25,000. The bank has issued a notice both to the borrower and the guarantor to repay forthwith. The borrower has no means to repay. When the guarantor is called upon to repay he requests the bank to sell the machinery and simultaneously file a suit against the borrower. He says he will definitely repay if the borrower fails to repay. Which one of the following is correct.

a. Guarantor's request can be acceded to

b. Gaurantor's request need not be acceded to because his/her liability is co-extensive with that of the borrower's

c. Guarantor need not repay as the machinery has become junk. It is neither his/her fault nor the borrower's

d. The borrower also need not repay as the industry has become sick

14. Mr. A has taken a loan of Rs. 20,000 with the joint and several guarantee of Mr. B & Mr. C. There is no other security. The loan has become overdue. The Bank sends recall notice to the guarantors. In reply Mr. B remits Rs.10,000 as his share and Mr. C. Rs. 5,000 stating that he is unable to pay more. Both Mr. A and C expressed that they are in great financial difficulties. The Bank can

a. Compel Mr. A to remit at least the balance of Rs. 5,000

b. Ask Mr. B only, to remit the balance of Rs. 5,000 as the liability is joint and several.

c. Ask Mr. C to raise through some source Rs. 5,000 and pay to cover his 50% of the guaranteed amount.

d. Write off the balance of Rs. 5000 as a Loss Asset.

15. Lords & Co. are merchandise traders. They send goods up country by trucks obtain lorry receipts and on their buyers draw usance bills of 60 days usance period with Documents to be delivered against Acceptance of the drawers. The bank finances by discounting such bills. One bill of Rs. 60,000 drawn on Sound & Co., Mysore, though accepted and documents delivered, came back dishonoured. The bank demanded payment from Lords & Co. And they came up with the following replies. Which one is acceptable to the bank?

a. the bank has committed a mistake in releasing the documents against Acceptance.

b. bank should represent the bill again and try to collect the money from sound & Co.

c. grant them a week's time to reimburse the amount. They are responsible for repayment.

d. the bank should file a suit against the Acceptor as he/she is in possession of the goods covered by Lorry Receipt.

16. MN & Co. receive a cheque of Rs. 50,000 from an upcountry customer of theirs drawn on his bank there. The cheque is dated 14th August, 2005 but they approach their bank on 27th July, 2005 with a request to discount the cheque. The bank considers the request and makes the payment on 27th July, 2005. On presenting the cheque on 14th August the cheque was returned with the reason, "Payment Stopped by the Drawer". The Bank asks MN & Co. to reimburse the amount of the cheque. MN & Co. came up with the following replies. Which one will be acceptable?

a. The bank should have presented the cheque immediately instead of waiting till 14th August, 2005

b. Stopping payment is not their fault.

c. They can represent and try to obtain the payment or whatever balance available in the account.

d. Give them a week's time to reimburse or accept some other cheques for discounting.

MODEL PAPER I

1. Ref: Banking Regulation Act, 1949. Identify odd item:
   a. Deposits
   b. Loans
   c. Investment
   d. Trading activity
2. "Account payee only" crossing is a direction to
   a. paying banker only
   b. collecting banker only
   c. both paying and collecting bankers
   d. payee only
3. Individuals who are engaged in trading or manufacturing activity can accept deposits.
   a. true; but they should report to RBI quarterly
   b. partly true; they can accept deposits from friends
   c. partly true; they can accept deposits from relatives
   d. partly true: both b & c
4. No banker issues a bearer draft. The reason is
   a. banking practice
   b. prohibited under BR Act
   c. prohibited under RBI Act
   d. prohibited under NI Act
5. Paying banker gets protection in case of payment of a bearer cheque under Sec. ... of NI Act.
   a. 25
   b. 65

   c. 85
   d. 128

6. Ten rupee note issued by RBI is
   a. currency note
   b. bank note
   c. bill of exchange
   d. all these

7. Under Section 131 of NI Act, the word conversion means
   a. transfer of title to a holder in due course
   b. transfer of title to a person who is not the true owner
   c. paying the value for a foreign currency instrument in Indian rupees
   d. changing the type of deposit

8. RBI can issue currency notes upto a maximum denomination of
   a. 1000
   b. 5000
   c. 10000
   d. 20000

9. Central Government has the power to issue directions to RBI in public interest as per provisions in the
   a. Constitution
   b. RBI Act
   c. BR Act
   d. All the above

10. A pay order issued by a bank is construed to be a
   a. promissory note
   b. bill of exchange
   c. IOU
   d. cheque

11. Identify the odd item (Ref: Sale of Goods Act)
   a. Goods
   b. Movable Property
   c. Stocks & Shares
   d. Currency Notes

12. Debenture is a document acknowledging
    a. Company's indebtedness
    b. Company's ownership
    c. Ownership of machinery
    d. None of the above
13. To commence or carrying on banking business in India, a company needs
    a. Licence from the Registrar of Companies
    b. Licence from the respective State Government
    c. Licence from the Reserve Bank
    d. No need for any licence
14. Voting rights of sharesholders is restricted to ___ % of total voting rights.
    a. 10%
    b. 20%
    c. 40%
    d. unlimited
15. The Director of a banking company can hold office continuously for
    a. 3 years
    b. 5 years
    c. 8 years
    d. for life.
16. The sole authority of Currency Note issue is
    a. Reserve Bank
    b. State Bank
    c. Consortium of banks
    d. Exim Bank
17. Banking Ombudsman is an authority for
    a. Resolution and Settlement of complaints of the public against banks without going to court
    b. Helping the banks for recovery of NPAs
    c. Finding ways and means to improve customer service
    d. Fixing rate of interest on deposits.
18. In respect of non-acceptance of small denomination notes complaint may be made to
    a. Reserve Bank

  b. District Consumer Forum
  c. DRT
  d. Banking Ombudsman

19. Scheduled Bank means
  a. A Bank with more than 100 Branches
  b. Bank with deposits beyond Rs. 1000 Crores
  c. Bank included in the Second Schedule of the RBI Act, 1934
  d. None of the above

20. Bank Rate means
  a. Fixed Deposit Rate
  b. Loans Rate
  c. Savings Bank Rate
  d. Standard Rate at which the Reserve Bank is prepared to buy eligible bills.

21. Under letter of Credit, Bill means
  a. Bill of Entry
  b. Bill of Lading
  c. Bill of Exchange
  d. Invoice

22. Unclaimed Deposit means a deposit not operated for
  a. 3 years
  b. 5 years
  c. 7 years
  d. 10 years

23. For return of paid instruments, a bank has to obtain permission from
  a. Reserve Bank
  b. Registrar of Companies
  c. Central Government
  d. None.

24. When the affairs of a bank are not satisfactory, a moratorium is imposed by
  a. Reserve Bank
  b. Central Government
  c. Registrar of Companies
  d. Bank's Board of Directors.

25. Bailment is the delivery of goods
    - *a.* as security
    - *b.* for safe custody
    - *c.* for using on rent
    - *d.* for sale or return
26. Partnership at will means
    - *a.* No specific duration for the partnership
    - *b.* No specific business
    - *c.* No specified number of partners
    - *d.* No understanding : Everybody acting at his will and pleasure
27. The first and the foremost duty of the partner is
    - *a.* To carry on some business
    - *b.* To carry on his personal business
    - *c.* To carry on the business of the firm
    - *d.* None of the above
28. All the partners can only decide on which of the following issues.
    - *a.* to issue notice to dissolve the partnership
    - *b.* issue a cheque to the suppliers
    - *c.* change of business
    - *d.* employee a clerk
29. Identify the odd item (Ref. Partnership)
    - *a.* Partnership deed
    - *b.* Goodwill
    - *c.* Dissolution
    - *d.* Authorised capital
30. A company is a
    - *a.* Legal person created under Law
    - *b.* Shareholders
    - *c.* Directors
    - *d.* Employees
31. Legally a company is
    - *a.* one person
    - *b.* many persons

c. number of persons equal to number of shares

d. no such limit

32. A company has to be registered basically under

a. Companies Act, 1956

b. Partnership Act, 1932

c. Banking Regulation Act, 1949

d. Reserve Bank of India Act, 1934

33. Income earned by a shareholder on a company's shareholding is called

a. Interest

b. Discount

c. Dividend

d. None of these

34. Common Seal of a Company is

a. Substitute for signature

b. Simply a seal

c. Identification mark of directors

d. Logo of the company

35. Private Limited Company must have the following as a part of its name:

a. Private Limited

b. Private

c. Company

d. Only the name

36. FEMA is applicable to

a. all foreign exchange transaction in India

b. to branches/offices/agencies outside India owned and controlled by a person resident in India

c. does not cover the transactions carried out by foreign citizens resident in India

d. a and b

37. A Bank authorised to deal in Foreign Exchange is officially called

a. Authorised Dealer

b. Foreign Bank

c. Dealer in Foreign Currency

d. Exchange Company

38. Under FEMA, Capital Account Transaction means a transaction resulting in increase or decrease of

a. Assets of a person resident in India but held abroad

b. Assets in India of a person resident outside India

c. Both a & b

d. a only.

39. Clauses in the Articles of Association can be made with the approval of...

a. Registrar of Companies

b. State Government

c. High Court

d. None of these

40. With reference to FEMA identify the odd item:

a. Current Account

b. Foreign Trade

c. Interest on loans given abroad

d. Salary earned by a resident Indian in India

41. Repatriate to India means

a. Bringing to India foreign exchange

b. Retaining foreign exchange abroad as per provisions of FEMA

c. Selling to authorised person

d. a & c

42. The Sub-Agent is responsible to

a. The Principal

b. The Agent

c. To both

d. To none

43. Under the Sale of Goods Act a condition means

a. Simply a stipulation

b. Stipulation essential to the main purpose

c. If violated confers a right for the cancellation of the contract

d. b & c

44. The Role of Ombudsman as an Arbitrator in respect of disputes is restricted to an amount of

a. Rs. 5 lakhs

b. Rs. 10 lakhs

c. Rs. 25 lakhs

d. No such limit

45. Max. Cash Reserve required to be maintained with the Reserve Bank under section 42(1) of the RBI Act, 1934 is

a. 2.1/2% on Demand liability

b. 10% on Demand & Time Liability

c. 5% on Demand & Time Liability

d. No ceiling at all

46. Memorandum & Articles of a company are

a. Public Documents

b. Secret Documents

c. Not documents

d. Meant only for the Company Directors.

47. Memorandum & Articles of any company are available for inspection in

a. The Printing Press where they are printed

b. All Public Libraries.

c. On the notice Board of Companies.

d. Office of the Registrar of Companies

48. A shareholder

a. can claim dividend as a matter of right

b. can receive only if the Board declares

c. can receive if approved in Annual General Body Meeting

d. b & c.

49. Act done by the Agent without the Principal's knowledge

a. can be ratified by the Principal

b. cannot be ratified

c. should always be ratified

d. results in the termination of the Agency.

50. The seller of goods is deemed to be an unpaid seller when

a. The price is paid but delivery not taken

b. Price is only quoted.

c. Price not paid

d. Price not settled.

51. Regional Rural Banks were set up
   a. to develop Rural Economy
   b. to act as bankers for the State Government
   c. to act as bankers for the Central Government
   d. work on behalf of the Reserve Bank in the rural areas.

52. To set up a RRB,
   a. Reserve Bank has to sponsor
   b. Another bank has to sponsor
   c. No bank need sponsor
   d. Anybody in the rural area can promote a RRB

53. A co-operative bank is registered under State Co-op. Societies Act
   a. if the Members so desire
   b. if it is operating in the same State
   c. if the depositors so desire
   d. if it is operating in more than one State

54. Identify the odd item: (Ref: Co-op. Bank)
   a. Primary Co-op. Bank
   b. Central Co-op. Bank
   c. State Co-op. Bank
   d. Primary Agricultural Co-op. Society

55. SARFAESI Act, 2002 is applicable to
   a. whole of India
   b. whole of India except Jammu & Kashmir
   c. major Cities of India
   d. only in the notified towns under Transfer of Property Act

56. SARFAESI Act, 2002 presupposes
   a. Loan taken has to be repaid
   b. Security cannot be sold
   c. If not, security is liable for being sold
   d. a & c

57. After the Mardia Chemicals case, the Government brought about an amendment stipulating the deposit amount for making an appeal under SARFAESI Act, 2002. Accordingly the amount to be deposited generally is
   a. 10%

b. 25%

c. 50%

d. 75%

58. The main provision of the SARFAESI Act, 2002 is realisation of securities

a. Through a Court of Law

b. Without the intervention of the Court

c. Through the Registrar of Companies

d. By Approaching the Police

59. Identify the odd item

a. Bank Guarantee

b. Performance Guarantee

c. Deferred Payment Guarantee

d. Credit Guarantee

60. Spurious Goods are defined under

a. Sale of Goods Act

b. Contract Act

c. Consumer Protection Act

d. Companies Act

61. Unfair Trade Practices mean

a. making use of a deceptive practice to promote sales

b. not participating in Trade Fairs

c. sale in an untidy shop

d. very high price and not a fair price

62. Consumer Protection Councils are constituted for the purpose of

a. running a grievance redressal machinery

b. receiving consumers complaints

c. tendering advice to Government

d. creating awareness among the consumers of their rights and protecting them

63. Identify the odd item: (Re : Consumers Protection Council)

a. Taluka Level

b. District Level

c. State Level

d. Central Level

64. BG issued favouring Courts, Customs, etc. guaranteeing payment by customers is called

a. financial guarantee

b. performance guarantee

c. DPG

d. statutory guarantee

65. In BG, the bank makes payment on

a. being convinced that the beneficiary has incurred loss.

b. on being sued by beneficiary

c. on the guarantee being invoked and after seeking concurrence of debtor

d. merely on demand by the beneficiary

66. A revocable LC is one which can be amended or cancelled by ..... without prior notice.

a. any or all parties to LC

b. the beneficiary

c. the issuing bank

d. all these

67. Foreign Exchange Management Act, 1999 (FEMA) treats letter of credit as

a. foreign currency

b. foreign exchange

c. both a & b

d. none

68. When documents are tendered under LC, the negotiating bank should

a. ensure that the documents are genuine.

b. take sufficient care to scrutinize

c. take reasonable care to scrutinize

d. should accept documents as tendered

69. If the LC prohibits transshipment, but BL contains a clause for transshipment,

a. banks should refuse the documents

b. banks will accept the documents

c. banks will accept the documents if LC is confirmed

d. banks will accept the documents under protest

70. "Corresponding new banks" is the term used for the banks constituted under
   a. Banking Companies 1980 (Acquisition & Transfer of Undertakings) Act, 1970 & 1980
   b. new generation banking companies registered under Companies Act
   c. a new bank formed by amalgamation of two banking companies
   d. Banking Regulation Act, 1949

71. In Agency agreement,
   a. the Principal should be a major
   b. the Agent should be a major
   c. anyone can be a minor
   d. both should be major

72. In Sale of Goods Act "quiet possession" means
   a. Buyer will get protection
   b. Seller will not make noise
   c. Buyer will remain quiet
   d. Buyer will possess and enjoy.

73. The income earned on a Debenture is
   a. dividend
   b. interest
   c. discount
   d. incentive

74. The bank receives the following four cheques through clearing. Which one of them is deemed to be a Crossed Cheque?
   a. On the top of the cheque the words, "Crossed Cheque" are written without any other marking.
   b. Two parallel transverse lines are drawn on the face of the cheque.
   c. On the back of the cheque two parallel transverse lines are drawn.
   d. A big "X" mark is made on the top of the cheque without any other marks.

75. Crossing means,
   a. cheque is cancelled.
   b. cash has to be paid on identification
   c. no cash can be paid across the counter.
   d. no balance in the account.

76. ABC Co. Ltd. have a current account operated by any one of the three directors A, B and C of which "A" dies. A cheque for Rs. 25,000 signed by "A" previously, is presented for payment.

The bank will

a. dishonour the cheque with the reason: "Signatory is dead."

b. honour the cheque as the Company, the account holder has perpetual life.

c. seek the Company's advice.

d. ask the Company to stop the payment and issue a new cheque.

77. Venu Sir is the Principal of Arunodaya College. He has received a cheque for Rs.1,00,000 in the name of the Principal, Arunodaya College crossed Account Payee and made to order. He wants to credit it to his personal account in the name of Venugopal Rao stating that he is the Principal. He approaches the bank manager to allow him to do it. State whether,

a. bank can accede to his request

b. cannot accede because the payee is the head of an educational institution and so it is meant for the principal of institution.

c. bank can accept only for the credit of the account of Arunodaya College.

d. left to the discretion of the Manager.

78. M/s.Venus & Co., a limited liability company approaches the bank to open a current account. They say theirs is not a private limited company and they produce the following documents for verification. Which one among them will give a conclusive proof of Public Limited company?

a. a resolution signed by all the directors that theirs is a Public Ltd.Co.

b. memorandum Association.

c. articles of Association.

d. certificate of Incorporation & Certificate to Commence Business issued by the Registrar of Companies of the state.

State whether the following is True or False :

79. An Agency is terminated by the Principal by revoking his authority, given earlier to the Agent

80. Agency is terminated by the Agent by renouncing it

81. A sale involves two persons

82. An agreement to sale becomes a sale when the parties perform mutual promises

83. A gift could be a sale

84. Branch licensing for Regional Rural Banks should be through NABARD

85. Under a contract of Guarantee, the surety has no liability at all
86. Surety is liable only for the Principal amount of the debt
87. Continuing Guarantee continues even after the debt is cleared
88. As soon as the surety clears the liability he will occupy the place of creditor
89. Bailee has to take care of the goods as if they are his own
90. Bailee need not return the goods unless claimed on the expiry of period
91. Partnership is a business relationship for sharing profits
92. Partnership business cannot be carried on by one partner acting for all
93. A shareholding in a company is a movable property of a shareholder
94. In its name a public limited company should invariably have the phrase, "Public Limited Company"
95. All the joint stock companies must have the word "limited" in their name unless the liability of the members is unlimited
96. Clauses of Memorandum of Association can be altered by special resolution and the sanction of company law board
97. A Member has no right to approach the Company Law Board to order investigation into the affairs of the Company
98. If a company commits an act of contravening the Memorandum it can be ratified by the shareholders at the general meeting of the Shareholders
99. Contravening the provisions of the Articles of Association can be ratified at the Annual General Meeting of the Shareholders
100. The property of the firm has to be held and used by the partners for the use of partnership
101. A partner is the Agent of the Firm
102. A statutory guarantee is given to a Court of Law
103. Letter of Credit is a negotiable Instrument
104. Some LCs enable the beneficiaries to avail loans
105. LC issuing bank undertakes to pay if the documents mentioned therein are tendered without any discrepancy
106. A private limited company has a perpetual life
107. In the case of a Joint Hindu Family, the Manager or the Karta, in the best interest of the family, can take a loan against the assets of the family without consulting the adult members
108. All Insurance Contracts are the contracts of Indemnity
109. The Agent is bound to conduct the business of the Principal
110. The Agency is terminated when the Principal is adjudicated as an insolvent

111. Under the Sale of Goods Act, "Future Goods" means Goods to be manufactured and sold

112. Donation by way of goods is a sale

113. In a sale ownership is passed on the buyer

114. An unpaid seller can stop the delivery of goods.

MODEL PAPER II

1. In Agency, the Principal is also called
   a. An Agent
   b. Businessman
   c. A person who engages another person to represent him/her while dealing with third party
   d. All the above

State True or False :

2. Agency is terminated when the business of the agent is being terminated
3. Agency is terminated at the Agent's death
4. A sale is not a contract
5. In a sale the delivery of goods is a must
6. Price is not the consideration for sale
7. Identify the document of title to goods from the following :
   a. Shares and stocks
   b. Invoice
   c. Bill of Lading
   d. Hypothecation deed
8. A debenture evidences
   a. debt due by the company
   b. share capital of the company
   c. rules of the company
   d. objects of the company
9. The document of title to goods enables the holder
   a. to transfer the goods

b. ownership by endorsement

c. possession of goods by delivery

d. all the above

10. Granting licence to carry on the banking business is the sole discretion of

a. Registrar of Companies

b. Respective State Government

c. High Court of the State

d. Reserve Bank of India

11. Foreign Bank means

a. a Bank carrying a foreign name

b. dealing in NRI deposits

c. dealing in Foreign Exchange

d. a Banking Company incorporated outside India

12. Identify the odd item in the following :

a. Bill of Lading

b. Bill of Exchange

c. Promissory note

d. Cheque

13. Demand Liability Means

a. Liability of a bank to be met on demand

b. Liability of the borrower of a bank to be repaid on demand

c. Liability against the demand promissory note

d. a or b.

State True or False

14. There is no ceiling for holding of shares in a banking company

15. Reserve Bank has the authority to regulate the rate of interest on advances.

16. Banking Ombudsman has the authority for the redressal of the grievances against the deficiency of banking services

17. A state co-operative bank is always a scheduled bank

18. Formats of Balance Sheet and Profit and Loss Account of bankers are prescribe by Reserve Bank of India

19. The total period of moratorium imposed on a bank should not exceed

a. 3 months

b. 6 months

c. 9 months

d. 12 months

20. In a contract of Guarantee there should be..... parties

a. Two

b. Three

c. No limit

d. One of the parties should be a bank.

21. Any variance in the terms of guarantee without the consent of the surety

a. Discharges the surety

b. Discharges the principal debtor

c. Discharges the debt

d. None of these

22. Pledge is the

a. bailment of goods

b. as a security for repayment of debt

c. bailment of goods as security for performance of a promise

d. all these

23. State True or False: Differences among the partners can be decided by the majority vote of partners.

24. Choose the correct one. (Ref : Partnership)

a. to carry on some lawful business

b. to go on a pleasure trip by contributing together

c. to pay voluntary donations making equal contributions

d. to play games bearing the expenses equally

State True or False

25. While returning paid instruments banks are not entitled for charges for taking out the copies

26. In a contract of Indemnity, one person promises to save the other from the loss

27. Death of Guarantor terminates the guarantee unless stipulated otherwise

28. In the contract of Bailment, period of bailment is essential

29. While selling pledged goods, notice has to be given to the borrower.

30. A Partnership at will can be dissolved by

a. any one of the partners by giving notice to all

b. all partner must give notice to all

c. no partner need give notice

d. by a creditor giving notice.

31. Identify the odd item. (Ref: Company)

a. legal Person

b. limited liability

c. shareholders

d. shareholder can take part in day to day business.

32. The Agent is responsible

a. for his/her actions

b. for the Acts of the Sub Agent

c. only for his action and not that of sub-agent's

d. a and b

33. Warranty is

a. collateral to the main purpose of the contract

b. a condition to fulfil

c. a rule to be observed

d. a Guarantee

34. Cash Reserve Ratio to be maintained with the Reserve Bank should be on average daily balance. Average is calculated for

a. Week

b. Fortnight

c. Month

d. Year

State True or False

35. A minor cannot be admitted as a partner in the partnership firm even when other partners give their consent.

36. The Consumer Protection Act does not have overriding effect on other laws.

37. A society registered under the Societies Registration Act, 1860 can hold shares in a company.

38. Under FEMA, payments due as interest on loans and as income from investments will be treated as current account transaction and not as capital account transaction.

39. A minor can give guarantee on behalf of a major.

40. A Surety is not discharged if the principal debtor is released by the creditor.

41. Every partner has a right to inspect and copy any of the books of the firm.

42. In an agreement to sell the seller can only sue for damages.

43. DRT Act is applicable to the whole of India including the State of Jammu and Kashmir.

44. The Banking Ombudsman has powers to handle cases where the disputed claim amount is beyond Rs.10 lacs.

45. Business of banking is permitted only if

a. Registrar of Companies grants certificate to commence Business

b. Reserve Bank Grants a licence

c. Central Government grants a permit

d. None of the above

46. Reserve Bank is supervising

a. banks

b. joint stock companies

c. only Govt.Companies

d. all trading activities in the country

47. Ref: Consumer Protection Act : If the complainant fails to appear on the date of hearing, the District Forum can

a. dismiss the complaint for failure/Decide on merit

b. levy a fine on the complainant

c. postpone the case

d. none of the above

48. In the above case if the opposite party fails to appear

The District Forum can,

a. postpone the case for a future date

b. ask the complainant to withdraw the complaint

c. decide the case ex-parte basing on the evidence.

d. none of the above

State True or false :

49. A bill of exchange is a document evidencing that the goods have been received for shipment.

50. A company owning more than 50% of share capital in another company is called a holding company

51. Where the beneficiary is entitled for advance before production of documents, it is called Green Clause Credit

52. The Chairman of the RRB is from the respective State Government

53. Foreign banks have to display in a prominent place in their principal office a copy of the last audited balance sheet not later than the first Friday in August of any year.

54. Selective credit control is used to prevent speculative holding of essential commodities

55. A stale cheque is defined under

a. NI Act (Negotiable Instruments Act)

b. BR Act (Banking Regulation Act)

c. TP Act (Transfer of Property Act)

d. None of the above

56. A cheque payable to order can be transferred by

a. delivery

b. endorsement

c. endorsement & delivery

d. none of these

57. Section 10 of NI Act deals with

a. promissory note

b. holder

c. holder in due course

d. payment in due course

58. Safe custody service of banks fall under the contract of

a. lease

b. indemnity

c. guarantee

d. bailment

59. A cheque in an individual's a/c is presented in clearing. Bank receives information that the drawer has passed away

a. the cheque can be passed

b. the cheque can be passed after confirmation from legal heirs

c. the cheque can be passed after confirmation from nominee

d. the cheque has to be returned

60. A cheque is signed by the Director of a limited company. Bank receives information that the drawer has passed away

a. the cheque can be passed

b. the cheque can be passed only after getting confirmation from Company's Board

c. the cheque can be passed after confirmation from legal heirs

d. the cheque has to be returned

61. Banker's general lien tantamounts to .....

a. mortgage

b. assignment

c. implied pledge

d. mortgage

62. Stop payment of a demand draft can be issued by

a. purchaser

b. issuing branch

c. head office of the bank

d. none of these

63. Banks execute standing instructions of the customers on the basis of relationship of

a. Creditor-debtor

b. Agent-principal

c. Principal-agent

d. Debtor-creditor

64. To give effect to an order of attachment, the banker customer relationship should be that of

a. bailor-bailee

b. debtor-creditor

c. creditor-debtor

d. lessee-lessor

65. "Account payee" crossing is defined in

a. NI Act

b. BR Act

c. Contract Act

d. None of these

66. In case the banker refuses payment wrongfully of a cheque, he is liable to

a. drawer

b. payee or endorsee

c. both a and b

d. a or b depending on circumstances

67. The law relating to payment of cheques and protection to a banker is contained in

a. BR Act

b. NI Act

c. Contract Act

d. All these

68. If the banker has to honour a cheque and also to exercise his right of set-off, he should

a. first honour the cheque and then go for set-off

b. first set-off and then honour the cheque

c. exercising right depends on the constitution of payee

d. exercising right depends on the quantum of set-off

69. A customer is bound to inform the bank about his lost cheque leaves. This statement is

a. true

b. not true

c. true, if the cheques were signed

d. true, if the cheques were issued to other than individuals

70. In a joint account, if one of the signature is forged and the instrument is paid, the bank and the customer are equally liable. This statement is

a. true

b. not true

c. true, if the genuine signature is that of higher authority

d. true, if the bank has paid the cheque in good faith

71. A minor can be admitted to the firm as

a. partner

b. agent

c. dormant partner

d. none of these

72. When a cheque is drawn by the borrower and made payable to the same bank branch

a. drawer and drawee are same

b. drawer and payee are same

c. drawee and payee are same

d. none of these

73. Hari has availed two loans from the bank on the personal guarantee of Guru and Ramesh separately. The loans have become overdue. To recover the liability through a Court of law

a. a single suit can be filed

b. 2 different suits to be filed

c. suits can be filed only against borrower

d. none

74. General Lien can be exercised by the bank on one of the following:

a. cash remitted for DD

b. credit balance in loan account

c. articles in safe custody

d. contents of locker

75. The tools of selective credit control are

a. margin requirements

b. specified ROI

c. ceiling on levels of credit

d. all these

76. Bank acts as ..... when standing instructions of customer are carried out

a. executant

b. principal

c. agent

d. creditor

77. When hypothecated goods are taken possession by the bank

a. fixed charge continues

b. floating charge becomes fixed charge

c. fixed charge becomes floating charge

d. none of the above

78. Usurious Loans Act has been enacted to protect ..... borrowers from powerful money lenders.

a. weaker

b. rural

c. agriculturist

d. all the above

79. Payment of a cheque is complete

a. when token is given

b. amount is debited

c. cheque passed

d. cash is given

80. Disclosure of information about the customer's account can be done

a. when customer expressly permits

b. bank is compelled under law

c. bank's own interest

d. all these circumstances

81. A Fixed Deposit Receipt can be transferred by

a. endorsement and delivery

b. by way of assignment

c. either a or b

d. none of these

82. Material alteration is one which varies

a. relationship of parties

b. rights of parties

c. liabilities of parties

d. b & c

83. Before honouring a claim under BG, the bank should ensure that

a. invocation is within validity period

b. claim amount is not more than guaranteed amount

c. authority invoking guarantee is empowered

d. all these

84. In a BG, bank is

a. debtor

b. creditor

c. surety

d. depends on the wordings

85. Statutory Corporations are established under
   a. Companies Act
   b. Act of Parliament
   c. Societies Registration Act
   d. All these

86. Right of set-off cannot be exercised in the following:
   a. loan account time barred
   b. loan account and deposit accounts are in two different branches
   c. loan account and deposit account are held under different rights
   d. loan account is recalled

87. A bearer cheque contains
   a. unconditional undertaking
   b. unconditional order
   c. both a and b
   d. conditional order to pay

88. In a special crossing of a cheque
   a. two parallel lines are important
   b. name of collecting banker is important
   c. both a and b are necessary
   d. words "not negotiable" is a must

89. Registration of charge with ROC need not be done
   a. for hypothecation of stocks
   b. for pledge of stocks
   c. for mortgage of property
   d. for hypothecation of vehicles

90. A private limited company need not submit the following document for opening the account:
   a. memorandum of association
   b. articles of association
   c. certificate of incorporation
   d. certificate of commencement of business

91. In a pronote with more than one borrower
   a. signature of all should appear across revenue stamp
   b. it is sufficient if one signs across revenue stamp

c. additional stamps should be pasted so that all will sign across the stamps

d. a & c

92. Under hypothecation agreement, the relationship between the customer and the banker is

a. bailor-bailee

b. lessor-lessee

c. creditor-debtor

d. debtor-creditor

93. Negative lien means

a. cancellation/release of lien marked on securities

b. prohibition of second encumbrance

c. prohibition of creating any charge

d. undertaking by executant not to encumber the unencumbered securities

94. Modification of charge is to be filed, where

a. same assets are taken as securities for limits granted subsequently

b. where loan facilities are transferred to another branch

c. where additional limits are granted and additional securities are taken

d. a & c above

95. *Pari passu* is a charge indicating

a. first charge over securities

b. second charge over securities

c. equal charge to charge holders

d. proportionate share to chargeholders

96. Limitation period for term loans repayable in instalments is

a. 3 years from date of loan document

b. 3 years from due date of each instalment

c. 3 years from date of disbursement

d. 12 years from date of loan documents

97. SARFAESI Act means

a. Securities & Reconstruction of Financial Assets & Enforcement of Security Interest Act

b. Securitisation & Reconstruction of Financial Assets & Enforcement of Securities Interest Act

c. Securitisation & Reconstruction of Financial Assets & Enforcement of Security Interest Act

d. None of these

98. Banks obtain security

a. to safeguard money advanced

b. to sell when need arises

c. both a and b

d. none

99. The objective of SARFAESI Act is

a. to improve recoveries

b. to exercise powers to take possession of securities

c. to sell them without intervention of Courts

d. all the above

100. As per the law existing today, mortgage security cannot be sold without Court intervention. Is this correct ?

a. Yes, Court intervention is required

b. No, SARFAESI Act has now made enabling provisions

c. Yes, since Contract Act has made no provision about court intervention

d. No, Due to recent amendments in TP Act, no court intervention is required

101. Under open cash credit, the goods are taken as security, without transferring

a. ownership of goods

b. possession of goods

c. both are transferred

d. both are not transferred

102. Under Keyshut cash credit/Pledge, the relationship between the borrower and the bank is

a. debtor-creditor

b. creditor-debtor

c. lessor-lessee

d. assignor-assignee

103. Upon admission of a new partner in a firm enjoying credit limits

a. fresh loan documents should be obtained from new partner

b. fresh loan documents should be obtained from the reconstituted firm *c.* letter of confirmation to be obtained from new partner

d. letter of confirmation to be obtained from all partners

104. Fixed charge means non registration of charge for the following:

a. book debts

b. supply bills

c. immovable property

d. pledge

105. Non-registration of charge with ROC makes a bank to

a. become unsecured creditor against other charge holders

b. share the securities with other charge holders

c. lose the remedy to file suit for the debt

d. lose both the security and the right to file suit

State True or False

106. Under FEMA an exporter can hold sale proceeds abroad

107. Under FEMA a person can continue to hold foreign securities acquired while he was a resident abroad.

108. A private limited company cannot invite general public to subscribe to its share capital

109. Under the Doctrine of Constructive Notice everyone who deals with a company is deemed to have read the

a. Memorandum & Association

b. Balance Sheet

c. Profit and loss account

d. Order Book

110. Every equity share holder is deemed to be a Member of the company

111. Doctrine of indoor management means outsiders are not required to see the compliance of Regulations

112. Doctrine of *ultra vires* lays down that a company cannot carry on with the objects other than the ones mentioned in Memorandum of Association

113. Under the Companies Act a member of the company is fully liable for the debts of the company

114. District Central Co-operative Bank supervises the activities of all the Co-operative Banks in the District

115. Transmission of share means a process by which the legal heir of a deceased shareholder becomes a shareholder of the company

116. "Compensate the drawer for the loss incurred by a wrongful dishonour of his cheque" This is a stringent provision in

a. Contract Act, 1872

b. Negotiable Instruments Act, 1881

c. Banking Ombudsman Scheme

d. Consumer Protection Act, 1986

117. Security Interest under SARFAESI Act means

a. interest on the Loan

b. interest on Govt. Security Papers

c. interest on Fixed Deposit

d. any interest created in the security for due repayment of the loan

118. SARFAESI Act is applicable to

a. all Banks

b. only Nationalised Banks

c. only State Bank group

d. not all Regional Banks are excluded.

119. M/s M & Co. has a regular Current Account and a cheque drawn by them for Rs. 50,000 is presented for payment when the balance in the account is Rs. 50,009. The party is not available on the phone to inform that by passing the cheque the account will have a balance of Rs. 9 only as against the minimum of Rs. 5,000 which is a rule by the bank to keep the account running

The cheque should be

a. returned with the Reason, "Minimum balance required"

b. returned with the Reason, "Full cover not received."

c. honoured as there is a balance sufficient to meet the cheque in full

d. send a messenger to the address of the party and collect minimum balance.

120. A cheque drawn by Mr. Kishore for Rs. 2,400 in favour of Telephones is presented for payment through clearing. But the drawer's signature is totally different from the one recorded with the bank. He is not available at the given address nor the bank has his telephone number on record. The bank should

a. return the cheque giving the exact reason.

b. honour the cheque, as otherwise the telephone line would be cut off.

c. issue its own cheque and pay the telephone bill.

d. hold back the cheque under Clearing Suspense Account till it meets the account holder.

ANSWERS FOR 100 QUESTIONS - 1									
1.a	2.d	3.d	4.c	5.c	7.b	8.d	9.c	10.c	
11.c	12.a	13.c	14.a	15.c	16.a	17.b	18.b	19.a	20.d
21.c	22.b	23.c	24.a	25.b	26.b	27.d	28.b	29.c	30.d
31.d	32.b	33.b	34.c	35.d	36.b	37.a	38.b	39.d	40.d
41.d	42.b	43.c	44.d	45.b	46.c	47.d	48.a	49.d	50.d
51.a	52.d	53.d	54.d	55.a	56.a	57.d	58.a	59.d	60.c
61.a	62.c	63.a	64.b	65.b	66.d.	67.a	68.d	69.c	70.b
71.d	72.d	—	73.a	74.a	75.c	76.c	77.a	78.d	79.c
80.d	81.b	82.c	83.b	84.a	85.a	86.d	87.c	88.a	89.b
90.b	91.a	92.d	93.d	94.b	95.b	96.d	97.d	98.c	99.c
ADDITIONAL 50 QUESTIONS - 2									
01.d	02.c	03.a	04.a	05.d	06.d	07.a	08.b	09.c	10.a
11.a	12.d	13.b	14.b	15.c	16.d	17.c	18.d	19.c	20.b
21.a	22.c	23.c	24.b	25.b	26.c	27.c	28.b	29.b	30.c
31.c	32.c	33.d	34.d	35.b	36.a	37.b	38.b	39.c	40.d
41.b	42.c	43.c	44.c	45.d	46.b	47.c	48.a	49.b	50.c
51.d	52.c	53.a	54.d	55.d	56.d	57.b	58.b	59.c	60.b
61.c	62.b	63.a	64.b	65.c	66.a	67.b	68.a	69.b	70.a
QUESTIONS - 3 CASES & CASE-LETS									
01.c	02.a	03.a.false	03.b.True	03.cFalse	03.d.False	04.d	05.b	06.b	07.b
08.d	09.a.false	09.b.true	09.c.false	10.d	11.c	12.a	13.b	14.b	15.c
16.d									
MODEL I									
1.d	2.c	3.d	4.c	5.c	6.a	7.b	8.c	9.d	10.c
11.f	12.d	13.a	14.c	15.a	16.c	17.a	18.a	19.d	20.c
21.d	22.c	23.d	24.d	25.b	26.g	27.d	28.a	29.c	30.c
31.d	32.a	33.a	34.a	35.c	36.a	37.a	38.d	39.a	40.c
41.d	42.d	43.d	44.b	45.d	46.b	47.b	48.a	49.d	50.d
51.a	52.c	53.a	54.b	55.b	56.d	57.a	58.e	59.c	60.b
61.d	62.c	63.a	64.d	65.a	66.d	67.d	—	—	—
71.c	72.c	73.c	74.b	75.a	76.d	77.d	78.b	79.b	80.c
81.d	82.c	83.d							
84.true	85.true	86.true	87.true	88.false	89.true	90.false	91.false	92.false	93.true
94.true	95.false	96.true	97.false	98.true	99.false	100.true	101.true	102.false	103.false

104.true	105.true	106.true	107.true	108.false	109.true	110.true	—	112.true	113.true
114.true	115.true	116.true	117.true	118.false	119.true	120.true			
MODEL II									
1.c	2.true	3.true	4.false	5.true	6.false	7.c	8.a	9.d	10.d
11.d	12.a	13.a	14.true	15.true	16.true	17.true	18.true	19.b	20.b
21.a	22.e	23.true	24.a	25.true	26.true	27.true	28.true	29.true	30.a
31.d	32.d	33.a	34.b	35.true	36.true	37.true	38.true	39.false	40.false
41.true	42.true	43.false	44.false	45.b	46.a	47.a	48.c	49.false	50.true
51.true	52.false	53.false	54.true	55.d	56.c	57.d	58.d	59.a	60.a
61.c	62.e	63.d	64.b	65.d	66.a	67.b	68.a	69.a	70.b
71.d	72.c	73.b	74.b	75.d	76.c	77.b	78.d	79.d	80.d
81.b	82.d	83.d	84.c	85.b	86.c	87.b	88.b	89.b	90.d
91.d	92.d	93.d	94.d	95.c	96.b	97.c	98.c	99.c	100.b
101.d	102.a	103.b	104.d	105.a	106.false	107.true	108.true	109.a	110.true
111.true	112.true	113.false	114.false	115.true	116.b	117.d	118.d	119.c	120.a